DISSERTATIONS IN THE HISTORY OF EDUCATION 1970-1980

by Edward R. Beauchamp

Scarecrow Press, Inc.
Metuchen, N.J., & London 1985

Library of Congress Cataloging in Publication Data

Beauchamp, Edward R., 1933-
  Dissertations in the history of education, 1970-1980.

  Includes index.
  1. Education--History--Bibliography. 2. Dissertations,
Academic--Bibliography. I. Title.
Z5811.B382 1985   [LA11]   011'.7   84-14125
ISBN 0-8108-1742-X

TABLE OF CONTENTS

ACKNOWLEDGEMENTS

I wish to publicly acknowledge the encouragement and cooperation of University Microfilms International, publishers of Dissertation Abstracts International, in the compilation of this volume. Researchers in all fields owe DAI a debt of gratitude for simplifying their research, and I hope that this volume will, in a modest way, contribute to that end.

Although he doesn't know it, the idea for this book was the result of a graduate historiography seminar taught by Professor Charles Burgess at the University of Washington. His insistence on thorough research led me to an early familiarity with DAI and the treasures which it contains.

Finally, my thanks to Nancy and Kevin for their patience while I spent too many weekends and evenings with my Apple rather than with them.

INTRODUCTION

Some of the best, most up-to-date scholarship on the history of education is found in dissertation form and often contains material on the cutting edge of historical scholarship. Although a number of these dissertations are eventually published as monographs, there is invariably a lengthy delay between dissertation completion and publication. In addition, many good dissertations are, for a variety of reasons, never published. Even dissertations not deemed worthy of publication by university or commercial presses, often contain valuable material, much of it not easily available elsewhere. Finally, many dissertations, mediocre as well as excellent, provide the careful researcher with new ideas, valuable leads, and useful bibliographical data.

For many years, University Microfilms of Ann Arbor, Michigan, has published a valuable research tool, Dissertation Abstracts International (DAI), used by thousands of diligent scholars and students searching for dissertations on all kinds of subjects. As valuable as DAI is to a researcher, however, few would claim that it is optimally organized to serve the needs of the historian of education. Each volume of DAI contains a section devoted to the history of education, but more than half of the dissertations found in my intensive search were discovered under other sections of the "Education" category, as well as in such categories as History, American Studies, Sociology, Political Science, Literature, and even Science.

As useful as computer searches are to the researcher, many of the most important and useful dissertations would not be identified in a computer search because they do not contain key words such as education, school, university, etc.

The entire set of Dissertation Abstracts International, covering dissertations written between 1970 and 1980, was personally searched and the abstracts of dissertations chosen examined to ensure their appropriateness to this bibliography. It would be difficult for anyone who has not closely examined DAI over a considerable period of time to be aware, not only of the large numbers of dissertations related to the history of education, but also of their great diversity.

The purpose of this bibliography is not to replace DAI, but to assist researchers in identifying dissertations written on a wide range of topics relevant to the history of education between 1970 and 1980. It is designed to encourage a wider use of dissertations through saving the researcher the laborious task of searching individual volumes for the proverbial needle in the haystack.

Obviously, some form of selection had to be exercised or this bibliography would be 2-3 times as long as it already is. The criteria used were simple and highly subjective. The dissertation topic had to treat education in an historical dimension, and the compiler had to judge it of reasonable significance to historians of education.

It was originally planned to provide a complete annotation for each dissertation cited, but that idea was abandoned when it quickly became apparent that it would result in two or three volumes. Also, a complete abstract of each dissertation is already available in DAI, a research tool found in virtually all college and university libraries. Complete information as to author, title, type of degree, institution awarding degree, volume, and number of the DAI in which the abstract can be found, along with its date and page number are listed. Finally, the University Microfilms' order number completes the citation. Please note that the order number format varies from citation-to-citation as University Microfilms used several different systems of numbering during the 1970-1980 period.

A vast majority of dissertation titles are content-specific enough to provide the reader with a general idea of the topic(s) covered. In a few cases, in which the reader cannot easily gain a general idea of the topic from the title, however, a few words have been added to provide assistance. There is, however, no substitute for going directly to the relevant volume of DAI for more detailed information on each individual dissertation. One can often arrange to borrow a copy of most dissertations, through interlibrary loan, or purchase a xerox or microfilm copy from the following address:

University Microfilms International
P.O. Box 1374
Ann Arbor, Michigan   48106

Accurate details for prices, postage, etc. can be found in a recent issue of DAI.

All dissertations in this volume have been categorized on the basis of their content, regardless of the type of degree they represent (Ph.D., Ed.D., et al.), or the department to which they have been submitted. In addition, specific cross-references have been made from other sections to the main entries when appropriate.

SAMPLE CITATION

Author   Degree   Title   Institution

Angelo, Richard M. Unassigned Frequencies: Four Essays in the History
of American Education. Ed.D. Dissertation. Temple University.
1979. 164 pp. DAI 39/11. (May 1979). Page 6853-A. Order # 7909980.

| Degree
Date | Number
of Pages | Volume 39
Number 11
of DAI | Date of
DAI | Page Number
Citation Found | Order
Number |

vii

HISTORY OF AMERICAN EDUCATION

General

---

1. Abbington, Gloria J. The Literary Contributions of Robert James Havighurst to the Process of Education and Educational Institutions as Reflected in His Books. Ph.D. Dissertation. St. Louis University. 1973. 151 pp. DAI 34/8. (February 1974). Page 4810-A. Order # 74-4461.

2. Berman, Barbara A. The Impenetrable Fortress: A Study of the Nineteenth Century American Social Values Inherent in United States Elementary and Secondary Public School Disciplinary Literature, 1830-1890. Ed.D. Dissertation. University of Rochester. 1971. 313 pp. DAI 32/6. (December 1971). Page 3065-A. Order # 72-789.

3. Boyd, Robert H. A Merging of the Concept of Egalitarianism and the Universal Guarantee of Minimum Competence in American Public Schools: A Historical Summary (1700-1978). Ed.D. Dissertation. University of North Dakota. 1979. 261 pp. DAI 40/11. (May 1980). Page 5758-A. Order # 8009790.

4. Chapman, Sara A. The Development of Movement Education in the Theoretical Bases. Ed.D. Dissertation. Temple University. 1974. 174 pp. DAI 35/6. (December 1974). Page 3490-A. Order # 74-28,163.

5. Ciarlante, Marjorie H. A Statistical Profile of Eminent American Inventors, 1700-1860: Social Opinions and Role. Ph.D. Dissertation. Northwestern University. 1978. 390 pp. DAI 39/10. (April 1979). Page 6295-A. Order # 7907859.

6. Comer, Stephen W. Contributions of Howard E. Wilson to Education for Citizenship and International Understanding. Ph.D. Dissertation. Duke University. 1974. 287 pp. DAI 35/8. (February 1975). Page 5070-A. Order # 75-2369.

7. Dehnick, Philip C. A History of the Literature on the Change Process in Education (1941-1976). Ed.D. Dissertation. Temple University. 1978. 163 pp. DAI 39/2. (August 1978). Page 561-A. Order # 7812267.

8. Dokes, Limuel C. A Historical and Critical Inquiry into the Educational Aspects of Equality of Educational Opportunity. Ph.D. Dissertation. University of Michigan. 1973. 225 pp. DAI 35/1. (July 1974). Page 97-A. Order # 74-15,703.

9. Donovan, Margaret E. And Let Who Must Achieve: High School Education and White-Collar Work in Nineteenth Century America. Ph.D.

Dissertation. University of California, Davis. 1977. 128 pp. DAI
38/10. (April 1978). Page 6341-A. Order # 7803607.

10. Falk, Ursula A. A History of the Development of the Discipline of Social Work in the United States. Ed. D. Dissertation. State University
of New York, Buffalo. 1976. 178 pp. DAI 37/9. (March 1977).
Page 5559-A. Order # 77-6136.

11. Fitzpatrick, Louise. A History of the National Organization for Public
Health Nursing, 1912-1952. Ed.D. Dissertation, Columbia University.
1972. 462 pp. DAI 34/5. (November 1973). Page 2351-A. Order
73-24,066.

12. Geiger, John O. H. J. Desmond: Catholic, Citizen, Reformer; The
Quest for Justice Through Education (1858-1932). Ph.D. Dissertation.
Marquette University. 1972. 347 pp. DAI 34/5. (November 1973).
Page 2351-A. Order # 73-27,503.

13. Goldfield, Emily D. Development of Creative Dance for Children in the
United States: 1903-1973. Ed.D. Dissertation. University of South-
ern California. 1977. n.p. DAI 38/10. (April 1978). Page 5989-A.
No Order #.

14. Goodman, David M. The American Institute of Instruction and the Con-
tours of Educational Association and Reforms in New England, 1830-
1918. Ph.D. Dissertation. Clark University. 1972. 276 pp. DAI
33/6. (December 1972). Page 2859-A. Order # 72-19,464.

15. Graff, Jr., Harvey F. Literacy and Social Structure in the Nineteenth
Century City. Ph.D. Dissertation. University of Toronto. 1975.
n.p. DAI 37/5. (November 1976). Page 2684-A. No Order #.

16. Gutowski, Thomas W. The High.School as an Adolescent-Raising Institution: An Inner History of Chicago Public Secondary Education, 1856-
1940. Ph.D. Dissertation. University of Chicago. 1978. n.p. DAI
39/6. (December 1978). Page 3417-A. No Order #.

17. Harris, Yvonne B. The History of the Penn School Under its Founder
at St. Helena Island, Frogmore, South Carolina, 1862-1908. Ph.D.
Dissertation. American University. 1979. 177 pp. DAI 40/7. (January 1980). Page 3808-A. Order # 8000753.

18. Morton, Robert J. The Influence of Selected Factors on the Job Sat-
isfaction and Career Development of the 1930-1973 Ph.D.'s from the
University of Wisconsin School of Education. Ph.D. Dissertation. University of Wisconsin. 1977. 271 pp. DAI 38/12. (June 1978). Page
7062-A. Order # 7804433.

19. Norberg, Arthur L. Simon Newcomb and Nineteenth Century Positional
Astronomy. Ph.D. Dissertation. University of Wisconsin. 1974. 441
pp. DAI 35/5. (November 1974). Page 2911-A. Order # 74-19,345.

20. Ortenzio, Paul J. The Problem of Purpose in American Education: The
Rise and Fall of the Educational Policies Commission (1935-1967). Ed.D.
Dissertation. Rutgers, the State University. 1977. 452 pp. DAI
38/11. (May 1978). Page 6572-A. Order # 7804601.

21. Pugh, David G. Virility's Virtue: The Making of the Masculine Cult in American Life, 1828-1890. Ph.D. Dissertation. Washington State University. 1978. 249 pp. DAI 39/2. (August 1978). Page 950-A. Order # 7811915.

22. Robbins, William A. The TVA as a Social and Educational Enterprise, 1933-1953. Ed.D. Dissertation. Columbia University. 1972. 178 pp. DAI 33/11. (May 1973). Page 6149-A. Order # 73-10,928.

23. Surles, Carol D. S. Historical Development of Alcoholism Control Programs in Industry from 1940-1978. Ph.D. Dissertation. University of Michigan. 1978. 119 pp. DAI 39/10. (April 1979). Page 5995-A. Order # 7907179.

24. Swerdlick, Steven R. The Life and Death of an Integrated School. Ph.D. Dissertation. Stanford University. 1977. 558 pp. DAI 38/6. (December 1977). Page 3335-A. Order # 77-25,735.

25. Taylor, Robert M. The Olin Tribe: Migration, Mutual Aid, and Solidarity of a Nineteenth Century Rural American Kin Group. Ph.D. Dissertation. Kent State University. 1979. 328 pp. DAI 40/6. (December 1979). Page 3162-A. Order # 7922729.

26. Van Hook, Barry L. The Contributions of Gladys Bahr to Consumer and Economic Education at the Secondary School Level. Ed.D. Dissertation. Northern Illinois University. 1973. 154 pp. DAI 34/8. (February 1974). Page 4816-A. Order # 74-2808.

27. Warren, C.F.X., Michael J. The Approach of Pierre Babin to Adolescent Catechists and its Influence on American Catholic Catechetical Literature, 1963-1972. Ph.D. Dissertation. Catholic University of America. 1974. 303 pp. DAI 35/3. (September 1974). Page 1518-A. Order # 74-20,165.

28. Weaver, Edwin B. The Social Foundations of Education: Present, Past and Future. Ed.D. Dissertation. Boston University. 1978. 276 pp. DAI 39/9. (March 1979). Page 5471-A. Order # 7905025.

29. Welsh, Catherine A. C. The Influence of Social Efficiency Education in the Twentieth Century: Education for Control Over, Not Autonomy of the Individual. Ph.D. Dissertation. University of Wisconsin. 1980. 147 pp. DAI 41/9. (March 1981). Page 3917-A. Order # 8025858.

30. Zehm, Stanley J. Educational Misfits: A Study of Poor Performers in the English Class, 1825-1925. Ph.D. Dissertation. Stanford University. 1973. 271 pp. DAI 34/6. (December 1973). Page 3106-A. Order # 73-30,498.

Historiography

---

31. Angelo, Richard M. Unassigned Frequencies: Four Essays in the History of American Education. Ed.D. Dissertation. Temple University. 1979. 164 pp. DAI 39/11. (May 1979). Page 6583-A. Order # 7909980.

32. Blaser, Lowell K. Between Science and Art: Henry Adams, Carl Becker
     and History in America. Ph.D. Dissertation. University of North
     Carolina. 1977. 376 pp. DAI 38/6. (December 1977). Page 3676-A.
     Order # 77-27,226.

33. Elchardus, Mark. The Modernization Complex: A Theoretical and In-
     ternationally Comparative Analysis with Special Reference to the Role
     of Education. Ph.D. Dissertation. Brown University. 1978. 383 pp.
     DAI 39/9. (March 1979). Page 5745-A. Order # 7906542.

34. Feigenbaum, Carl E. American Educational Historiography, 1900-1920:
     Review and Synthesis. Ph.D. Dissertation. Cornell University. 1973.
     386 pp. DAI 34/1. (July 1973). Page 156-A. Order # 73-16,109.

35. Flood, Gerald J. Herbert Baxter Adams and the Study of Education.
     Ph.D. Dissertation. Johns Hopkins University. 1970. 270 pp. DAI
     33/5. (November 1972). Page 2139-A. Order # 72-28,955.

36. Fonsino, Frank J. Oral History as a Research and Teaching Tool.
     D.A. Dissertation. Illinois State University. 1979. 342 pp. DAI
     40/7. (January 1980). Page 3939-A. Order # 8001282.

37. Randolph, Scott K. An Analysis of the Committee on the Role of Edu-
     cation in American History and Lawrence Cremin's Revisionist View of
     the Nature of the History of American Education. Ed.D. Dissertation.
     Rutgers, the State University. 1976. 181 pp. DAI 37/12. (June
     1977). Page 7578-A. Order # 77-13,286.

38. Russo, John B. Educational Revisionism and Recent School Reform:
     The Case of Rochester (New York). Ed.D. Dissertation. University
     of Massachusetts. 1977. 251 pp. DAI 38/3. (September 1977).
     Page 1938-A. Order # 77-21,501.

39. Sine, Thomas W. Images of the Future in the American Past: Visions
     for Education. Ph.D. Dissertation. University of Washington. 1978.
     446 pp. DAI 349/5. (November 1978). Page 2787-A. Order # 7820772.

40. Thum, Gladys E. Bias Against Women in American Educational History:
     A Propoganda Analysis. Ph.D. Dissertation. St. Louis University.
     1975. 573 pp. DAI 36/7. (January 1976). Page 4307-A. Order #
     76, 880.

The Colonial Heritage, 1607-1800

---

41. Beales, Rose W. Cares for the Rising Generation: Youth and Religion
     in Colonial New England. Ph.D. Dissertation. University of California,
     Davis. 1971. 260 pp. DAI 32/9. (March 1972). Page 5139-A. Order
     # 72-9875.

42. Davis, Leroy A. A Comparative Investigation of Certain Similarities of
     Educational Concern Between New England Puritanism and the Propo-
     sals for National Systems of Education in the Eighteenth Century.

Ph.D. Dissertation. Ohio University. 1973. 341 pp. DAI 34/5. (November 1973). Page 2350-A. Order # 73-25,739.

43. Enger, William R. Samuel Eusebius McCorkele: North Carolina Educator (1746-1811). Ed.D. Dissertation. Oklahoma State University. 1973. 312 pp. DAI 34/10. (April 1974). Page 6424-A. Order # 74-8004.

44. Hay, Carla H. Crusading Schoolmaster: James Burgh, 1714-1775. Ph.D. Dissertation. University of Kentucky. 1972. 342 pp. DAI 33/5. (November 1972). Page 2286-A. Order # 72-29,275.

45. Hornick, Nancy S. Anthony Benezat: Eighteenth Century Social Critic, Educator and Abolitionist. Ph.D. Dissertation. University of Maryland. 1974. n.p. DAI 35/11. (May 1975). Page 7206-A. No Order #.

46. Innes, Stephen C. A Patriachal Society: Economic Dependency and Social Order in Springfield, Massachusetts, 1636-1702. Ph.D. Dissertation. Northwestern University. 1977. 251 pp. DAI 38/11. (May 1978). Page 6894-A. Order # 7805284.

47. Kelly, Richard E. A Study of the Schoolmaster of Seventeenth Century Newbury, Massachusetts. Ph.D. Dissertation. Michigan State University. 1971. 368 pp. DAI 32/6. (December 1971). Page 3069-A. Order # 71-31,241.

48. Murphy, Julie N. Schools and Schooling in Eighteenth-Century Philadelphia. Ph.D. Dissertation. Bryn Mawr College. 1977. 246 pp. DAI 38/9. (October 1978). Page 5295-A. Order # 7801383.

49. Myres, William V. The Public and Private Political Thought of Ezra Stiles, 1760-1795. Ph.D. Dissertation. University of Dallas. 1973. 381 pp. DAI 35/2. (August 1974). Page 1185-A. Order # 74-18,753.

50. Potts, Jr., Heston N. The Dutch Schools in North America, 1620-1750. Ed.D. Dissertation. Rutgers, the State University. 1973. 629 pp. DAI 34/7. (January 1974). Page 3938-A. Order # 73-32,234.

51. Schaffer, Michael D. The Good Citizen of the American Republic, 1789-1900. Ph.D. Dissertation. Yale University. 1973. 219 pp. DAI 34/6. (December 1973). Page 3322-A. Order # 73-29,246.

52. Seed, Patricia P. Parents Versus Children: Marriage Opposition in Colonial New Mexico, 1610-1779. Ph.D. Dissertation. University of Wisconsin. 1980. 343 pp. DAI 41/12. (June 1981). Page 5217-A. Order # 8106529.

53. Shereshewskjy, Murray S. Academy Keeping and the Great Awakening: The Presbyterian Academies, College of New Jersey and Revivalism, 1727-1768. Ph.D. Dissertation. New York University. 1980. 304 pp. DAI 41/12. (June 1981). Page 5004-A. Order # 8110685.

54. Wenrick, Jon S. For Education and Entertainment--Almanacs in the Early American Republic, 1783-1815. Ph.D. Dissertation. Claremont Graduate School. 1974. 354 pp. DAI 35/8. (January 1975). Page 5326-A. Order # 75-2282.

Forming a New Nation, 1800-1865

55. Albanese, Anthony G. The Plantation as a School: The Sea Islands of Georgia and South Carolina, A Test Case, 1800-1860. Ed.D. Dissertation. Rutgers, the State University. 1970. 403 pp. DAI 31/7. (January 1971). Page 3308-A. Order # 71-471.

56. Booth, Daniel J. Popular Educational Thought of the Early National Period in America. 1776-1830: A Survey and Analysis of Published Essays and Addresses. Ed.D. Dissertation. University of Colorado. 1974. 296 pp. DAI 35/4. (October 1974). Page 2023-A. Order # 74-22,316.

57. Brooke, Jr., Victor D. Education and Politics in the New Nation--A Study of the Educational Policies of the Federalists. Ed.D. Dissertation. University of Pennsylvania. 1974. 322 pp. DAI 35/8. (February 1975). Page 5070-A. Order # 75-3703.

58. Figliomeni, Michelle P. A Study of Educational Reform in the Common Schools of Orange County: An Investigation of the Common Schools of Orange County, New York, from 1843 to 1853. Ph.D. Dissertation. New York University. 1972. 296 pp. DAI 33/10. (April 1973). Page 5528-A. Order # 73-8164.

59. Finkelstein, Barbara J. Governing the Young: Teacher Behaviour in American Primary Schools, 1820-1880: A Documentary History. Ph.D. Dissertation. 1970. 436 pp. DAI 32/6. (December 1972). Page 3068-A. Order # 71-27,999.

60. Foster, Claudia C. Motives, Means, and Ends in Gradual Abolitionist Education, 1785-1830. Ph.D. Dissertation. Columbia University. 1977. 260 pp. DAI 38/1. (July 1977). Page 132-A. Order # 77-14796.

61. Fraser, James W. Pedagogue for God's Kingdom: Lyman Beecher and the Second Great Awakening. Ph.D. Dissertation. Columbia University. 1975. 512 pp. DAI 36/6. (December 1975). Page 3467-A. Order # 75-27,407.

62. Frisch, John R. Youth Culture in America, 1790-1865. Ph.D. Dissertation. 1970. 439 pp. DAI 36/3. (September 1975). Page 1755-A. Order # 75-20,1131.

63. Gordon, Mary M. Union with the Virtuous Past: The Development of School Reform in Massachusetts, 1789-1837. Ph.D. Dissertation. University of Pittsburgh. 1974. 352 pp. DAI 35/9. (March 1975). Page 6058-A. Order # 75-6362.

64. Gross, Walter E. The American Philosophical Society and the Growth of Science in the United States, 1835-1850. Ph.D. Dissertation. University of Pennsylvania. 1970. 429 pp. DAI 32/1. (July 1971). Page 356-A. Order # 71-19,230.

65. Hermann, Christopher. Regionalism and Development: A Socio-Economic

History of New York, 1835-1875. Ph.D. Dissertation. Cornell University. 1979. 322 pp. DAI 40/6. (December 1979). Page 3542-A. Order # 7926909.

66. Kersey, Shirley N. The Formative Years of the Wisconsin Common School Movement as Revealed in the Annual Reports of the State School Superintendent of Public Instruction, 1849-1861. Ph.D. Dissertation. Marquette University. 1970. 219 pp. DAI 32/2. (August 1971). Page 761-A. Order # 71-20,735.

67. Kohlstedt, Sally L. G. The Formation of the American Scientific Community: The Association for the Advancement of Science, 1848-1860. Ph.D. Dissertation. University of Illinois. 1972. 425 pp. DAI 34/2. (August 1973). Page 704-A. Order # 73-17,286.

68. Mariampolski, Hyman. The Dilemmas of Utopian Communities: A Study of the Owenite Community at New Harmony, Indiana. Ph.D. Dissertation. Purdue University. 1977. 309 pp. DAI 38/10. (April 1978). Page 6336-A. Order # 7803261.

69. McPherson, Donald S. The Fight Against Free Schools in Pennsylvania: Popular Opposition to the Common School System, 1834-1874. Ph.D. Dissertation. University of Pittsburgh. 1977. 406 pp. DAI 38/12. (June 1978). Page 7181-A. Order # 7803261.

70. Naylor, Natalie A. Raising a Learned Ministry: The American Education Society, 1815-1860. Ed.D. Dissertation. Columbia University. 1971. 430 pp. DAI 32/10. (April 1972). Page 5581-A. Order # 72-12,805.

71. Pascu, Elaine W. From the Philanthropic Tradition to the Common School Ideal: Schooling in New York City, 1815-1832. Ph.D. Dissertation. Northern Illinois University. 1980. 594 pp. 41/3. (September 1980). Page 1189-A. Order # 8020674.

72. Pippin, Kathryn A. The Common School Movement in the South, 1840 to 1860. Ph.D. Dissertation. University of North Carolina. 1977. 310 pp. DAI 38/6. (December 1977). Page 3683-A. Order # 77-27,295.

73. Rich, Thomas R. The Western Literacy Institute and College of Professional Teachers in the West, 1830-1840. Ed.D. Dissertation. Northern Illinois University. 1973. 210 pp. DAI 34/5. (November 1973). Page 2356-A. Order # 73-27,606.

74. Royfe, Ephraim H. A Systems Analysis of an Historic Mental Retardation Institution: A Case Study of Elwyn (Pennsylvania) Institute, 1852-1870. Ed.D. Dissertation. Temple University. 1972. 413 pp. DAI 33/4. (October 1972). Page 1474-A. Order # 72-20,211.

75. Shur, Irene G. Emergence of Free Common Schools in Chester County, Pennsylvania: 1834-1874. Ed.D. Dissertation. University of Pennsylvania. 1976. 326 pp. DAI 37/7. (January 1977). Page 4175-A. Order # 76-29,711.

76. Smith, Shirley A. L. Educational Developments on the Spoon River Frontier: Edge of American Civilization in the Early Romantic Era,

1812-1860. Ph.D. Dissertation. St. Louis University. 1970. 123 pp.
DAI 31/8. (February 1971). Page 3915-A. Order # 71-3291.

77. Smith, Tom W. The Dawn of the Urban Industrial Age: The Social
Structure of Philadelphia, 1790-1830. Ph.D. Dissertation. University
of Chicago. 1980. n.p. DAI 41/1. (July 1980). Page 371-A. No
Order #.

78. Stillman, Rachel B. Education in the Confederate States of America,
1861-1865. Ph.D. Dissertation. University of Illinois. 1972. 485 pp.
DAI 33/6. (December 1972). Page 2873-A. Order # 72-19,937.

79. Stone, Bruce W. The Role of Learned Societies in the Growth of Scientific Boston, 1780-1848. Ph.D. Dissertation. Boston University. (1974).
Page 1606-A. Order # 74-20,405.

80. Teplitz, Carole. The Informal Education of Southern Children as Revealed in the Literature of the Period, 1830-1860. Ph.D. Dissertation.
University of North Carolina. 1970. 167 pp. DAI 31/5. (November
1971). Page 2143-A. Order # 70-21,237.

81. Thomas, Jr., Robert D. The Development of a Utopian Mind: A Psycho-
Analytic Study of John Humphrey Noyes, 1828-1869. Ph.D. Disserta-
tion. State University of New York, Stony Brook. 1973. 333 pp.
DAI 34/10. (April 1974). Page 6551-A. Order # 74-8942.

82. Weber, William M. Before Horace Mann: Elites and Boston Public
Schools, 1800-1822. Ed.D. Dissertation. Harvard University. 1974.
168 pp. DAI 35/5. (November 1974). Page 2741-A. Order # 74-
24,967.

83. Webster, Laraine M. American Educational Innovators: A Sub-Committee
of the Boston School Committee of 1820. Ed.D. Dissertation. Arizona
State University. 1970. 198 pp. DAI 31/5. (November 1971). Page
2143-A. Order # 70-20,912.

84. Wertheim, Sally H. Educational Periodicals: Propaganda Sheets for
the Ohio Common Schools, 1831-1861. Ph.D. Dissertation. Case Western Reserve University. 1970. 215 pp. DAI 31/7. (January 1971).
Page 3313-A. Order # 71-1764.

85. Woodburn, Robert O. An Historical Investigation of the Opposition to
Jefferson's Educational Proposals in the Commonwealth of Virginia.
Ph.D. Dissertation. American University. 1974. 231 pp. DAI 35/11.
(May 1975). Page 7096-A. Order # 75-11,123.

An Era of Transition, 1865-1919

---

86. Adams, Paul K. James Pyle Wickersham and Educational Reform in
Pennsylvania, 1866-1881. Ph.D. Dissertation. Kent State University.
1978. 370 pp. DAI 39/12. (June 1979). Page 7193-A. Order #
7912504.

87. Bonner, Marianne W. The Politics of the Introduction of the Gary Plan to the New York City School System. Ph.D. Dissertation. Rutgers, the State University. 1978. 317 pp. DAI 39/7. (January 1979). Page 4087-A. Order # 7901235.

88. Bower, Stephen E. The Child, the School, and the Progressive Education Concept of Community: 1890-1920. Ph.D. Dissertation. 1980. 193 pp. DAI 41/5. (November 1980). Page 1978-A. Order # 8024565.

89. Coles, Gerald S. Political Economy and Education in Progressivism and Socialism, 1905-1932: Scott Nearing. Ph.D. Dissertation. State University of New York, Buffalo. 1974. 362 pp. DAI 35/3. (September 1974). Page 1473-A. Order # 74-19,972.

90. Collins, Cherry W. Schoolmen, Schoolma'ams and School Boards: The Struggle for Power in Urban School Systems in the Progressive Era. Ed.D. Dissertation. Harvard University. 1976. 329 pp. DAI 37/6. (December 1976). Page 3462-A. Order # 76-26,745.

91. Couvares, Francis G. Work, Leisure and Reform in Pittsburgh: The Transformation of an Urban Culture, 1860-1920. Ph.D. Dissertation. University of Michigan. 1980. 308 pp. DAI 41/5. (November 1980). Page 2257-A. Order # 8025668.

92. Crimmins, Timothy J. The Crystal Star: A Study of the Effects of Class, Race and Ethnicity on Secondary Education in Atlanta, 1872-1925. Ph.D. Dissertation. Emory University. 1972. (December 1972). Page 2854-A. Order # 72-32,661.

93. Deantoni, Edward P. Coming of Age in an Industrial State--The Ideology and Implementation of Rural School Reforms. 1893-1925: New York State as a Case Study. Ph.D. Dissertation. Cornell University. 1971. 273 pp. DAI 31/12. (June 1971). Page 6373-A. Order # 71-15,622.

94. Dreyer, Barbara A. The Influence of the Mental Hygiene Movement on the Education of Children During the Early Decades of the Twentieth Century in America. Ph.D. Dissertation. Johns Hopkins University. 1972. 310 pp. DAI 33/4. (October 1972). Page 1471-A. Order # 72-25,016.

95. Fisher, Robert B. The People's Institute of New York City, 1897-1934: Culture, Progressive Democracy and the People. Ph.D. Dissertation. New York University. 1974. 471 pp. DAI 35/2. (August 1974). Page 1003-A. Order # 74-18,156.

96. Ford, Judith A. B. Innovative Methods in Elementary Education: A Description and Analysis of Individualized Instruction in the Progressive Movement in Comparison with the Innovative Modern Elementary Schools. Ph.D. Dissertation. University of Oklahoma. 1977. 226 pp. DAI 38/9. (March 1978). Page 5293-A. Order # 7732861.

97. Furner, Mary O. Advocacy and Objectivity: The Professionalization of Social Science, 1865-1905. Ph.D. Dissertation. Northwestern University. 1972. 356 pp. DAI 33/6. (December 1972). Page 2858-A. Order # 72-32,437.

98. Gannon, Joseph A. Lillian D. Wald: A Study of Education at the
     Henry Street Settlement Based on her Writings and Papers. Ph.D.
     Dissertation. Fordham University. 1979. 366 pp. DAI 39/11.
     (May 1979). Page 6585-A. Order # 7911204.

99. Garrison, Lora D. Cultural Missionaries: A Study of American Pub-
     lic Library Leaders, 1876-1910. Ph.D. Dissertation. University of
     California, Irvine. 1973. 375 pp. DAI 34/7. (January 1974).
     Page 4152-A. Order # 73-31,432.

100. Geltner, Sharon O. The Common Schools of Los Angeles, 1850-1900:
     Variations on a National Pattern. Ed.D. Dissertation. University of
     California, Los Angeles. 1972. 310 pp. DAI 33/10. (April 1973).
     Page 5529-A. Order # 73-10,423.

101. Gold, Oliver D. The Soldiers' Orphan Schools of Pennsylvania, 1864-
     1889. Ph.D. Dissertation. University of Maryland. 1971. DAI
     32/7. (January 1972). Page 3738-A. Order # 72-2593.

102. Hammack, David C. Participation in Major Decisions in New York City,
     1890-1900: The Creation of Greater New York and the Centralization
     of the Public School System. Ph.D. Dissertation. Columbia Univer-
     sity. 1973. 484 pp. DAI 35/11. (May 1975). Page 7222-A. Order
     # 75-7499.

103. Handler, Kyoko S. Angel's Flight. Ph.D. Dissertation. Claremont
     Graduate School. 1975. 195 pp. DAI 37/1. (July 1976). Page
     156-A. Order # 76-15,759.

104. Haskell, Thomas L. Safe Haven for Sound Opinion: The American
     Social Science Association and the Professionalization of Social Thought
     in the United States, 1865-1909. Ph.D. Dissertation. Stanford Uni-
     versity. 1973. 405 pp. DAI 33/12. (June 1973). Page 6840-A.
     Order # 73-14,903.

105. Haywood, Jacqueline S. The American Missionary Association in Louis-
     iana During Reconstruction. Ph.D. Dissertation. University of Cal-
     ifornia, Los Angeles. 1974. 262 pp. DAI 35/2. (August 1974).
     Page 1010-A. Order # 74-18,773.

106. Hires, William L. Josiah Harmar Penniman, Educator, 1868-1941. Ph.D.
     Dissertation. University of Pennsylvania. 1972. 267 pp. DAI 33/4.
     (October 1972). Page 1472-A. Order # 72-25,587.

107. Hogan, David J. Capitalism and Schooling: A History of the Polit-
     ical Economy of Education in Chicago, 1880-1930. Ph.D. Dissertation.
     University of Illinois. 1978. 503 pp. DAI 39/5. (November 1978).
     Page 2785-A. Order # 7820964.

108. Howell, Sarah H. M. Scholars of the Urban-Industrial Frontier, 1880-
     1889. Ph.D. Dissertation. Vanderbilt University. 1970. 374 pp.
     DAI 31/6. (December 1970). Page 2715-A. Order # 70-24,872.

109. Humphrey, Robert E. Children of Fantasy: The Rebels of Greenwich
     Village, 1910-1920. Ph.D. Dissertation. University of Iowa. 1975.
     398 pp. DAI 36/4. (October 1975). Page 2366-A. Order # 75-
     23,050.

110. Keesbury, Forrest E. Radical Republicans and the Congressional Abandonment of the Mixed School Idea, 1870-1875. Ed.D. Dissertation.
Leigh University. 1971. 166 pp. DAI 32/9. (March 1972). Page
5002-A. Order # 72-9299.

111. Keller, Arnold J. An Historical Analysis of the Arguments for and
Against Coeducational Public High Schools in the United States (1850-
1920). Ed.D. Dissertation. Columbia University. 1971. 407 pp.
DAI 32/2. (August 1971). Page 761-A. Order # 71-20,016.

112. King, William E. The Era of Progressive Reform in Southern Educa-
tion: The Growth of Public Schools in North Carolina, 1885-1910.
Ph.D. Dissertation. Duke University. 1970. 336 pp. DAI 31/5.
(November 1970). Page 2310-A. Order # 70-21,993.

113. Kussick, Marilyn R. Social Reform as a Tool of Urban Reform: The
Emergence of the Twentieth Century Public Schools in Newark, New
Jersey, 1890-1920. Ph.D. Dissertation. Rutgers, the State Univer-
sity. 1974. 367 pp. DAI 35/6. (December 1974). Page 3480-A.
Order # 74-27,621.

114. Landers, Mary G. Public Pre-Collegiate Education in Alabama During
Reconstruction, 1868-1875. Ed.D. Dissertation. University of Ala-
bama. 1975. 179 pp. DAI 36/12. (June 1976). Page 7907-A.
Order # 76-13,918.

115. Leach, Eugene E. Concepts of Human Sociality in American Social
Science and Social Philosophy, 1890-1915. Ph.D. Dissertation. Yale
University. 1977. 597 pp. DAI 39/4. (October 1978). Page 2376-
A. Order # 7817598.

116. Lee, Arthur E. Public Education in Post-Bellum Missouri. Ph.D.
Dissertation. University of Missouri. 1976. 221 pp. DAI 37/9.
(March 1977). Page 5647-A. Order # 77-5624.

117. Levy, Richard M. The Professionalization of American Architects and
Civil Engineers, 1865-1917. Ph.D. Dissertation. University of California, Berkeley. 1980. 441 pp. DAI 41/7. (January 1981). Page
3218-A. Order # 8029465.

118. MacLeod, David I. Good Boys Made Better: The Boy Scouts of
America Boys' Brigades, and YMCA Boys' Work, 1880-1920. Ph.D.
Dissertation. University of Wisconsin. 1973. 511 pp. DAI 34/5.
(November 1973). Page 2521-A. Order # 73-20,265.

119. Marley, Owen G. Thomas Henry Briggs: Philosopher and Educator.
Ed.D. Dissertation. University of Massachusetts. 1974. 278 pp.
DAI 35/5. (November 1974). Page 2542-A. Order # 74-25,850.

120. McClellan, Bernard E. Education for an Industrial Society: Chang-
ing Conceptions of the Role of Public Schooling, 1865-1900. Ph.D.
Dissertation. Northwestern University. 1972. 174 pp. DAI 33/6.
(December 1972). Page 2864-A. Order # 72-32,509.

121. McClellan, Michael E. Implementation and Administration of Radical
Education in Texas: Politics or Reform in Education from 1870-1873.
Ph.D. Dissertation. North Texas State University. 1976. 117 pp.
DAI 37/6. (December 1976). Page 3464-A. Order # 76-29,153.

122. Miller, Janet A. Urban Education and the New City: Cincinnati's Elementary Schools, 1870-1914. Ed.D. Dissertation. University of Cincinnati. 1974. 522 pp. DAI 35/8. (February 1975). Page 5071-A. Order # 75-2336.

123. Moreo, Domenic W. Public Schools in Search of Legitimacy: Mandarin Schools and Folk Teachers, 1900-1929. Ph.D. Dissertation. University of Washington. 1971. 243 pp. DAI 32/5. (November 1971). Page 2452-A. Order # 71-28,451.

124. Mulder, John M. The Gospel of Order: Woodrow Wilson and the Development of his Religious, Political, and Educational Thought, 1865-1910. Ph.D. Dissertation. Princeton University. 1974. 440 pp. DAI 35/2. (August 1974). Page 1022-A. Order # 74-17,480.

125. Nelson, Bryce E. Good Schools: The Development of Public Schooling in Seattle, 1901-1922. Ph.D. Dissertation. University of Washington. 1981. 356 pp. DAI 42/12. (June 1982). Page 5043-A. Order # 8212598.

126. O'Keefe, J. Paul. The Bond of Perfection: Empirical Method in American Social Reform, 1860's-1880's. Ph.D. Dissertation. University of Wisconsin. 1979. 345 pp. DAI 40/6. (December 1979). Page 3494-A. Order # 7922829.

127. Pennoyer, John C. The Harper Report of 1899: Administrative Progressivism and the Chicago Public Schools. Ph.D. Dissertation. University of Denver. 1978. 320 pp. DAI 39/11. (May 1979). Page 6919-A. Order # 7910665.

128. Randall, Prudence B. The Meaning of Progressivism in Urban School Reform: Cleveland, 1901-1909. Ph.D. Dissertation. Case Western Reserve University. 1971. 266 pp. DAI 32/8. (February 1972). Page 4391-A. Order # 72-00094.

129. Reese, William J. Progressivism and the Grass Roots: Social Change and Urban Schooling, 1840-1920. Ph.D. Dissertation. University of Wisconsin. 1980. 576 pp. DAI 41/12. (June 1981). Page 5004-A. Order # 8106524.

130. Schubert, Florence M. The Emergence of Preparation for Psychiatric Nursing in Professional Nursing Education Programs in the United States, 1873-1918. Ed.D. Dissertation. Columbia University. 1972. 165 pp. DAI 33/8. (February 1973). Page 4143-A. Order # 73-2630.

131. Speakman, Joseph M. Unwillingly to School: Child Labor and its Reform in Pennsylvania in the Progressive Era (1889-1918). Ph.D. Dissertation. Temple University. 1976. 573 pp. DAI 37/4. (October 1976). Page 2385-A. Order # 76-22,127.

132. Stein, Francis J. Ernest Horn's Ideas on Education Within the Context of the Progressive Education Movement in America. Ph.D. Dissertation. University of Iowa. 1973. 122 pp. DAI 34/6. (December 1973). Page 3105-A. Order # 73-30,989.

133. Stevens, Jr., Edward W. The Political Education of Children in the

Rochester (New York) Public Schools, 1899-1917: An Historical Perspective on Social Control in American Education. Ed.D. Dissertation.
University of Rochester. 1971. 322 pp. DAI 32/3. (September
1971). Page 1313-A. Order # 71-22,334.

134. Tien, Joseleyne S. The Educational Theories of American Socialists,
1900-1920. Ph.D. Dissertation. Michigan State University. 1972.
201 pp. DAI 33/11. (May 1973). Page 6149-A. Order # 73-12,836.

135. Tyler, Bruce M. The American Political Theory of Equality in the
Operation of Public Schools as Perceived by Five Educational Leaders.
1890-1915. (W. Harris, C. Eliot, N. M. Butler, F. Parker, J. Dewey).
Ph.D. Dissertation. University of Connecticut. 1979. 352 pp. DAI
40/1. (July 1979). Page 91-A. Order # 7915050.

136. Tyor, Peter L. Segregation or Surgery: The Mentally Retarded in
America, 1850-1920. Ph.D. Dissertation. Northwesern University.
1972. 254 pp. DAI 33/6. (December 1972). Page 2876-A. Order #
72-32,598.

137. Utlaut, Robert L. The Role of the Chatauqua Movement in Shaping
Progressive Thought in America at the End of the Nineteenth Century.
Ph.D. Dissertation. University of Minnesota. 1972. Page 2876-A.
Order # 72-32,332.

138. Vertinsky, Patricia A. Education for Sexual Morality: Moral Reform
and the Regulation of American Sexual Behavior in the Nineteenth Century. Ed.D. Dissertation. University of British Columbia. 1975.
n.p. DAI 36/7. (January 1976). Page 4308-A. No Order #.

139. Weiss, Nancy P. Save the Children: A History of the Children's
Bureau, 1903-1918. Ph.D. Dissertation. University of California,
Los Angeles. 1974. 332 pp. DAI 35/3. (September 1974). Page
1474-A. Order # 74-19,115.

140. Wilder, Joan K. Charles William Eliot and American Education Reform,
1909-1926. Ph.D. Dissertation. University of Wisconsin. 1970.
332 pp. DAI 31/6. (December 1970). Page 2718-A. Order # 70-
13,946.

141. Willard, George-Anne. Charles Lee Coon (1868-1927): North Carolina
Crusader for Educational Reform. Ph.D. Dissertation. University
of North Carolina. 1974. 323 pp. DAI 35/8. (February 1975).
Page 5328-A. Order # 75-4887.

142. Wright, Evelyn C. School English and Social Order: Nineteenth Century Background to the Work of the Committee of Ten and its Conference on English. Ph.D. Dissertation. Northwestern University. 1977.
242 pp. DAI 38/8. (February 1978). Page 4622-A. Order # 7732370.

143. Yaillen, Earl. R. Progressive Education and Social Group Work: An
Historical Analysis. Ph.D. Dissertation. University of Pittsburgh.
1977. 248 pp. DAI 38/9. (March 1978). Page 5298-A. Order #
7801884.

144. Yulish, Stephen M. The Search for Civic Religion: A History of the
Character Education Movement in America, 1890-1935. Ph.D.

Dissertation. University of Illinois. 1975. 292 pp. DAI 36/9.
(March 1976). Page 5888-A. Order # 76-7021.

145. Zaretsky, Eli S. Progressive Thought on the Impact of Industrializa-
      tion on the Family and its Relation to the Emergence of the Welfare
      State, 1890-1920. Ph.D. Dissertation. University of Maryland. 1979.
      234 pp. DAI 40/10. (April 1980). Page 5564-A. Order # 8008261.

Education Between the Wars, 1919-1941

---

146. Akin, William H. Technology and the American Dream: The Technol-
      ogy Movement, 1919-1936. Ph.D. Dissertation. University of Roches-
      ter. 1972. 326 pp. DAI 33/5. (November 1972). Page 2274-A.
      Order # 72-28,719.

147. Barthell, Daniel W. The Committee on Militarism in Education, 1925-
      1940. Ph.D. Dissertation. University of Illinois. 1972. 348 pp.
      DAI 33/10. (April 1973). Page 5647-A. Order # 73-9876.

148. Depaola, Pier L. G. Managing National Educational Change: The Case
      of the Eight Year Study. Ph.D. Dissertation. University of Indiana.
      1977. 262 pp. DAI 39/11. (May 1978). Page 6570-A. Order #
      7805567.

149. Fass, Paula S. The Fruits of Transition: American Youth in the
      1920's. Ph.D. Dissertation. Columbia University. 1974. 672 pp.
      DAI 37/6. (December 1976). Page 3849-A. Order # 76-29,054.

150. Finn, Mary E. Schools and Society in Buffalo, N.Y., 1918-1936: The
      Effects of Progressivism. Ph.D. Dissertation. State University of
      New York, Buffalo. 1980. 416 pp. DAI 41/1. (July 1980). Page
      132-A. Order # 8016190.

151. Gearity, James L. The First Brain Trust: Academic Reform and the
      Wisconsin Idea. Ph.D. Dissertation. University of Minnesota. 1979.
      355 pp. DAI 40/6. (December 1979). Page 3488-A. Order # 7926127.

152. Grauls, Paul A. A Historical Study: The Essentialist Committee for
      the Advancement of American Education. Ed.D. Dissertation. State
      University of New York, Albany. 1974. 400 pp. DAI 35/8. (Feb-
      ruary 1975). Page 5215-A. Order # 75-5010.

153. Hirsch, Maxine E. Caroline Pratt and the City and Country School,
      1914-1945. Ed.D Dissertation. Rutgers, the State University. 1978.
      120 pp. DAI 40/1. (July 1979). Page 132-A. Order # 7941119.

154. Iversen, Joan N. S. The Origin and History of the Workshop Move-
      ment in Education, 1936-1945. Ed. Dissertation. Columbia Univer-
      sity. 1973. 240 pp. DAI 34/4. (October 1973). Page 1667-A.
      Order # 73-22,711.

155. Kennedy, James R. The Mental Hygiene Movement in American Edu-
      cation. Ph.D. Dissertation. University of Pittsburgh. 1975. 146
      pp. DAI 36/9. (March 1976). Page 5887-A. Order # 76-5449.

156. Kurriger, Patricia A. Philosophy of Art in Progressive Education: 1919-1940. P.H.D. Dissertation. Loyola University, Chicago. 1973. 227 pp. DAI 34/1. (June 1973). Page 68-A. Order # 73-16,817.

157. Kurshan, Neil. The Eight Year Study: Origins, Impact and Implications. Ed.D. Dissertation. Harvard University. 1973. 184 pp. DAI 34/11. (May 1974). Page 7015-A. Order # 74-11,313.

158. Lawton, William H. A History of the Persistency and Consistency of Progressive Education Principles in Planning for Pre-Adolescent Children from 1920 to 1971. Ph.D. Dissertation. University of Connecticut. 1973. 123 pp. DAI 34/5. (November 1973). Page 2273-A. Order # 73-26,579.

159. Pavlak, Raymond T. The New Deal and Public Schooling in Connecticut, 1933-1939. Ph.D. Dissertation. University of Connectituct 1977. 152 pp. DAI 38/8. (February 1978). Page 4621-A. Order # 7731210.

160. Pulda, Arnold H. Better Todays: The American Public Culture in the 1930's. Ph.D. Dissertation. University of North Carolina. 1978. 240 pp. DAI 39/7. (January 1979). Page 4452-A. Order # 7900498.

161. Runge, Janis M. Professional Educational Reform in Comparative Perspective (U.S.-Canada). Ph.D. Dissertation. University of Toronto. 1979. n.p. DAI 40/2. (August 1979). Page 817-A. No Order #.

162. Treacy, Robert E. Progressivism and Corrine Seeds: UCLA and the University Elementary School. Ph.D. Dissertation. University of Wisconsin. 1972. 460 pp. DAI 33/7. (January 1973). Page 3340-A. Order # 72-23,340.

163. Weinberg, Daniel E. The Foreign Language Information Service and the Foreign Born, 1918-1939: A Case Study of Cultural Assimilation Viewed as a Problem of Social Technology. Ph.D. Dissertation. University of Minnesota. 1973. 277 pp. DAI 34/5. (November 1973). Page 2495-A. Order # 73-25,686.

164. Wilkes, James D. Power and Pedagogy: The National Electric Light Association and Public Education, 1919-1928. Ph.D. Dissertation. University of Tennessee. 1973. 342 pp. DAI 34/6. (December 1973). Page 3329-A. Order # 73-27,756.

World War II

---

165. Brown, Hubert O. The Impact of War Worker Migration on the Public School System of Richmond, California from 1940-1945. Ph.D. Dissertation. Stanford University. 1973. 339 pp. DAI 34/6. (September 1973). Page 3100-A. Order # 73-30,373.

166. Doyle, Frederick J. German Prisoners of War in Southwest United States During World War II: An Oral History. Ph.D. Dissertation. University of Denver. 1979. 345 pp. DAI 39/11. (May 1979). Page 6912-A. Order # 7910045.

167. Ugland, Richard M. The Adolescent Experience During World War II: Indianapolis as a Case Study. Ph.D. Dissertation. University of Indiana. 1977. 452 pp. DAI 38/11. (May 1978). Page 6899-A. Order # 7805584.

Post-World War II

168. Allen, Dan C. Franklin D. Roosevelt and the Development of an American Occupation Policy in Europe. Ph.D. Dissertation. Ohio State University. 1976. 351 pp. DAI 37/2. (August 1976). Page 1167-A. Order # 76-17,957.

169. Berg, Thomas R. The Modern Romantic Critics of Education (Paul Goodman, Edgar Friedenberg, John Holt and Jonathan Kozol). Ph.D. Dissertation. Ohio State University. 1972. 133 pp. DAI 33/8. (February 1973). Page 4138-A. Order # 73-1943.

170. Botzenhart-Viehe, Verena. The German Reaction to the American Occupation, 1944-1947. Ph.D. Dissertation. University of California, Santa Barbara. 1980. 232 pp. DAI 41/10. (April 1981). Page 4476-A. Order # 8107698.

171. Buss, Dennis C. The Ford Foundation and the Exercise of Power in American Public Education, 1951-1971. Ed.D. Dissertation. Rutgers, The State University. 1972. 617 pp. DAI 33/9. (March 1973). Page 4787-A. Order # 73-6431.

172. Caliguire, Arthur G. A History of Cooperation Between the Cleveland Public Schools and the Cleveland Catholic Diocesan Schools, 1966-1976. Ed.D Dissertation. University of Akron. 1980. 313 pp. DAI 40/12. (June 1980). Page 6172-A. Order # 8012115.

173. Chislett, Howard J. "Nothing Will Stop Us": The Climax of Racial Segregation in the Boston Public Schools, 1963-1974. Ed.D. Dissertation. Columbia University. 1979. 230 pp. DAI 40/4. (October 1979). Page 1937-A. Order # 7923574.

174. Clark, Michael A. Critiques of Education and Responses from Educators at Mid-Century. Ph.D. Dissertation. Michigan State University. 1977. 164 pp. DAI 38/5. (November 1977). Page 2609-A. Order # 77-25,227.

175. Engler, William H. Radical School Reformers in the Late 1960's. Ed.D. Dissertation. Rutgers, the State University. 1973. 389 pp. DAI 34/7. (January 1974). Page 3933-A. Order # 73-32,210.

176. Fischer, Lawrence. A Study of Criticisms of American Public Education from 1949 to 1969, with Emphasis on Selected Teacher-Authored Criticisms. Ed.D. Dissertation. University of Rochester. 1971. 151 pp. DAI 32/3. (September 1971). Page 1310-A. Order # 71-22,332.

177. Foley, Fred J. Community Control and the Philadelphia Public Schools:

The Failure of Urban School Reform. Ph.D. Dissertation. Princeton University. 1979. 337 pp. DAI 39/11. (May 1979). Page 6960-A. Order # 7910109.

178. Hanson, David C. The Historical Roots of Evolution of the Alternative Education Movement. Ed.D. Dissertation. Ball State University. 1980. 183 pp. DAI 41/12. (June 1981). Page 5003-A. Order # 8111636.

179. Litz, Charles E. The Growth of American Business Interests in Educational Reform, 1945-1968. Ph.D. Dissertation. University of Michigan. 1970. 144 pp. DAI 32/3. (September 1970). Page 1312-A. Order # 71-23,810.

180. McCune, Robert P. Origins and Development of the National Science Foundation and its Division of Social Sciences, 1945-1961. Ed.D. Dissertation. Ball State University. 1971. 312 pp. DAI 32/3. (September 1971). Page 1448-A. Order # 71-23,026.

181. McKay, Sandra L. T. An Historical Analysis of the Intellectual and Socio-Cultural Matrix of Linguistic Diversity, 1945-1970. Ph.D. Dissertation. University of Minnesota. 1971. 261 pp. DAI 32/8. (February 1972). Page 4390-A. Order # 72-5554.

182. Morris, Robert C. Era of Anxiety: An Historical Account of the Effects of and Reaction to Right Wing Forces Affecting Education During the Years 1949 to 1954. Ph.D. Dissertation. Indiana State University. 1976. 382 pp. DAI 38/3. (September 1977). Page 1937-A. Order # 77-20,662.

183. Polsky, Richard M. The Children's Television Workshop, 1966-1968. Ed.D. Dissertation. Columbia University. 1973. 231 pp. DAI 34/5. (November 1973). Page 2355-A. Order # 73-25,168.

184. Schmid, William T. A Historical Analysis of the Educators' Request for Non-Commercial Television Channel Reservations in the United States. Ph.D. Dissertation. Ohio State University. 1970. 412 pp. DAI 31/9. (March 1971). Page 4505-A. Order # 71-7557.

185. Self, Nancy S. An Analysis of the Stated Definitions, Goals and Methods of Humanistic Public Education, 1962-1976. Ph.D. Dissertation. University of North Carolina. 1978. 338 pp. DAI 40/1. (July 1979). Page 151-A. Order # 7914403.

186. White, Patricia C. Educational Attainment Levels and State Personal Income: Changing Relationships Between 1960 and 1970 in the United States. Ph.D. Dissertation. Illinois State University. 1977. 126 pp. DAI 38/9. (March 1978). Page 5186-A. Order # 7800558.

187. Woods, Samuel B. Censorship Involving Educational Institutions in the United States, 1966-75. Ph.D. Dissertation. University of Texas. 1977. n.p. DAI 39/11. (May 1979). Page 6521-A. No Order #.

Adult-Community Education

188. Berman, Martin L. Arthurdale Nambe, and the Developing Community
      School Model: A Comparative Study (New Mexico and Virginia in
      1930's). Ph.D. Dissertation. University of New Mexico. 1979.
      306 pp. DAI 40/4. (October 1979). Page 1918-A. Order # 7922863.

189. Cameron, Henry T. The Story of the Development of the Total Com-
      munity School in the City of New Haven, Connecticut for the Period
      1962-1971. Ed.D. Dissertation. University of Massachusetts. 1972.
      196 pp. DAI 33/9. (March 1973). Page 4662-A. Order # 73-5545.

190. Cook, Nancy C. A State of the Art of Community Education in South
      Carolina: The Historical Basis and Current Status. Ph.D. Disserta-
      tion. University of South Carolina. 1977. 240 pp. DAI 39/4.
      (July 1978). Page 79-A. Order # 7807894.

191. Cook, Wanda D. A History of Adult Literacy in the United States.
      Ed.D. Dissertation. Florida State University. 1971. 256 pp. DAI
      33/2. (August 1972). Page 544-A. Order # 72-21,304.

192. Davis, Esther R. G. The Transition of Gemeinschaft to Gessellschaft
      (1870-1920) and the Revival of Community Participation in Schools.
      Ph.D. Dissertation. Northwestern University. 1974. 179 pp. DAI
      35/10. (April 1975). Page 6382-A. Order # 75-7898.

193. Days, Everett A. Alain Leroy Locke (1886-1954): Pioneer in Adult
      Education and Catalyst in the Adult Education Movement for Black
      Americans. Ed.D. Dissertation. North Carolina State University.
      1978. 159 pp. DAI 39/10. (April 1979). Page 5870-A. Order #
      7905502.

194. Duncan, Robert C. Descent from Utopia: A Study of Community
      Education, 1848-1966. Ph.D. Dissertation. Syracuse University.
      1971. 469 pp. DAI 32/3. (September 1971). Page 1217-A. Order
      # 71-23,443.

195. Geiger, Bernard R. A History of Adult Education in the Omaha Pub-
      lic Schools, 1873-1946. Ph.D. Dissertation. University of Nebraska.
      1975. 297 pp. DAI 36/12. (June 1976). Page 7807-A. Order #
      76-13,328.

196. Grady, Marilyn L. A History of the Twilight School of the Ohio State
      University. Ph.D. Dissertation. Ohio State University. 1980. 207
      pp. DAI 41/10. (April 1981). Page 4232-A. Order # 8107332.

197. Hilton, Thomas B. A Historical Analysis of Non-Credit Adult Educa-
      tion Program Development at the University of Georgia, 1904-1968.
      Ed.D. Dissertation. University of Georgia. 1979. 432 pp. DAI
      30/8. (February 1970). Page 3270-A. Order # 70-1142.

198. Johnson, Mary S. Political Cleavages and Public Policy: Adult Edu-
      cation in France and the United States. Ph.D. Dissertation. Univer-
      sity of Virginia. 1978. 270 pp. DAI 40/2. (August 1979). Page
      1052-A. Order # 7916281.

199. Lape, Keith R. The Historical Development of Adult Education in Illinois From 1966-1975. Ph.D. Dissertation. Southern Illinois University. 1977. 172 pp. DAI 38/10. (April 1978). Page 5886-A. Order # 7804284.

200. Pfeiffer, Hadley J. A Historical Perspective of the Growth and Development of Adult Education of the Springfield (Illinois) Public Schools from 1933 to 1970. Ph.D. Dissertation. Southern Illinois University. 1977. 216 pp. DAI 38/10. (April 1978). Page 5892-A. Order # 7804298.

201. Portman, David N. The Origin and Development of Higher Adult Education in the United States (1865-1970's). Ph.D. Dissertation. Syracuse University. 1972. 290 pp. DAI 33/9. (March 1973). Page 4889-A. Order # 73-7760.

202. Rockwell, Jean A. A History of Evening Business Education in the Four Year Colleges and Universities of New Jersey. Ph.D. Dissertation. New York University. 1970. 257 pp. DAI 31/7. (January 1971). Page 3451-A. Order # 70-26,441.

203. Rogers, James K. Community School Legislation in Utah in 1970, and the Historical Antecedents. Ph.D. Dissertation. Michigan State University. 1971. 336 pp. DAI 32/9. (March 1972). Page 5003-A. Order # 72-8771.

204. Selavan, Ida C. The Columbian Council of Pittsburgh, 1894-1909: A Case Study of Adult Immigrant Education. Ph.D. Dissertation. University of Pittsburgh. 1976. 161 pp. DAI 37/3. (September 1976). Page 1354-A. Order # 76-19,928.

205. Sessoms, Barbara R. James S. McKimmon: His Influence Upon Adult Education in North Carolina. Ed.D. Dissertation. North Carolina State University. 1980. 193 pp. DAI 41/12. (June 1981). Page 4938-A. Order # 8111048.

206. Stubblefield, Harold W. Adult Education for Civic Participation: A Historical Analysis. Ed.D. Dissertation. University of Indiana. 1972. 205 pp. DAI 33/11. (May 1973). Page 6047-A. Order # 73-10,788.

207. Taylor, Barbara M. A Historical Study of the Antecedents of Community Education in Nevada, 1864-1975. Ed.D. Dissertation. Brigham Young University. 1976. 163 pp. DAI 37/9. (March 1977). Page 5648-A. Order # 77-4854.

208. Wilcox, Dan L. The Educational Implications of the Chatauqua Movement on Nebraska Education, 1874-1932. Ed.D. Dissertation. 1970. 304 pp. DAI 31/10. (April 1971). Page 5113-A. Order # 71-9593.

American Education Abroad

---

209. Acierto, Maria G. American Influence in Shaping Philippine Secondary Education. Ed.D. Dissertation. Loyola University, Chicago. 1980.

300 pp. DAI 41/3. (September 1980). Page 1012-A. Order #
8019009.

210. Ajjawi, Mahmoud M. American Missions and Their Educational Activities in Lebanon, 1819-1959. Ph.D. Dissertation. Southern Illinois
University. 1979. 178 pp. DAI 40/8. (February 1980). Page
4467-A. Order # 8004022.

211. Amayo, Gersham N. A History of the Adventist Christian Education
in Kenya: Illustrated in the Light of its Impact on the Africans' Social, Economic, Religious, and Political Development, 1906-1963. Ph.D.
Dissertation. Howard University. 1973. 397 pp. DAI 36/1. (July
1975). Page 469-A. Order # 75-2175.

212. Antakly, Waheeb G. American Protestant Educational Missions: Their
Influence on Syria and Arab Nationalism, 1820-1923. Ph.D. Dissertation. American University. 1976. 161 pp. DAI 37/3. (September
1976). Page 1420-A. Order # 76-19,776.

213. Augustus, Amelia. Penn School at Home and Overseas: A Study of
a Unique American Educational Institution and Model for Foreign Vis-
itors. Ed.D. Dissertation. Columbia University. 1970. 125 pp.
DAI 34/4. (October 1970). Page 1590-A. Order # 70-18,132.

214. Bailen, Frank G. Mutual Educational and Cultural Exchange Act of
1961: An Historical Analysis and Chronological Review, 1938-1964.
Ed.D. Dissertation. Loyola University, Chicago. 1980. 207 pp.
DAI 40/8. (February 1980). Page 4427-A. Order # 8005355.

215. Bantug, Victoria P. Elements of Propagandistic Bias in Philippine
History Textbooks Used in Philippines Schools During the American
Era and the Era of the Philippine Republic--A Comparative Analysis.
Ph.D. Dissertation. New York University. 1976. 249 pp. DAI
37/9. (March 1977). Page 5999-A. Order # 77-5287.

216. Berman, Edward H. Education in Africa and America: A History of
the Phelps-Stokes Fund, 1911-1945. Ed.D. Dissertation. Columbia
University. 1970. 326 pp. DAI 31/2. (August 1970). Page 621-
A. Order # 70-13,764.

217. Bose, Anima. American Missionaries' Involvement in Higher Education
in India in the Nineteenth Century. Ph.D. Dissertation. University
of Kansas. 1971. 445 pp. DAI 32/4. (October 1971). Page 2019-
A. Order # 71-27,126.

218. Boyle, Michael J. The Planning of the Occupation of Japan and the
American Reform Tradition. Ph.D. Dissertation. University of Wyo-
ming. 1979. 266 pp. DAI 41/2. (August 1980). Page 769-A.
Order # 8018000.

219. Brown, Harold C. A History of the Department of Defense Dependent
Schools, Okinawa, Japan, 1946-1978. Ph.D. Dissertation. Oregon
State University. 1981. 157 pp. DAI 41/10. (April 1981). Page
4222-A. Order # 8108200.

220. Bullock, Mary H. B. The Rockefeller Foundation in China: Philanthropy, Peking Union Medical College, and Public Health. Ph.D.

Dissertation. Stanford University. 1973. 494 pp. DAI 34/9. (March 1974). Page 5854-A. Order # 74-6454.

221. Campfield, Mary T. Oberlin-in-China, 1881-1951. Ph.D. Dissertation. University of Virginia. 1974. 404 pp. DAI 36/8. (February 1976). Page 5464-A. Order # 75-22,168.

222. Clifton, Denzil T. Bremen Under U.S. Military Occupation, 1945-1949: The Reform of Education. Ph.D. Dissertation. University of Delaware. 1973. 281 pp. DAI 34/10. (April 1974). Page 6559-A. Order # 74-8722.

223. Connolly, Yolanda E. Roots of Divergency: American Protestant Missionaries in Kenya, 1923-1946. Ph.D. Dissertation. University of Illinois. 1975. 231 pp. DAI 36/5. (November 1976). Page 2682-A. Order # 75-24,285.

224. Dastrup, Boyd L. U.S. Military Occupation of Nuremberg, Germany, 1945-1949. Ph.D. Dissertation. Kansas State University. 1980. 248 pp. DAI 42/11. (June 1981). Page 5219-A. Order # 801248.

225. Dodge, Herbert W. A History of U.S. Assistance to Korean Education, 1953-1966. Ed.D. Dissertation. George Washington University. 1971. 326 pp. DAI 32/6. (December 1971). Page 3067-A. Order # 72-456.

226. Douglas, Donald E. American Education in the Creation of an Independent Philippines: The Commonwealth Period, 1935-1941. Ph.D. Dissertation. University of Michigan. 1979. 334 pp. DAI 40/5. (November 1979). Page 2514-A. Order # 7925139.

227. Fisher, Donald. The Impact of American Foundations on the Development of British University Education, 1900-1939. Ph.D. Dissertation. University of California, Berkeley. 1977. 803 pp. DAI 38/8. (February 1978). Page 5073-A. Order # 7731353.

228. Fritz, David L. The Philippine Question: American Civil/Military Policy in the Philippines, 1898-1905. Ph.D. Dissertation. University of Texas. 1977. 768 pp. DAI 38/7. (January 1978). Page 4324-A. Order # 77-29,029.

229. Gannon, Peter S. The Ideology of Americanization in Puerto Rico, 1898-1909: Conquest and Disestablishment. Ph.D. Dissertation. New York University. 1979. 510 pp. DAI 40/3. (September 1979). Page 1644-A. Order # 7918960.

230. Gill, Jerry L. Oklahoma State University and the Great Adventure International Education, 1951-1976. Ph.D. Dissertation. Oklahoma State University. 1976. 228 pp. DAI 38/9. (March 1978). Page 5664-A. Order # 7801255.

231. Gorman, Michael B. Language Policy in Puerto Rican Education. Ph.D. Dissertation. American University. 1973. 223 pp. DAI 34/6. (December 1973). Page 3102-A. Order # 73-28,817.

232. Hager, Jerry D. The Schooling of Third Culture Children: The Case of the American School of The Hague. Ph.D. Dissertation. Michigan

State University. 1978. 368 pp. DAI 39/10. (April 1979). Page
6050-A. Order # 7907336.

233. Heyman, Richard D. The Role of the Carnegie Corporation in African
Education, 1925-1960. Ed.D. Dissertation. Columbia University.
1970. 229 pp. DAI 31/4. (October 1970). Page 1592-A. Order #
70-18,139.

234. Maniago, Jo Ann B. The First Peace Corps: The Work of the Amer-
ican Teachers in the Philippines, 1900-1910. Ph.D. Dissertation.
Boston University. 1971. 324 pp. DAI 32/4. (October 1971).
Page 2013-A. Order # 71-26,450.

235. Marks, Marguerite M. The American Influence on the Development of
Universities in the Kingdom of Saudi Arabia (from the late 1930's to
1980). Ph.D. Dissertation. University of Oregon. 1980. 163 pp.
DAI 41/4. (October 1980). Page 1431-A. Order # 8018856.

236. Mason, Sarah M. R. Missionary Conscience and the Comprehension
of Imperialism: A Study of the Children of American Missionaries
in China, 1900-1949. Ph.D. Dissertation. Northern Illinois University. 1978. 428 pp. DAI 39/8. (February 1979). Page 5105-A.
Order # 7902454.

237. May, Glenn A. America in the Philippines: The Shaping of a Colonial
Policy, 1898-1913. Ph.D. Dissertation. Yale University. 1975.
396 pp. DAI 36/6. (December 1975). Page 3932-A. Order # 75-
27,024.

238. Mengitsu, Betta. A Survey and Analysis of Four Major United States
Based Evangelical Missionary Organizations' Educational Enterprises
in Africa. Ed.D. Dissertation. Northern Illinois University. 1979.
135 pp. DAI 41/5. (November 1980). Page 2041-A. Order #
8011169.

239. Miller, Kathryn S. E. The American School of Kinshasa, Republic of
Zaire: A Case Study of Growth and Development, 1961-1975. Ph.D.
Dissertation. Miami University. 1978. 222 pp. DAI 39/8. (Feb-
ruary 1979). Page 4772-A. Order # 7903172.

240. Muniwoki, Samson M. The Impact of Western Education on Kenyans
in the United States. Ed.D. Dissertation. University of South Dakota. 1979. 105 pp. DAI 40/11. (May 1980). Page 5796-A. Order
8009978.

241. Myers, Judy A. Education Intentions and Practices of the Presbyterian
Church of the United States in Northeast Brazil: A Case Study of
the Agnes Erskine School and the Quinze School. Ph.D. Dissertation.
Georgia State University. 1980. 232 pp. DAI 41/9. (March 1981).
Page 3915-A. Order # 8106829.

242. Naughton, Ezra A. The Origin and Development of Higher Education
in the Virgin Islands. Ph.D. Dissertation. Catholic University of
America. 1973. 347 pp. DAI 34/7. (January 1974). Page 3919-A.
Order # 73-23,182.

243. Nguyen-Van-Khoi, F.S.C., Brother Joseph. A Study of the Impact

of Christian Missionaries on Education in Thailand, 1662-1910. Ph.D. Dissertation. St. Louis University. 1972. 375 pp. DAI 33/6. (December 1972). Page 2746-A. Order # 72-23,983.

244. Ninkovich, Frank A. U.S. Foreign Policy and Cultural Relations, 1938-1950. Ph.D. Dissertation. University of Chicago. 1978. n.p. DAI 39/4. (October 1978). Page 2488-A. No Order #.

245. Nishi, Toshio. Politics of Freedom: American Occupation of Japan, 1945-1952. Ph.D. Dissertation. University of Washington. 1976. 350 pp. DAI 37/5. (November 1976). Page 2685-A. Order # 76-25,441.

246. Nkongola, Muyumba F. English for Speakers of Other Languages: A Historical Study of the Development of the English Language Teaching Program in the United States' Binational Center from 1953 to 1975. Ph.D. Dissertation. University of Indiana. 1977. 385 pp. DAI 38/8. (February 1978). Page 4633. Order # 7730310.

247. Olsen, Frederick H. The Navy and the White Man's Burden: Naval Administration of (Eastern/American) Samoa. Ph.D. Dissertation. Washington University. 1976. 228 pp. DAI 37/4. (October 1976). Page 2370-A. Order # 76-23,088.

248. Pankake, Marcia J. Americans Abroad: A Bibliographical Study of American Travel Literature, 1625-1800. Ph.D. Dissertation. University of Minnesota. 1975. 177 pp. DAI 37/1. (July 1976). Page 522-A. Order # 76-14,998.

249. Perry, Alan F. The American Board of Commissioners for Foreign Missions and the London Missionary Society in the Nineteenth Century: A Study of Ideas. Ph.D. Dissertation. Washington University. 1974. 592 pp. DAI 35/9. (March 1975). Page 6071-A. Order # 75-6615.

250. Rasmussen, Jr., John C. The American Forces in Germany and Civil Affairs, July 1919-January 1923. Ph.D. Dissertation. University of Georgia. 1972. 266 pp. DAI 33/12. (June 1973). Page 6849-A. Order # 73-5768.

251. Rêgo, George B. The Influence of John Dewey's Educational Philosophy on the University Reform of 1968 in Brazil. Ph.D. Dissertation. Tulane University. 1977. 182 pp. DAI 38/12. (June 1978). Page 7207-A. Order # 7807665.

252. Remick, John E. American Influence on the Education of Ouimbundu (The Benguela and Bie Highlands) of Angola, Africa, from 1880-1914. Ph.D. Dissertation. Miami University. 1977. 132 pp. DAI 37/7. (January 1977). Page 4041-A. Order # 77-994.

253. Rich, Evelyn J. United States Government Sponsored Higher Educational Programs for Africans: 1957-1970 with Special Attention to the Role of the African-American Institute. Ph.D. Dissertation. Columbia University. 1978. 316 pp. DAI 39/1. (July 1978). Page 416-A. Order # 7809920.

254. Rubinstein, Murray A. Zion's Corner: Origins of the American Protestant Missionary Movement in China, 1827-1839. Ph.D. Dissertation.

New York University. 1976. 497 pp. DAI 37/9. (March 1977).
Page 6001-A. Order # 77-5462.

255. Sahraie, Hasheen and Janet. Educational Development in Afghanistan:
History of the Teachers College, Columbia University Assistance Program, 1954-1971. Ph.D. Dissertation. Columbia University. 1975.
543 pp. DAI 36/1. (July 1975). Page 49-A. Order # 75-13,909.

256. Shalom, Stephen R. US-Philippine Relations: A Study of Neo-
Colonialism. Ph.D. Dissertation. Boston University. 1976. 688 pp.
DAI 37/3. (September 1976). Page 1783-A. Order # 76-21,311.

257. Slind, Marvin G. Democratization in Occupied Germany: Pursuit of
an American Ideal. Ph.D. Dissertation. Washington State University.
1978. 118 pp. DAI 39/2. (August 1978). Page 1049-A. Order #
7811919.

258. Smith, Ralph R. "In Every Destitute Place": The Mission Program
of the American Sunday School Union, 1817-1834. Ph.D. Dissertation.
University of Southern California. 1973. 312 pp. DAI 34/7. (January 1974). Page 4173-A. Order # 74-944.

259. Stein, Charlotte D. The Influence of Missions on Women's Education
in India: The American Marathi Mission in Ahmadnagar, 1830-1930.
Ph.D. Dissertation. University of Michigan. 1977. 349 pp. DAI
38/3. (September 1977). Page 1582-A. Order # 77-18,125.

260. Soleimani, Mansoor. The Educational Impact of American Church Missionaries on the Educational Programs of Iran (1834-1925 C.E.).
Ed.D. Dissertation. University of the Pacific. 1980. 102 pp. DAI
41/3. (September 1980). Order # 8019378.

261. Sudsawasd, Saovakon. An Analysis of the Use of Educated and Trained
Thai Returnees Who Attended Iowa State University. Ph.D. Dissertation. Iowa State University. 1980. 138 pp. DAI 41/3. (September 1980). Page 964-A. Order # 8019667.

262. Thomas, Edward J. F. The European Advisory Commission and Allied
Planning for a Defeated Germany, 1943-1945. Ph.D. Dissertation.
American University. 1981. 281 pp. DAI 42/11. (May 1982). Page
4897-A. Order # 8209078.

263. Thomas, Ethel N. Mary Mills Patrick and the American College for
Girls at Istanbul in Turkey. Ed.D. Dissertation. Rutgers, the State
University. 1979. 165 pp. DAI 40/11. (May 1980). Page 5761-
A. Order # 8011432.

264. Treadway, Sandra G. Terra Incognita: The Philippine Islands and
the Establishment of American Colonial Policy, 1898-1904. Ph.D. Dissertation. University of Virginia. 1978. 295 pp. DAI 40/2. (August 1979). Page 1034. Order # 7916292.

265. Walters, John W. A Political History of the United States Virgin Islands, 1917-1967. Ph.D. Dissertation. Princeton University. 1979.
233 pp. DAI 40/7. (January 1980). Page 4175-A. Order # 7928493.

266. Wayland, Cora A. The Development of Institutions of Higher Educa-

tion of the Korea Mission, Presbyterian Church, U.S. Ed.D. Dissertation. University of Georgia. 1972. 476 pp. DAI 33/7. (January
1973). Page 3341-A. Order # 72-34,161.

267. Willis, Arthur C. Attitudes of American Philanthropic Organizations
and Missionary Societies Toward African Education, 1880-1935. Ph.D.
Dissertation. Harvard University. 1973. 280 pp. DAI 36/2. (August 1975). Page 1018-A. Order # 75-2192.

Athletics/Physical Education

268. Boerigter, Robert J. A History of the American College of Sports
Medicine. Ph.D. Dissertation. University of Utah. 1978. 289 pp.
DAI 39/9. (March 1979). Page 5391-A. Order # 7905074.

269. Broom, Gipsie J. An Historical Study of the Mississippi Association
for Health, Physical Education and Recreation (1932-1970). Ed.D.
Dissertation. University of Southern Mississippi. 1971. 224 pp.
DAI 32/5. (November 1971). Page 2451-A. Order # 71-28,825.

270. Buckles, Eddie. A History of Physical Education and Athletics at Al-
corn (Mississippi) Agricultural and Mechanical College (1871-1971).
Ph.D. Dissertation. Ohio State University. 1972. 238 pp. DAI
33/4. (October 1972). Page 1483-A. Order # 72-26,984.

271. Churovia, Robert M. An Intercollegiate Athletic History: The Geneva
(Pennsylvania) Story. Ph.D. Dissertation. University of Pittsburgh.
1978. 126 pp. DAI 39/3. (September 1978). Page 1362-A. Order
7816782.

272. Cohen, Steven D. More Than Fun and Games: A Comparative Study
of the Role of Sport in English and American Society at the Turn of
the Century. Ph.D. Dissertation. Brandeis University. 1980. 378
pp. DAI 41/5. (November 1980). Page 2242-A. Order # 8024534.

273. Cunningham, Lee C. A History of the Southern Intercollegiate Gym-
nastic League from its Beginning in 1949 to its Demise in 1977. Ph.D.
Dissertation. Florida State University. 1980. 371 pp. DAI 41/3.
(September 1980). Page 1167-A. Order # 8020330.

274. Franks, Marie S. A History of the Department of Health and Physical
Education of the East Texas State University from 1889 through 1969.
Ph.D. Dissertation. East Texas State University. 1970. 320 pp.
DAI 31/9. (March 1970). Page 4516-A. Order # 71-8640.

275. Furuichi, Suguru. A Comparative Study of the Intercollegiate Athletic
Programs Between Two Selected Universities (Ohio State and Waseda)
in the United States and Japan. Ph.D. Dissertation. Ohio State University. 1980. 156 pp. DAI 41/1. (July 1980). Page 154-A.
Order # 8015876.

276. Gay, Robert E. A History of the American Football Coaches Association. Ph.D. Dissertation. University of North Carolina. 1971.
183 pp. DAI 31/9. (March 1972). Page 5016-A. Order # 72-10,683.

277. Grice, John W. The History of the Ohio Association for Health, Physical Education and Recreation. Ph.D. Dissertation. Ohio State University. 1971. 247 pp. DAI 32/3. (September 1971). Page 1320-A. Order # 71-22,482.

278. Hardy, Stephen H. Organized Sport and the Search for Community: Boston, 1865-1915. Ph.D. Dissertation. University of Massachusetts. 1980. 320 pp. DAI 40/12. (June 1980). Page 6391-A. Order # 8012608.

279. Harms, William B. An Analysis of the Major Issues Confronting the National Collegiate Athletic Association, 1973-1976. Ph.D. Dissertation. Kansas State University. 1977. 204 pp. DAI 38/9. (March 1978). Page 5294-A. Order # 7800813.

280. Holmberg, Sharon M. Valerie Colvin: Pioneer Physical Educator in Oklahoma. Ed.D. Dissertation. Oklahoma State University. 1978. 172 pp. DAI 39/8. (February 1979). Page 4807-A. Order # 7903681.

281. Kearney, June F. The History of Women's Intercollegiate Athletics in Ohio, 1945-1972. Ph.D. Dissertation. Ohio State University. 1973. 173 pp. DAI 34/8. (February 1974). Page 4838-A. Order # 74-3218.

282. Knipping, Paul A. Clair E. Turner and the Growth of Health Education. Ph.D. Dissertation. University of Wisconsin. 1970. 245 pp. DAI 31/11. (May 1971). Page 5813-A. Order # 71-3468.

283. Kupersanin, Michael. Intercollegiate Athletics at Duquesne University in Historical Perspective (1874-1980). Ph.D. Dissertation. University of Pittsburgh. 1980. 162 pp. DAI 41/2. (August 1980). Page 555-A. Order # 8018314.

284. Land, Carroll B. A History of the National Association of Intercollegiate Athletics. Ph.D. Dissertation. University of Southern California. 1977. n.p. DAI 38/10. (April 1978). Page 5991-A. No Order #.

285. Leaf, Carol A. History of the American Academy of Physical Education, 1850-1970. Ph.D. Dissertation. University of Utah. 1974. 413 pp. DAI 35/7. (January 1975). Page 4229-A. Order # 74-29,554.

286. Lewis, Robert M. Rational Recreation: The Ideology of Recreation in the Northern United States in the Nineteenth Century. Ph.D. Dissertation. The Johns Hopkins University. 1980. 412 pp. DAI 41/31. (September 1980). Page 1188-A. Order # 8020132.

287. Lumpkin, Angela. The Contributions of Women to the History of Competitive Tennis in the United States (1874-1974). Ph.D. Dissertation. Ohio State University. 1974. 239 pp. DAI 35/7. (January 1975). Page 4230-A. Order # 74-24,364.

288. Nelson, Allen E. A Biographical Analysis of Historical Leaders in Health, Physical Education and Recreation. Ed.D. Dissertation. Brigham Young University. 1972. 491 pp. DAI 32/9. (March 1972). Page 5024-A. Order # 72-9832.

289. Newcomer, Arthur R. The History and Development of the National Council of Secondary School Athletic Directors. Ed.D. Dissertation. 1975. 74 pp. DAI 36/7. (January 1976). Page 4306-A. Order # 75-30,070.

290. Nightingale, Thomas W. A History of Physical Education, Sport, Recreation and Amusement, in Cincinnati, Ohio in the Nineteenth Century. Ph.D. Dissertation. Ohio State University. 1979. 286 pp. DAI 40/8. (February 1980). Page 4475-A. Order # 8001794.

291. Nyikos, Michael S. A History of the Relationship Between Athletic Administration and Faculty Governance at the University of Michigan, 1945-1968. Ph.D. Dissertation. University of Michigan. 1970. 211 pp. DAI 31/12. (June 1971). Page 6366-A. Order # 71-15,252.

292. O'Hanlon, Timothy P. Interscholastic Athletics, 1900-1940: Shaping Citizens for Unequal Roles in the Modern Industrial State. Ph.D. Dissertation. University of Illinois. 1979. 364 pp. DAI 40/1. (July 1979). Page 133-A. Order # 7915405.

293. Pappas, Nina K. History and Development of the International Olympic Academy, 1927-1977. Ph.D. Dissertation. University of Illinois, 1978. 310 pp. DAI 39/5. (November 1978). Page 3084-A. Order # 7821220.

294. Park, Roberta J. Legislated Provision for State-Mandated Physical Education in the Public Schools of California, 1866-1968. Ph.D. Dissertation. University of California, Berkeley. 1970. 354 pp. DAI 31/11. (May 1971). Page 5815-A. Order # 71-9886.

295. Parker, Giles E. A History of the Rocky Mountain, Skyline and Western Athletic Conferences, 1909-1976. Ed.D. Dissertation. Brigham Young University. 1976. 987 pp. DAI 37/9. (March 1977). Page 5683-A. Order # 77-4845.

296. Pinkston, Dorothy. A History of Physical Therapy Education in the United States: An Analysis of the Development of the Curricula. Ph.D. Dissertation. Case Western Reserve University. 1978. 238 pp. DAI 39/3. (September 1978). Page 1302-A. Order # 7816554.

297. Rice, Cyrus N. The History of the Society of State Directors of Health, Physical Education and Recreation, 1953-1976. Ed.D. Dissertation. University of Alabama. 1977. 205 pp. DAI 39/1. (July 1978). Page 142-A. Order # 7809874.

298. Robertson, David F. The History and Development of Men's Intercollegiate Swimming in the United States from 1897 to 1970. Ph.D. Dissertation. Ohio State University. 1977. 520 pp. DAI 38/8. (February 1978). Page 4659-A. Order # 7731961.

299. Rocker, Jack L. Major Themes of Undergraduate Professional Preparation in Physical Education from 1860 to 1962. Ph.D. Dissertation. University of Southern California. 1971. 235 pp. DAI 32/12. (June 1972). Page 6797-A. Order # 72-17,504.

300. Soare, Warren G. A History from 1820 to 1890 of Two Theories of Physical Training: The Collegiate Gymnastics Movement After the

28   American Education

Rise of Intercollegiate Athletic Teams at Amherst, Harvard, Princeton
and Yale. Ed.D. Dissertation. Columbia University. 1979. 364 pp.
DAI 40/10. (April 1980). Page 5341-A. Order # 8006859.

301. Spokane, Harold L. Health and Education: Views Held by American
     Educators. Ph.D. Dissertation. University of Pittsburgh. 1975.
     274 pp. DAI 36/12. (June 1976). Page 7908-A. Order # 76-14,169.

302. Stout, Billy H. A History of Intercollegiate Athletics at Milligan Col-
     lege, 1887-1973. Ed.D. Dissertation. East Tennessee State Univer-
     sity. 1974. 282 pp. DAI 35/8. (February 1975). Page 4949-A.
     Order # 75-5008.

303. Thompson, Charles H. The History of the National Basketball Tourna-
     ment for Black High Schools. Ph.D. Dissertation. Louisiana State
     University and Agricultural and Mechanical College. 1980. 270 pp.
     DAI 41/4. (October 1980). Page 1476-A. Order # 8021762.

304. Twin, Stephanie L. Jock and Jill: Aspects of Women's Sports in His-
     tory in America, 1870-1940. Ph.D. Dissertation. Rutgers, the State
     University. 1978. 315 pp. DAI 39/11. (May 1979). Page 6924-A.
     Order # 7910447.

305. Usher, III, Mildred M. A History of Women's Intercollegiate Athletics
     at Florida State University from 1905 to 1972. Ph.D. Dissertation.
     Florida State University. 1980. 328 pp. DAI 41/5. (November
     1980). Page 2010-A. Order # 8021109.

306. Waters, Carlinda O. S. A Century of Health Instruction in the Pub-
     lic Schools of Maryland, 1872-1972. Ph.D. Dissertation. University
     of Maryland. 1972. 528 pp. DAI 33/11. (May 1973). Page 6164-
     A. Order # 73-11,417.

307. Wiggins, David K. Sport and Popular Pastimes in the Plantation Com-
     munity: The Slave Experience. Ph.D. Dissertation. University of
     Maryland. 1979. 317 pp. DAI 41/2. (August 1980). Page 588-A.
     Order # 8017194.

308. Willoughby, Avalee. Historical and Philosophical Foundations of
     Health, Physical Education, Recreation and Athletics at Samford (Ho-
     ward College) University (Alabama), 1900-1970. Ed.D. Dissertation.
     University of Alabama. 1972. 906 pp. DAI 33/9. (March 1973).
     Page 4925-A. Order # 73-8018.

309. Zingale, Donald P. A History of the Involvement of the American
     Presidency in School and College Physical Education and Sports Dur-
     ing the Twentieth Century. Ph.D. Dissertation. Ohio State Univer-
     sity. 1973. 237 pp. DAI 34/2. (August 1973). Page 609-A.
     Order # 73-18,967.

Biographies

310. Ansbro, James B. Albion Woodbury Small and Education. Ph.D.

Dissertation. Loyola University, Chicago. 1978. 216 pp. DAI 38/12. (June 1978). Page 7180-A. Order # 7807060.

311. Bittista, Frank T. Charles H. Bohem: His Contributions and Activities as Superintendent of Public Instruction in Pennsylvania (1956-1964). Ed.D. Dissertation. Pennsylvania State University. 1971. 322 pp. DAI 32/9. (March 1972). Page 4858-A. Order # 72-9436.

312. Buckley, Kerry W. Behaviorism and the Professionalization of American Psychology: A Study of John Broadus Watson, 1878-1958. Ph.D. Dissertation. University of Massachusetts. 1982. 320 pp. DAI 42/12. (June 1982). Page 5219-A. Order # 8210301.

313. Burrs, C. Thomas. James Pyle Wickersham: A Biography of a Nineteenth Century Educator. Ed.D. Dissertation. Rutgers, the State University. 1978. 236 pp. DAI 39/5. (November 1978). Page 2784-A. Order # 7820315.

314. Clover, Haworth A. Oscar Letson Matthews: Education and Morality in the Nineteenth Century. Ed.D. Dissertation. University of the Pacific. 1977. 190 pp. DAI 38/2. (August 1977). Page 668-A. Order # 77-16,209.

315. Cole, Brian A. Hutchins and his Critics, 1936-1953. Ph.D. Dissertation. University of Maryland. 1976. 192 pp. DAI 37/11. (May 1977). Page 6991-A. Order # 77-9498.

316. Conerly, Evelyn N. Thomas Ray Landry, Louisiana Educator. Ph.D. Dissertation. The Louisiana State University and Agricultural and Mechanical College. 1973. 236 pp. DAI 34/9. (March 1974). Page 5674-A. Order # 74-7214.

317. Dahlstrand, Frederick C. Amos Bronson Alcott: An Intellectual Biography. Ph.D. Dissertation. University of Kansas. 1977. 609 pp. DAI 38/12. (June 1978). Page 7509-A. Order # 7809342.

318. Davis, Frances T. The Role of Senator A.M. Aikin, Jr., in the Development of Public Education in Texas, 1932-1974. Ed.D. Dissertation. East Texas State University. 1975. 160 pp. DAI 36/11. (May 1976). Page 7247-A. Order # 76-11,946.

319. Davis, James A. Dr. Curtis V. Bishop: Focus on a Junior College Career, 1930-1960. Ph.D. Dissertation. Florida State University. 1973. 319 pp. DAI 34/6. (December 1973). Page 3102-A. Order # 73-30,275.

320. Dawidoff, Robert. The Education of John Randolph (1773-1833). Ph.D. Dissertation. Cornell University. 1975. 397 pp. DAI 36/4. (October 1975). Page 2358-A. Order # 75-22,985.

321. Deschamps, Daniel R. Aldophe Unruh, Ph.D.: An Examination of his Career in Education and Major Ideas as Revealed through his Writing for Professional Journals, 1932-1937. Ph.D. Dissertation. St. Louis University. 1979. 221 pp. DAI 40/11. (May 1980). Page 5759-A. Order # 8010718.

322. Dorgan, Jane N. Eighteenth-Century Voices of Educational Change: Mary Wollstonecraft and Judith Sargent Murray. Ed.D. Dissertation.

Rutgers, the State University. 1976. 217 pp. DAI 37/2. (August 1976). Page 843-A. Order # 76-17,312.

323. Dorris, Jr., William G. The Educational Thought of George Albert Coe (1862-1951). Ed.D. Dissertation. Columbia University. 1970. 409 pp. DAI 32/3. (September 1971). Page 1309-A. Order # 71-24,142.

324. Doss, George M. Hugo L. Black and the Concept of Education. Ed.D. Dissertation. University of Alabama. 1972. 82 pp. DAI 33/9. (March 1973). Page 4667-A. Order # 73-7995.

325. Ferguson, Janice L. A Critical Study of the Social and Educational Perspective of Walter Lippman. Ph.D. Dissertation. University of Oklahoma. 1971. 121 pp. DAI 32/7. (January 1972). Page 3737-A. Order # 72-3388.

326. Fisher, Sue H. The Education of Elizabeth Peabody. Ed.D. Dissertation. Harvard University. 1980. 263 pp. DAI 41/7. (January 1981). Page 2968-A. Order # 8100347.

327. Foster, Charles R. Horace Bushnell on Education. Ed.D. Dissertation. Columbia University. 1971. 210 pp. DAI 32/10. (April 1972). Page 5579-A. Order # 72-12,803.

328. Freeman, William W. The Life and Educational Contributions of John Rufi (University of Missouri, 1928-1962). Ed.D. Dissertation. University of Missouri. 1977. 387 pp. DAI 39/2. (August 1978). Page 566-A. Order # 7814115.

329. Friedman, Belinda B. Orie Latham Hatcher and the Southern Women's Alliance. Ph.D. Dissertation. Duke University. 1981. 242 pp. DAI 42/11. (May 1982). Page 4702-A. Order # 8207848.

330. Gaston III, Robert H. Dr. William Bass Hatcher, Louisiana Educator. Ed.D. Dissertation. The Louisiana State University and Agricultural and Mechanical College. 1971. 207 pp. DAI 32/2. (August 1971). Page 760-A. Order # 71-20,593.

331. Glascoe, Myrtle G. The Educational Thought of William Edward Burghardt Dubois: An Evolutionary Perspective. Ed.D. Dissertation. Harvard University, 1980. 291 pp. DAI 41/7. (January 1981). Page 2969-A. Order # 8100349.

332. Goodman, Helen E. Robert Henri: The Teacher. Ph.D. Dissertation. New York University. 1975. 248 pp. DAI 36/4. (October 1975). Page 2072-A. Order # 75-21,148.

333. Graber, Paul N. A Biography of Eliwood Craig Davis: Philosopher, Educator, Scholar. Ph.D. Dissertation. University of Utah. 1979. DAI 40/6. (December 1979). Page 3185-A. Order # 7927072.

334. Griffin, Jan A. Winifred Ward: A Critical Biography (Northwestern faculty member). Ph.D. Dissertation. Duke University. 1976. 265 pp. DAI 37/2. (August 1976). Page 844-A. Order # 76-18,95

335. Hadley, Jr., Worth. Rosco Dunjee on Education: The Improvement of Black Education in Oklahoma, 1930-1955. Ed.D. Dissertation. University of Oklahoma. 1981. 165 pp. DAI 42/11. (May 1982). Page 4759-A. Order # 8209425.

336. Hancock, Judith A. Jonathan Baldwin Turner (1805-1899): A Study of an Educational Reformer. Ph.D. Dissertation. University of Washington. 1971. 355 pp. DAI 32/3. (September 1971). Page 1310-A. Order # 71-24,040.

337. Horrigan, Donald C. Frederick G. Hochwalt: Builder of the National Catholic Educational Association, 1944-1966. Ed.D. Dissertation. Columbia University. 1977. 244 pp. DAI 38/1. (July 1977). Page 133-A. Order # 77-14,727.

338. Hughes, Arthur J. Carlton J. H. Hayes: Teacher and Historian. Ph.D. Dissertation. Columbia University. 1970. 426 pp. DAI 33/7. (January 1973). Page 3509-A. Order # 72-33,426.

339. Johnson, Ronald M. Captain of Education: An Intellectual Biography of Andrew S. Draper, 1848-1913. Ph.D. Dissertation. University of Illinois. 1970. 260 pp. DAI 31/5. (November 1971). Page 2309-A. Order # 70-20,989.

340. King, Jim L. Neil C. Aslin--Educator (Missouri). Ed.D. Dissertation. University of Missouri. 1979. 388 pp. DAI 41/5. (November 1980). Page 2049-A. Order # 8024368.

341. Krasenbaum, Burt R. Charles William Bardeen: Educational Progressive. Ph.D. Dissertation. Syracuse University. 1970. 215 pp. DAI 31/11. (May 1971). Page 5813-A. Order # 71-10,936.

342. Lee, Michael M. S. Melvil Dewey (1851-1931): His Educational Contributions and Reforms. Ph.D. Dissertation. Loyola University, Chicago. 1979. 309 pp. DAI 39/11. (May 1979). Page 6586-A. Order # 7910342.

343. McDonald, Judith L. Mari Sandoz and Educational History. Ph.D. Dissertation. University of Nebraska. 1980. 325 pp. DAI 41/12. (June 1981). Page 5003-A. Order # 8111680.

344. McDougall, James A. Abbott Lawrence Lowell, Educator and Innovator. Ph.D. Dissertation. New York University. 1980. 322 pp. DAI 41/6. (December 1980). Page 2469-A. Order # 8027461.

345. McHugh, Thomas F. Thomas Woody: Teacher, Scholar, Humanist. Ph.D. Dissertation. University of Pennsylvania. 1973. 343 pp. DAI 34/12. (June 1974). Page 7563-A. Order # 74-14,103.

346. Miller, Mark F. David Calwell: The Forming of a Southern Educator (1725-1824). Ph.D. Dissertation. University of North Carolina. 1979. 264 pp. DAI 41/1. (July 1980). Page 370-A. Order # 8013971.

347. Monson, Jr., Robert J. F. Louis Soldan: A Case Study of the School Administrator as Philosopher-Educator. Ph.D. Dissertation. St. Louis University. 1975. 224 pp. DAI 36/6. (December 1975). Page 3469-A. Order # 75-26,289.

348. Moser, Maynard. Jacob Gould Schurman: Scholar, Political Activist and Ambassador of Good Will, 1892-1942. Ph.D. Dissertation. University of California, Santa Barbara. 1976. 256 pp. DAI 37/3. (September 1976). Page 1724-A. Order # 76-20,510.

349. Newland, George. The Educational Philosophy of William Ernest Hock-
      ing. Ph.D. Dissertation. University of Arizona. 1970. 149 pp.
      DAI 31/6. (December 1970). Page 2717-A. Order # 70-23,661.

350. Oliver, William L. Doak S. Campbell, Educator. Ph.D. Dissertation.
      Florida State University. 1978. 282 pp. DAI 39/3. (September
      1978). Page 1384-A. Order # 7815473.

351. Patti, Frank J. The Life and Work of Edwin Lewis Stephens. Ed.D.
      Dissertation. The Louisiana State University and Agricultural and
      Mechanical College. 1971. 279 pp. DAI 32/2. (August 1971).
      Page 763-A. Order # 71-20,613.

352. Quintana, Patricio G. The Image of Tom Wiley in New Mexico Educa-
      tion. Ed.D. Dissertation. New Mexico State University. 1973. 132
      pp. DAI 34/9. (March 1974). Page 5545-A. Order # 74-7089.

353. Racz, Ernest B. (Alexander) Meiklejohn. Ed.D. Dissertation. Co-
      lumbia University. 1979. 205 pp. DAI 41/9. (March 1981). Page
      3916-A. Order # 8105909.

354. Reed, Germaine M. David Boyd: Southern Educator. Ph.D. Disser-
      tation. The Louisiana State University and Agricultural and Mechan-
      ical College. 1970. 712 pp. DAI 33/11. (May 1973). Page 5969-
      A. Order # 71-12,431.

355. Reid, John Y. The Public Career of James Earl McGrath: Vindicating
      Education for Holistic Man. Ph.D. Dissertation. University of Ari-
      zona. 1978. 324 pp. DAI 39/2. (August 1978). Page 709-A. Order
      # 7813589.

356. Romanish, Bruce A. An Historical Analysis of the Educational Ideas
      and Career of George S. Counts. Ed.D. Dissertation. Pennsylvania
      State University. 1980. 228 pp. DAI 41/9. (March 1981). Page
      3916-A. Order # 8105800.

357. Smith, Joan K. Ella Flagg Young: Portrait of a Leader. Ph.D. Dis-
      sertation. Iowa State University. 1976. 331 pp. DAI 37/7. (Jan-
      uary 1977). Page 4176-A. Order # 77-1482.

358. Spalding, Sharon B. A Study of the Contributions of Mary Lizzie
      McCord to Drama Education at Southern Methodist University. Ph.D.
      Dissertation. North Texas State University. 1976. 163 pp. DAI
      37/6. (December 1976). Page 3279-A. Order # 76-29,172.

359. Steckman, Midrid C. Harl Roy Douglass: A Biography. Ed.D. Dis-
      sertation. University of Colorado. 1970. 353 pp. DAI 31/9. (March
      1971). Page 4392-A. Order # 71-5934.

360. Taylor, Michael W. Ben Darrow and the Ohio School of the Air. Ph.D.
      Dissertation. Ohio State University. 1974. 253 pp. DAI 35/11.
      (May 1975). Page 7039-A. Order # 75-11,435.

361. Thompson, George H. The Winnetka Superintendency of Carleton
      Washburne: A Study in Educational Statesmanship. Ph.D. Disserta-
      tion. Michigan State University. 1970. 364 pp. DAI 31/12. (June
      1971). Page 6376-A. Order # 71-2175.

362. Weeks, Sandra R. Anne Schley Duggan: Portrait of a Dance Educa-
     tor. Ph.D. Dissertation. Texas Women's University. 1980. 331 pp.
     DAI 41/5. (November 1980). Page 2010-A. Order # 8025590.

363. Weimer, Charles E. John Easterly Coxe, Louisiana Educator. Ph.D.
     Dissertation. Louisiana State University and Agricultural and Mechan-
     ical College. 1974. 91 pp. DAI 35/8. (February 1975). Page 5073-
     A. Order # 75-1963.

364. Westbrook, Douglas C. Victor Leandor Roy: Louisiana Educator.
     Ed.D. Dissertation. Louisiana State University and Agricultural and
     Mechanical College. 1970. 245 pp. DAI 31/10. (April 1971). Page
     5163-A. Order # 71-10,593.

Church and State

---

365. Bolick, Jr., Ernest B. A Historical Account of the Controversy Over
     State Support of Church-Related Higher Education in the Fifty States.
     Ed.D. Dissertation. University of North Carolina, Greensboro. 1978.
     420 pp. DAI 39/6. (December 1978). Page 3393-A. Order # 7824293.

366. Freeman, Thomas R. The Opinions Expressed Toward the United
     States Supreme Court Decisions on Bible Reading and Prayer. Ed.D.
     Dissertation. Auburn University. 1978. 289 pp. DAI 39/10. (April
     1979). Page 6044-A. Order # 7007814.

367. Garrahan, John F. Church-State Issues in Education as Seen in the
     Light of Selected Supreme Court Decisions. Ed.D. Dissertation. Uni-
     versity of Pennsylvania. 1969. DAI 30/7. (January 1970). 419 pp.
     DAI 30/7. (January 1970). Page 2870-A. Order # 69-21,631.

368. Royse, Phillip N. The Warren Court: The Establishment of Religion
     and Schools. Ed.D. Dissertation. University of Cincinnati. 1979.
     153 pp. DAI 40/7. (January 1980). Page 3682-A. Order # 8002137.

369. Ruiz, A. Jorge. Treatment of Church-State Relations in Primary and
     Secondary Colombian History Textbooks, 1952-1976. Ph.D. Disserta-
     tion. University of Maryland. 1979. 265 pp. DAI 40/7. (January
     1980). Page 3829-A. Order # 8002069.

Citizenship Education

---

370. Franson, Jerome D. Citizenship Education in the South Carolina Sea
     Islands, 1954-1966. Ph.D. Dissertation. George Peabody College
     for Teachers. 1977. 129 pp. DAI 38/9. (March 1975). Page
     5384-A. Order # 7725100.

371. O'Neal, Roland L. Citizenship Education in the Twenties: The Port-
     land (Maine) Experience. Ed.D. Dissertation. Columbia University.

34 American Education

1973. 346 pp. DAI 34/8. (February 1974). Page 4814-A. Order # 74-2132.

372. Siverston, Sidney C. Community Civics: Education for Social Efficiency. Ph.D. Dissertation. University of Wisconsin. 1972. 584 pp. DAI 32/12. (June 1972). Page 6792-A. Order # 72-13,111.

373. Smith, Raymond E. Educating for American Liberties: The Civil Liberties Educational Foundation, the National Assembly for Teaching the Principles of the Bill of Rights, and the Center for Research and Education in American Liberties, 1956-1970. Ed.D. Dissertation. Columbia University. 1980. 687 pp. DAI 41/4. (October 1980). Page 1443-A. Order # 8022162.

374. Stubblefield, Harold W. Adult Education for Civic Participation: A Historical Analysis. Ed.D. Dissertation. University of Indiana. 1972. 205 pp. DAI 33/11. (May 1973). Page 6047. Order # 73-10,788.

375. Sweet, Douglas H. Church and Community: Town Life and Ministerial Ideals in Revolutionary New Hampshire. Ph.D. Dissertation. Columbia University. 1978. 350 pp. DAI 41/7. (January 1981). Page 2971-A. Order # 8028808.

376. Tafel, Jonathon L. The Historical Development of Political and Patriotic Images of America: A Visual Analysis of Fourth of July Cartoons in Five Newspapers. Ph.D. Dissertation. Ohio State University. 1979. 202 pp. DAI 40/4. (October 1979). Page 1996-A. Order # 7922568.

377. Yazawa, Melvin M. The Forming of a Republican Identity: Politics and Education in Revolutionary America. Ph.D. Dissertation. Johns Hopkins University. 1977. 457 pp. DAI 41/2. (August 1980). Page 776-A. Order # 8018418.

Collective Bargaining

378. Abel, William B. The Historical Development of Collective Bargaining in the Flint Community Schools. Ph.D. Dissertation. Michigan State University. 1977. 300 pp. DAI 38/10. (April 1978). Page 5808-A. Order # 7803458.

379. Byrd, William L. Teacher Collective Bargaining and Strikes in Public Elementary and Secondary Education. Ed.D. Dissertation. St. Louis University. 1979. 119 pp. DAI 40/5. (November 1979). Page 2370-A. Order # 7923812.

380. Crosby, Chester G. Collective Bargaining in Public Education, 1960-1975. Ph.D. Dissertation. St. Louis University. 1979. 153 pp. DAI 40/5. (November 1979). Page 2361-A. Order # 7923817.

381. Goldberg, Jerry D. Lincoln Park: The Effect of Collective Bargaining on a Teachers' Organization, 1965-1975. Ed.D. Dissertation.

University of Michigan. 1979. 281 pp. DAI 40/5. (November 1979). Page 2380-A. Order # 7925097.

382. Green, Clarence D. Collective Bargaining and Power at Wayne State University from 1969 to 1976. Ph.D. Dissertation. 1978. 229 pp. DAI 39/11. (May 1979). Page 6568-A. Order # 7908914.

383. Harlan, William L. An Historical Study of the Trends Toward Collective Bargaining in Public Education in Texas. Ed.D. Dissertation. East Texas State University. 1978. 194 pp. DAI 39/11. (May 1979). Page 6680-A. Order # 7909656.

384. Manney, Bernard J. An Analysis of Empirical Data Relating to Collective Negotiations Among Boards of Education and Teachers in New Jersey Public School Districts: 1969-1970 to 1973-1974. Ed.D. Dissertation. Rutgers, the State University. 1976. 172 pp. DAI 37/2. (August 1976). Page 846-A. Order # 76-17,314.

Compulsory School Attendance

---

385. Koch Jr., Carl. A Historical Review of Compulsory School Attendance Laws and Child Labor Laws. Ed.D. Dissertation. University of Wyoming. 1972. 225 pp. DAI 33/4. (October 1972). Page 1473-A. Order # 72-26,508.

386. Mrozinski, Ronald R. Compulsory Education: An Historical Review of its Origins, Growth and Challenges. Ph.D. Dissertation. University of Michigan. 1977. 368 pp. DAI 38/11. (May 1978). Page 6571-A. Order # 7804778.

387. Rosenfeld, R. William. Custodian of All the Children: The Evolution of the Universal Custodianship of Ohio's Children by Schools, 1803-1921. Ph.D. Dissertation. Case Western Reserve University. 1976. 489 pp. DAI 38/2. (August 1977). Page 668-A. Order # 77-12,010.

388. Schumacher, Carolyn S. School Attendance in Nineteenth Century Pittsburgh: Wealth, Ethnicity and Occupational Mobility of School Age Children, 1855-1865. Ph.D. Dissertation. University of Pittsburgh. 1977. 230 pp. DAI 38/5. (November 1977). Page 2978-A. Order # 77-23,598.

Correctional Institutions

---

389. Norcott, Alan G. A Documentation and Analysis of the Historical Development of Educational Programs in the State Prisons of New Jersey (1798-1976). Ed.D. Dissertation. Rutgers, the State University. 1979. 164 pp. DAI 40/7. (January 1980). Page 3828-A. Order # 8000871.

390. Olson, Richard F. A Study of the Formal Academic Program in Connecticut's Correctional Institutions, 1968-1975. Ph.D. Dissertation. University of Connecticut. 1978. 119 pp. DAI 39/11. (May 1979). Page 6683-A. Order # 7911398.

391. Remick, Cecile P. The House of Refuge of Philadelphia. Ed.D. Dissertation. University of Pennsylvania. 1975. 508 pp. DAI 36/11. (May 1976). Page 7249-A. Order # 76-11,196.

392. Sullivan, Robert D. A Historical Perspective of Education in Massachusetts' Correctional Institutions. Ed.D. Dissertation. 1975. 155 pp. DAI 35/12. (June 1975). Page 7596-A. Order # 75-12,233.

Courts and Education

---

393. Baily, Joseph R. History of the Child-Benefit Doctrine as a Means of Providing Governmental Financial Aid for Non-Public Education. Ed.D. Dissertation. University of Massachusetts. 1979. 168 pp. DAI 40/8. (February 1980). Page 4312-A. Order # 8004894.

394. Boggs, Timothy J. An Analysis of the Opinions in the United States Supreme Court Decisions on Religion and Education from 1948 through 1972. Ed.D. Dissertation. University of Colorado. 1973. 899 pp. DAI 34/7. (January 1974). Page 3931-A. Order # 73-32,517.

395. Boles, David C. A Historical Study of Court Decisions Which Originated in Relation to the Middle Level and Senior High School Students. Ed.D. Dissertation. University of Colorado. 1978. 165 pp. DAI 39/5. (November 1978). Page 2639-A. Order # 7820489.

396. Brooke, Jr., William O. Assessing the Impact of Title IX and Other Factors on Women's Intercollegiate Athletic Programs, 1972-1977: A National Study of Four-Year AIAW Institutions. Ed.D. Dissertation. Arizona State University. 1979. 154 pp. DAI 40/4. (October 1979). Page 1947-A. Order # 7919171.

397. Chait, Richard P. The Desegregation of Higher Education: A Legal History. Ph.D. Dissertation. University of Wisconsin. 1972. 316 pp. DAI 33/12. (June 1973). Page 6883-A. Order # 73-9190.

398. Craig, Robert C. California Supreme Court Decisions Affecting Administration of Public Schools, 1950-1970. Ed.D. Dissertation. University of Southern California. 1974. 149 pp. DAI 35/4. (October 1974). Page 1901-A. Order # 74-21,466.

399. Crowley, Donald W. The Impact of Serrano v. Priest: A Study in Judicial Policy. Ph.D. Dissertation. University of California, Riverside. 1979. 289 pp. DAI 40/5. (November 1979). Page 2857-A. Order # 7924280.

400. Drouin, Edmond G. The United States Supreme Court and Religious Freedom in American Education in its Decisions Affecting Church-Related Elementary and Secondary Schools During the First Three

Quarters of the Twentieth Century. Ph.D. Dissertation. The Catholic
University of America. 1980. 502 pp. DAI 41/10. (April 1981).
Page 4310-A. Order # 8107975.

401. Dunn, Jr., John C. American Educational Jurisprudence: A Study
of the Influence of State Statutes and Federal Courts on Public
Schools and the Desegregation Process in the United States. Ph.D.
Dissertation. The Ohio State University. 1978. 214 pp. DAI 39/8.
(February 1979). Page 4620-A. Order # 7902112.

402. Frey, Peter W. U.S. Supreme Court Dissenting Opinions Since McCollum:
Their Role in the Continuing Controversy Over Religion and Education.
Ed.D. Dissertation. Temple University. 1981. 276 pp. DAI 42/12.
(June 1982). Page 5053-A. Order # 8210483.

403. Gribbin, William G. The So-Called Child Benefit Theory: Parochiad
and the Establishment Clause. Ph.D. Dissertation. Pennsylvania
State University. 1977. 291 pp. DAI 38/10. (April 1978). Page
5822-A. Order # 7803327.

404. Harris, James T. Alabama Reaction to the Brown Decision, 1954-1956:
A Case Study in Early Massive Resistence. D.A. Dissertation. Middle Tennessee State University. 1978. 327 pp. DAI 39/6. (December 1978). Page 3774-A. Order # 7822621.

405. Heike, Susan J. Federal District Judges and Public School Desegregation: A Study of Judicial Decision-Making (1954-1975). Ph.D.
Dissertation. Emory University. 1977. 249 pp. DAI 38/8. (February 1978). Page 5023-A. Order # 7732378.

406. Hennessey, Gary J. An Unfulfilled Dream: A Catalogue and Analysis
of the Different Perceptions of Busing, 1954-1956. Ph.D. Dissertation.
The Ohio State University. 1976. 159 pp. DAI 37/5. (November
1976). Page 2684-A. Order # 76-24,613.

407. Herman, Carl S. A Historical and Legal Analysis of the Role of School
Bus Drivers in the Public Transportation of North Carolina, 1911-1979.
Ed.D. Dissertation. University of North Carolina, Greensboro. 1980.
272 pp. DAI 41/4. (October 1980). Page 1443-A. Order # 8021774.

408. Hirschberger, Emma J. A Study of the Development of the In Loco
Parentis Doctrine, its Application and Emerging Trends. Ph.D. Dis-
sertation. University of Pittsburgh. 1971. 284 pp. DAI 32/8.
(February 1972). Page 4389-A. Order # 72-7887.

409. Hogancamp, Richard L. The Historical Significance of the Michigan
Tenure Decisions Since 1964. Ed.D. Dissertation. Wayne State Uni-
versity. 1971. 183 pp. DAI 32/5. (November 1971). Page 2347-
A. Order # 2347.

410. Houck, Robert F. The Impact of Federal Judicial and Legislative Decisions on Educational Practices During the Warren Years--1953 to
1969. Ph.D. Dissertation. St. Louis University. 1978. 255 pp.
DAI 39/3. (September 1978). Page 1226-A. Order # 7814576.

411. Iamnone, Ronald H. The 1975 Wood v. Strickland Supreme Court Decision: Its Impact on School Board Members and School Board

Candidates in Los Angeles County, California. Ed.D. Dissertation.
Brigham Young University. 1978. 345 pp. DAI 39/2. (August
1978). Page 547-A. Order # 7813814.

412. Iovacchini, Eric V. A Study of Academic Due Process in Public
Higher Education Subsequent to Dixon v. Alabama State Board of
Education, through 1977. Ph.D. Dissertation. University of Wyo-
ming. 1978. 81 pp. DAI 39/4. (October 1978). Page 2497-A.
Order # 7818937.

413. Kelly, Cynthia A. Due Process in the Schools: The View from Inside.
Ph.D. Dissertation. Northwestern University. 1979. 299 pp. DAI
40/6. (December 1979). Page 3498-A. Order # 7927383.

414. Kesselman, Michael N. An Historical Analysis of Desegregation on Mi-
ami Beach Public Secondary Schools, 1968-1977. Ed.D. Dissertation.
University of Miami. 1979. 405 pp. DAI 40/8. (February 1980).
Page 4443-A. Order # 8001665.

415. Kirk, Robert L. A Descriptive Survey of Public Elementary School
Liability Cases in the United States from 1945 through 1970. Ed.D.
Dissertation. American University. 1974. 94 pp. DAI 35/9.
(March 1974). Page 5731-A. Order # 75-5197.

416. Kmetz, Joseph I. An Analysis of the Appellate Court Decisions Concerning Student Rights, 1961 to Date (1973). Ph.D. Dissertation.
University of Pittsburgh. 1973. 299 pp. DAI 34/8. (February
1974). Page 4635-A. Order # 74-1543.

417. McNeill, Paul W. School Desegregation in South Carolina, 1963-1970.
Ed.D. Dissertation. University of Kentucky. 1979. 134 pp. DAI
40/11. (May 1980). Page 5760-A. Order # 8010510.

418. Middleton, Joanne M. The History of Singleton v. Jackson Municipal
Separate School District: Southern School Desegregation from the
Perspective of the Black Community. Ed.D. Dissertation. Harvard
University. 1978. 176 pp. DAI 39/6. (December 1978). Page
3436-A. Order # 7823682.

419. O'Donnell, Jr., Thomas F. Religion, Basic Education and the First
Amendment: The Supreme Court from Fuller to Warren. Ed.D. Dissertation. Lehigh University. 1973. 238 pp. DAI 34/4. (October
1973). Page 1669-A. Order # 73-23,814.

420. Quesenberry, Guy H. A Study of the Newport News Pupil Desegregation Process. Ed.D. Dissertation. Virginia Polytechnic Institute
and State University. 1977. 159 pp. DAI 39/1. (July 1978). Page
161-A. Order # 7810002.

421. Rabold, Ted F. Educational Malpractice Litigation: The Evolution of
Judicial Pronouncements from 1950 through 1976. Ed.D. Dissertation.
Lehigh University. 1976. 119 pp. DAI 39/3. (September 1978).
Page 1243-A. Order # 7815828.

422. Runkel, H. John. An Historical Study and Analysis: Public Law
874. Ed.D. Dissertation. University of Denver. 1969. 184 pp.
DAI 30/7. (January 1970). Page 2776-A. Order # 69-22,245.

423. Santiago Santiago, Isaura. Aspira v. Board of the City of New York: A
     History and Policy Analysis. Ph.D. Dissertation. Fordham University.
     1978. 410 pp. DAI 38/12. (June 1978). Page 7199-A. Order # 7809014.

424. Schwartz, Frank. The Changing Concept Constitutional Culpability in
     School Desegregation Cases: A Search for Judicial Justification of
     Remedial Action, 1954-1977. Ph.D. Dissertation. University of North
     Carolina. 1979. 309 pp. DAI 40/5. (November 1979). Page 2874-
     A. Order # 7925962.

425. Sheets, Carl G. A History of the Legislative Acts of the State of Ar-
     kansas that Pertain to Elementary Education (1836-1977). Ph.D. Dis-
     sertation. University of Arkansas. 1979. 343 pp. DAI 40/3. (Sep-
     tember 1979). Page 1266-A. Order # 7919235.

426. Soder, Scott. Tinker v. Des Moines Independent School Community
     School District: The Marketplace of Ideas Applied to Primary and
     Secondary Schools. Ph.D. Dissertation. Cornell University. 1979.
     184 pp. DAI 40/6. (December 1979). Page 3182-A. Order #
     7926965.

427. Stacey, Charles E. The Supreme Court and the Elevation of Education
     to the Status of a Fundamental Right. Ph.D. Dissertation. Univer-
     sity of Pittsburgh. 1974. 333 pp. DAI 35/12. (June 1975). Page
     7585-A. Order # 75-13,217.

428. Stephens, Ronald W. A Study of U.S. Supreme Court Decisions from
     1970 to 1977 as the Basis for Developing Policy for Censorship of Cur-
     riculum Materials by American Public Schools. Ph.D. Dissertation.
     University of Nebraska. 1978. 405 pp. DAI 39/9. (March 1979).
     Page 5251-A. Order # 7901945.

429. Strope, John L. The Impact of the United States Supreme Court on
     the Educational Policies of the States with Particular Emphases on
     Goss v. Lopez in Nebraska. Ph.D. Dissertation. University of Ne-
     braska. 1979. 284 pp. DAI 40/2. (August 1979). Page 1037-A.
     Order # 7918024.

430. Thompson, John M. School Desegregation in Jefferson County, Ken-
     tucky, 1954-1975. Ed.D. Dissertation. University of Kentucky. 1976.
     383 pp. DAI 37/9. (March 1977). Page 5519-A. Order # 77-5707.

431. Turman, Ira N. United States Supreme Court Decisions Affecting
     Compulsory School Attendance Laws. Ed.D. Dissertation. North
     Texas State University. 1975. 92 pp. DAI 37/11. (May 1976).
     Page 7123-A. Order # 76-11,156.

432. Vega, Jose E. The Enactment of Bilingual Education Legislation in
     Texas, 1969-1973. Ph.D. Dissertation. University of Illinois. 1980.
     301 pp. DAI 41/2. (August 1980). Page 567-A. Order # 8018212.

433. Walker, Jr., James G. A Study of the History and Development of
     the Parochiaid Movement in the United States. Ph.D. Dissertation.
     University of Michigan. 1975. 204 pp. DAI 36/6. (December 1975).
     Page 3322-A. Order # 75-27,609.

434. Walker, John H. A Historical Comparative Study of Participation in

Educational Policy Development by Selected State Appellate Courts.
Ph.D. Dissertation. University of Texas. 1973. 376 pp. DAI 34/5.
(November 1973). Page 2357-A.

435. Williams, Sr., Theodore R. Educational Policy Implications (K-12) of
the U.S. Supreme Court Decision in the Tinker v. Des Moines Case.
Ph.D. Dissertation. University of Iowa. 1978. 332 pp. DAI 39/8.
(February 1979). Page 4651-A. Order # 7902960.

436. Wollenberg, Charles M. All Deliberate Speed: Segregation and Exclu-
sion in California Schools, 1855-1975. Ph.D. Dissertation. University
of California, Berkeley. 1975. 240 pp. DAI 37/1. (July 1976).
Page 158-A. Order # 76-15,425.

Curriculum--General Subjects

---

437. Clarke, Christopher R. The Influence of the Idea of Progress on the
Curriculum Theories of Experimentalism, Essentialism, and Reconstruc-
tionism. Ed.D. Dissertation. East Tennessee State University. 1975.
188 pp. DAI 36/9. (March 1976). Page 5885-A. Order # 76-6478.

438. Dobson, Edward C. An Analytical Review of Representative Studies
in Curriculum Evaluation from 1929 to 1970. Ph.D. Dissertation.
Florida State University. 1972. 317 pp. DAI 33/6. (December 1972).
Page 2744-A. Order # 72-31,392.

439. Fraley, Angela E. Core Curriculum: An Epic in the History of Educational Reform. Ed.D. Dissertation. Columbia University. 1977.
243 pp. DAI 38/10. (April 1978). Page 5883-A. Order # 7804457.

440. Hansen, Jessie M. Kimball Wiles' Contribution to Curriculum and Instruction: An Analysis within an Historical Context. Ph.D. Dissertation. University of Texas. 1971. 243 pp. DAI 32/11. (May
1972). Page 6165-A. Order # 72-15,770.

441. Hinkemeyer, Michael T. Democracy and the Curriculum: An Historical Survey, 1918-1968. Ph.D. Dissertation. Northwestern University. 1971. 276 pp. DAI 32/6. (December 1971). Page 2910-A.
Order # 71-30,832.

442. Huber, Margaret A. The Renewal of Curriculum Theory in the 1970's:
An Historical Study. Ph.D. Dissertation. University of Michigan.
1979. 192 pp. DAI 40/2. (August 1979). Page 711-A. Order #
7916731.

443. Jackson, Byron H. The Covenant Life Curriculum within its Historical Setting (1963-1978). Ed.D. Dissertation. Columbia University.
1980. 219 pp. DAI 41/4. (October 1980). Page 1515-A. Order #
8022120.

444. Kaufhold, John A. Factors Which Influenced the Use of Programmed
Instruction in American Public Schools, 1926-1973. Ed.D. Dissertation. University of Virginia. 1974. 236 pp. DAI 35/7. (January
1975). Page 4133-A. Order # 74-29,205.

445. Keienburg, III, John W. Epperson v. Arkansas: A Question of Control Over Curriculum and Instruction Decision-Making in the Public Schools. Ph.D. Dissertation. Texas A & M University. 1978. 208 pp. DAI 39/12. (June 1979). Page 7194-A. Order # 7909213.

446. Kozak, Michael R. A Critical Analysis of Individualized Instruction Since 1944. Ed.D. Dissertation. Texas A & M University. 1974. 269 pp. DAI 35/8. (February 1975). Page 5218-A. Order # 75-2912.

447. Lucas, Verlene D. The Development of Public Elementary School Curriculum in Calfornia, 1930-1970. Ed.D. Dissertation. University of Southern California. 1973. 841 pp. DAI 34/7. (January 1974). Page 3934-A. Order # 73-31,368.

448. Morman, Marilyn D. An Historical Review of the Development and Improvement of Elementary and Secondary School Curriculum in the State of Florida with Emphasis on the Course of Study Committee. Ph.D. Dissertation. Florida State University. 1978. 173 pp. DAI 39/11. (May 1979). Page 6587-A. Order # 7909780.

449. Mullen, Gregory J. The Development of the Curriculum Field, 1940-1975. Ph.D. Dissertation. Northwestern University. 1976. 215 pp. DAI 37/7. (January 1977). Page 4101-A. Order # 77-1309-A.

450. Paulos, Katherine M. An Historical Review of Curriculum Research, 1918-1975. Ph.D. Dissertation. University of Florida. 1976. 502 pp. DAI 37/10. (April 1977). Page 6249-A. Order # 77-8210.

451. Rambo, Wayne H. An Historical-Analytical Study of the Formulation of, the Sources of, and Functions of Educational Objectives, 1900-1979. Ed.D. Dissertation. Temple University. 1982. 185 pp. DAI 42/12. (June 1982). Page 5015-A. Order # 8210544.

452. Rosen, Kenneth J. The Historical Development of Individually Gifted Education in America: The Case of Wisconsin I.G.E. (Individually Guided Education). Ed.D. Dissertation. Rutgers, the State University. 1978. 229 pp. DAI 39/1. (July 1978). Page 101-A. Order # 7810236.

453. Rosenbaum, Karen J. Curricular Innovation in Federal Youth Programs: A Comparison of New Deal and War on Poverty Education Efforts. Ph.D. Dissertation. Johns Hopkins University. 1973. 763 pp. DAI 34/1. (July 1973). Page 153-A. Order # 73-16,622.

454. Rutherford, Millicent A. Feminism and the Secondary School Curriculum, 1890-1920. Ph.D. Dissertation. Stanford University. 1977. 211 pp. DAI 38/3. (September 1977). Page 1205-A. Order # 77-18,243.

455. Weldon, John W. The Evolution of Curriculum Developments in the United States as Revealed through Selected Writings (1890-1970). Ph.D. Dissertation. Southern Illinois University. 1970. 194 pp. DAI 31/10. (April 1971). Page 5162-A. Order # 71-10,072.

Art Education

456. Dobbs, Stephen M. Paradox and Promise: Art Education in the Public Schools. Ph.D. Dissertation. Stanford University. 1972. 231 pp. DAI 33/5. (November 1972). Page 2139-A. Order # 72-30,622.

457. Wilson, Mildred M. A Historical Inquiry into Early Development of Art Education in the American Public Schools. Ed.D. Dissertation. Wayne State University. 1980. 113 pp. DAI 41/4. (October 1980). Page 1354-A. Order # 8022827.

Business Education

458. Bowman, Vernon L. A Historical Study of Business Education and Secretarial Science at Oregon State University (1868-1970). Ed.D. Dissertation. Oregon State University. 1974. 163 pp. DAI 34/7. (January 1974). Page 3932-A. Order # 73-32,750.

459. Brantley, Gloria A. (Charles). An Historical Analysis and Present Position of Business Education in the Public Secondary Schools of Louisiana, 1956-1968. Ed.D. Dissertation. Oklahoma State University. 1971. 189 pp. DAI 33/2. (August 1972). Page 600-A. Order # 72-21,835.

460. Gwatney, Martha B. The Contributions of Paul Sanford Lomax to Business Education. Ed.D. Dissertation. University of Mississippi. 1972. 166 pp. DAI 33/7. (January 1973). Page 3336-A. Order # 73-1267.

461. Sedlak, Michael W. The Emergence and Development of Collegiate Business Education in the United States, 1881-1974: Northwestern University as a Case Study. Ph.D. Dissertation. Northwestern University. 1977. 479 pp. DAI 38/11. (May 1978). Page 6898-A. Order # 7805326.

462. Thompson, Claud C. The Influence of Social Conditions and Curriculum Trends on Consumer Education Before World War II. Ph.D. Dissertation. University of Wisconsin. 1970. 366 pp. DAI 31/11. (May 1971). Page 5817-A. Order # 71-2252.

463. Weiss, Janice H. Educating for Clerical Work: A History of Commercial Education in the United States Since 1850. Ed.D. Dissertation. Harvard University. 1978. 301 pp. DAI 39/6. (December 1978). Page 3420-A. Order # 7823695.

464. White, Gayle W. The Contributions of Russell J. Hosler to Business Education. Ed.D. Dissertation. University of Mississippi. 1972. 174 pp. DAI 33/7. (January 1973). Page 3341-A. Order # 73-1297.

465. Wise, Sarah B. A Study of the Development of Business Education in the Public Schools of South Carolina, 1900-1970. Ph.D. Dissertation. University of South Carolina. 1971. 206 pp. DAI 32/5. (November 1971). Page 2454-A. Order # 71-28,900.

English Education

466. Criscoe, Betty L. An Historical Analysis of Spelling Instruction in the United States, 1644-1973. Ph.D. Dissertation. Syracuse University. 1973. 229 pp. DAI 34/11. (May 1974). Page 7014-A. Order # 74-10,138.

467. Flaherty, Terrance J. Charles W. Eliot and the Teaching of Composition. Ph.D. Dissertation. Northwestern University. 1978. 261 pp. DAI 39/10. (April 1979). Page 5985-A. Order # 7907873.

468. Gibson, James C. An Examination of Speech Teaching in Selected Georgia Educational Institutions, 1732-1900. Ed.D. Dissertation. University of Georgia. 1971. 203 pp. DAI 32/7. (January 1972). Page 3738-A. Order # 72-2485.

469. Kraus, Joanna H. A History of the Children's Theater Association of Baltimore, Maryland from 1943-1966. Ed.D. Dissertation. 1972. 408 pp. DAI 33/11. (July 1972). Page 175-A. Order # 72-19,518.

470. Schwartz, Philip J. A Historical Analysis of Creative Dramatics in American Schools. Ed.D. Dissertation. Rutgers, the State University. 1979. 145 pp. DAI 40/7. (January 1980). Page 3830-A. Order # 8000880.

471. Smith, Jr., Rodney P. Contributions to Reading in Elementary English, 1924-1973. Ph.D. Dissertation. Florida State University. 1973. 330 pp. DAI 35/2. (August 1974). Page 730-A. Order # 74-18,042.

472. Sykes, George. The Humanities Movement and the Search for Curriculum Unity in Secondary Education. Ed.D. Dissertation. Columbia University. 1973. 158 pp. DAI 35/9. (March 1975). Page 5890-A. Order # 75-6477.

Foreign Languages

473. Ameruoso, Frank A. Latin in the American Public High School--A Struggle for Survival in the Twentieth Century. Ph.D. Dissertation. University of Pittsburgh. 1974. 180 pp. DAI 35/9. (March 1975). Page 5883-A. Order # 75-6337.

474. Aronson, Jack L. Classical and Modern Foreign Languages in American Secondary Schools and Colleges--An Historical Analysis. Ed.D.

Dissertation. Boston University. 1975. 171 pp. DAI 35/12. (June 1975). Page 7601-A. Order # 75-12,224.

475. Arum, Stephen M. Early Stages of Foreign Language and Area Studies in the United States: 1915-1941. Ed.D. Dissertation. Columbia University. 1975. 678 pp. DAI 37/3. (September 1976). Page 1421-A. Order # 76-20,864.

476. Chanover, E. Pierre. A History of the Teaching of French in Public and Private Schools of Nassau County from 1898 to 1930, Grades K-12. Ph.D. Dissertation. New York University. 1975. 245 pp. DAI 36/4. (October 1975). Page 2070-A. Order # 75-21,137.

477. Coleman, Rosalie M. An Historical Analysis of the French/English Bilingual Education Programs Conducted in Connecticut by the Daughters of the Holy Spirit. Ph.D. Dissertation. University of Connecticut. 1978. 263 pp. DAI 39/11. (May 1979). Page 6404-A. Order # 7911350.

478. Hildebrand, Janet E. Methods for Teaching College German in the United States, 1753-1903: An Historical Study. Ph.D. Dissertation. University of Texas. 1977. 230 pp. DAI 38/7. (January 1978). Page 3996-A. Order # 77-29,044.

479. Javert, Richard I. Lawrence Augustus Wilkins and the Advancement of High School Spanish Teaching in the United States, 1914-1942. Ed.D. Dissertation. Columbia University. 1973. 204 pp. DAI 33/12. (June 1973). Page 6703-A. Order # 73-15,022.

Home Economics Education

---

480. Liddell, Marian B. Home Economics: Past, Present and Future. Ed.D. Dissertation. West Virginia University. 1978. 207 pp. DAI 39/11. (May 1979). Page 6589-A. Order # 7910877.

Mathematics Education

---

481. Bell, James A. Trends in Secondary Mathematics in Relation to Psychological Theories, 1893-1970. Ed.D. Dissertation. University of Oklahoma. 1971. 191 pp. DAI 32/4. (October 1971). Page 1890-A. Order # 71-26,540.

482. Hayden, Robert W. A History of the 'New Math' Movement in the United States. Ph.D. Dissertation. Iowa State University. 1981. 278 pp. Page 4753-A. Order # 8209127.

Science Education

483. Blank, Efrom I. The History of the Development of the Earth Science
     Course in the Secondary Schools of New York State, 1894 to 1966.
     Ph.D. Dissertation. New York University. 1972. 371 pp. DAI 33/1.
     (July 1972). Page 174-A. Order # 72-20,619.

484. Boekenkamp, Richard P. Geological Education in the United States
     During the Late Nineteenth Century. Ph.D. Dissertation. Ohio State
     University. 1974. 189 pp. DAI 35/5. (November 1974). Page 2792-
     A. Order # 74-24,299.

485. Gough, Jerry B. The Foundations of Modern Chemistry: The Origin
     and Development of the Concept of the Gaseous State and its Role in
     the Chemical Revolution of the Eighteenth Century. Ph.D. Disserta-
     tion. Cornell University. 1971. 222 pp. DAI 32/4. (October 1971).
     Page 2012-A. Order # 71-27,382.

486. Lynch, Francis P. Growth of Environmental Awareness in Connecti-
     cut and the Curriculum Response in Public Secondary Schools, 1950-
     1970. Ph.D. Dissertation. University of Connecticut. 1973. 326 pp.
     DAI 34/7. (January 1974). Page 3935-A. Order # 74-26.

487. Minton, Tyree G. The History of the Nature-Study Movement and its
     Role in the Development of Environmental Education. Ed.D. Disser-
     tation. University of Massachusetts. 1980. 223 pp. DAI 41/3.
     (September 1980). Page 967-A. Order # 8019480.

488. Ogden, William R. A Chronological History of the Objectives for
     Teaching Chemistry in the High Schools of the United States During
     the Period 1918-1967, as Reflected in Selected Professional Periodicals.
     Ph.D. Dissertation. University of Wisconsin. 1972. 515 pp. DAI
     33/8. (February 1973). Page 4142-A. Order # 72-29,509.

489. Root-Bernstein, Robert S. The Ionists: Founding of Physical Chem-
     istry, 1872-1890. Ph.D. Dissertation. Princeton University. 1980.
     667 pp. DAI 41/7. (January 1981). Page 3238-A. Order # 8101554.

490. Roy, Robert H. Secondary School Earth Science Teaching, 1918-
     1972: Objectives as Stated in Periodical Literature. Ed.D. Disser-
     tation. East Texas State Universtiy. 1979. 570 pp. DAI 40/2.
     (August 1979). Page 781-A. Order # 7918463.

Social Sciences (Including History)

491. Biddle, Thelma S. The Development of the Social Studies Program in
     Richmond, Virginia, 1869-1971. Ed.D. Dissertation. University of
     Virginia. 1973. 192 pp. DAI 34/2. (August 1973). Page 552-A.
     Order # 73-18,992.

492. Bronson, Judith A. C. Ellen Semple: Contributions to the History
      of American Geography. Ph.D. Dissertation. St. Louis University.
      1973. 269 pp. DAI 35/5. (November 1974). Page 2877-A. Order
      # 74-24,049.

493. Browne, Joseph L. The Role of the Historian in the Development of
      History in the Secondary School Social Studies Curriculum, 1959-
      1969. Ph.D. Dissertation. University of Maryland. 1972. 238 pp.
      DAI 33/1. (July 1972). Page 139-A. Order # 72-18,943.

494. Casey, Michael T. Economic Education in American High Schools,
      1894-1924. Ed.D. Dissertation. Columbia University. 1971. 310 pp.
      DAI 32/6. (December 1971). Page 3066-A. Order # 72-1227.

495. Cavallini, Donald J. Using Oral History in College and High School:
      A Model for Studying the Great Depression. D.A. Dissertation.
      Illinois State University. 1980. 325 pp. DAI 41/5. (November
      1980). Page 2257-A. Order # 8024302.

496. Clemmer, Janice W. A Portrayal of the American Indian in Utah State
      Approved United States History Textbooks. Ph.D. Dissertation. Uni-
      versity of Utah. 1979. 103 pp. DAI 40/5. (November 1979).
      Page 2526-A. Order # 7924346.

497. Cornbleth, Catherine R. Inquiry Theory and New Social Studies Cur-
      ricula, 1910-1972. Ph.D. Dissertation. University of Texas. 1974.
      145 pp. DAI 35/1. (July 1974). Page 318-A. Order # 74-14,680.

498. Dodge, Ellen E. A Study of the Articulation of American History
      Courses in High Schools and Colleges in the Twentieth Century.
      Ed.D. Dissertation. Columbia University. 1979. 173 pp. DAI 40/4.
      (October 1979). Page 1920-A. Order # 7923584.

499. Dority, John F. Evolution of New York State Education Department's
      Sylabuses (sic) in Social Studies, 1930-1970, with a Content Analysis
      of Syllabuses (sic) Published in the 1960's. Ed.D. Dissertation.
      Syracuse University. 1971. 407 pp. DAI 32/8. (February 1972).
      Page 4238-A. Order # 72-6660.

500. Dudley, Richard E. History and the Social Sciences in Nebraska Pub-
      lic Schools During the Quarter Century of the National Committee
      Movement, 1892-1918. Ph.D. Dissertation. University of Nebraska,
      1970. 421 pp. DAI 31/4. (October 1970). Page 1590-A. Order #
      70-17,718.

501. Fleming, Daniel B. A Legislative History of Federally Supported Teacher
      Institutes in History and the Social Sciences. Ed.D. Dissertation.
      George Washington University. 1970. 112 pp. DAI 31/5. (Novem-
      ber 1970). Page 2138-A. Order # 70-20,106.

502. Glasheen, Patricia. The Advent of Social Studies, 1916: An Historic
      Study. Ed.D. Dissertation. Boston University. 1973. 227 pp.
      DAI 34/4. (October 1973). Page 1666-A. Order # 73-23,563.

503. Grier, Lee W. The History of the Teaching of Sociology in the Sec-
      ondary School. Ed.D. Dissertation. Duke University. 1971. 277
      pp. DAI 32/10. (April 1972). Page 5580-A. Order # 72-11,094.

504. Le Riche, Leo W. The Widening Horizon Concept in Elementary Social
      Studies Education, 1903-1965. Ph.D. Dissertation. University of
      Washington. 1974. 219 pp. DAI 35/9. (March 1975). Page 5888-
      A. Order # 75-6605.

505. Little, Timothy H. A History of the Law in American Society Project.
      Ph.D. Dissertation. Northwestern University. 1971. 409 pp. DAI
      32/8. (February 1972). Page 4390-A. Order # 72-7813.

506. McCann, Mary B. A Description of Social Studies in the Catholic Sec-
      ondary Schools of the Archdiocese of Philadelphia, 1890-1976. Ed.D.
      Dissertation. Temple University. 1978. 153 pp. DAI 39/11. (May
      1979). Page 6682-A. Order # 7910012.

507. Muschinske, David J. Social Ideas and Social Studies: Relationships
      Between Social Thought and Proposals for Social Science Education in
      American Public Schools as Revealed in the Writings of John Dewey,
      G. Stanley Hall, Harold Rugg, Charles McMurray, Frank McMurray,
      Charles De Garmo and the American Historical Association's Commit-
      tee on the Study and Teaching of History in Elementary Schools.
      Ed.D. Dissertation. Boston University. 1971. 305 pp. DAI 32/4.
      (October 1971). Page 1892-A. Order # 71-26,724.

508. Rampton, George O. The Development of Secondary Social Studies
      Content in the Public Schools of Utah from 1874 to 1969. Ed.D. Dis-
      sertation. Utah State University. 1969. 273 pp. DAI 30/8. (Feb-
      ruary 1970). Page 3296-A. Order # 70-2443.

509. Robinson, David P. Historical Models of the Emergence of the Social
      Studies. Ph.D. Dissertation. Stanford University. 1977. 251 pp.
      DAI 38/9. (March 1978). Page 5386-A. Order # 7802224.

510. Samec, Charles E. A History of the Amherst Project: Revising the
      Teaching of American History, 1959-1972. Ph.D. Dissertation. Loyola
      University, Chicago. 1976. 141 pp. DAI 37/5. (November 1976).
      Page 2688-A. Order # 76-24,457.

511. Schwartz, John J. The Work of Harold Rugg and the Question of Ob-
      jectivity. Ph.D. Dissertation. University of Rochester. 1978. 219
      pp. DAI 39/4. (October 1978). Page 2041-A. Order # 7818285.

512. Secrist, Philip L. The Public Pays the Piper: The People and Social
      Studies in Georgia Schools, 1930-1970. Ed.D. Dissertation. Univer-
      sity of Georgia. 1971. 154 pp. DAI 32/7. (January 1972). Page
      3740-A. Order # 72-2538.

513. Smolens, Richard. The Source Study Method of Teaching History in
      Nebraska (1891-1920): An Attempt at Large Scale Teaching Innovation.
      Ed.D. Dissertation. Columbia University. 1970. 414 pp. DAI 32/7.
      (January 1972). Page 3741-A. Order # 72-4188-A.

514. Stearns, Harold J. American History in Montana High Schools: Past
      and Present. Ed.D. Dissertation. University of Montana. 1978.
      618 pp. DAI 39/5. (November 1978). Page 2677-A. Order #
      7821910.

515. Streb, Richard W. A History of the Citizenship Education Project:
      A Model Curricular Study. Ed.D. Dissertation. Columbia University.

1979. 396 pp. DAI 40/5. (November 1979). Page 2516-A. Order # 7923624.

516. Wilson, Virginia. Harold Rugg's Social and Educational Philosophy as Reflected in his Textbook Series, "Man and His Changing Society." Ph.D. Dissertation. Duke University. 1975. 269 pp. DAI 36/6. (December 1975). Page 3470-A. Order # 75-29,486.

517. Wilson, Yvonna A. Curricular Materials for Teaching Post-Secondary Students about Notable American Women, 1920-1970. Ed.D. Dissertation. University of Arkansas. 1977. 348 pp. DAI 38/5. (November 1977). Page 2539-A. Order # 77-23,394.

Education and Culture

518. Bynack, Vincent P. Language and the Order of the World: Noah Webster and the Idea of American Culture. Ph.D. Dissertation. Yale University. 1978. 292 pp. DAI 39/4. (October 1978). Page 2375-A. Order # 7818587.

519. Geschwind, Norman. The History of Anthropology and Education--From the Doctrine of Recapitulation to the Culture Concept: The Impact of a Paradigm Shift. Ed.D. Dissertation. University of Hawaii. 1980. 155 pp. DAI 41/12. (June 1981). Page 5003-A. No Order #.

520. Hayatt, Marshall. The Emergence of a Discipline: Franz Boas and the Study of Man. Ph.D. Dissertation. University of Delaware. 1979. 363 pp. DAI 40/2. (August 1979). Page 1028-A. Order # 7918803.

521. Kendall, Cynthia. Anglo-Saxonism and the Reaction of the American Public Schools, 1870-1915. Ed.D. Dissertation. Columbia University. 1975. 264 pp. DAI 36/3. (September 1975). Page 1344-A. Order # 75-18,688.

522. Wolf, Ronald H. The Influence of Cultural Anthropology Upon American History as Reflected in the American Indian Case. Ed.D. Dissertation. Columbia University. 1977. 484 pp. DAI 38/3. (September 1977). Page 1939-A. Order # 77-22,313.

Education in Literature

523. Ainsworth, Charles P. Academia in Recent American Fiction: An Exploration of Main Themes in Novels Related to Higher Education, 1961-1971. Ed.D. Dissertation. University of Kentucky. 1973. 342 pp. DAI 35/3. (September 1973). Page 1455-A. Order # 74-19,607.

524. Chalpin, Lila. Dystopia as Viewed by Social Scientists and Novelists. Ed.D. Dissertation. Boston University. 1977. 232 pp. DAI 38/9. (March 1978). Page 5383-A. Order # 7732759.

525. Click, Donald W. The Image of Higher Education in American Novels, 1920-1966. Ed.D. Dissertation. University of Southern California. 1970. 208 pp. DAI 31/3. (September 1970). Page 1032-A. Order # 70-16,858.

526. Colozzi, John J. Educational Values as Reflected in Some Best-Selling American Fiction, 1895-1916. Ed.D. Dissertation. George Peabody College for Teachers. 1976. 141 pp. DAI 37/9. (March 1977). Page 6011-A. Order # 76-21,620.

527. Daniels, Dalia R. Utopia: Literacy and Educational Implications. Ph.D. Dissertation. University of Texas. 1977. 167 pp. DAI 38/7. (January 1978). Page 3994-A. Order # 77-29,015.

528. Di Fazio, John S. A Content Analysis to Determine the Presence of Selected American Values Found in Comic Books During Two Time Periods, 1946-1950, and 1966-1970. Ph.D. Dissertation. University of Iowa. 1973. 302 pp. DAI 34/9. (March 1974). Page 5578-A. Order # 74-7366.

529. Finn, Thomas. College Teaching as Portrayed in the American College Novel, 1962-1972. Ph.D. Dissertation. University of California, Berkeley. 1979. 232 pp. DAI 41/1. (July 1980). Page 123-A. Order # 8014675.

530. Floyd, Jo Ann. The Journey Home: The Intellectual's Search for Identity in Five Spanish-American Novels. Ed.D. Dissertation. Columbia University. 1979. 334 pp. DAI 40/9. (March 1980). Page 4927-A. Order # 8006808.

531. Gardiner, Helen J. American Utopian Fiction, 1885-1910: The Influence of Science and Technology. Ph.D. Dissertation. University of Houston. 1978. 207 pp. DAI 39/11. (May 1979). Page 6840-A. Order # 7910490.

532. Hearn, Betty H. An Interpretative Study of the Relationship Between Political and Educational Theory in Four Literary Utopias. Ph.D. Dissertation. University of Mississippi. 1972. 195 pp. DAI 33/11. (May 1973). Page 6148-A. Order # 73-11,425.

533. Hetherington, Edith W. Education in Eighteenth Century English Novels. Ph.D. Dissertation. University of Kansas. 1976. 175 pp. DAI 37/8. (February 1977). Page 4912-A. Order # 77-2228.

534. King, James B. The Persona of the College Professor in the American Novel, 1928-1968. Ph.D. Dissertation. University of Michigan. 1970. 303 pp. DAI 31/8. (February 1970). Page 3902-A. Order # 71-4652.

535. Lauffer, Carolyn G. The Satiric Treatment of College Teaching in the Novel, 1960-1972. Ph.D. Dissertation. Duke University. 1977. 239 pp. DAI 38/12. (June 1978). Page 7172-A. Order # 7807611.

536. Mac Leod, Anne S. A Moral Tale: Children's Fiction and American Culture. Ph.D. Dissertation. University of Maryland. 1973. 259 pp. DAI 34/6. (December 1973). Page 3308-A. Order # 73-28,868.

537. Nichols, Edward L. The Image of the College Professor as a Protagonist

in Selected American Novels from 1945 through 1965. Ed.D. Dissertation. Tulsa University. 1970. 217 pp. DAI 31/8. (February 1971).
Page 3787-A. Order # 71-4450.

538. Noble, Judith A. The Home, the Church, and the School as Portrayed
      in American Realistic Fiction for Children, 1965-1969. Ph.D. Dissertation. Michigan State University. 1971. 320 pp. DAI 32/6. (December 1971). Page 2918-A. Order # 71-31,271.

539. Parks, Gail A. Adolescence in the Twenties as Represented in American Novels, Popular Magazines and Literature Anthologies of the
      Decade. Ph.D. Dissertation. 1977. 275 pp. DAI 38/10. (April
      1978). Page 5986-A. Order # 7804110.

540. Poteet, George H. A Computer-Assisted Content Analysis of Film
      Criticism in Popular American Periodicals from 1933 through 1977.
      Ed.D. Dissertation. Columbia University. 1971. 121 pp. DAI 32/6.
      (December 1971). Page 2920-A. Order # 72-1257.

541. Seaton, Chadwick L. The Image of College Life as Reflected in a
      Sampling of American Novels, 1950-1969. Ed.D. Dissertation. Indiana University. 1974. 218 pp. DAI 35/10. (April 1975). Page
      6486-A. Order # 75-5663.

542. Sundstrand, Lyndon D. The Academic Community as Reflected in Selected American Novels. Ph.D. Dissertation. University of Southern
      California. 1977. n.p. DAI 38/8. (February 1978). Page 4617-A.
      No Order #.

543. Young, James M. How Bright the Vision: Social and Educational
      Structures in Modern Utopian Literature. Ph.D. Dissertation. University of Minnesota. 1980. 146 pp. DAI 41/5. (November 1980).
      Page 2245-A. Order # 8025529.

544. Zellhoffer, Gregor F. The Image of the Public High School Teacher
      in the American Novel, 1920-1970. Ph.D. Dissertation. Loyola University, Chicago. 1980. 237 pp. DAI 40/11. (May 1980). Page
      5815-A. Order # 8011029.

Family, Mothers and Childhood

---

545. Boozer, Julie L. Early Childhood as Portrayed in Women's Magazines,
      1945-1970. Ph.D. Dissertation. University of Pittsburgh. 1971.
      250 pp. DAI 32/4. (October 1971). Page 1891-A. Order # 71-
      26,152.

546. Brickman, Jane P. Mother Love--Mother Death: Maternal and Infant
      Care; Social Class and the Role of Government (in 19th Century America). Ph.D. Dissertation. City University of New York. 1978. 757
      pp. DAI 39/4. (October 1978). Page 2482-A. Order # 7818810.

547. Candela, Jr., Joseph L. Concern for Family Stability in American
      Opinion, 1880-1920. Ph.D. Dissertation. University of Chicago.
      1978. n.p. DAI 39/1. (July 1978). Page 425-A. No Order #.

548. Censer, Jane T. Parents and Children: North Carolina Planter Families, 1800-1860. Ph.D. Dissertation. Johns Hopkins University. 1980. 395 pp. DAI 41/3. (September 1980). Page 1185-A. Order # 8020128.

549. Chapman, Jimmy C. Changes in the Concepts of Childhood Education in America, 1607-1860. Ph.D. Dissertation. University of Texas. 1972. 235 pp. DAI 34/2. (August 1973). Page 592-A. Order # 73-18,411.

550. Covotsos, Louis J. Child Welfare and Social Progress: A History of the United States Children's Bureau, 1912-1935. Ph.D. Dissertation. University of Chicago. 1976. n.p. DAI 37/6. (December 1976). Page 3848-A. No Order #.

551. Frankel, Gusti W. Between Parent and Child in Colonial New England: An Analysis of the Religious Child-Oriented Literature and Selected Children's Works. Ph.D. Dissertation. University of Minnesota. 1976. 280 pp. DAI 38/3. (September 1977). Page 1572-A. Order # 77-18,986.

552. Klos, Sarah F. Reform Initiatives in American Maternal Health Services, 1900-1940. Ed.D. Dissertation. Harvard University. 1979. DAI 40/6. (December 1979). Page 3161-A. Order # 7927949.

553. Leyden, Martha C. An Analysis of the Advice Given to Parents About Preschooler's Play from 1930 to 1970 through Popular Magazines. Ed.D. Dissertation. Columbia University. 1971. 105 pp. DAI 32/7. (January 1972). Page 3562-A. Order # 72-4173.

554. McGlone, Robert E. Suffer the Children: The Emergence of Modern Middle-Class Family Life in America, 1820-1870. Ph.D. Dissertation. University of California, Los Angeles. 1971. DAI 32/7. (January 1972). Page 3927-A. Order # 72-3183.

555. Mulligan, Jane S. The Madonna and the Child in American Culture, 1830-1916. Ph.D. Dissertation. University of California, Los Angeles. 1975. DAI 36/7. (January 1976). Page 4679-A. Order # 76-1156.

556. Reinier, Jacqueline R. Attitudes Toward and Practices of Child-Rearing: Philadelphia, 1790 to 1830. Ph.D. Dissertation. University of California, Berkeley. 1977. 476 pp. DAI 39/2. (August 1978). Page 1063-A. Order # 7812749.

557. Rosenberg, Gary L. Family and Society in the Early Seventeenth Century Massachusetts Bay Area. Ph.D. Dissertation. State University of New York, Buffalo. 1980. 283 pp. DAI 41/2. (August 1980). Page 774-A. Order # 8016241.

558. Ross, Elizabeth D.F. The Kindergarten Movement in the United States, 1870-1914. Ph.D. Dissertation. Johns Hopkins University. 1971. 190 pp. DAI 34/7. (January 1974). Page 3939-A. Order # 73-31,233.

559. Slater, Peter Gregg. Views of Children and of Child-Rearing During the Early National Period: A Study in the New England Intellect. Ph.D. Dissertation. University of California, Berkeley. 1970. 336 pp. DAI 31/12. (June 1971). Page 6532-A. Order # 71-15,888.

560. Smallwood, Mary A. N. Childhood on the Southern Plains Frontier,
     1870-1910. Ph.D. Dissertation. Texas Tech University. 1975. 242
     pp. DAI 37/2. (August 1976). Page 1181-A. Order # 76-17,763.

561. Smith, Daniel B. Family Experience and Kinship in Eighteenth-Century
     Chesapeake Society. Ph.D. Dissertation. University of Virginia.
     1978. 416 pp. DAI 39/8. (February 1978). Page 5107-A. Order #
     7903532.

562. Stowe, Steven M. All the Relations of Life: A Study in Sexuality,
     Family and Social Values in the Southern Planter Class. Ph.D. Dis-
     sertation. State University of New York, Stony Brook. 1979. 481
     pp. DAI 39/11. (May 1979). Page 6923-A. Order # 7911329.

563. Tank, Robert M. Young Children, Families and Society in America
     Since the 1820's: The Evolution of Health, Education, and Child
     Care Programs for Preschool Children. Ph.D. Dissertation. Univer-
     sity of Michigan. 1980. 477 pp. DAI 41/9. (March 1981). Page
     4144-A. Order # 8106233.

564. Tueth, S. J., Michael W. The Image of the Family in Popular Ameri-
     can Theater, 1945-1960. Ph.D. Dissertation. New York University.
     1977. 284 pp. DAI 38/12. (June 1978). Page 7409-A. Order #
     7808566.

Government, Politics and Education

---

565. Adams, David W. The Federal Indian Boarding School: A Study of
     Environment and Response, 1879-1918. Ed.D. Dissertation. Univer-
     sity of Indiana. 1975. 275 pp. DAI 36/9. (March 1976). Page
     5885-A. Order # 76-6261.

566. Benenati, Carl G. The State Politics of Decision Making for K-12
     Public Education in New York State, 1920-1970. Ph.D. Dissertation.
     Syracuse University. 1971. 395 pp. DAI 32/8. (February 1972).
     Page 4266-A. Order # 72-6553.

567. Biebel, Charles D. Politics, Pedagogues and Statesmanship: James
     B. Conant and the Public Schools, 1933-1948. Ph.D. Dissertation.
     University of Wisconsin. 1971. 313 pp. DAI 32/6. (December 1971).
     Page 3194-A. Order # 71-24,448.

568. Briggs, Ernest E. The Educational Policies of Richard M. Nixon.
     Ed.D. Dissertation. Auburn University. 1973. 172 pp. DAI 34/3.
     (September 1973). Page 996-A. Order # 73-19,648.

569. Broder, Dorothy E. Life Adjustment Education: A Historical Study
     of a Program in the United States Office of Education, 1945-1954.
     Ed.D. Dissertation. Columbia University. 1977. 272 pp. DAI 37/12.
     (June 1977). Page 7500. Order # 77-13,015.

570. Citron, Henry. The Study of the Arguments of Interest Groups Which
     Opposed Federal Aid to Education from 1945-1965. Ph.D. Dissertation.

New York University. 1977. 253 pp. DAI 38/3. (September 1977). Page 2298-A. Order # 77-20,739.

571. Clowse, Barbara B. Education as an Instrument of National Security: The Cold War Campaign to "Beat the Russians" from Sputnik to the National Defense Education Act of 1958. Ph.D. Dissertation. University of North Carolina. 1977. 381 pp. DAI 38/11. (May 1978). Page 6892-A. Order # 7807122.

572. Cox, Charles W. The Congressional Struggle to Create a Separate Department of Education, 1918-1930. Ed.D. Dissertation. Ball State University. 1971. 269 pp. DAI 32/10. (April 1972). Page 5579-A. Order # 72-12,667.

573. Dobbin, Sister M. Teresita. Childhood Emancipation: The United States Federal Government and Education, 1880-1930. Ph.D. Dissertation. Catholic University of America. 1970. 181 pp. DAI 30/12. (June 1970). Page 5260-A. Order # 70-10,572.

574. Esquith, Stephen L. Liberal Political Philosophy and the Problem of Political Education. Ph.D. Dissertation. Princeton University. 1979. 412 pp. DAI 39/11. (May 1979). Page 6936-A. Order # 7910108.

575. Freedman, Irving H. The Issue of Public Support for Church-Related Education in the 1967 New York State Constitutional Convention: A Study in the Decision-Making Process. Ed.D. Dissertation. State University of New York, Albany. 1969. n.p. DAI 30/8. (February 1970). Page 3294-A. Order # 70-1886.

576. Hill, John W. The Elementary and Secondary Education Act of 1965. Ed.D. Dissertation. Boston University. 1971. 176 pp. DAI 32/4. (October 1971). Page 1785-A. Order # 71-26,704.

577. Huckabee, Ray M. A Study of Change in the Administration of Federal Level Apprenticeship Policy (1937-1978). Ph.D. Dissertation. New York University. 1979. 210 pp. DAI 40/7. (January 1970). Page 3827-A. Order # 7925270.

578. Jarman, Beth S. Political Activism: Does it Impact on the Quality of Education? Ph.D. Dissertation. University of Utah. 1977. 191 pp. DAI 38/5. (November 1977). Page 2610-A. Order # 77-23,430.

579. Jeffrey, Julie R. Education for Children of the Poor: A Study of the Origins and Implementation of the Elementary and Secondary Education Act of 1965. Ph.D. Dissertation. Rice University. 1972. 288 pp. DAI 33/4. (October 1972). Page 1647-A. Order # 72-26,429.

580. Jones, Kenneth M. Science, Scientists, and Americans: Images of Science and the Formation of Federal Science Policy, 1945-1950. Ph.D. Dissertation. Cornell University. 1975. 430 pp. DAI 36/5. (November 1975). Page 3070-A. Order # 75-24,202.

581. Judd, Elliot L. Factors Affecting the Passage of the Bilingual Education Act of 1967. Ph.D. Dissertation. New York University. 1977. 284 pp. DAI 38/12. (June 1978). Page 7198-A. Order # 7808471.

582. Lindenberg, Terrance W. An Historical Analysis of the Conceptual
      Development of Federal Aid to Elementary and Secondary Education,
      1890-1939. Ph.D. Dissertation. University of Illinois. 1974. 504
      pp. DAI 35/7. (January 1975). Page 4214-A. Order # 72-29,618.

583. Marden, David L. The Cold War and American Education. Ph.D. Dis-
      sertation. University of Kansas. 1975. 489 pp. DAI 37/1. (July
      1976). Page 548-A. Order # 76-16,749.

584. Martin, Don T. The Public Statements of Presidents Truman and Ei-
      senhower on Federal Aid to Education. Ph.D. Dissertation. Ohio
      State University. 1970. 263 pp. DAI 31/9. (March 1971). Page
      4502-A. Order # 71-7513.

585. Marver, James D. Consultants Can Help: The Use of Outside Ex-
      perts in the U.S. Office of Child Development. Ph.D. Dissertation.
      University of California, Berkeley. 1979. 347 pp. DAI 40/1. (July
      1979). Page 453-A. Order # 7914691.

586. McBride, Ruth T. The Concept of Political Education: An Exercise
      in Republican Thought. Ph.D. Dissertation. University of Arizona.
      1979. 96 pp. DAI 40/5. (November 1979). Page 2861-A. Order #
      7923186.

587. McCann, Maurice J. The Truman Administration and Education. Ph.D.
      Dissertation. Southern Illinois University. 1976. 287 pp. DAI
      39/1. (August 1978). Page 721-A. Order # 7813560.

588. McDougall, Daniel J. McCarthyism and Academia: Senator Joe Mc-
      Carthy's Political Investigations of Education, 1950-54. Ph.D. Dis-
      sertation. Loyola University, Chicago. 1977. 372 pp. DAI 38/3.
      (September 1977). Page 1936-A. Order # 77-22,346.

589. Murray, Michael A. The House Education-Labor Committee and the
      1967 Poverty Controversy: A Study of Congressional Avoidance.
      Ph.D. Dissertation. University of Illinois. 1969. 266 pp. DAI
      30/7. (January 1970). Page 3066-A. Order # 70-939.

590. Nozicka, George J. Distributional Analysis of Federally Funded Re-
      search and Development at Universities and Colleges (1973-1977).
      Ph.D. Dissertation. American University. 1979. 196 pp. DAI
      40/5. (November 1979). Page 2862-A. Order # 7924360.

591. Robinson, Imogene G. An Historical Study of the Impact of the Edu-
      cation Professions Development Act and Other Acts on the Problem
      of Personnel Displacement in Segregated Schools. Ed.D. Disserta-
      tion. George Washington University. 1977. 235 pp. DAI 38/6.
      (December 1977). Page 3199-A. Order # 77-25,548.

592. Rogers, Nancy L. D. The Development of Federal Policy for the
      Elimination of Discrimination in the Postsecondary Education of Women.
      Ph.D. Dissertation. University of Michigan. 1979. 168 pp. DAI
      40/2. (August 1979). Page 712-A. Order # 7916802.

593. Ross, Naomi V. Congresswoman Edith Green on Federal Aid to Schools
      and Colleges. Ed.D. Dissertation. Pennsylvania State University.
      1980. 319 pp. DAI 41/5. (November 1980). Page 1974-A. Order
      #8024488.

594. Smith III., Gilbert E. The Limits of Reform: Politics and Federal Aid
to Education, 1937-1950. Ph.D. Dissertation. Columbia University.
1975. 442 pp. DAI 36/5. (November 1975). Page 3075-A. Order
75-25,722.

595. Sorenson, Dale R. The Anticommunist Consensus in Indiana, 1945-
1958. Ph.D. Dissertation. University of Indiana. 1980. 242 pp.
DAI 41/3. (September 1980). Page 1191-A. Order # 8020040.

596. Stanley, III., William O. The [American] Communist Party and Education, 1928-1939: The Union of Theory and Practice. Ph.D. Dissertation. University of Illinois. 1974. 421 pp. DAI 35/11. (May
1975). Page 7095-A. Order # 75-11,674.

597. Sullivan, Harold J. De Facto School Segregation: Private Choice or
Public Policy? Ph.D. Dissertation. City University of New York.
1978. 247 pp. DAI 39/7. (January 1979). Page 4477-A. Order #
7900812.

598. Sullivan, Samuel. President Lyndon Baines Johnson and the Common
School, 1963-1969. Ed.D. Dissertation. Oklahoma State University.
1973. 334 pp. DAI 34/10. (April 1974). Page 6425-A. Order #
74-8127.

599. Sutherland, James H. Federal Grants to State Departments of Education for the Administration of the Elementary and Secondary Education Acts of 1965. Ph.D. Dissertation. University of Michigan.
1974. 198 pp. DAI 35/8. (February 1975). Page 5072-A. Order #
75-829.

600. Trusz, Andrew R. The Activities of Governmental Education Bodies
in Refining the Role of Post-Secondary Education Since 1945: A Comparative Case Study of New York and the Province of Ontario, 1945-
1972. Ed.D. Dissertation. State University of New York, Buffalo.
1977. 402 pp. DAI 39/2. (August 1978). Page 716-A. Order #
7813994.

601. Van Wormer, James W. Sputnik and American Education. Ph.D. Dissertation. Michigan State University. 1976. 201 pp. DAI 37/12.
(June 1977). Page 7579-A. Order # 77-11,728.

602. Weaver, Samuel H. The Truman Administration and Federal Aid to
Education. Ph.D. Dissertation. American University. 1972. 359 pp.
DAI 33/5. (November 1972). Page 2311-A. Order # 72-30,117.

603. Whitmore, Bonnie C. Early Childhood Education: A Bibliography of
Federal Legislation (1910-1970). Ed.D. Dissertation. University of
Arkansas, 1973. 98 pp. DAI 34/5. (November 1973). Page 2358-
A. Order # 73-27,400.

604. Wilson, Jr., Samuel P. The Politics of Funding State Senior High Ed-
ucation in Texas: An Analysis of the Pressure Group--Policy Process.
Ph.D. Dissertation. North Texas State University. 1980. 211 pp.
DAI 41/4. (October 1980). Page 1756-A. Order # 8021927.

605. Wrigley, Julia C. The Politics of Education in Chicago (ca. 1900-
1950): Social Conflicts and the Public Schools. Ph.D. Dissertation.

University of Wisconsin. 1977. 360 pp. DAI 38/10. (April 1978).
Page 6341-A. Order # 7725854.

Higher Education

606. Altenbaugh, Richard J. Forming the Structure of a New Society Within
the Shell of the Old: A Study of Three Labor Colleges (Brookwood
Labor College in Katonah, N.Y.; Commonwealth College near Mena,
Arkansas; and Work People's College in Duluth, Minnesota) and Their
Contributions to the American Labor Movement. Ph.D. Dissertation.
University of Pittsburgh. 1980. 396 pp. DAI 41/2. (August 1980).
Page 565-A. Order # 8018284.

607. Barbeau, Joseph E. The Historical Development of Cooperative Education in American Higher Education. Ed.D. Dissertation. Boston University. 1973. 231 pp. DAI 34/4. (October 1973). Page 1637-A.
Order # 73-23,533.

608. Bell, Dorothy E. A Phoenix in Our Midst: The Carnegie Foundation
for the Advancement of Teaching and its Relationship to American
Higher Education, (1950-1970). Ph.D. Dissertation. University of
Illinois. 1972. 479 pp. DAI 34/2. (August 1973). Page 576-A.
Order # 73-17,115.

609. Bushko, Andrew A. Religious Revivals at American Colleges, 1783-
1860: An Exploratory Study. Ed.D. Dissertation. Columbia University. 1974. 251 pp. DAI 35/9. (March 1975). Page 5844-A. Order
75-6460.

610. Carr, George A. Relationships Between the Political and Educational
Progressives. Ed.D. Dissertation. Cornell University. 1972. 199
pp. DAI 33/12. (June 1973). Page 6702-A. Order # 73-14,695.

611. Carrig, Anne T. The English Contribution to Higher Educational Reform in the Post-Civil War Period. Ph.D. Dissertation. Boston College. 1971. 521 pp. DAI 32/2. (August 1971). Page 858-A.
Order # 71-19,791.

612. Cook, Anne W. A History of the Indiana University Audio-Visual Center: 1913-1975. Ph.D. Dissertation. Indiana University. 1980.
334 pp. DAI 41/1. (July 1980). Page 69-A. Order # 8016402.

613. Davis, Eugene D. The Rise and Development of Farmers' Institutes
in Michigan in Relationship to Michigan Agricalatural College from
1876 to 1889. Ph.D. Dissertation. Michigan State University. 1974.
199 pp. DAI 35/9. (March 1975). Page 5883-A. Order # 75-7149.

614. Davis, Mollie C. Quest for a New America: Ferment in Collegiate
Culture, 1921-1929. Ph.D. Dissertation. University of Georgia.
1972. 382 pp. DAI 33/7. (January 1973). Page 3530-A. Order #
72-34,063.

615. Dobrunz, Carol A. The History, Development and Contributions of

Delta Psi Kappa from 1916 to 1970. Ph.D. Dissertation. University of Oregon. 1973. 180 pp. DAI 34/9. (March 1974). Page 5685-A. Order # 74-6821.

616. Erenberg, Phyliss V. Change and Continuity: Values in American Higher Education, 1750-1800. Ph.D. Dissertation. University of Michigan. 1974. 302 pp. DAI 35/7. (January 1975). Page 4349-A. Order # 75-681.

617. Faurer, Judson C. The Granting of Academic Degrees by Federal Institutions: A History, 1775-1964. Ph.D. Dissertation. University of Denver. 1974. 368 pp. DAI 35/12. (June 1975). Page 7698-A. Order # 75-1324.

618. Gibson, J'nelle S. The Eight Year Study: A Limited View of College Admission Reform. Ph.D. Dissertation. University of Michigan. 1974. 261 pp. DAI 35/11. (May 1975). Page 7094-A. Order # 75-10,176.

619. Granade, Samuel R. Higher Education in Antebellum Alabama. Ph.D. Dissertation. Florida State University. 1972. 262 pp. DAI 33/2. (August 1972). Page 600-A. Order # 72-21,313.

620. Huehner, David R. Reform and the Pre-Civil War American College. Ph.D. Dissertation. University of Illinois. 1972. 378 pp. DAI 33/10. (April 1973). Page 5637-A. Order # 73-9952.

621. Jackson, Glenn W. History of the Salem (Ohio) School of Technology. Ed.D. Dissertation. University of Akron. 1979. 237 pp. DAI 40/3. (September 1979). Page 1310-A. Order # 7919411.

622. Janzen, Fred G. A Historical Study of the Campus Ombudsman in United States Higher Education. Ed.D. Dissertation. Texas Tech University. 1971. 265 pp. DAI 32/4. (October 1971). Page 1787-A. Order # 71-25,625.

623. Lang, Daniel W. The People's College: An Experiment in Nineteenth Century Higher Education. Ph.D. Dissertation. University of Toronto. 1976. n.p. Comprehensive Dissertation Index. Volume 18. 1979. Page 408. No Order #.

624. Lee, Jr., James L. A Century of Military Training at Iowa State University, 1870-1970. Ph.D. Dissertation. Iowa State University. 1972. 480 pp. DAI 33/4. (October 1972). Page 1368-A. Order # 72-26,926.

625. Low, Mortimer E. A History of the Bureau of Audio-Visual Instruction at the University of Colorado, 1923 to 1975. Ph.D. Dissertation. University of Colorado. 1973. 349 pp. DAI 34/7. (January 1974). Page 3839-A. Order # 73-32,568.

626. May, Russell A. A History of the Association of University Summer Sessions: Fifty Years of Progress. Ed.D. Dissertation. University of Indiana. 1971. 209 pp. DAI 32/1. (July 1971). Page 134-A. Order # 71-17,875.

627. McCarthy, John R. The Slavery Issue in Selected Colleges and Universities in Illinois, Ohio, Kentucky and Indiana, 1840-1869. Ph.D. Dissertation. Florida State University. 1974. 205 pp. DAI 35/12. (June 1975). Page 7700-A. Order # 75-12,656.

628. Meredith, Thomas C.   Migratory Trends of Students in Senior Colleges
      and Universities in the United States, by States, 1949 through 1968.
      Ed.D. Dissertation. University of Mississippi. 1971. 162 pp. DAI
      32/7. (January 1972). Page 3726-A. Order # 72-3928.

629. Michalik, Craig A.   The Southern State University During the Progres-
      sive Era. Ph.D. Dissertation. University of Arkansas. 1978. 255
      pp. DAI 40/3. (September 1979). Page 1651-A. Order # 7919251.

630. Miller, Guy H.   A Contracting Community: American Presbyterians,
      Social Conflict and Higher Education, 1730-1820. Ph.D. Dissertation.
      University of Michigan. 1970. 562 pp. DAI 31/12. (June 1971).
      Page 6523-A. Order # 71-15,239.

631. Nichols, Scott G.   Volunteerism in Higher Education: A History of
      Bucknell University Alumni. Ed.D. Dissertation. University of
      Pennsylvania. 1977. 386 pp. DAI 38/5. (November 1977). Page
      2611-A. Order # 77-24,168.

632. Pease, Harold W.   The History of the Alumni Association and its Influ-
      ence on the Development of Brigham Young University. Ph.D. Dis-
      sertation. Brigham Young University. 1974. 569 pp. DAI 35/7.
      (January 1975). Page 4399-A. Order # 75-545.

633. Ragan, Gaylord B. L.   The Emergence of the Graduate Fellow, 1865-
      1910: Changing Conceptions and Changing Roles. Ph.D. Dissertation.
      University of Oregon. 1978. DAI 39/2. (August 1978). Page 722-
      A. Order # 7814325.

634. Reeves, Dorothy E.   British Commentary on American Culture and
      Higher Education, 1814-1914. Ed.D. Dissertation. George Peabody
      College for Teachers. 1974. 848 pp. DAI 35/8. (February 1975).
      Page 5064-A. Order # 74-29,151.

635. Ritchie, Linda C. S.   History of the University of Nebraska Summer
      Sessions: 1891-1915. Ph.D. Dissertation. University of Nebraska.
      1980. 142 pp. DAI 41/7. (January 1981). Page 2970-A. Order #
      8100776.

636. Robson, David W.   Higher Education in the Emerging American Repub-
      lic, 1750-1800. Ph.D. Dissertation. Yale University. 1974. 325 pp.
      DAI 35/5. (November 1974). Page 2915-A. Order # 74-24,564.

637. Shawen, Neil M.   The Casting of a Lengthening Shadow: Thomas Jef-
      Ferson's Role in Determining the Site of a State University in Virginia.
      Ed.D. Dissertation. George Washington University. 1980. 479 pp.
      DAI 41/2. (August 1980). Page 567-A. Order # 8017730.

638. Tachikawa, Akira.   The Two Sciences and Religion in Ante-Bellum New
      England: The Founding of the Museum of Comparative Zoology and
      the Massachusetts Institute of Technology. Ph.D. Dissertation. Uni-
      versity of Wisconsin. 1978. 300 pp. DAI 39/9. (March 1979).
      Page 5368-A. Order # 7823089.

639. Tolles, Bryant F.   College Architecture in Northern New England
      Before 1860: A Social and Cultural History. Ph.D. Dissertation.
      Boston University. 1970. 462 pp. DAI 31/5. (November 1970).
      Page 2326-A. Order # 70-22,396.

640. Warriner, David R. The Veterans of World War II at Indiana University. Ph.D. Dissertation. University of Indiana. 1978. 284 pp. DAI 39/2. (August 1978). Page 1066-A. Order # 7813197.

641. Wechsler, Harold S. The Selective Function of American College Admission Policies, 1870-1970. Ph.D. Dissertation. Columbia University. 1974. 481 pp. DAI 35/10. (April 1975). Page 6649-A. Order # 75-7546.

Academic Freedom

---

642. Aby, Stephen H. The Political Economy of Academic Freedom. Ph.D. Dissertation. State University of New York, Buffalo. 1979. 312 pp. DAI 40/4. (October 1979). Page 1751-A. Order # 7921843.

643. Anderson, Jr., Stanley D. An Analysis of the Meaning of Academic Freedom in American Higher Education, 1860-1920. Ph.D. Dissertation. University of Minnesota, 1980. 297 pp. DAI 41/7. (January 1981). Page 2951-A. Order # 8102063.

644. Beauregard, Erving E. History of Academic Freedom in Ohio: Case Studies, 1808-1975. Ph.D. Dissertation. Union Graduate School. 1976. 424 pp. DAI 38/1. (July 1977). Page 436-A. Order # 77-13,830.

645. Bock, Leon. The Control of Alleged Subversive Activities in the Public Schools of New York City, 1949-1956. Ed.D. Dissertation. Columbia University, 1971. 287 pp. DAI 32/3. (September 1971). Page 1210-A. Order # 71-24,137.

646. Cox, Alice C. The Rainey Affair: A History of the Academic Freedom Controversy at the University of Texas, 1938-1946. Ph.D. Dissertation. University of Denver. 1970. 163 pp. DAI 31/10. (April 1971). Page 5158-A. Order # 71-8770.

647. Dinniman, Andrew E. Academic Freedom at West Chester: The Controversy of 1927. D.Ed. Dissertation. Pennsylvania State University. 1978. 211 pp. DAI 39/10. (April 1979). Page 5974-A. Order # 7909058.

648. Harris, Benedict O. A Review of Some Aspects of Academic Freedom in Colleges and Universities in the Perspective of the 1915 Declaration of the American Association of University Professors. Ph.D. Dissertation. State University of New York, Buffalo. 1978. 110 pp. DAI 39/1. (July 1978). Page 149-A. Order # 7810627.

649. Hartsell, Lee E. An Analysis of Judicial Decisions Regarding Academic Freedom in Public and Private Elementary and Secondary Schools and the Institutions of Higher Education, 1960-1975. Ed.D. Dissertation. Auburn University. 1977. 154 pp. DAI 38/5. (November 1977). Page 2450-A. Order # 77-24,497.

650. Metzger, Loya F. Professors in Trouble: A Quantitative Analysis of Academic Freedom and Tenure Cases (1913-1957). Ph.D. Dissertation.

Columbia University. 1978. 427 pp. DAI 39/4. (October 1978).
Page 2571-A. Order # 7819393.

651. Nass, Deanna R. The Image of Academic Freedom Conveyed by Select
Scholarly Journals of the McCarthy Era. Ph.D. Dissertation. Columbia University. 1979. 455 pp. DAI 40/10. (April 1980). Page
5560-A. Order # 8009359.

652. Nicholas III, William E. Academic Dissent in World War I, 1917-1918.
Ph.D. Dissertation. Tulane University. 1970. 264 pp. DAI 31/9.
(March 1971). Page 4685-A. Order # 71-8076.

653. Sanders, Jane A. Academic Freedom at the University of Washington
During the Cold War Years; 1946-1964. Ph.D. Dissertation. Univer-
sity of Washington. 1976. 384 pp. DAI 37/7. (January 1977).
Page 4175-A. Order # 77-617.

654. Schaehrer, Peter C. McCarthyism and Academic Freedom: Three
Case Studies. Ed.D. Dissertation. Columbia University. 1974.
314 pp. DAI 35/4. (October 1974). Page 2026-A. Order # 74-
23,532.

655. Snyder, Sam R. Academic Freedom at the University of Michigan:
The Nickerson Case (1954). Ph.D. Dissertation. University of
Michigan. 1970. 312 pp. DAI 32/1. (July 1971). Page 215-A.
Order # 71-15,312.

656. Steinberg, Philip A. Communism, Education, and Academic Freedom:
Philadelphia, A Case Study. Ed.D. Dissertation. Temple University.
1978. 335 pp. DAI 39/4. (October 1978). Page 2101-A. Order #
7817410.

657. Summerscales, William. Academic Affirmation and Dissent: Columbia's
Response to the Crisis of World War I. Ph.D. Dissertation. Columbia University. 1969. 298 pp. DAI 32/3. (September 1971). Page
1313-A. Order # 71-23,630.

658. Violas, Paul C. Academic Freedom in the Public School, 1930-1960.
Ed.D. Dissertation. University of Rochester. 1969. 315 pp. DAI
30/8. (February 1970). Page 3296-A. Order # 70-2944.

659. Wiley, Wayne H. Academic Freedom at the University of Virginia:
The First Hundred Years--From Jefferson through Alderman (1819-
WWI). Ph.D. Dissertation. University of Virginia. 1973. 399 pp.
DAI 34/8. (February 1974). Page 4817-A. Order # 73-31,174.

660. Zimmerman, Norman A. A Triumph of Orthodoxy: The University of
Wisconsin During World War I. Ph.D. Dissertation. University of
Minnesota. 1971. 243 pp. DAI 32/6. (December 1971). Page 3237-
A. Order # 72-384.

Accreditation

---

661. Allen, Jr., George J. A History of the Commission on Colleges of

the Southern Association of Colleges and Schools, 1949-1975. Ph.D. Dissertation. Georgia State University. 1978. 320 pp. DAI 39/8. (February 1980). Page 4770-A. Order # 7901820.

662. Harper, William S. G. A History of Criticisms of "Extra-Legal" Accrediting of Higher Education in the United States from 1890 to 1970. Ed.D. Dissertation. University of Missouri. 1972. 430 pp. DAI 34/5. (November 1973). Page 2352-A. Order # 73-21,430.

663. Williams, David. A Historical Study of the Involvement of the North Central Association with Higher Education in the United States. Ph.D. Dissertation. Wayne State University. 1972. 202 pp. DAI 33/11. (May 1973). Page 6146-A. Order # 73-12,619.

Administration/Governance

---

664. Born, William M. The Historical Development of Governing Boards at State Universities in the United States: An Analysis of Some Trends and Portents. Ph.D. Dissertation. Michigan State University. 1974. 205 pp. DAI 35/6. (December 1974). Page 3446-A. Order # 74-27,390.

665. Laird, Jr., David B. The Regents of the University of Michigan and the Legislature of the State, 1920-1950. Ph.D. Dissertation. University of Michigan. 1972. 225 pp. DAI 33/5. (November 1972). Page 2140-A. Order # 72-29,126.

666. Lefebvre, Jeanne M. Toward Credible Authority: Selected National Efforts to Renew Academic Governance Structures Between 1964 and 1974. Ph.D. Dissertation. Georgetown University. 1978. 324 pp. DAI 39/11. (May 1979). Page 6917-A. Order # 7909317.

667. Mills, Thomas J. Historical Study of the Dean of Men and the Major Issues They Faced at the University of Oregon, 1920-1968. Ph.D. Dissertation. University of Oregon. 1974. 217 pp. DAI 35/6. (December 1974). Page 3461-A. Order # 74-26,550.

668. Rice, Abbott E. The Revolutionary Process at Belknap College (New Hampshire): A Historical Study in Campus Governance. Ed.D. Dissertation. Boston University. 1978. 222 pp. DAI 39/5. (November 1978). Page 2779-A. Order # 7819775.

669. Rosenthal, Michael L. The Founding of the Office of the Dean of Faculty. Undergraduate Life at the College of New Jersey: An Anthropological View of History. Ed.D. Dissertation. Rutgers, the State University. 1974. 385 pp. DAI 35/6. (December 1974). Page 3612-A. Order # 74-27,341.

670. Summers, Kurt. A Study of Decisions Made by the Board of Trustees of Kent State University from 1968 through 1977. Ph.D. Dissertation. Kent State University. 1978. 143 pp. DAI 39/12. (June 1979). Page 7104-A. Order # 7912528.

671. Walsh, James P. Regent Peter C. Yorke and the University of

California, 1900-1912. Ph.D. Dissertation. University of California, Berkeley. 1970. 303 pp. DAI 31/7. (January 1971). Page 3488-A. Order # 71-862.

672. Weaver, Mary L. Policy and its Consequences: Higher Education in the United States and Great Britain, 1957-1977. Ph.D. Dissertation. Cornell University. 1980. 516 pp. DAI 41/3. (September 1980). Page 1204-A. Order # 8020901.

673. Wilson, Alton J. Analysis of Board Policies in Relation to District of Columbia Teachers College and Federal City College of the District of Columbia. Ed.D. Dissertation. University of Southern California. 1978. n.p. DAI 39/5. (November 1978). Page 2682-A. No Order #.

Adult and Extension

---

674. Bird, Nancy K. The Conference on College Composition and Communication: A Historical Study of its Continuing Education and Professionalization Activities, 1949-1975. Ed.D. Dissertation. Virginia Polytechnic Institute and State University. 1977. 250 pp. DAI 38/12. (June 1978). Page 7078-A. Order # 7808114.

675. Fearing, Bertie E. A History of the Department of Adult and Community College Education at North Carolina State University: A Need, a Response, and a Model. Ed.D. Dissertation. North Carolina State University. 1978. 184 pp. DAI 39/5. (November 1978). Page 2686-A. Order # 7820027.

676. Fiske, Emmett P. The College and its Constituency: Rural and Community Development at the University of California, 1875-1978. Ph.D. Dissertation. University of California, Davis. 1979. 490 pp. DAI 41/2. (August 1980). Page 816-A. Order # 8016755.

677. Fowler, Quuen E. D. Educating Adults: A History of University College at Washington University, Saint Louis, its Purposes and Implications for the Future, 1908-1970. Ph.D. Dissertation. 1974. 178 pp. DAI 36/6. (December 1975). Page 3331-A. Order # 75-26,252.

678. Gerrity, Thomas W. College-Sponsored Correspondence Instruction in the United States: A Comparative History of its Origins (1873-1915) and its Recent Developments (1960-1975). Ed.D. Dissertation. Columbia University. 1976. 214 pp. DAI 37/2. (August 1976). Page 844-A. Order # 76-17,282.

679. Hall, James C. A History of Special Baccalaureate Programs for Adults, 1945-1970. Ph.D. Dissertation. University of Chicago. n.p. DAI 36/7. (January 1976). No Order #.

680. Hayden, Dale L. A History of the External Degree in Britain and the United States. Ph.D. Dissertation. University of Alabama. 1979. 128 pp. DAI 40/1. (July 1979). Page 131-A. Order # 7915013.

681. Kobasky, Michael G. A History of the General Extension Division of

Florida at the University of Florida, 1919-1961. Ph.D. Dissertation. Florida State University. 1971. 275 pp. DAI 32/12. (May 1972). Page 6791-A. Order # 72-18,604.

682. Powell, John B. A History of Louisiana State University Division of Continuing Education, 1924-1973. Ph.D. Dissertation. Louisiana State University and Agricultural and Mechanical College. 1977. 148 pp. DAI 38/12. (June 1978). Page 7141-A. Order # 7807554.

683. Van Arsdall, James E. The Stated and Operative Objectives of the University of Nebraska Extension High School Program, 1929-1975. Ed.D. Dissertation. University of Nebraska. 1977. 205 pp. DAI 38/5. (November 1977). Page 2611-A. Order # 77-23,165.

684. Woytanowitz, George M. "To Train Good Citizens": The Early Years of University Extension in the United States: 1885-1915. Ph.D. Dissertation. Johns Hopkins University. 1970. 358 pp. DAI 32/1. (July 1971). Page 216-A. Order # 71-16,756.

Biographies

---

685. Chambers, Carole Z. The Presidential Years of Sister Ann Ida Gannon, BVM, Mundelein College, 1957-1975. Ph.D. Dissertation. Loyola University, Chicago. 1978. 188 pp. DAI 38/12. (June 1978). Page 7488-A. Order # 7807064.

686. Curley, Thomas E. Robert I. Gannon: President of Fordham University, 1936-1949: A Jesuit Educator. Ph.D. Dissertation. New York University. 1974. 237 pp. DAI 35/2. (August 1974). Page 834-A. Order # 74-17,136.

687. Denbo, Marilyn. The Nineteenth Century Presidents of the College of William and Mary. Ph.D. Dissertation. New York University. 1974. 223 pp. DAI 35/5. (November 1974). Page 2714-A. Order # 74-24,985.

688. Dixon, T. O. R., Reverend and Blaise P. The Catholic University of America, 1909-1928, The Rectorship of Thomas Joseph Shahan. Ph.D. Dissertation. Catholic University of America. 1972. 403 pp. DAI 33/2. (August 1972). Page 681-A. Order # 72-21,566.

689. Eichlin, Arthur S. An Historical Analysis of the Fellowships Program at the Johns Hopkins University, 1876-1889: Daniel Gilman's Unique Contribution. Ph.D. Dissertation. Loyola University, Chicago. 1976. 182 pp. DAI 37/5. (November 1976). Page 2683-A. Order # 76-24,439.

690. Gawrysiak, Kenneth J. The Administration of Albert C. Fox, S. J.: A Portrait of Educational Leadership at Marquette University, 1922-1928. Ed.D. Dissertation. Marquette University. 1973. 192 pp. DAI 35/2. (August 1974). Page 858-A. Order # 74-18,228.

691. Grisso, Karl M. David Kinley, 1861-1944: The Career of the Fifth

President of the University of Illinois. Ph.D. Dissertation. University of Illinois. 1980. 717 pp. DAI 41/11. (May 1981). Page 4618-A. Order # 8108525.

692. Jones, Lewis L. Carl Emil Seashore: Dean of the Graduate College of the University of Iowa, 1908 to 1936, Dean Pro Tempore, 1942 to 1946: A Study of his Ideas on Graduate Education. Ph.D. Dissertation. University of Iowa. 1978. 239 pp. DAI 39/8. (February 1979). Page 4759-A. Order # 7902915.

693. Joyce, Walter E. Noah Porter as President of Yale, 1871-1886: A Conservative Response in a Time of Transition. Ph.D. Dissertation. New York University. 1972. 272 pp. DAI 33/10. (April 1973). Page 5530-A. Order # 73-8173.

694. Keating, James M. Seth Low and the Development of Columbia University, 1889-1901. Ed.D. Dissertation. Columbia University. 1973. 308 pp. DAI 34/5. (November 1973). Page 2333-A. Order # 73-24,072.

695. Lipping, Alar. Charles W. Eliot's Views on Education, Physical Education, and Intercollegiate Athletics. Ph.D. Dissertation. Ohio State University. 1980. 366 pp. DAI 41/7. (January 1981). Page 2996-A. Order # 8100189.

696. McGovern, James H. College Presidents and Community Leadership: Brown University, 1764-1897. Ph.D. Dissertation. Boston College. 1975. 334 pp. DAI 36/10. (April 1976). Page 6508-A. Order # 75-21,287.

697. McSweeney, John P. The Chancellorship of Reuben G. Gustavson at the University of Nebraska, 1946-53. Ph.D. Dissertation. University of Nebraska. 1971. 198 pp. DAI 32/7. (January 1972). Page 3739-A. Order # 72-3971.

698. Morrissey, Robert S. David Ross Boyd and the University of Oklahoma: An Analysis of the Educational Contributions of the First President (1892-1908). Ed.D. Dissertation. University of Oklahoma. 1973. 277 pp. DAI 34/9. (March 1974). Page 5666-A. Order # 74-6975.

699. Newman, George C. The Morgan Years: Politics of Innovative Change, Antioch College in the 1920's. Ph.D. Dissertation. University of Michigan. 1978. 270 pp. DAI 39/10. (April 1979). Page 6299-A. Order # 7907146.

700. Read, James C. The Williams Chancellorship at the University of Mississippi, 1946-1968. Ed.D. Dissertation. University of Mississippi. 1978. 340 pp. DAI 39/6. (December 1978). Page 3408-A. Order # 7824061.

701. Sonner, Ray V. Madison College: The Miller Years, 1949-1970. Ed.D Dissertation. University of Virginia. 1974. 153 pp. DAI 35/7. (January 1975). Page 4103-A. Order # 74-29,212.

702. Stein, Lloyd E. Hutchins of Chicago: Philosopher-Administrator. Ed. D. Dissertation. University of Massachusetts. 1971. 295 pp. DAI 32/4. (October 1971). Page 1816-A. Order # 71-25,082.

703. Taylor, Richard S. Seeking the Kingdom: A Study in the Career of Jonathan Blanchard, 1811-1892. Ph.D. Dissertation. Northern Illinois University. 1977. 603 pp. DAI 39/1. (July 1978). Page 430-A. Order # 7811196.

704. Traxler, Joseph M. The Contribution of Delyte W. Morris to Southern Illinois University (1948-1970). Ph.D. Dissertation. Southern Illinois University. 1971. 184 pp. DAI 32/8. (February 1972). Page 4315-A. Order # 72-5400.

705. Van de Water, Peter E. "Peace Maker": President Alexander G. Ruthven of Michigan and his Relationship to his Faculty, Students and Regents. Ph.D. Dissertation. University of Michigan. 1970. 231 pp. DAI 31/8. (Feburary 1971). Page 3910-A. Order # 71-4756.

Community Colleges/Junior Colleges

---

706. Alford, Stanley C. The Historical Development of Hagerstown Junior College, 1945-1975. Ed.D. Dissertation. George Washington University. 1976. 238 pp. DAI 37/4. (October 1976). Page 2006-A. Order # 76-23,540.

707. Ballard, Robert M. Tyler (Texas) Junior College: Its Founding, Growth and Development (1926-ca. 1970). Ph.D. Dissertation. East Texas State University. 1971. 192 pp. DAI 33/2. (August 1972). Page 582-A. Order # 72-22,740.

708. Beshara, Anthony W. An Educational History of the St. Louis--St. Louis County Junior College District. Ph.D. Dissertation. St. Louis University. 1972. 364 pp. DAI 34/8. (February 1974). Page 4770-A. Order # 74-4478.

709. Caserta, John A. A History of the Community College Movement in Nevada, 1967-1977. Ed.D. Dissertation. University of Nevada, Reno. 205 pp. DAI 40/12. (June 1980). Page 6172-A. Order # 8011911.

710. Cox, James N. The Urban Community College: A Case Study of Los Angeles City College from 1929 to 1970. Ed.D. Dissertation. University of California, Los Angeles. 1971. 584 pp. DAI 32/7. (January 1972). Page 3716-A. Order # 72-2794.

711. Evans, James M. The Organization and Promotion of Sacramento Junior College, 1916-1940. Ph.D. Dissertation. University of Southern California. 1974. 432 pp. DAI 35/5. (November 1974). Page 2716-A. Order # 74-23,582.

712. Goodwin, Gregory L. The Historical Development of the Community-Junior College Ideology: An Analysis and Interpretation of the Writings of Selected Community-Junior College National Leaders from 1890 to 1970. Ph.D. Dissertation. University of Illinois. 1971. (April 1972). Page 5566-A. Order # 72-12,178.

713. Hall, Reginald W. The History of Alexander City State Junior College:

Its Beginnings, Foundation and Progress, 1963-1980. Ed.D. Dissertation. Auburn University. 1980. 175 pp. DAI 40/10. (April
1981). Page 4311-A. Order # 8107118.

714. Hinsdale, Rosejean C. Maricopa (Arizona) Community College District:
First Decade of Growth of a Multicollege District, 1962-1972. Ph.D.
Dissertation. Arizona State University. 1973. 184 pp. DAI 34/7.
January 1973). Page 3933-A. Order # 74-1096.

715. House, Lloyd L. The Historical Development of Navajo (Arizona) Community College. Ph.D. Dissertation. Arizona State University. 1974.
169 pp. DAI 35/4. (October 1974). Page 2024-A. Order # 72-21,532.

716. Klotz, Richard R. The Hershey Junior College, Hershey, Pennsylvania,
1938-1965. Ed.D. Dissertation. Pennsylvania State University. 1970.
406 pp. DAI 32/2. (August 1971). Page 762-A. Order # 71-21,764.

717. Louden, Lois M. R. A Comparison of the Development of the American
Community Junior College and the English Sixth Form College. Ph.D.
Dissertation. University of North Carolina. 1974. 315 pp. DAI
35/6. (December 1974). Page 3481/A. Order # 74-26,906.

718. Meisterheim, Matthew J. A History of the Public Junior College in
Illinois, 1900-1965. Ed.D. Dissertation. University of Illinois. 1974.
199 pp. DAI 35/1. (July 1974). Page 234-A. Order # 74-11,742.

719. Nutter, Larry W. A History of Junior Colleges in Oklahoma. Ph.D.
Dissertation. University of Oklahoma. 1974. 118 pp. DAI 35/9.
(March 1975). Page 5869-A. Order # 75-6544.

720. Oakley, Jesse R. The Origins and Development of the Public Junior
College Movement, 1850-1921. Ed.D. Dissertation. University of
North Carolina, Greensboro. 1979. 239 pp. DAI 40/4. (October
1979). Page 1921-A. Order # 7922417.

721. Reid, Hubert D. Phenomena Affecting the Community Junior College
in the United States: 1960-1975. Ph.D. Dissertation. Wayne State
University. 1978. 854 pp. DAI 39/3. (September 1978). Page
1281-A. Order # 7816075.

722. Stanley, Larry D. The Historical Development of the Two-Year Col-
leges in Kentucky, 1903-1964. Ph.D. Dissertation. University of
Kentucky. 1974. 236 pp. DAI 35/9. (March 1975). Page 6068-A.
Order # 75-5856.

723. Van Horne, James E. A History of the Alabama Public Junior Colleges (1958-1970). Ed.D. Dissertation. University of Alabama. 1971.
206 pp. DAI 32/9. (March 1972). Page 5003-A. Order # 72-8475.

724. Wainwright, Frank N. A History of the Early Development of an Urban Community College: The Story of Los Angeles Southwest College:
1967-1974. Ed.D. Dissertation. University of Southern California.
1978. n.p. DAI 39/5. (November 1978). Page 2680-A. No
Order #.

725. Washington, Walter. Utica (Mississippi) Junior College, 1903-1957:
A Half-Century of Education for Negroes. Ed.D. Dissertation.

University of Southern Mississippi. 1970. 202 pp. DAI 31/9. (March 1971). Page 4506-A. Order # 71-5402.

726. Wiebe, Jeffrey J. Trinity (British Columbia) Junior College: Its History, Development and Institutional Mission. Ph.D. Dissertation. University of North Dakota. 1970. 176 pp. DAI 32/12. (June 1972). Page 6788-A. Order # 72-16,375.

727. Willoughby, Glenn E. Promises vs. Performance: An Historical Analysis of the Pledge of Equal Educational Opportunity and Washington's Community Colleges. Ph.D. Dissertation. Washington State University. 1980. 355 pp. DAI 41/1. (July 1980). Page 373-A. Order # 8015171.

728. Wright, Richard G. Professionalization of Administrators: Developments in the Community College Field, 1917-1975. Ed.D. Dissertation. Columbia University. 1976. 201 pp. DAI 37/3. (September 1976). Page 1366-A. Order # 76-21,042.

Curriculum

---

729. Batchellor, Robert W. The Development of the General Chemistry Program at the Ohio State University (since 1895). Ph.D. Dissertation. Ohio State University. 1973. 290 pp. DAI 35/1. (July 1974). Page 206-A. Order # 74-3116.

730. Buchan, Robin G. Lecture-Production: Technique for Teaching Western History in Community Colleges. D.A. Dissertation. Illinois State University. 1979. 196 pp. DAI 40/12. (June 1980). Page 6389-A. Order # 8012341.

731. Connors, Jr., Manning A. Curricular Changes and Innovation in Selected Church-Related Institutions of Higher Education, 1961-1970. Ph.D. Dissertation. Indiana University. 1971. 157 pp. DAI 32/6. (December 1971). Page 3048-A. Order # 72-1539.

732. Dwyer, Richard E. An Examination of the Development of Labor Studies at Rutgers University. 1931-1974: A Study in Union-University Cooperation. Ed.D. Dissertation. Rutgers, the State University. 1975. 339 pp. DAI 36/7. (January 1976). Page 4304-A. Order # 76-1110.

733. Heinrichs, Mary A. The Initiation and Development of Instruction in American Literature During the Nineteenth Century in Five Ohio Colleges Established Before 1860. Ph.D. Dissertation. University of Toledo. 1973. 232 pp. DAI 35/2. (August 1974). Page 843-A. Order # 74-16,921.

734. Lagow, Larry D. A History of the Center for Vietnamese Studies at Southern Illinois University, 1969-1976. Ph.D. Dissertation. Southern Illinois University. 1978. 669 pp. DAI 39/4. (October 1978). Page 2088-A. Order # 7817533.

735. McMaster, Robert K. A History of the Department of Philosophy at

the State University of Iowa from Jared Stone to Herbert Martin. Ph.D. Dissertation. University of Iowa. 1979. 343 pp. DAI 40/5. (November 1979). Page 2536-A. Order # 7924504.

736. Patterson, Robert M. The Development of Academic Sociology at the University of Chicago, 1892-1920. Ph.D. Dissertation. Vanderbilt University. 1973. 290 pp. DAI 34/7. (January 1974). Page 4164-A. Order # 74-1353.

737. Pruitt, Franklin B. A Historical Study of the Teaching of History in American Colleges. Ed.D. Dissertation. Texas Tech University. 1978. 256 pp. DAI 39/5. (November 1978). Page 2787-A. Order # 7819897.

738. Seidel, Robert W. Physics Research in California: The Rise of a Leading Sector in American Physics. Ph.D. Dissertation. University of California, Berkeley. 1978. 603 pp. DAI 39/9. (March 1979). Page 5685-A. Order # 7904599.

739. Stafford, Frances J. An Historical Examination of the Goals for History Instruction in Courses Required as Part of the General Education of Students in Post-Secondary Institutions. Ph.D. Dissertation. Florida State University. 1978. 191 pp. DAI 39/3. (September 1978). Page 1385-A. Order # 7815485.

Economics and Finance

---

740. Beck, Norman E. A History of Modern Student Financial Aid. Ph.D. Dissertation. Ball State University. 1971. 380 pp. DAI 32/3. (September 1971). Page 1309-A. Order # 71-23,025.

741. Dane, John H. An Analysis of the Trends of Financial Support by Philanthropic Foundations to General Programs in U.S. Higher Education, 1955-1970. Ph.D. Dissertation. University of Pittsburgh. 1974. 195 pp. DAI 35/4. (October 1974). Page 2003-A. Order # 74-21,670.

742. Follbaum, Terry D. An Historical Analysis of National Budgetary Trends, Circa 1920 to 1970, with Major Emphasis on Budgeting Trends for Higher Education, State of Michigan, 1970-1977. Ed.D. Dissertation. Wayne State University. 1980. 220 pp. DAI 41/4. (October 1980). Page 1424-A. Order # 8022812.

743. Jones, Alan H. Philanthropic Foundations at the University of Michigan, 1922-1965. Ph.D. Dissertation. University of Michigan. 1971. 236 pp. DAI 32/11. (May 1972). Page 6165-A. Order # 72-14,905.

744. Gray, Charles E. Student Financial Support at Southern Illinois University at Carbondale: 1874-1974. Ph.D. Dissertation. Southern Illinois University. 1976. 383 pp. DAI 37/9. (March 1977). Page 5627-A. Order # 76-28,741.

745. Hayes, Jr., Richard A. Selected Characteristics of Michigan Legislators Related to Financial Support of Institutions of Higher Education:

1919-1969. Ph.D. Dissertation. Wayne State University. 1971. 262
pp. DAI 32/11. (May 1972). Page 6253-A. Order # 72-14,567.

746. Hirsh, James B. The Response of Selected Urban Private Universities
to the Forces of Economic Depression of the 1930's. Ph.D. Dissertation.
University of Denver. 1976. 358 pp. DAI 37/5. (November 1976).
Page 2668-A. Order # 76-24,415.

747. McFarland, William E. A History of Student Financial Assistance Programs at Oklahoma State University, 1891-1978, with an Emphasis on
the Creation and Administration of the Lew Wentz Foundation. Ph.D.
Dissertation. Oklahoma State University. 1979. 200 pp. DAI 40/6.
(December 1979). Page 3455-A. Order # 7928219.

748. Okugawa, Yoshihasa. Higher Education and Earnings in the United
States and Japan. Ed.D. Dissertation. Oklahoma State University.
1979. 145 pp. DAI 41/1. (July 1980). Page 128-A. Order #
8013037.

749. Orr, Kenneth B. The Impact of the Depression Years, 1929-1939, on
Faculty in American Colleges and Universities. Ph.D. Dissertation.
University of Michigan. 1978. 418 pp. DAI 39/2. (August 1978).
Page 708-A. Order # 7813714.

750. Rainsburger, Richard A. Sources of Current Operating Income in
Ohio's Colleges Before 1960. Ph.D. Dissertation. University of To-
ledo. 1977. 235 pp. DAI 37/7. (January 1977). Page 4168-A.
Order # 77-380.

General Education/Liberal Arts

751. Braxton, Harold E. A History of the General Education Program at
Virginia State College Since 1950. Ed.D. Dissertation. University of
Virginia. 1973. 121 pp. DAI 34/8. (February 1974). Page 4687-A.
Order # 73-32,426.

752. Cook, John F. A History of Liberal Education at the University of
Wisconsin, 1862-1918. Ph.D. Dissertation. University of Wisconsin.
1970. 439 pp. DAI 31/9. (March 1971). Page 466-A. Order #
70-22,044.

753. Guyotte, III, Roland L. Liberal Education and the American Dream:
Public Attitudes and the Emergence of Mass Higher Education, 1920-
1952. Ph.D. Dissertation. Northwestern University. 1980. 356 pp.
DAI 41/6. (December 1980). Page 2735-A. Order # 8026818.

754. Hanks, Paul A. Changes and Trends in Private Liberal Arts Colleges:
1930-1966. Ed.D. Dissertation. University of Southern California.
1972. 231 pp. DAI 32/12. (June 1972). Page 6779-A. Order #
72-17,470.

755. Kass, Amy A. Radical Conservatives for Liberal Education. Ph.D.
Dissertation. Johns Hopkins University. 1973. n.p. DAI 34/1.
(July 1973). Page 157-A. No Order #.

756. Koch, Gail A. The General Education Movement in American Higher
      Education: An Account and an Appraisal of its Principles and Prac-
      tices and Their Relation to Democratic Thought in Modern American
      Society. Ph.D. Dissertation. University of Minnesota. 1979. 313
      pp. DAI 40/11. (May 1980). Page 5749A. Order # 8011837.

757. Kulkis, Robert D. General Education and the Social Sciences at Am-
      herst College: A Case Study of Inquiry and Learning. Ed.D. Dis-
      sertation. Columbia University. 1973. 445 pp. DAI 34/2. (August
      1973. Page 593-A. Order # 73-19,349.

758. LeBlanc, M. Elizabeth. The Concept of General Education in Colleges
      and Universities, 1945-1979. Ed.D. Dissertation. Rutgers, the State
      University. 1980. 780 pp. DAI 41/4. (October 1980). Page 1288-
      A. Order # 8023605.

759. Lyons, Mack D. The Liberal Arts as Viewed by Faculty Members in
      Nine Professional Schools and Three Types of Universities. Ph.D.
      Dissertation. University of Alabama. 1978. 258 pp. DAI 40/1.
      (July 1979). Page 51-A. Order # 7915015.

760. Moore, David W. Liberalism and Liberal Education at Columbia Uni-
      versity: The Columbia Careers of Jacques Barzun, Lionel Trilling,
      Richard Hofstadter, Daniel Bell and C. Wright Mills. Ph.D. Disserta-
      tion. University of Maryland. 1978. 456 pp. DAI 40/1. (July
      1979). Page 324-A. Order # 7915794.

761. Riccio, Gregory J. The History of Loyola University of Chicago's
      Rome Center of Liberal Arts, 1962-1977. Ph.D. Dissertation. Loyola
      University, Chicago. 1978. 161 pp. DAI 39/3. (September 1978).
      Page 1376-A. Order # 7815878.

762. Thomas, Richard K. A History of General Education at the Florida
      State University in National Perspective, 1935-1969. Ph.D. Disserta-
      tion. Florida State University. 1970. 191 pp. DAI 31/9. (March
      1971). Page 4498-A. Order # 71-7118.

Individual Colleges and Universities

---

763. Ancelet, LeRoy. A History of Southeastern Louisiana College (1925-
      1967). Ph.D. Dissertation. Louisiana State University and Agricul-
      tural and Mechanical College. 1971. 150 pp. DAI 32/7. (January
      1972). Page 3736-A. Order # 72-3455.

764. Arthur, David J. The University of Notre Dame, 1919-1933: An Ad-
      ministrative History. Ph.D. Dissertation. University of Michigan.
      1973. 452 pp. DAI 35/1. (July 1974). Page 205-A. Order # 74-
      15,660.

765. Barlow, Andrew L. Coordination and Control: The Rise of Harvard
      University, 1825-1910. Ph.D. Dissertation. Harvard University.
      1979. 464 pp. DAI 40/2. (August 1979). Page 1097-A. Order #
      7916362.

766. Berquist, David H. The Latin School and the Emergence of a State
     University in Nebraska: A History of Preparatory Education at the
     University of Nebraska, 1871-1897. Ed.D. Dissertation. University
     of Nebraska. 1973. 223 pp. DAI 34/7. (January 1974). Page
     3930-A. Order # 74-629.

767. Bern, Paula R. Point Park College: A History. Ph.D. Dissertation.
     University of Pittsburgh. 1980. 463 pp. DAI 41/2. (August 1980).
     Page 565-A. Order # 8018287.

768. Berrian, George R. Manhattan College: Tradition vs. Transition--A
     Case Study. Ed.D. Dissertation. Columbia University. 1975. 211
     pp. DAI 36/10. (April 1976). Page 6517-A. Order # 76-7769.

769. Beutler, Albert J. The Founding (1947) and History of Bethel College
     of Indiana. Ph.D. Dissertation. Michigan State University. 1970.
     207 pp. DAI 31/5. (November 1970). Page 2137-A. Order # 70-
     20,436.

770. Bledsoe, Bonnie G. The Origin and Development of Henderson (Ar-
     kansas) State College (1890-1970). Ph.D. Dissertation. North Texas
     State University. 1973. 468 pp. DAI 35/1. (July 1974). Page
     230-A. Order # 74-14,807.

771. Byrnes, Lawrence W. Ferris Institute (Michigan) as a Private School,
     1884-1952. Ph.D. Dissertation. Michigan State University. 1970.
     306 pp. DAI 32/1. (July 1972). Page 210-A. Order # 71-18,178.

772. Campbell, Bruce A. Law and Experience in the Early Republic: The
     Evolution of the Dartmouth College Doctrine, 1780-1819. Ph.D. Dis-
     sertation. Michigan State University. 1973. 420 pp. DAI 34/3.
     (September 1983). Page 1201-A. Order # 73-20,320.

773. Campbell, Clarice T. History of Tougaloo (Mississippi) College. Ph.D.
     Dissertation. Universty of Mississippi. 1970. 410 pp. DAI 31/3.
     (September 1970). Page 1181-A. Order # 70-16,392.

774. Campbell, Sharon A. C. A History of the Development of the Flint
     and Dearborn Branches of the University of Michigan. Ph.D. Disser-
     tation. University of Michigan. 1973. 336 pp. DAI 34/8. (Feb-
     ruary 1974). Page 4775-A. Order # 74-3591.

775. Caton, Lewis H. Washington and Jefferson College: In Pursuit of
     the Uncommon Man (1802-1972). Ph.D. Dissertation. University of
     Pittsburgh. 1972. 685 pp. DAI 33/12. (June 1973). Page 6682-A.
     Order # 73-13,286.

776. Cavanna, Robert C. A History of Sheridan College, 1948-1973. Ed.D.
     Dissertation. University of Wyoming. 1977. 232 pp. DAI 38/9.
     (March 1978). Page 5148-A. Order # 7800166.

777. Chambers, Frederick. Historical Study of Arkansas Agricultural,
     Mechanical, and Normal College, 1873-1943. Ed.D. Dissertation. 1970.
     442 pp. DAI 31/10. (April 1971). Page 5158-A. Order # 71-9046.

778. Clees, William J. Duquesne University: Its Years of Struggle, Sac-
     rifice and Service (1878-1970). Ed.D. Dissertation. University of

Pittsburgh. 1970. 204 pp. DAI 31/5. (November 1970). Page 2138-A. Order # 70-20,323.

779. Conway, G. Allan. Columbia and New York Universities Consolidation: A Study in Urban Social Consciousness. Ph.D. Dissertation. New York University. 1974. 262 pp. DAI 35/10. (April 1975). Page 6490-A. Order # 75-8537.

780. Cornell, Frederic. A History of the Rand School of Social Science-- 1906 to 1956. Ed.D. Dissertation. Columbia University. 1976. 271 pp. DAI 39/2. (August 1978). Page 720-A. Order # 7812007.

781. Cronin, Kathleen J. An Historical Perspective of the College of Great Falls (Montana), 1932-1974. Ed.D. Dissertation. Boston University. 1974. 393 pp. DAI 35/1. (July 1974). Page 232-A. Order # 74-14,230.

782. Davis, Lenwood G. A History of Livingston College, 1879-1957. D.A. Dissertation. Carnegie-Mellon University. 1979. 323 pp. DAI 40/5. (November 1979). Page 2819-A. Order # 7919137.

783. Dayton, David M. Building 'Mid the Pines: An Historical Study of Grove City (Pennsylvania) College. Ph.D. Dissertation. University of Pittsburgh. 1971. 440 pp. DAI 32/9. (March 1972). Page 4999-A. Order # 72-7867.

784. Dillingham, Jr., George A. Peabody Normal College (Tennessee) in Southern Education, 1875-1909. Ph.D. Dissertation. George Peabody College for Teachers. 1970. 227 pp. DAI 31/6. (December 1970). Page 2839-A. Order # 70-23,349.

785. Doran, Micheileen J. A History of Marymount College, Tarrytown (New York). Ed.D. Dissertation. Columbia University. 1979. 393 pp. DAI 40/10. (April 1980). Page 5333-A. Order # 8006802.

786. Dorrance, David B. Cleveland College: Genesis, Ethos, Exodus (mid-1920's to mid-1950's). Ph.D. Dissertation. Case Western Reserve University. 1977. 195 pp. DAI 38/8. (February 1978). Page 4601-A. Order # 7730983.

787. Epting, James B. A Chronological Review of the Development of Judson College, Marion, Alabama, 1838-1978. Ed.D. Dissertation. University of Alabama. 1978. 159 pp. DAI 39/9. (March 1979). Page 5348-A. Order # 7905404.

788. Fancher, Evelyn P. Tennessee State University (1912-1974): A History of an Institution with Implications for the Future. Ed.D. Dissertation. George Peabody College for Teachers. 1975. 302 pp. DAI 36/8. (February 1976). Page 5098-A. Order # 76-3721.

789. Fisher, Michael P. The Turbulent Years, the University of Kansas, 1960-1975: A History. Ph.D. Dissertation. University of Kansas. 1979. 270 pp. DAI 40/5. (November 1979). Page 2500-A. Order # 7925868.

790. Foley, Patrick J. The Antecedents and Early Development of the University of California, 1849-1875. Ph.D. Dissertation. University

of California, Berkeley. 1970. 224 pp. DAI 31/8. (February 1971).
Page 3914-A. Order # 71-772.

791. Forst, Jr., Arthur C. From Normal School to State College: The
Growth and Development of Eastern Connecticut State College from
1889 to 1959. Ph.D. Dissertation. University of Connecticut. 1980.
258 pp. DAI 41/8. (February 1981). Page 3453-A. Order # 8103167.

792. Foster, Elaine E. "A Great School of Fine Arts for New York City":
A Study of the Development of Art in the Regular Undergraduate
Curriculum of Columbia College and University, Including Affiliations
with the National Academy of Design and the Metropolitan Museum of
Art, 1860-1914. Ed.D. Dissertation. 1970. 215 pp. DAI 32/9.
(March 1972). Page 4981-A. Order # 72-8821.

793. Friel, Mary E. History of Emmanuel College, 1919-1974. Ph.D. Dissertation. Boston College. 1980. 308 pp. DAI 40/11. (May 1980).
Page 5745-A. Order # 8003731.

794. Gantner, Elliot S. Long Island: The History of a Relevant and Re-
sponsive University, 1926-1968. Ed.D. Dissertation. Columbia University. 1975. 732 pp. DAI 35/12. (June 1975). Page 7679-A. Order
75-13,887.

795. Gardner, Frederick P. Institutional Histories: Their Contribution to
Understanding the American College and University. Ed.D. Disser-
tation. State University of New York, Buffalo. 1976. 252 pp.
DAI 37/9. (March 1977). Page 5626-A. Order # 77-6137.

796. Garren, Charles M. The Educational Program at Black Mountain College, 1933-1943. Ph.D. Dissertation. University of North Carolina.
1980. 261 pp. DAI 41/4. (October 1980). Page 1425-A. Order #
8022455.

797. George, Melvin R. Northeastern Illinois University: The History of
a Comprehensive State University. Ph.D. Dissertation. University
of Chicago. 1979. n.p. DAI 40/6. (December 1979). Page 3141-
A. No Order #.

798. Gibson, DeLois. A Historical Study of Philander Smith (Arkansas)
College (ca. 1887-1970). Ed.D. Dissertation. University of Arkansas.
1972. 200 pp. DAI 33/5. (November 1972). Page 2140-A. Order
72-29,699.

799. Gordon, Ann D. The College of Philadelphia, 1749-1779: Impact of
an Institution. Ph.D. Dissertation. University of Wisconsin. 1975.
342 pp. DAI 37/1. (July 1976). Page 544-A. Order # 76-10,660.

800. Gordon, Shelia. The Transformation of the City University of New
York, 1945-1970. Ph.D. Dissertation. Columbia University. 1975.
322 pp. DAI 38/7. (January 1978). Page 4325-A. Order # 77-
27,856.

801. Hall, John G. Henderson State College (Arkansas): The Methodist
Years, 1890-1929. Ph.D. Dissertation. University of Mississippi.
1972. 364 pp. DAI 33/7. (January 1973). Page 3509-A. Order
73-1268.

802. Hanley, Francis X. Duquesne University: Evolution from College to
      University, Administration of Martin A. Hehir, C.S. SP., 1899-1931.
      Ph.D. Dissertation. University of Pittsburgh. 1979. 351 pp. DAI
      40/8. (February 1980). Page 4325-A. Order # 8004808.

803. Hibbard, Janet G. Eastern Kentucky University, 1906-1960: Adminis-
      trative Problems. Ed.D. Dissertation. University of Indiana. 1973.
      164 pp. DAI 34/8. (February 1974). Page 4624-A. Order # 74-2668.

804. Hill, Jack D. Critical Decisions in the Organization and Development
      of John A. Logan College: A Historical Analysis of the Years 1965
      through 1972. Ph.D. Dissertation. Southern Illinois University.
      1978. 379 pp. DAI 39/4. (October 1978). Page 2100-A. Order #
      7817525.

805. Hoffman, Allan M. History of an Idea: Skidmore College, 1903-1925.
      Ed.D. Dissertation. Columbia University. 1976. 267 pp. DAI 37/
      10. (April 1977). Page 6312-A. Order # 77-6714.

806. Horn, Larry. A History of West Los Angeles College. Ph.D. Disserta-
      tion. University of Southern California. 1971. 722 pp. DAI 32/1.
      (July 1971). Page 212-A. Order # 71-16,415.

807. Jeppson, Joseph H. The Secularization of the University of Utah to
      1929. Ph.D. Dissertation. University of California, Berkeley. 1973.
      357 pp. DAI 34/3. (September 1973). Page 1108-A. Order # 73-
      19,729.

808. Johnson, Alandus C. The Growth of Paine College (Georgia), A Suc-
      cessful Interracial Venture, 1903-1946. Ph.D. Dissertation. Univer-
      sity of Georgia. 1970. 423 pp. DAI 31/10. (April 1971). Page
      5321-A. Order # 71-3747.

809. Jones, Glendell A. A History of Lon Morris College (Texas). Ph.D.
      Dissertation. North Texas State University. 1973. 359 pp. DAI
      34/4. (October 1973). Page 1668-A. Order # 73-23,737.

810. Jordahl, Donald C. Greensville (Illinois) College--The Antecedents:
      A History of Almira College. Ph.D. Dissertation. Southern Illinois
      University. 1974. 259 pp. DAI 35/7. (January 1975). Page 4214-
      A. Order # 75-122.

811. Kubik, Jan B. Migrational Patterns of College Students from Harvard,
      Princeton and Yale, 1915-1965. with Special Reference to the Out Mi-
      gration of Students from the South. Ph.D. Dissertation. University
      of Illinois. 1978. 141 pp. DAI 39/12. (June 1979). Page 7536-A.
      Order # 7913520.

812. Kujawa, Rose M. Madonna College: Its History of Higher Education,
      1937-1977. Ph.D. Dissertation. Wayne State University. 1979. 289
      pp. DAI 40/4. (October 1979). Page 1905-A. Order # 7921683.

813. Lane, Ulysses S. The History of Southern Illinois University: 1879-
      1960. Ed.D. Dissertation. Utah State University. 1970. 189 pp.
      DAI 32/3. (September 1971). Page 1229-A. Order # 71-19,131.

814. Lang, Elizabeth H. Colonial Colleges and Politics: Yale, King's

College, and the College of Philadelphia, 1740-1764. Ph.D. Dissertation. Cornell University. 1976. 356 pp. DAI 38/3. (September 1977). Page 1267-A. Order # 77-20,002.

815. Leslie, William B. A Comparative Study of Four Middle Atlantic Colleges, 1870-1915: Bucknell University, Franklin and Marshall College, Princeton University, and Swarthmore College. Ph.D. Dissertation. Johns Hopkins University. 1971. 282 pp. DAI 32/2. (August 1971). Page 762-A. Order # 71-21,027.

816. Logsdon, Guy W. The University of Tulsa: A History from 1882 to 1972. Ed.D. Dissertation. University of Oklahoma. 381 pp. DAI 37/1. (July 1976). Page 157-A. Order # 76-15,814.

817. McGrath, Gary L. The Establishment and Early Development of the University of Minnesota, Morris. Ed.D. Dissertation. 1974. 150 pp. DAI 35/9. (March 1975). Page 5865-A. Order # 75-5566.

818. Merryman, Sr., John E. Indiana University of Pennsylvania: From Private Normal School to Public University (1871-1968). Ph.D. Dissertation. University of Pittsburgh. 1972. 506 pp. DAI 33/8. (February 1973). Page 4142-A. Order # 73-1676.

819. Molen, Jr., Clarence T. The Evolution of a State University into a Teachers College: The University of Northern Iowa, 1876-1916. Ph.D. Dissertation. University of Iowa. 1974. 426 pp. DAI 35/12. (June 1975). Page 7686-A. Order # 75-13,797.

820. Moore, Kathryn S. M. Old Saints and Young Sinners: A Study of Student Discipline at Harvard College, 1636-1734. Ph.D. Dissertation. University of Wisconsin. 1972. 345 pp. DAI 32/12. (June 1972). Page 6782-A. Order # 72-15,372.

821. Morrison, Betty L. A History of Our Lady of Holy Cross College, New Orleans, Louisiana. Ph.D. Dissertation. Louisiana State University and Agricultural and Mechanical College. 1976. 183 pp. DAI 37/5. (November 1976). Page 2685-A. Order # 76-25,276.

822. Morrison, Jr., James L. The United States Military Academy, 1833-1866: Years of Progress and Turmoil. Ph.D. Dissertation. Columbia University. 1970. 377 pp. DAI 31/9. (March 1970). Page 4684-A. Order # 71-6230.

823. Muck, Steven J. The History of El Camino (California) College, 1946-1966. Ed.D. Dissertation. University of California, Los Angeles. 1971. 358 pp. DAI 32/7. (January 1972). Page 3728-A. Order # 72-2871.

824. Pedtke, Dorothy A. H. A History of Kaskaskia College. Ph.D. Dissertation. Southern Illinois University. 1979. 154 pp. DAI 40/8. (February 1980). Page 4444-A. Order # 8004079.

825. Ranson, Leonard B. The Vocational Basis for the Founding of Harvard College: An Alternative to Samuel Morison and Winthrop Hudson. Ph.D. Dissertation. University of Iowa. 1979. 177 pp. DAI 40/5. (November 1979). Page 2515-A. Order # 7924519.

826. Richardson, Frederick. A Power for Good in Society: The History of
      Benedict College (South Carolina). Ph.D. Dissertation. Florida State
      University. 1973. 275 pp. DAI 35/2. (August 1974). Page 1028-A.
      Order # 74-18,039.

827. Roberts, Norene A. D. An Early Political and Administrative History
      of the University of Minnesota, 1851-84. Ph.D. Dissertation. Uni-
      versity of Minnesota. 1978. 561 pp. DAI 39/12. (June 1979). Page
      7188-A. Order # 7912069.

828. Rolph, Rebecca S. Emmanuel College, Cambridge and the Puritan
      Movements of Old and New England. Ph.D. Dissertation. University
      of Southern California. 1979. n.p. DAI 40/4. (October 1979).
      Page 2202-A. No Order #.

829. Rowen, William A. The Emerging Identity of Wagner College (1848-
      1970). Ed.D. Dissertation. Indiana University. 1972. 124 pp.
      DAI 33/11. (May 1973). Page 6136-A. Order # 73-10,862.

830. Salie, Robert D. The Harvard Annex Experiment in the Higher Edu-
      cation of Women: Separate But Equal? Ph.D. Dissertation. Emory
      University. 1976. 399 pp. DAI 37/7. (January 1977). Page 4174-
      A. Order # 77-979.

831. Serinko, Regis J. California State College of Pennsylvania: From
      Private Normal College to Multi-Purpose Public Institution (1852-1972).
      Ph.D. Dissertation. University of Pennsylvania. 1974. 557 pp.
      DAI 35/4. (October 1974). Page 2026-A. Order # 74-21,675.

832. Sheehan, Patrick M. Harvard Alumni in Colonial America: Demo-
      graphic, Theological and Political Perspectives. Ph.D. Dissertation.
      Case Western Reserve University. 1972. 237 pp. DAI 32/12. (June
      1972). Page 6792-A. Order # 72-18,736.

833. Simpson, Lowell. The Little Republics: Undergraduate Literary So-
      cieties at Columbia, Dartmouth, Princeton and Yale, 1753-1865. Ed.D.
      Dissertation. Columbia University. 1976. 194 pp. DAI 37/2. (Au-
      gust 1976). Page 847-A. Order # 76-17,294.

834. Skelton, Phillip D. A History of Southern Arkansas University from
      1909 to 1976. Ed.D. Dissertation. University of Mississippi. 1979.
      230 pp. DAI 40/4. (October 1979). Page 1914-A. Order # 7921523.

835. Smedley, Margaret A. A History of the East-West Cultural and Tech-
      nical Interchange Center Between 1960 and 1966. Ph.D. Dissertation.
      Catholic University. 1970. 201 pp. DAI 31/5. (November 1970).
      Page 2142-A. Order # 70-22,694.

836. Smith, Keith L. A History of Brigham Young University--The Early
      Years, 1875-1921. Ph.D. Dissertation. Brigham Young University.
      1972. 281 pp. DAI 33/3. (September 1972). Page 1002-A. Order
      # 72-23,193.

837. Stameshkin, David M. The Town's College: Middlebury College, 1800-
      1915. Ph.D. Dissertation. University of Michigan. 1978. 690 pp.
      DAI 39/2. (August 1978). Page 1064-A. Order # 7813738.

838. Stetar, Joseph M. Development of Southern Higher Education, 1865-1910: Selected Case Studies of Six Colleges. Ph.D. Dissertation. State University of New York, Buffalo. 1975. 208 pp. DAI 36/3. (September 1975). Page 1345-A. Order # 75-18,848.

839. Synnott, Marcia G. A Social History of Admissions Policies at Harvard, Yale and Princeton, 1900-1930. Ph.D. Dissertation. University of Massachusetts. 1974. 791 pp. DAI 35/5. (November 1974). Page 2920-A. Order # 74-25,906.

840. Szymczak, Donald R. Origin and Development of the Southeastern Illinois College, 1960-1976. Ph.D. Dissertation. Southern Illinois University. 1977. 252 pp. DAI 38/5. (November 1977). Page 2604-A. Order # 77-24,041.

841. Taliaferro, Cecil R. Virginia Union University, The First One Hundred Years, 1865-1965. Ph.D. Dissertation. University of Pittsburgh. 1975. 144 pp. DAI 36/4. (October 1975). Page 2065-A. Order # 75-22,468.

842. Thomas, Mary M. Southern Methodist University, the First Twenty-Five Years, 1915-1940. Ph.D. Dissertation. Emory University. 1971. 373 pp. DAI 32/4. (October 1971). Page 2045-A. Order # 71-27,802.

843. Thurman, Francis A. The History of Saint Paul's College in Lawrenceville, Virginia, 1888-1959. Ph.D. Dissertation. Howard University. 1978. 320 pp. DAI 40/3. (September 1979). Page 1655-A. Order # 7917010.

844. Tinsley, Samuel J. A History of Mississippi Valley State College. Ph.D. Dissertation. University of Mississippi. 1972. 293 pp. DAI 33/7. (January 1973). Page 3339-A. Order # 73-1295.

845. Tipton, Elizabeth H. A Descriptive Analysis of Selected Forces and Events Which Influenced the Founding, Growth, and Development of Bowie State College from 1865 to 1975. Ed.D. Dissertation. George Washington University. 1976. 266 pp. DAI 37/4. (October 1976). Page 2022-A. Order # 76-23,561.

846. Tobias, Marilyn I. Old Dartmouth on Trial: The Transformation of the Academic Community in Nineteenth Century America. Ph.D. Dissertation. New York University. 1977. 367 pp. DAI 38/10. (April 1978). Page 5965-A. Order # 7803036.

847. Trares, Thomas F. Ecumenical Action: A History of Springfield College in Illinois, 1929-1969. Ph.D. Dissertation. St. Louis University. 1972. 87 pp. DAI 34/9. (March 1974). Page 5499-A. Order # 74-4585.

848. Troutman, R. Dwight. Hazard Yet Forward: A History of Seton Hill College. Ph.D. Dissertation. University of Pittsburgh. 1978. 323 pp. DAI 39/3. (September 1978). Page 1385-A. Order # 7816819.

849. Tyler, Francis L. Blue Mountain College (Mississippi) Under the Administration of Lawrence Tyndale Lowrey, 1925-1960. Ph.D. Dissertation. University of Mississippi. 1974. 192 pp. DAI 35/11. (May 1975). Page 7095-A. Order # 75-10,688.

850. Vosper, James M. A History of Selected Factors in the Development
     of Creighton University. Ph.D. Dissertation. University of Nebraska.
     1976. 268 pp. DAI 37/7. (January 1977). Page 4176-A. Order #
     77-955.

851. Warden, James E. Bridgewater (Virginia) College, 1880-1972. Ed.D.
     Dissertation. University of Pittsburgh. 1973. 279 pp. DAI 34/7.
     (January 1974). Page 4126-A. Order # 73-29,370.

852. Watson, Robert J. Slippery Rock's Journey from Normal School to
     Multi-Purpose State College. Ph.D. Dissertation. University of Pitts-
     burgh. 1979. 210 pp. DAI 40/5. (November 1979). Page 2517-A.
     Order # 7924745.

853. Welch, Joe B. A History of the Growth and Development of Lamar Uni-
     versity from 1949-1973. Ed.D. Dissertation. McNeese State Univer-
     sity. 1974. 217 pp. DAI 35/7. (January 1975). Page 4108-A.
     Order # 74-29,281.

854. Whitehead, John S. The Separation of College and State: The Trans-
     formation of Columbia, Dartmouth, Harvard and Yale from Quasi-Public
     to Private Institutions, 1776-1876. Ph.D. Dissertation. Yale Univer-
     sity. 1971. 317 pp. DAI 32/12. (June 1972). Page 6914-A. Order
     # 72-17,197.

855. Williams, Earl R. John Brown University (Arkansas): Its Founder
     and its Founding, 1919-1957. Ed.D. Dissertation. University of Ar-
     kansas. 1971. 284 pp. DAI 32/5. (November 1971). Page 2448-
     A. Order # 71-27,670.

856. Wilson, Wilbert R. An Historical Analysis of Events and Issues Which
     Have Led to the Growth and Development of the University of Mary-
     land Eastern Shore from 1886-1975. Ed.D. Dissertation. George
     Washington University. 1976. 195 pp. DAI 37/8. (February 1977).
     Page 4914-A. Order # 77-2966.

857. Witt, Michael J. The Devolution of Christian Brothers College (St.
     Louis), 1900-1931. Ph.D. Dissertation. St. Louis University. 1980.
     270 pp. DAI 41/7. (January 1981). Page 3220-A. Order # 8101279.

858. Zaidenberg, Arthur. From Reforms to Professionalization: The Tran-
     sition of Attitudes Toward Scientific Education at Harvard. Ph.D.
     Dissertation. University of California, Los Angeles. 1974. 231 pp.
     DAI 35/9. (March 1975). Page 5890-A. Order # 75-5701.

Individual States

---

859. Alston, Jerry G. The Role of the State Legislature in Public Higher
     Education in Kentucky. 1950-1968. Ph.D. Dissertation. Southern
     Illinois University. 1970. 167 pp. DAI 31/7. (January 1970).
     Page 3285-A. Order # 71-2362.

860. Bounds, Stuart M. Environment and Political Correlates of Appropria-
     tions for Higher Education in Virginia, 1950-1972. Ed.D. Dissertation

College of William and Mary. 1974. 137 pp. DAI 35/7. (January 1975). Page 4178-A. Order # 75-540.

861. Castro, Apolinario. Higher Education in Puerto Rico, 1898-1956. Ed.D. Dissertation. Lehigh University. 1975. 256 pp. DAI 36/11. (May 1976). Page 7247-A. Order # 76-10,363.

862. Conrad, Erik P. A History of Kansas' Closed Colleges. Ph.D. Dissertation. University of Oklahoma. 1970. 219 pp. DAI 31/7. (January 1971). Page 3309-A. Order # 71-1483.

863. Cook, Jr., James F. Politics and Education in the Talmadge Era: The Controversy Over the University System of Georgia, 1941-42. Ph.D. Dissertation. University of Georgia. 1972. 336 pp. DAI 33/7. (January 1973). Page 3528-A. Order # 72-34,057.

864. Dooher, Philip M. Higher Education and the Veterans: An Historical Study of Change in a Select Number of Massachusetts' Colleges and Universities, 1944-1949. Ph.D. Dissertation. Boston College. 1980. 153 pp. DAI 41/2. (August 1980). Page 549-A. Order # 8017833.

865. Hair, Mary J. S. History of the Efforts to Coordinate Higher Education in Utah. Ph.D. Dissertation. University of Utah. 1974. 422 pp. DAI 35/7. (January 1975). Page 4187-A. Order # 75-587.

866. Hoig, Stanley W. A History of the Development of Institutions of Higher Education in Oklahoma. Ph.D. Dissertation. University of Oklahoma. 1971. 395 pp. DAI 32/5. (November 1972). Page 2451-A. Order # 71-27,617.

867. Johnson, Daniel T. Puritan Power in Illinois Higher Education Prior to 1870. Ph.D. Dissertation. University of Wisconsin, 1974. 234 pp. DAI 35/10. (April 1975). Page 6491-A. Order # 74-30,109.

868. Kalb, John M. The Florida State University System, 1859-1974: A History through Student Distribution. Ph.D. Dissertation. Florida State University. 1978. 217 pp. DAI 40/2. (August 1979). Page 1029-A. Order # 7917049.

869. Lightfoot, Frank K. The History of the Alabama Collegiate Conference, 1959-1972. Ed.D. Dissertation. University of Alabama. 1978. 131 pp. DAI 39/9. (March 1979). Page 5394-A. Order # 7905418.

870. Muscatell, Toni G. P. An Historical Analysis of Instructional Television in Public Higher Learning in the State of Florida. Ed.D. Dissertation. Florida Atlantic University. 1973. 258 pp. DAI 34/11. (May 1974). Page 7016-A. Order # 74-11,604.

871. Norris, Timmerman H. Public Higher Education and the Alabama Legislature, 1901-1960. Ed.D. Dissertation. University of Alabama. 1973. 141 pp. DAI 34/10. (April 1974). Page 6414-A. Order # 74-9377.

872. Pernal, Michael E. A Study of State Legislation in the Development of Public Higher Education in Connecticut from 1849 to 1970. Ph.D. Dissertation. University of Connecticut. 1975. 397 pp. DAI 36/3. (September 1975). Page 1333-A. Order # 75-18,338.

873. Pilver, Erika E. The Politics and Administration of Higher Education
      in Connecticut (1965-1977). Ph.D. Dissertation. University of Con-
      necticut. 1977. 269 pp. DAI 38/8. (February 1978). Page 5044-
      A. Order # 7731213.

874. Ranker, Irene K. Major Studies of Higher Education in California
      1962-1974. Ed.D. Dissertation. University of Southern California.
      1976. n.p. DAI 38/1. (July 1977). Page 129-A. No Order #.

875. Roper, Dwight D. Founders and Renovators: Presidents During the
      Beginning and Change of a California State College (San Francisco
      State Normal School/San Francisco State College). Ph.D. Disserta-
      tion. Stanford University. 1976. 212 pp. DAI 37/5. (November
      1976). Page 2687. Order # 76-26,067.

876. Sherwood, Philip K. A Historical Study of the Associated Colleges
      of Indiana. Ed.D. Dissertation. University of Indiana. 1973. 250
      pp. DAI 34/8. (February 1974). Page 4801-A. Order # 74-2705.

877. Waddell, Frederic J. A Historical Review of the Coordination of Higher
      Education in Texas. Ed.D. Dissertation. North Texas State Univer-
      sity. 1972. 195 pp. DAI 33/8. (February 1973). Page 4135-A.
      Order # 73-2931.

878. Wilson, Marlene R. The History of Developmental Education in Public
      Higher Education Institutions in Ohio: The First Decade, 1968-1978.
      Ph.D. Dissertation. Kent State University. 1980. 426 pp. DAI
      41/6. (December 1980). Page 2474-A. Order # 8024609.

879. Yarish, La Vera M. Twenty Years of Developmental Education in Flor-
      ida Community Colleges (1957-1977). Ed.D. Dissertation. Florida
      State University. 1977. 116 pp. DAI 40/6. (December 1979).
      Page 3160-A. Order # 7926841.

Minorities

---

880. Bethel, Leonard L. The Role of Lincoln University (Pennsylvania) in
      the Education of African Leadership: 1854-1970. Ed.D. Dissertation.
      Rutgers, the State University. 1975. 391 pp. DAI 36/7. (January
      1976). Page 4304-A. Order # 76-1101.

881. Blackwell, Velma L. A Black Institution Pioneering Adult Education:
      Tuskegee Institute Past and Present (1881-1973). Ph.D. Dissertation.
      Florida State University. 1973. 235 pp. DAI 35/1. (August 1974).
      Page 783-A. Order # 74-18,027.

882. Brodsky, Paul L. Radical Factors in the Administration of Morgan
      State College, 1937-1961. Ph.D. Dissertation. University of Mary-
      land. 1976. 239 pp. DAI 37/11. (May 1977). Page 6991-A. Order
      # 77-10,269.

883. Browning, Jane E. S. The Origins, Development and Desegregation
      of Traditionally Black Public Colleges and Universities: 1837-1975.

Ed.D. Dissertation. Harvard University. 1975. 273 pp. DAI 36/11. (May 1976). Page 7229-A. Order # 76-10,557.

884. Cheek, Neal K. An Historical Study of the Administrative Actions in the Racial Desegregation of the University of North Carolina at Chapel Hill, 1930-1955. Ph.D. Dissertation. University of North Carolina. 1973. 235 pp. DAI 34/9. (March 1974). Page 5655-A. Order # 74-5905.

885. Fletcher, Juanita D. Against the Consensus: Oberlin College and the Education of American Negroes, 1835-1865. Ph.D. Dissertation. American University. 1974. 321 pp. DAI 35/4. (October 1974). Page 2005-A. Order # 74-20,887.

886. Hanle, Robert V. A History of Higher Education Among the German Baptist-Brethren: 1708-1908. Ph.D. Dissertation. University of Pennsylvania. 1974. 345 pp. DAI 36/1. (July 1975). Page 159-A. Order # 75-14,569.

887. Hatcher, Cleophus C. An Historical Study of the Integration of Students and Faculty at Bowie (Maryland) State College (1911-1977). Ed.D. Dissertation. George Washington University. 1977. 196 pp. DAI 38/3. (September 1977). Page 1149-A. Order # 77-20,070.

888. High, Juanita J. Black Colleges as Social Intervention: The Development of Higher Education Within the African Methodist Episcopal Church. Ed.D. Dissertation. Rutgers, the State University. 1978. 251 pp. DAI 39/1. (July 1978). Page 160-A. Order # 7810230.

889. Preer, Jean L. Law and Social Policy: Desegregation in Public Higher Education. Ph.D. Dissertation. George Washington University. 1980. 595 pp. DAI 41/5. (November 1980). Page 2265-A. Order # 8023864.

890. Robinson, Jr., Walter G. Blacks in Higher Education in the United States Before 1865. Ph.D. Dissertation. Southern Illinois University. 1976. 220 pp. DAI 37/11. (May 1977). Page 6984-A. Order # 76-28,773.

891. Williams, David A. The History of Higher Education for Black Texans, 1872-1977. Ed.D. Dissertation. Baylor University. 1978. 192 pp. DAI 39/6. (December 1978). Page 3298-A. Order # 7822691.

Organization, Structure, Programs

---

892. Blockstein, Zaga. Graduate School of Public Health, University of Pittsburgh, 1948-1973. Ph.D. Dissertation. University of Pittsburgh. 1974. 369 pp. DAI 35/12. (June 1975). Page 7697-A. Order # 75-51114.

893. Buerki, Robert A. Historical Development of Continuing Pharmaceutical Education in American Universities. Ph.D. Dissertation. Ohio State University. 1972. 542 pp. DAI 73-1954. (February 1973). Page 4139-A. Order # 73-1954.

894. Burns, Ralph E. A History of the Department of Health, Physical Ed-
     ucation, and Recreation at Jackson State University, Mississippi, from
     1877 to 1973. Ed.D. Dissertation. East Texas State University. 1976.
     264 pp. DAI 37/7. (January 1977). Page 4209-A. Order # 77-475.

895. Carter, Gayvon D. A History of the Physical Education Program at
     Florida State University, 1901-1978. Ph.D. Dissertation. Florida
     State University. 1980. 330 pp. DAI 41/7. (January 1981). Page
     2993-A. Order # 8100636.

896. Ellsworth, Frank L. Developments in American Legal Education at the
     Turn of the Century: The Founding of the University of Chicago
     Law School. Ph.D. Dissertation. University of Chicago. 1976.
     n.p. DAI 37/6. (December 1976). Page 3463-A. No Order #.

897. Emerson, Bruce. A History of the Relationships Between the State of
     Virginia and its Public Normal Schools, 1869-1930. Ed.D. Disserta-
     tion. College of William and Mary. 1973. 201 pp. DAI 34/7. (Jan-
     uary 1974). Page 3905-A. Order # 74-83.

898. Ewing, James W. An Historical Investigation of the Training Programs
     in Counseling and Psychotherapy in American Higher Education: 1880-
     1941. Ph.D. Dissertation. St. Louis University. 1972. 239 pp.
     DAI 33/3. (September 1972). Page 983-A. Order # 72-23,924.

899. Fouché, James F. The Tulane University Graduate School of Business
     Education: An Oral Institutional History. Ph.D. Dissertation. Uni-
     versity of Florida. 1978. 228 pp. DAI 39/11. (May 1979). Page
     6584-A. Order # 7907742.

900. Herron, John B. History of the School of Education, University of
     Pittsburgh, 1953-1972. Ph.D. Dissertation. University of Pittsburgh.
     1974. 202 pp. DAI 35/9. (March 1975). Page 5887-A. Order # 75-
     5134.

901. Jenkins, Edwin G. History and Development of the Southern College
     Personnel Association as a Professional Organization, 1949-1972. Ed.D.
     Dissertation. Auburn University. 1974. 214 pp. DAI 35/3. (Sep-
     tember 1974). Page 1462-A. Order # 74-19,386.

902. Johnson, Henry J. The Preparation of Teachers as a University Func-
     tion: The Case of the University of Illinois. Ph.D. Dissertation.
     University of Illinois. 1970. 565 pp. DAI 31/9. (March 1971).
     Page 4501-A. Order # 71-5137.

903. Johnson, William R. The University of Wisconsin Law School: 1868-
     1930. Ph.D. Dissertation. University of Wisconsin. 1972. 403 pp.
     DAI 33/12. (June 1973). Page 6704-A. Order # 73-2546.

904. Levitt, Leon. A History of the School of Education at the University
     of Southern California. Ed.D. Dissertation. University of Southern
     California. 1970. 523 pp. DAI 31/5. (November 1970). Page 2140-
     A. Order # 70-23,160.

905. Mackey, James A. A History of the Louisiana State University Labo-
     ratory School, 1915-1965. Ed.D. Dissertation. Louisiana State Uni-
     versity and Agricultural and Mechanical College. 1971. 277 pp.
     DAI 32/12. (June 1972). Page 6791. Order # 72-17,786.

906. Marsh, Joseph T. A History of Teacher Education at Northern Illi-
      nois University: An Example of the Development of Teacher Prepa-
      ration Institutions from Normal Schools to State Universities in the
      United States. Ed.D. Dissertation. University of Indiana. 1971.
      261 pp. DAI 32/6. (December 1971). Page 3053-A. Order # 72-
      11,347.

907. Neff, William B. History of the School of Education, University of
      Pittsburgh, 1910-1950. Ph.D. Dissertation. University of Pittsburgh.
      1974. 302 pp. DAI 35/8. (February 1975). Page 5060-A. Order #
      75-4080.

908. Patterson, Richard H. Harris (Missouri) Teachers College, 1904-1966.
      Ph.D. Dissertation. St. Louis University. 1972. 173 pp. DAI
      33/3. (September 1972). Page 1096-A. Order # 72-23,994.

909. Pierson, Charles L. A History of the Southern Illinois University
      School of Music, 1874-1970. Ph.D. Dissertation. Southern Illinois
      University. 1971. 400 pp. DAI 32/9. (March 1972). Page 5135-
      A. Order # 72-10,284.

910. Reed, George R. The Contributions of Thomas Milton Carter to
      Teacher Education, Albion (Michigan) College, 1923-1962. Ed.D.
      Dissertation. Michigan State University. 1970. 198 pp. DAI 32/1.
      (July 1971). Page 213-A. Order # 71-18,278.

911. Richards, John D. A History of the Organization, Development, and
      Administration of the Cadet Counseling Center, United States Military
      Academy (1802-1980). Ed.D. Dissertation. University of Southern
      California. 1980. n.p. DAI 41/6. (December 1980). Page 2390.
      No Order #.

912. Sammis, George F. A History of the Maine Normal Schools. Ph.D.
      Dissertation. University of Connecticut. 1970. 305 pp. DAI 31/12.
      (June 1972). Page 6375-A. Order # 71-16,035.

913. Shuchman, Hedvah L. Professionalism and Political Influence: A Po-
      litical History of the University of Connecticut Health Center. Ph.D.
      Dissertation. George Washington University. 1978. 281 pp. DAI
      39/1. (July 1978). Page 452-A. Order # 7810158.

914. Thompson, Wade H. Historical Development of Student Personnel Serv-
      ices Administration at Ball State University, 1918-1968. Ed.D. Dis-
      sertation. University of Indiana. 1971. 278 pp. DAI 32/11. (July
      1971). Page 208-A. Order # 71-17,889.

915. Wertheim, Carl Y. The Doctoral Program in Education for the Depart-
      ment of Defense Dependents Schools Personnel in Europe. Ph.D. Dis-
      sertation. University of Southern California. 1978. n.p. DAI 39/7.
      (January 1979). Page 4092-A. No Order #.

916. Wine, Margaret A. M. A Narrative History of the University High
      School: University of Iowa, 1916-1972. Ph.D. Dissertation. Univer-
      sity of Iowa. 1979. 380 pp. DAI 40/5. (November 1979). Page
      2584-A. Order # 7924543.

917. Woodward, George R. History of the C.O.E. (College of Education),

University of Wyoming: 1887-1945. Ed.D. Dissertation. University of Wyoming. 1971. 161 pp. DAI 33/3. (September 1972). Page 1003-A. Order # 72-13,056.

Professors

918. Beardsley, Wallace R. Samuel Pierpoint Langley--His Early Academic Years at the Western University of Pennsylvania. Ph.D. Dissertation. University of Pittsburgh. 1978. 173 pp. DAI 40/2. (August 1979). Page 690-A. Order # 7917409.

919. Bergen, Jr., Timothy J. A Critical Comparison of the Educational Theories of Five Sociologists (Ross Finney, E. G. Payne, Charles Peters, Walter Smith, and David Snedden). Ph.D. Dissertation. University of Oklahoma. 1974. 299 pp. DAI 35/9. (March 1975). Page 5883-A. Order # 75-6500.

920. Daggy, Robert E. Measures for Yalensia: Naphtali Daggett and Yale College, 1766-1788. Ph.D. Dissertation. University of Wisconsin. 1971. 379 pp. DAI 32/6. (December 1971). Page 3067-A. Order # 71-25,185.

921. Falk, Gerhard. The Immigration of the European Professors and Intellectuals to the United Sttes and Particularly the Niagara (New York) Frontier During the Nazi Era (1933-1941). Ed.D. Dissertation. State University of New York, Buffalo. 1970. 301 pp. DAI 31/4. (October 1970). Page 1584-A. Order # 70-10,306.

922. Finkelstein, Martin J. Three Decades of Research on American Academics: A Descriptive Portrait and Synthesis of Findings. Ph.D. Dissertation. State University of New York, Buffalo. 1978. 446 pp. DAI 39/3. (September 1978). Page 1364-A. Order # 7817031.

923. Fisher, Philip A. Emerson's Vision in "The American Scholar" as Recapitualted in the Inaugural Addresses of Andrew D. White and Charles W. Eliot. Ed.D. Dissertation. University of Southern California. 1978. n.p. DAI 38/10. (April 1978). Page 5943-A. No Order #.

924. Grayson, Gerald H. Professors Unite: A History of the Legislative Conference of City University of New York, 1938-1971. Ph.D. Dissertation. New York University. 1973. 489 pp. DAI 34/12. (June 1974). Page 7548-A. Order # 74-12,841.

925. Green, James M. Alexander Meiklejohn--Innovator in Undergraduate Education (1900-1930). Ph.D. Dissertation. University of Michigan. 1970. 411 pp. DAI 31/8. (February 1971). Page 3914-A. Order # 71-4614.

926. Grossman, David N. Professors and Public Service, 1885-1925: A Chapter in the Professionalization of the Social Sciences. Ph.D. Dissertation. Washington University. 1973. 376 pp. DAI 34/12. (June 1974). Page 7676-A. Order # 74-13,775.

927. Jaquith, L. Paul. The University Seminars at Columbia University: A Living Monument to Frank Tannenbaum. Ed.D. Dissertation. Columbia University. 1973. 155 pp. DAI 34/2. (August 1973). Page 583-A. Order # 73-19,348.

928. Marotta, Gary M. Professors and Imperialism: A Study of the American Academic Community in the Great Debate, 1898-1902. Ph.D. Dissertation. New York University. 1973. 459 pp. DAI 34/8. (February 1974). Page 5037-A. Order # 74-1928.

929. Murphy, Donald J. Professors, Publicists and Pan Americanism: A Study in the Origins of the Use of "Experts" in Shaping American Foreign Policy (in the early 20th century). Ph.D. Dissertation. University of Wisconsin. 1970. 516 pp. DAI 31/11. (May 1971). Page 5992-A. Order # 70-24,808.

930. Nolan, John P. Genteel Attitudes in the Formation of the American Scientific Community: The Career of Benjamin Silliman of Yale. Ph.D. Dissertation. Columbia University. 1978. 235 pp. DAI 39/10. (April 1979). Page 5986-A. Order # 7908623.

931. Saunders, Bruce D. Herbert Baxter Adams and the Development of American Higher Education, 1876-1901. Ph.D. Dissertation. University of Texas. 1975. 303 pp. DAI 36/2. (August 1975). Page 1050-A. Order # 75-16,736.

932. Schoepflin, Gary L. Dennison Olmsted (1791-1859), Scientist, Teacher, Christian: A Biographical Study of the Connection of Science with Religion in Antebellum America. Ph.D. Dissertation. Oregon State University. 1977. 437 pp. DAI 38/7. (January 1978). Page 4336-A. Order # 77-29,426.

933. Vujnovich, Miles M. Ray S. Musgrave: A Biography of a Dedicated Educator (Millsaps College and University of Southern Mississippi in Educational Psychology). Ph.D. Dissertation. University of Southern Mississippi. 1976. 249 pp. DAI 37/9. (March 1977). Page 5647-A. Order # 77-5978.

934. Walsh, Thomas R. Charles E. Bessey: Land-Grant College Professor. Ph.D. Dissertation. University of Nebraska. 1972. 245 pp. DAI 33/6. (December 1972). Page 2748-A. Order # 72-31,882.

Religion

---

935. Anderson, Willis B. A History of Methodist Higher Education in Arkansas, 1836-1933. Ed.D. Dissertation. University of Arkansas. 1971. (August 1971). Page 758-A. Order # 71-19,528.

936. Galvin, C. M. Reverend James M. Secularizing Trends in Roman Catholic Colleges and Universities. Ed.D. Dissertation. University of Indiana. 1971. 124 pp. DAI 32/6. (December 1971). Page 3050-A. Order # 72-1545.

937. McKevitt, Gerald. The History of Santa Clara College: A History of
      Jesuit Education in California, 1851-1912. Ph.D. Dissertation. Uni-
      versity of California, Los Angeles. 1972. 372 pp. DAI 33/4. (Oc-
      tober 1972). Page 1654-A. Order # 72-25,811.

938. Stokes, Arthur P. Daniel Alexander Payne (1811-1893): Churchman
      and Educator. Ph.D. Dissertation. Ohio State University. 1973.
      262 pp. DAI 34/11. (May 1974). Page 7137-A. Order # 74-11,057.

939. Trindade, Father Armando D. Roman Catholic Worship at Stanford
      University, 1891-1971. Ph.D. Dissertation. Stanford University.
      1971. 387 pp. DAI 32/8. (February 1972). Page 4392-A. Order
      # 72-6012.

Student Politics and Activities

940. Armistead, Timothy W. The Criminalization of Political Protest in Berk-
      eley, 1960-1970. D. Crim. Dissertation. University of California,
      Berkeley. 1977. 796 pp. DAI 38/8. (February 1978). Page 796-
      A. Order # 7731242.

941. Baker, John H. The Relationship of Student Activism at the Univer-
      sity of Puerto Rico to the Struggle for Political Independence in Puerto
      Rico, 1923-1971. Ph.D. Dissertation. Boston College. 1973. 250
      pp. DAI 34/3. (September 1973). Page 1092-A. Order # 73-21,722.

942. Bolinder, Calvin H. A Theoretical Analysis of Student Protest in Mod-
      ern America (1960-1972). Ph.D. Dissertation. University of Wiscon-
      sin. 1973. 374 pp. DAI 34/11. (May 1974). Page 6992-A. Order
      # 74-7458.

943. Donnelly, Thomas H. Student Activists Seven Years Later: A Study
      of Change in Political Attitudes and Activity. Ph.D. Dissertation.
      New York University. 1978. 389 pp. DAI 39/12. (June 1979).
      Page 7528-A. Order # 7912268.

944. Eagan, Eileen M. The Student Peace Movement in the U.S., 1930-
      1941. Ph.D. Dissertation. Temple University. 1979. 345 pp. DAI
      39/11. (May 1979). Page 6913-A. Order # 7910045.

945. Horn, Max. The Intercollegiate Socialist Society, 1905-1921: Origins
      of the Modern American Student Movement. Ph.D. Dissertation. Co-
      lumbia University. 1975. 348 pp. DAI 36/6. (December 1975).
      Page 3468-A. Order # 75-27,426.

946. Huntley, Richard T. Events and Issues of the Angela Davis Dismissal.
      Ed.D. Dissertation. University of Southern California. 1976. n.p.
      DAI 37/9. (March 1977). Page 5630-A. No Order #.

947. Jaffe, Jr., Joseph L. Isolation and Neutrality in Academe, 1938-1941.
      Ph.D. Dissertation. Case Western Reserve University. 1979. 426
      pp. DAI 39/11. (May 1979). Page 6915-A. Order # 7909358.

948. Malek-Madani, Firouz. American College Student Unrest from Colonial
      to 1976, in Relation to the Kondratieff Theory of Business Cycles.
      Ph.D. Dissertation. Southern Illinois University. 1977. 157 pp.
      DAI 38/10. (April 1978). Page 5953-A. Order # 7804289.

949. Metzger, Jerome C. Litigation, 1960-1970. Involving Students and
      Higher Education Institutions. Ed.D. Dissertation. University of
      Indiana. 1971. 325 pp. DAI 32/6. (December 1971). Page 3050-
      A. Order # 71-24,557.

950. Murray, Neil D. A Comparative Historical Study of Student Protest
      at the University of Oregon and Oregon State University During the
      Sixties. Ph.D. Dissertation. University of Oregon. 1971. 196 pp.
      DAI 32/9. (March 1971). Page 4844-A. Order # 72-8579.

951. Palcic, James L. The History of the Black Student Union at Florida
      State University, 1968-1978. Ph.D. Dissertation. Florida State Uni-
      versity. 1979. 376 pp. DAI 40/6. (December 1979). Page 3151-
      A. Order # 7926796.

952. Persico, Connell F. The Student Movement and Institutional Disrup-
      tion: An Historical Case Study of San Francisco State College (1966-
      1969). Ph.D. Dissertation. Stanford University. 1974. 179 pp.
      DAI 35/3. (September 1974). Page 1467-A. Order # 74-20,223.

953. Phelps, Marianne R. The Response of Higher Education to Student
      Activism, 1933-1938. Ph.D. Dissertation. George Washington Uni-
      versity. 1980. 340 pp. DAI 41/5. (November 1980). Page 2183-
      A. Order # 8023863.

954. Pollak, Peter G. Socialism and Social Science in the Formation of the
      American University: The Intercollegiate Socialist Society and the
      Case of Wisconsin. Ph.D. Dissertation. State University of New
      York, Albany. 1977. 401 pp. DAI 38/11. (May 1978). Page 6572-
      A. Order # 7805711.

955. Rappaport, Margaret M. Perspectives on University Student Activism
      in America, 1960-1970. Ph.D. Dissertation. University of Colorado.
      1971. 347 pp. DAI 32/4. (October 1971). Page 1758-A. Order #
      71-25,867.

956. Rosenbrier, Gilbert M. An Historical Analysis of Student Unrest.
      Ed.D. Dissertation. Boston University. 1971. 332 pp. DAI 32/4.
      (October 1971). Page 1884-A. Order # 71-26,734.

957. Schnell, Rodolph L. National Activist Student Organizations in Amer-
      ican Higher Education, 1905-1944. Ph.D. Dissertation. University of
      Michigan. 1975. 263 pp. DAI 36/10. (April 1976). Page 6519-A.
      Order # 76-9506.

958. Schreiber, Stephen T. American College Student Riots and Disorders
      Between 1815 and the Civil War. Ed.D. Dissertation. University of
      Indiana. 1979. 311 pp. DAI 40/7. (January 1980). Page 3830-
      A. Order # 8000649.

959. Schwerner, Stephen A. An Historical Study of the Changing Empha-
      sis on Social, Political, and Economic Issues Since World War I in

Undergraduate Newspapers at Four Eastern Colleges. (CCNY, Princeton, Columbia, Vassar). Ph.D. Dissertation. New York University. 1970. 130 pp. DAI 31/11. (May 1971). Page 5802-A. Order # 71-13,622.

960. Swisher, Randall S. Student Activists in the Seventies: The Public Interest Research Group Movement. Ph.D. Dissertation. George Washington University. 1978. 589 pp. DAI 39/8. (February 1979). Page 5086-A. Order # 7903793.

961. Winterbauer, Nancy S. An Analysis of the 1968-69 Black Student Disturbances at Rutgers University. Ed.D. Dissertation. Rutgers, the State University. 1980. 179 pp. DAI 41/4. Page 1460-A. Order # 8023634.

Student Life

---

962. Burke, Colin B. The Quiet Influence: The American Colleges and Their Students, 1800-1860. Ph.D. Dissertation. Washington University. 1973. 388 pp. DAI 34/12. (June 1974). Page 7662-A. Order #74-13,766.

963. Cipic, Margaret S. A History of Gamma Chapter, Delta Pi Epsilon, 1940-1978. Ed.D. Dissertation. University of Pittsburgh. 1980. 181 pp. DAI 41/2. (August 1980). Page 755-A. Order # 8018293.

964. Frank, Frederick J. Student Life in Selected Colleges in the Early Nineteenth Century. Ph.D. Dissertation. University of Pittsburgh. 1975. 332 pp. DAI 36/9. (March 1976). Page 5886-A. Order # 76-5438.

965. Gilson, James E. Changing Student Lifestyle at the University of Iowa, 1800-1900. Ph.D. Dissertation. University of Iowa. 1980. 396 pp. DAI 41/4. (October 1980). Page 1664-A. Order # 8022025.

966. Lenn, Marjorie P. A Study of Residence Hall Development: Shifting Organizational Patterns and Roles of Residence Hall Staff from 1961 to 1976. Ed.D. Dissertation. University of Massachusetts. 1978. 173 pp. DAI 39/4. (October 1978). Page 2089-A. Order # 7818015.

967. Saslaw, Rita S. Student Societies: Nineteenth Century Establishment. Ph.D. Dissertation. Case Western Reserve University. 1971. 249 pp. DAI 32/6. (December 1971). Page 3070-A. Order # 72-101.

968. Stentz, Oren W. Evolution of Residence Hall Administration at Ohio University, 1883-1969. Ph.D. Dissertation. Ohio University. 1975. 183 pp. DAI 36/10. (April 1976). Page 6490-A. Order # 76-8896.

969. Thompson, William E. The Impact of College Socialization: Phase I of a Longitudinal Cohort Analysis. Ph.D. Dissertation. Ohio State University. 1979. 188 pp. DAI 40/6. (December 1979). Page 3557-A. Order # 7928239.

970. Wall, Jr., Charles C. Students and Student Life at the University of
      Virginia, 1825-1861. Ph.D. Dissertation. University of Virginia.
      1978. 341 pp. DAI 40/2. (August 1979). Page 1035-A. Order #
      7916286.

971. Zicklin, Gilbert. Case Studies in the Culture and Practice of Com-
      munes of the Late 1960's and Early 1970's. Ph.D. Dissertation. Uni-
      versity of California, Davis. 1977. 239 pp. DAI 38/12. (June
      1978). Page 7576-A. Order # 7809265.

972. Zimmerman, Joan G. College Culture in the Midwest, 1890-1930. Ph.D.
      Dissertation. University of Virginia. 1978. 275 pp. DAI 40/2.
      (August 1979). Page 1036-A. Order # 7916278.

Theory and Philosophy

---

973. Adams, Stephanie M. The Creative Adjustment of Higher Education
      to Social and Philosophical Tensions in the United States: 1865-1915.
      Ed.D. Dissertation. University of Southern California. 1975. n.p.
      DAI 37/11. (May 1976). Page 7227-A. No Order #.

974. Coughlin, Neil P. Dewey and the University. Ph.D. Dissertation.
      University of Wisconsin. 1970. 176 pp. DAI 32/11. (May 1972).
      Page 6332-A. Order # 72-11,234.

975. Dixon, Henry W. An Historical Survey of Jesuit Higher Education in
      the United States with Particular Reference to the Objectives of Edu-
      cation. Ed.D. Dissertation. Arizona State University. 1974. 196
      pp. DAI 35/3. (September 1974). Page 1473-A. Order # 74-19,282.

976. Hoffman, Lars. William Rainey Harper and the Chicago Fellowship.
      Ph.D. Dissertation. University of Iowa. 1978. 327 pp. DAI 39/12.
      (June 1979). Page 7483-A. Order # 7912856.

977. Jarech, Leon N. Two Contrasting Views of the Uses of the University:
      Robert M. Hutchins and Clark Kerr. Ph.D. Dissertation. University
      of Illinois. 1978. 359 pp. DAI 39/12. (June 1979). Page 7216-A.
      Order # 7913500.

978. Jones, Richard B. Higher Learning for America: A Comparison of
      Abraham Flexner and Robert Maynard Hutchins and Their Views on
      Higher Education. Ph.D. Dissertation. St. Louis University. 1978.
      327 pp. DAI 39/3. (September 1978). Page 1370-A. Order #
      7814586.

979. Keenan, Hubert J. A View from the Tower: An Investigation of the
      Writings of John Huston Finley on the School and Higher Education
      from 1921 to 1940. Ph.D. Dissertation. New York University. 1970.
      332 pp. DAI 31/5. (November 1970). Page 2139-A. Order # 70-
      21,135.

980. Maldonado-Rivera, Manual. The Historical and Philosophical Founda-
      tions of Ortega's Concept of the University. Ph.D. Dissertation.

University of Texas. 1971. 381 pp. DAI 32/11. (May 1972). Page
6008-A. Order # 72-15,798.

981. Masson, Margaret W. The Premise and Purpose of Higher Education in
American Society, 1745-1770. Ph.D. Dissertation. University of Wash-
ington. 1971. 295 pp. DAI 32/11. (May 1972). Page 6346-A.
Order # 72-15,121.

982. Ravitch, Harold. Robert Maynard Hutchins: Philosopher of Education.
Ph.D. Dissertation. University of Southern California. 1980. n.p.
DAI 41/4. (October 1980). Page 1470-A. No Order #.

983. Roeske, Clarence E. The Land-Grant Philosophy: Historical Implications of its Changing Definition through the American Experience.
Ph.D. Dissertation. Ohio State University. 1973. 164 pp. DAI
34/5. (November 1973). Page 2356-A. Order # 73-26,899.

984. Stuart, Mary C. Clark Kerr: Biography of an Action Intellectual.
Ph.D. Dissertation. University of Michigan. 1980. 388 pp. DAI
41/2. (August 1980). Page 563-A. Order # 8017376.

985. Warford, Malcolm L. Piety, Politics and Pedagogy: An Evangelical
Protestant Tradition in Higher Education at Lane, Oberlin and Beria,
1834-1904. Ed.D. Dissertation. Columbia University. 1973. 231 pp.
DAI 34/10. (April 1974). Page 6425-A. Order # 74-9654.

986. Warren, Charles F. Higher Education in the Ancient Roman Empire
and its Implications for Contemporary Higher Education in the United
States. Ph.D. Dissertation. University of Alabama. 1976. 120 pp.
DAI 37/12. (June 1977). Page 7573-A. Order # 77-12,250.

Women

---

987. Adair, Alice J. L. A Study of Women at the University of Utah from
1953 to 1964. Ph.D. Dissertation. University of Utah. 1980. 186
pp. DAI 41/11. (May 1981). Page 4615-A. Order # 8109566.

988. Gordon, Lynn D. Women with Missions: Varieties of College Life in
the Progressive Era. Ph.D. Dissertation. University of Chicago.
1980. n.p. DAI 41/7. (January 1981). Page 3233-A. No Order #.

989. Horn, Marcia A. Ideas of the Founders of the Early Colleges for
Women on the Role of Women's Education in American Society. Ed.D.
Dissertation. Rutgers, the State University. 1977. 157 pp. DAI
37/12. (June 1977). Page 7577-A. Order # 77-13,465.

990. Ihle, Elizabeth L. The Development of Coeducation in Major Southern
State Universities. Ed.D. Dissertation. University of Tennessee.
1976. 205 pp. DAI 37/11. (May 1977). Page 6992-A. Order # 77-
10,776.

991. Monahan, Danno R. Educating Women Religioses: The History of
Marilloc (Missouri) College, 1955-69. Ph.D. Dissertation. St. Louis

University. 1972. 127 pp. DAI 33/6. (December 1972). Page
2745-A. Order # 72-31,474.

992. Russ, Anne J. Higher Education for Women: Intent, Reality, and
Outcomes: Wells College, 1968-1913. Ph.D. Dissertation. Cornell
University. 1980. 138 pp. DAI 41/1. (July 1980). Page 135-A.
Order # 8015732.

993. Strobel, Marian E. Ideology and Women's Higher Education, 1945-
1960. Ph.D. Dissertation. Duke University. 1975. 291 pp. DAI
36/10. (April 1976). Page 6903-A. Order # 76-9148.

994. Wilcox, Reba A. A Study of the Education of Women at the University
of Utah, 1915-1916 to 1924-1925. Ph.D. Dissertation. University of
Utah. 1979. 168 pp. DAI 40/11. (November 1980). Page 5761-
A. Order # 8009806.

995. Wills, Lynette A. H. Peabody Women Doctorates: 1961-1975. Ph.D.
Dissertation. George Peabody College for Teachers. 1978. 230 pp.
DAI 39/8. (February 1979). Page 4651-A. Order # 7902516.

Ideology and Education

---

996. Anderson, Lynn F. Crisis Ideology in American Social Thought: Its
Implications and Impact Upon Education. Ph.D. Dissertation. Ohio
State University. 1971. 226 pp. DAI 32/9. (March 1972). Page
4833-A. Order # 72-4482.

997. Balter, Robert. The Merchant in the Classroom: The Influence of
Bourgeoise Thought on American Education. Ph.D. Dissertation.
Cornell University. 1977. 235 pp. DAI 38/7. (January 1978).
Page 4015-A. Order # 77-28,185.

998. Bosak, Beverly W. A Decade of Radical Education Trends: The
1960's. Ph.D. Dissertation. Arizona State University. 1977. 552
pp. DAI 38/2. (August 1977). Page 533-A. Order # 77-17,251.

999. Browning, Robert G. Ideology and Educational Philanthropy: An
Historical Analysis. Ph.D. Dissertation. Ohio State University.
1979. 251 pp. DAI 40/1. (July 1979). Page 131-A. Order #
7915959.

1000. Hebert, Michael R. The Social Purpose of American Education Con-
sidered from the Class Relativist Point of View. Ph.D. Dissertation.
University of Indiana. 1974. 313 pp. DAI 35/7. (January 1975).
Page 4313-A. Order # 75-1705.

1001. Hootman, Richard S. The Romantic Critics of the Sixties: John
Holt and Company. Ph.D. Dissertation. University of Iowa. 1976.
183 pp. DAI 37/5. (November 1976). Page 2684-A. Order # 76-
26,290.

1002. Lennon, James H. Romanticism in Education. Ed.D. Dissertation.

Wayne State University. 1980. 293 pp. DAI 41/4. (October 1980). Page 1468-A. Order # 8022816.

1003.   Mark, Arthur. Two Libertarian Educators: Elizabeth Byrne Ferm and Alexis Constantine Ferm (1857-1971). Ed.D. Dissertation. Columbia University. 1974. 372 pp. DAI 36/1. (July 1975). Page 160-A. Order # 75-13,899.

1004.   Mendelson, Robert. The Ideological Debate in the Public Schools Guidance Movement, 1900-1970. Ph.D. Dissertation. New York University. 1974. 170 pp. DAI 35/10. (April 1975). Page 6491-A. Order # 75-8554.

1005.   Phillips, Norman R. Neo-Conservatism and Educational Excellence, 1918-1970. Ph.D. Dissertation. Loyola University, Chicago. 1975. 183 pp. DAI 36/1. (July 1975). Page 160-A. Order # 75-14,522.

1006.   Rogers, Lawrence E. Anarchism and Libertarian Education. Ph.D. Dissertation. University of Nebraska. 1975. 274 pp. DAI 36/8. (February 1976). Page 5100-A. Order # 76-4536.

1007.   Shapiro, Harvey S. Education and Ideology: A Sociological Study of Educational Thought in the American Radical Movement, 1900-1925. Ed.D. Dissertation. Boston University. 1978. 314 pp. DAI 39/5. (November 1978). Page 3166-A. Order # 7819781.

1008.   Shea, Christine M. The Ideology of Mental Health and the Emergence of the Therapeutic Liberal State: The American Mental Hygiene Movement, 1900-1930. Ph.D. Dissertation. University of Illinois. 1980. 465 pp. DAI 41/6. (December 1980). Page 2476-A. Order # 8026596.

1009.   Tager, Florence M. S. A Radical Approach to Education: American Schooling--The Modern School of New York and Stelton. Ph.D. Dissertation. Ohio State University. 1979. 328 pp. DAI 40/1. (July 1979). Page 134-A. Order # 7916033.

1010.   Wake, Wilma E. Anarchism and Education: Development of a Framework for Non-Authoritarian Education. Ph.D. Dissertation. University of Maryland. 1977. 284 pp. DAI 38/9. (March 1978). Page 5328-A. Order # 7800399.

Immigrants and Education

1011.   Alexander, Sylvia J. G. The Immigrant Church and Community: The Formation of Pittsburgh's Slovak Religious Institutions, 1880-1914. Ph.D. Dissertation. University of Minnesota. 1980. 696 pp. DAI 41/7. (January 1981). Page 3231-A. Order # 8102061.

1012.   Crispino, James A. The Assimilation of Ethnic Groups: The Italian Case. Ph.D. Dissertation. Columbia University. 1979. 310 pp. DAI 40/6. (December 1979). Page 3540-A. Order # 7924865.

1013. Dann, Martin E. "Little Citizens": Working Class and Immigrant
      Childhood in New York City, 1890-1915. Ph.D. Dissertation. City
      University of New York. 1978. 494 pp. DAI 39/4. (October 1978).
      Page 2482-A. Order # 7818811.

1014. Edson, C. H. Immigrant Perspectives on Work and Schooling: East-
      ern European Jews and Southern Italians, 1880-1920. Ph.D. Disser-
      tation. Stanford University. 1979. 287 pp. DAI 40/7. (January
      1980). Page 3826-A. Order # 8001909.

1015. Eisele, Jack C. The Immigrants and the Educational Thought of One
      Progressive, John Dewey. Ph.D. Dissertation. Ohio State Univer-
      sity. 1974. DAI 35/8. (February 1975). Page 5071-A. Order #
      75-3054.

1016. Gorlick, Sherry. Social Control, Social Mobility, and Eastern Euro-
      pean Jews: An Analysis of Public Education in New York City,
      1880-1924. Ph.D. Dissertation. Columbia University. 1975. 374
      pp. DAI 36/12. (June 1975). Page 8333-A. Order # 76-12,809.

1017. Jaros, James A. The Gospel of Americanization: The Influence of
      the Protestant Economy of Salvation in Defining the Ideal Immigrant
      Experience. Ph.D. Dissertation. Case Western Reserve University.
      1973. 297 pp. DAI 34/8. (February 1974). Page 5062-A. Order
      # 74-2531.

1018. Kopan, Andrew T. Education and Greek Immigrants in Chicago, 1892-
      1979: A Study in Ethnic Survival. Ph.D. Dissertation. University
      of Chicago. 1974. n.p. DAI 36/2. (August 1975). Page 751-A.
      No Order #.

1019. Kristufek, Richard. The Immigrant and the Pittsburgh Public Schools:
      1870-1940. Ph.D. Dissertation. University of Pittsburgh. 1975.
      177 pp. DAI 36/9. (March 1976). Page 5887-A. Order # 76-5453.

1020. Kronish, Ronald. The Influence of John Dewey on Jewish Education
      in America. Ed.D. Dissertation. Harvard University. 1979. 306
      pp. DAI 40/8. (February 1980). Page 4443-A. Order # 7927950.

1021. Kuyper, Susan J. The Americanization of German Immigrants: Lan-
      guage, Religion and Schools in Nineteenth Century Rural Wisconsin.
      Ph.D. Dissertation. University of Wisconsin. 1980. 228 pp. DAI
      42/1. (July 1981). Page 111-A. Order # 8107844.

1022. Kuznicki, CSSF, Sister Ellen M. An Ethnic School in American Edu-
      cation: A Study of the Origin, Development, and Merits of the Ed-
      ucational System of the Felician Sisters in the Polish-American Cath-
      olic Schools of Western New York. Ph.D. Dissertation. Kansas State
      University. 1973. 288 pp. DAI 33/12. (June 1973). Page 6845-A.
      Order # 73-13,353.

1023. Lagios, George A. The Development of Greek-American Education
      in the United States, 1908-1973: Its Theory, Curriculum, and Prac-
      tice. Ph.D. Dissertation. University of Connecticut. 1977. 379
      pp. DAI 38/2. (August 1977). Page 613-A. Order # 77-16,718.

1024. Lapham, James S. The German-Americans of New York City. 1860-

1890. Ph.D. Dissertation. St. John's University. 1977. 295 pp. DAI 38/7. (January 1978). Page 4330-A. Order # 77-29,447.

1025. Leuca, Mary. Development in Ethnic Heritage Curriculum: A Case Study of Romanian-Americans in Lake County, Indiana. Ph.D. Dissertation. Purdue University. 1979. 226 pp. DAI 40/6. (December 1979). Page 3087-A. Order # 7926403.

1026. Light, Dale B. Class, Ethnicity and the Urban Ecology in a Nineteenth Century City: Philadelphia's Irish, 1840-1890. Ph.D. Dissertation. University of Pennsylvania. 1979. 259 pp. DAI 40/6. (December 1979). Page 3490-A. Order # 7928150.

1027. Linask, Kersti L. An Historical Study of Selected Estonian Supplementary Schools in the United States and Canada from 1950 to the Present (1978). Ph.D. Dissertation. University of Connecticut. 1978. 198 pp. DAI 39/11. (May 1979). Page 6613-A. Order # 7911388.

1028. Linkh, Richard M. Catholicism and the European Immigrant, 1900-1924: A Chapter in American Catholic Social Thought. Ed.D. Dissertation. Columbia University. 1973. 361 pp. DAI 34/7. (January 1974). Page 3934-A. Order # 73-31,283.

1029. Markus, Daria. Education of Ethnic Leadership: A Case Study of the Ukrainian Ethnic Group in the United States (1970-1974). Ph.D. Dissertation. Loyola University, Chicago. 1977. 336 pp. DAI 37/12. (June 1977). Page 7578-A. Order # 77-13,422.

1030. Nazeri, Janet F. Views of Leading American Educators Concerning the Schooling of Immigrant Children. Ed.D. Dissertation. Southern Illinois University. 1981. 143 pp. DAI 42/11. (May 1982). Page 4745-A. Order # 8207105.

1031. Rivers, Richard R. American Biological Opposition to Southeastern European Immigration, 1900-1924: Ideas, Policies and Implications for Teaching. D.A. Dissertation. Illinois State University. 1978. 179 pp. DAI 39/9. (March 1979). Page 5682-A. Order # 7905104.

1032. Stibili, Edward C. The St. Raphael Society for the Protection of Italian Immigrants, 1887-1923. Ph.D. Dissertation. University of Notre Dame. 1977. 350 pp. DAI 38/3. (September 1977). Page 1588-A. Order # 77-19,154.

1033. Wieder, Alan V. Immigration, the Public Schools, and the Twentieth Century American Ethos: The Jewish Immigrant as a Case Study. Ph.D. Dissertation. Ohio State University. 1977. 157 pp. DAI 38/5. (November 1977). Page 2612-A. Order # 77-24,726.

Individual Cities and States

1034. Abraham, Cleo. Protests and Expedients in Response to Failures in Urban Education: A Study of New Haven, 1950-1970. Ed.D. Dis-

sertation. University of Massachusetts. 1971. 178 pp. DAI 32/4.
(October 1971). Page 1738-A. Order # 71-25,423.

1035. Ainsworth, David B. The Public Elementary Schools of Montana, 1860-
1920. Ph.D. Dissertation. University of Montana. 1971. 201 pp.
DAI 32/7. (January 1972). Page 3736-A. Order # 72-4121.

1036. Alexander, George D. The Historical Development of State Aid in
Texas, 1930-1968. Ph.D. Dissertation. East Texas State Univer-
sity. 1970. 165 pp. DAI 33/7. (January 1971). Page 3191-A.
Order # 71-219.

1037. Arvid, Jr., Edward N. A History of the Policies, Rules and Regula-
tions of the Public Schools of Omaha, Nebraska from 1870 to 1964.
Ed.D. Dissertation. University of Nebraska. 1969. 491 pp. DAI
30/7. (January 1970). Page 2772-A. Order # 69-22,292.

1038. Black, Paul F. A Historical Study of the Structures and Major Functions of the Pittsburgh Board of Public Education. Ph.D. Dissertation. University of Pittsburgh. 1972. 279 pp. DAI 33/8. (February 1973). Page 4139-A. Order # 73-4130.

1039. Bresnahan, Daniel J. The Springfield Plan in Retrospect. Ed.D.
Dissertation. Columbia University. 1971. 203 pp. DAI 32/7.
(January 1972). Page 3736-A. Order # 72-4163.

1040. Bryson, Norris C. The Response of the Cooperative Extension Service in the Great Depression in Michigan, 1929-1938. Ph.D. Dissertation. Michigan State University. 1979. 170 pp. DAI 40/12.
(June 1980). Page 6171-A. Order # 8013705.

1041. Burns, Hugh J. The History of the Francis Howell (Missouri) School
District. Ph.D. Dissertation. St. Louis University. 1977. 167 pp.
DAI 39/3. (September 1978). Page 1208-A. Order # 7814540.

1042. Carpenter, Edward F. The Development of an Alternative School:
Harlem Prep. 1967-1972. Ed.D. Dissertation. University of Massa-
chusetts. 1973. 167 pp. DAI 34/1. (July 1973). Page 63-A.
Order # 73-14,626.

1043. Casdorph, Paul D. Legislative Politics and the Public Schools in
West Virginia, 1933-1958: A Twenty-Five Year History. Ed.D. Dis-
sertation. University of Kentucky. 1970. 414 pp. DAI 32/2.
(August 1971). Page 759-A. Order # 71-19,359.

1044. Chenette, Edward B. The Montana State Board of Education: A
Study of Higher Education in Conflict, 1884-1959. (2 Vols). Ed.D.
Dissertation. University of Montana. 1972. 507 pp. DAI 33/11.
(May 1973). Page 6110-A. Order # 73-11,310.

1045. Chilton, Jr., John F. Changing Public Attitudes Toward Pre-Collegiate
Education in the Nashville Basin, Tennessee, 1800-1860. Ph.D. Dis-
sertation. George Peabody College for Teachers. 1975. 183 pp.
DAI 36/4. (October 1975). Page 2070-A. Order # 75-22,254.

1046. Chipman, Donald D. The Development of the Florida State System of
Public Education, 1922-1948. Ph.D. Dissertation. Florida State

University. 1972. 236 pp. DAI 33/9. (March 1973). Page 4901-A.
Order # 73-185.

1047. Connelly, Thomas F. Historical Development of Educational Decentralization in Selected (Chicago, St. Louis, Detroit and Cleveland) Mid-
western Urban Centers. Ph.D. Dissertation. Loyola University,
Chicago. 1974. 249 pp. DAI 35/4. (October 1974). Page 1900-
A. Order # 74-22,421.

1048. Curran, Patrick J. T. A History of Public Education in the Town of
Islip, New York. Ph.D. Dissertation. North Texas State University.
1971. 258 pp. DAI 32/12. (June 1972). Page 6790-A. Order #
72-17,001.

1049. Dial, Henry C. Historical Development of School Finance in Arkansas, 1819-1970. Ed.D. Dissertation. University of Arkansas. 1971.
555 pp. DAI 32/5. (November 1971). Page 2339-A. Order # 71-
27,651.

1050. Dicker, Saul S. The Theory and Practice of Corporal Punishment in
the Public and Private Secondary Schools of Boston, 1821-1890.
Ph.D. Dissertation. Catholic University of America. 1970. 224 pp.
DAI 31/3. (September 1970). Page 1047-A. Order # 70-16,456.

1051. Donnan, Annette W. A Study of the History of Capiah-Lincoln Agricultural High School (Mississippi) and Junior College from 1914 to
May 31, 1976. Ed.D. Dissertation. University of Southern Mississippi. 1977. 241 pp. DAI 38/5. (November 1977). Page 2691-A.
Order # 77-22,866.

1052. Draper, Owen H. Contributions of Governor Braxton Bragg Comer
to Public Education in Alabama, 1907-1911. Ed.D. Dissertation.
University of Alabama. 1970. 257 pp. DAI 31/10. (April 1971).
Page 5158-A. Order # 71-9080.

1053. Dubose, Peggy H. Explanation of Public Policy: Environment and
Power in Public Education Policy in Georgia, 1930-1970. Ph.D. Dissertation. Vanderbilt University. 1977. 164 pp. DAI 38/8. (February 1978). Page 5021-A. Order # 7730357.

1054. Ecton, Gayle W. A History of the Lincoln School, Sampsonville, Kentucky, 1966-1970. Ed.D. Dissertation. University of Kentucky.
1979. 223 pp. DAI 40/6. (December 1979). Page 3229-A. Order
7927672.

1055. Eidt, Mary B. Fifty Years of Public Education in Concordia Parish,
1927-1978. Ed.D. Dissertation. Northeast Louisiana University.
1979. 254 pp. DAI 40/9. (March 1980). Page 4926-A. Order #
8005605.

1056. Eisenberg, Carolyn W. The Parents Movement at P.S. 201 (New York
City): From Integration to Black Power, 1958-1966: A Case Study
of Developing Ideology. Ph.D. Dissertation. Columbia University.
1971. 376 pp. DAI 35/2. (August 1974). Page 1002-A. Order
74-17,860.

1057. Ellard, Robert M. A History of Clarksdale, Mississippi, Public

Schools from 1905 to 1975. Ed.D. Dissertation. University of Mississippi. 1977. 223 pp. DAI 38/3. (September 1977). Page 1266-A. Order # 77-20,178.

1058. Farmers, William W. The Anti-Evolution Crusade in Missouri, 1922-1971. Ph.D. Dissertation. University of Missouri. 1974. 294 pp. DAI 35/9. (March 1975). Page 5884-A. Order # 75-5742.

1059. Findley, Eugene M. The Historical Development of Standards for the Accreditation of Public Secondary Schools in Texas (to 1970). Ed.D. Dissertation. Baylor University. 1973. 417 pp. DAI 35/2. (August 1974). Page 747-A. Order # 74-7286.

1060. Flanagan, Jr., Henry E. Aspirando Et Perserverando: The Evolution of the Avon (Connecticut) Old Farmers School as Influenced by its Founder. Ph.D. Dissertation. University of Michigan. 1978. 1959 pp. DAI 39/2. (August 1978). Page 564-A. Order # 7813652.

1061. Foley, Virginia M. The Establishment of the City Superintendency of Public Schools in Five Nineteenth Century American Cities (Buffalo, St. Louis, Los Angeles, Savannah, Salt Lake). Ed.D. Dissertation. State University of New York, Buffalo. 1972. 234 pp. DAI 32/11. (May 1972). Page 6164-A. Order # 72-15,624.

1062. Ginevan, Anne V. The Evolution of the Home and School Visitor Service in the Pittsburgh Public Schools: Sociological and Economic Influences. Ph.D. Dissertation. University of Pittsburgh. 1974. 123 pp. DAI 35/12. (June 1975). Page 7698-A. Order # 75-13,185.

1063. Giordano, Paul A. The Italians of Louisiana: Their Cultural Background and their Many Contributions in the Fields of Literature, the Arts, Education, Politics, Business and Labor. Ph.D. Dissertation. Indiana University. 1978. 256 pp. DAI 39/7. (January 1979). Page 4445-A. Order # 7900390.

1064. Giovacchini, Larry. History of the Public School System of Ebensburg, Pennsylvania, from 1834 to 1973. D.Ed. Dissertation. Pennsylvania State University. 1976. 445 pp. DAI 37/6. (December 1976). Page 3463-A. Order # 76-27,359.

1065. Glauert, Ralph E. Education and Society in Ante-Bellum Missouri. Ph.D. Dissertation. University of Missouri. 1973. 267 pp. DAI 35/2. (August 1974). Page 1006-A. Order # 74-18,534.

1066. Gordon, Richard L. The Development of Louisiana's Public Mental Health Institutions, 1735-1940. Ph.D. Dissertation. Louisiana State University and Agricultural and Mechanical College. 1978. 510 pp. (2 Vols.). DAI 39/11. (May 1979). Page 6913-A. Order # 7911570.

1067. Greene, Richard E. A Historical Study of the Massachusetts Association of School Committees: A Philosophic Basis for Development of an Organizational Model for the Future. Ed.D. Dissertation. Boston University. 1971. 337 pp. DAI 32/4. (October 1971). Page 1784-A. Order # 71-26,701.

1068. Hales, William M. Technological In-Migration and Curricular Change: Educational Policies in Albuquerque, 1945-1965. Ph.D. Dissertation.

University of New Mexico, 1970.   325 pp.   DAI 31/10.   (April 1971).
Page 5074-A.   Order # 71-9299.

1069. Hall, Waverly H.   History of the Organization and Administration of
       Public Schools in Tulare County, California, 1852-1970.   Ed.D. Dis-
       sertation.   University of Southern California.   1972.   276 pp.   DAI
       33/5.   (November 1972).   Page 2021-A.   Order # 72-27,663.

1070. Hannon, Donald F.   The Political and Legislative Role of the Pennsyl-
       vania State Education Association, 1968-1979.   Ph.D. Dissertation.
       University of Pittsburgh.   1980.   349 pp.   DAI 41/12.   (June 1981).
       Page 4908-A.   Order # 8112674.

1071. Harder, Peter J.   An Analysis of the Evolution of Public Responsibil-
       ity for Secondary Education in the Town of Madison, Connecticut,
       1821-1922.   Ph.D. Dissertation.   University of Connecticut.   1977.
       276 pp.   DAI 38/10.   (April 1978).   Page 5964-A.   Order # 7803682.

1072. Harris, Johnny L.   A Historical Analysis of Education, Economics,
       and Political Changes in Fayette, Mississippi from 1954 to 1971.
       Ph.D. Dissertation.   Florida State University.   1972.   179 pp.   DAI
       33/5.   (November 1972).   Page 2264-A.   Order # 72-27,915.

1073. Hatch, Rodney P.   Maine School Finance: Past, Present and Future.
       Ed.D. Dissertation.   George Peabody College for Teachers.   1979.
       157 pp.   DAI 42/2.   (August 1981).   Page 577-A.   Order # 8116044.

1074. Heck, Glenn E.   The Constitutional and Legal Development of the
       State Board of Education as a Central Educational Agency in Michi-
       gan.   Ph.D. Dissertation.   Michigan State University.   1973.   302
       pp.   DAI 34/12.   (June 1974).   Page 7561-A.   Order # 74-13,901.

1075. Heicler, Sidney J.   The Development of State Funding of Teachers'
       Salaries in Louisiana, 1921-1973.   Ph.D. Dissertation.   The Louisiana
       State University and Agricultural and Mechanical College.   1974.
       157 pp.   DAI 35/5.   (November 1974).   Page 2578-A.   Order # 74-
       24,778.

1076. Hiett, Joseph H.   The Florida State-wide Governing Board for Higher
       Education, 1905-1969: A Study of the Personal Characteristics of
       the Members and Selected Trends in the History of the Board.   Ph.D.
       Dissertation.   Florida State University.   1971.   187 pp.   DAI 32/11.
       (May 1972).   Page 6154-A.   Order # 72-13,517.

1077. Hill, Ralph L.   A View of the Hill--A Study of Experiences and At-
       titudes in the Hill District of Pittsburgh, Pennsylvania from 1900 to
       1973.   Ph.D. Dissertation.   University of Pittsburgh.   1973.   250
       pp.   DAI 35/2.   (August 1974).   Page 843-A.   Order # 74-15,626.

1078. Hinkle, Lonnie J.   A History of Public Secondary Education in Fair-
       fax County, Virginia (1870-1970).   Ed.D. Dissertation.   George
       Washington University.   1971.   313 pp.   DAI 32/3.   (September
       1971).   Page 1310-A.   Order # 71-22,421.

1079. Jackson, James W.   A History of School Desegregation in Lee County,
       Florida (1954-1969).   Ph.D. Dissertation.   University of Miami.   1970.
       281 pp.   DAI 32/2.   (August 1971).   Page 701-A.   Order # 71-19,872.

1080. Jones, Helen S. A Historical Study of Public Education in Stafford
County, Virginia, from 1865 through 1965. Ed.D. Dissertation.
American University. 1970. 430 pp. DAI 32/3. (September 1971).
Page 1311-A. Order # 71-22,115.

1081. Jones, Merrill O. Contributions of Selected Private Foundations to
Florida's Public Schools, 1907-1947. Ph.D. Dissertation. Florida
State University. 1074. 306 pp. DAI 35/9. (March 1975). Page
5729-A. Order # 75-6284.

1082. Kaegi, Mona G. An Historical Study of an Educational Microcosm:
Hardin County, Illinois, 1839-1977. Ph.D. Dissertation. Southern
Illinois University. 1978. 227 pp. DAI 39/10. (April 1979).
Page 5985-A. Order # 7908046.

1083. Kelly, Robert F. Influences Related to the Continuation of the Nor-
wich Free Academy as the Agency for High School Education in Nor-
wich, Connecticut, 1932-1965. Ph.D. Dissertation. University of
Connecticut. 1973. 289 pp. DAI 35/2. (August 1974). Page 859-
A. Order # 74-16,776.

1084. Kirk, Marcella. An Examination and Analysis of the Chicago Model
Cities Educational Project, from 1967 through 1971. Ed.D. Disser-
tation. Loyola University, Chicago. 1973. 273 pp. DAI 34/3.
(September 1973). Page 1109-A. Order # 73-19,855.

1085. Klibaner, Irwin. The Southern Conference Educational Fund: A
History. Ph.D. Dissertation. University of Wisconsin. 1971. 477
pp. DAI 32/6. (December 1971). Page 3211-A. Order # 71-25,480.

1086. Lash, Hoyt H. Role of the Indiana Township Trustee in Educational
Administration, 1859-1959. Ed.D. Dissertation. Ball State Univer-
sity. 1973. 134 pp. DAI 34/3. (September 1973). Page 1033-A.
Order # 73-19,990.

1087. Laughlin, Richard L. A Historical Study: The County Superintendent of Schools in Wyoming from 1869 to 1969. Ed.D. Dissertation.
University of Wyoming. 1973. 219 pp. DAI 34/5. (November
1973). Page 2354-A. Order # 73-25,556.

1088. Leach, Leslie L. School District Organization in Pennsylvania, 1834-
1970. Ed.D. Dissertation. Pennsylvania State University. 1972.
185 pp. DAI 33/12. (June 1973). Page 6620-A. Order # 73-
14,008.

1089. Le Count, Jr., Roscoe D. The Politics of Public Education: New
York State, 1795-1851. Ed.D. Dissertation. Columbia University.
1971. 332 pp. DAI 33/2. (September 1971). Page 1311-A. Order
71-24,154.

1090. Liptzin, Stanley S. The Modern School of Skelton, New Jersey: A
Libertarian Educational Experiment Examined. Ed.D. Dissertation.
Rutgers, the State Univesity. 1976. 332 pp. DAI 37/12. (June
1977). Page 7577-A. Order # 77-13,274.

1091. LoPate, Carol B. Power and Authority in a Rural School: A History of the Green Valley (New York) Central School System. Ph.D.

Dissertation. Columbia University. 1974. 296 pp. DAI 35/9.
(March 1975). Page 5889-A. Order # 75-5231.

1092. Ludwick, James W. The History of the Rochelle, Illinois Public
Schools, 1837-1930. Ed.D. Dissertation. Northern Illinois Univer-
sity. 1980. 194 pp. DAI 41/2. (September 1980). Page 967-A.
Order # 8020671.

1093. Macauley, Howard K. A Social and Intellectual History of Elementary
Education in Pennsylvania to 1850. Ph.D. Dissertation. University
of Pennsylvania. 1972. 1079 pp. DAI 33/12. (June 1973). Page
6704-A. Order # 73-13,433.

1094. MacLennan, Carol A. Plantation Capitalism and Social Policy in Hawaii. Ph.D. Dissertation. University of California, Berkeley. 1979.
310 pp. DAI 41/1. (July 1980). Page 306-A. Order # 8014788.

1095. Mansfield, Jr., Henry. Articulation in California: An Historical
Study of the Historical Liaison Committee of the California Articulation
Conference, 1947-1972. Ed.D. Dissertation. University of California,
Los Angeles. 1974. 177 pp. DAI 35/5. (November 1974). Page
2740-A. Order # 74-24,597.

1096. McGrath, Kristin S. American Values and the Slums: A Chicago
Case Study. Ph.D. Dissertation. University of Minnesota. 1977.
373 pp. DAI 38/6. (December 1977). Page 3577-A. Order # 77-
26,135.

1097. Meinert, James D. A History of the Oregon State Scholarship Committee. Ph.D. Dissertation. University of Oregon. 1974. 127 pp.
DAI 35/8. (February 1975). Page 5071-A. Order # 75-4516.

1098. Mentzer, Elmo L. A History of the Public School System of Carlisle,
Pennsylvania (1751-1969). Ed.D. Dissertation. Pennsylvania State
University. 1970. 305 pp. DAI 32/2. (August 1971). Page 763-
A. Order # 71-21,773.

1099. Moberly, Arthur W. The Grier (Pennsylvania) School (1957-ca. 1970).
Ed.D. Dissertation. Pennsylvania State University. 1971. 154 pp.
DAI 32/9. (March 1972). Page 5002-A. Order # 72-9508.

1100. Mowrer, Sherwyn W. An Historical Analysis of the Michigan Public
School Employees' Retirement System, 1915-1975. Ph.D. Dissertation.
University of Michigan. 473 pp. DAI 37/6. (December 1976).
Page 3317-A. Order # 76-27,554.

1101. Muir, Kenneth K. A School System and its Students Come to Terms:
A Description of Student Activism in the Montgomery County, Maryland, Public Schools, 1960-1969. Ed.D. Dissertation. George Washington University. 1974. 244 pp. DAI 35/4. (October 1974).
Page 1924-A. Order # 74-23,494.

1102. Murray, Rebecca J. The Development of the Kindergarten Program
in the Public School System of North Carolina. Ed.D. Dissertation.
Duke University. 1973. 203 pp. DAI 34/7. (January 1974).
Page 3937-A. Order # 74-1150.

1103. Oakley, Wesley E. Education in the Missouri Ozark Region: One
       School's Story, 1807-1975. Ph.D. Dissertation. Southern Illinois
       University. 1976. 123 pp. DAI 37/6. (December 1976). Page
       3464-A. Order # 76-28,766.

1104. Pablo, Jean M. Washington, D,C. and its School System, 1900-1906.
       Ph.D. Dissertation. Georgetown University. 1973. 595 pp. DAI
       35/1. (July 1974). Page 349-A. Order # 74-16,420.

1105. Przybyszewski, Robert J. A History of Politics and Education: The
       Junior High School Comes to Buffalo. Ed.D. Dissertation. State
       University of New York, Buffalo. 1973. 219 pp. DAI 34/1. (July
       1973). Page 158-A. Order # 73-15,470.

1106. Quillen, Isaac J. Industrial City: A History of Gary, Indiana to
       1929. Ph.D. Dissertation. Yale University. 1942. 531 pp. DAI
       41/5. (November 1980). Page 2244-A. Order # 8024808.

1107. Rankin, Aneta P. M. The Development of Educational Media in Lou-
       isiana, 1908-1976. Ph.D. Dissertation. Louisiana State University
       and Agricultural and Mechanical College. 1977. 206 pp. DAI 38/6.
       (December 1977). Page 3229-A. Order # 77-25,400.

1108. Rasnake, Marshall E. The Impact of Commissioners of Education Upon
       the Development of Public Education in Tennessee, 1945 through
       1970. Ed.D. Dissertation. Memphis State University. 1971. 398
       pp. DAI 32/8. (February 1972). Page 4304-A. Order # 72-7569.

1109. Ravitch, Diane S. The Great School Wars: New York City, 1805-
       1973. Ph.D. Dissertation. Columbia University. 1975. no. pp.
       DAI 37/1. (July 1976). Page 158-A. No Order #.

1110. Ray, James A. Equal Education Opportunities in the Detroit Appren-
       tice Schools from 1962 to 1976. Ph.D. Dissertation. University of
       Michigan. 1979. 228 pp. DAI 40/5. (November 1979). Page
       2519-A. Order # 7925214.

1111. Rider, Samuel R. A Historical Review of the Hendry County, Florida
       School System with Emphasis on Secondary Education. Ph.D. Dis-
       sertation. University of Wyoming. 1973. 274 pp. DAI 34/8.
       (February 1974). Page 4815-A. Order # 74-2161.

1112. Robson, John H. The Western New York School Study Council--
       Analysis and Summary of a Twenty-Year Period, 1949-1969. Ed.D.
       Dissertation. State University of New York, Buffalo. 1971. 258 pp.
       DAI 32/5. (November 1971). Page 2369-A. Order # 71-28,046.

1113. Rowe, Roy H. Educational Policy-Makers in the North Carolina Gen-
       eral Assembly, 1933-1974. Ed.D. Dissertation. Duke University.
       1975. 210 pp. DAI 36/7. (January 1976). Page 4182-A. Order
       # 75-29,531.

1114. Rumbley, Rose-Mary. The History of Speech and Drama Education
       in the Dallas Public Schools (1884-1970). Ph.D. Dissertation. North
       Texas State University. 1971. 377 pp. DAI 32/12. (June 1972).
       Page 6693-A. Order # 72-17,023.

1115. Rynearson, Jr. Elton J. The History of the Anchor Bay [Michigan] School System. Ph.D. Dissertation. University of Michigan. 1973. 488 pp. DAI 35/1. (July 1974). Page 234-A. Order # 74-15,846.

1116. Schumacher, Corinne L. Oversell: Educational Innovation in a Chicago Suburb: An Historical Case Study of the Winnetka Public Schools. Ph.D. Dissertation. Northwestern University. 1972. 245 pp. DAI 33/6. (December 1972). Page 2747-A. Order # 72-32,570.

1117. Shradar, Victor L. Ethnic Politics, Religion, and the Public Schools of San Francisco, 1849-1933. Ph.D. Dissertation. Stanford University. 1974. 240 pp. DAI 35/6. (December 1974). Order # 74-27,113.

1118. Silva, Edwin L. Community Politics and the Public Schools of Paradise, California, 1961-1969. Ed.D. Dissertation. 1971. 211 pp. DAI 32/11. (May 1972). Page 6166-A. Order # 72-14,760.

1119. Simmons, Hugh G. A Historical Account and Analysis of a Short-lived Regional Educational Laboratory in the Rocky Mountain West. Ed.D. Dissertation. University of Wyoming. 1971. 210 pp. DAI 33/6. (December 1972). Page 2747-A. Order # 72-32,804.

1120. Smith, Laurence M. A History of the Junior High School in Omaha, Nebraska, 1917-1965. Ed.D. Dissertation. University of Nebraska. 1970. 286 pp. DAI 31/4. (October 1970). Page 1594-A. Order # 70-17,759.

1121. Smith, Stewart D. Schools and Schoolmen: Chapters in Texas Education, 1870-1900. Ph.D. Dissertation. North Texas State University. 1974. 324 pp. DAI 35/7. (January 1975). Page 4350-A. Order # 75-902.

1122. Sperounis, Frederick P. The Cambridge Alternative Public School: A Case Study in School Reform. Ph.D. Dissertation. Brandeis University. 1978. 326 pp. DAI 39/5. (November 1978). Page 3155-A. Order # 7819961.

1123. Stange, Karl H. A Short Season of Reform: The Regina School of Social Work, 1971-1978. Ph.D. Dissertation. University of Wisconsin. 1979. 272 pp. DAI 40/6. (December 1979). Page 3157-A. Order # 7922838.

1124. Stephenson, Ralph S. A History of School Guidance in Maine to 1965. Ed.D. Dissertation. University of Maine. 1972. 342 pp. DAI 34/2. (August 1973). Page 595-A. Order # 73-13,080.

1125. Taggart, Robert J. Programs of City Superintendents for Schools in Michigan, 1870-1915. Ph.D. Dissertation. University of Michigan. 1970. 323 pp. DAI 32/1. (July 1971). Page 216-A. Order # 71-17,172.

1126. Vitone, Samuel F. Community, Identity, and Schools: Educational Experiences of Italians in San Francisco from the Gold Rush to the Second World War. Ph.D. Dissertation. University of California.

1981. 420 pp. DAI 42/12. (June 1982). Page 5043-A. Order #
8212139.

1127. White, Lee W. Popular Education and the State Superintendent of
Public Instruction in Texas, 1860-1899. Ph.D. Dissertation. Uni-
versity of Texas. 1974. 276 pp. DAI 35/5. (November 1974).
Page 2742-A. Order # 74-24,949.

1128. Williams, John R. Nebraska Governors and Education--1905-1915 and
1955-1965. Ed.D. Dissertation. University of Nebraska. 1970.
255 pp. DAI 31/10. (April 1971). Page 5163-A. Order # 71-9594.

Industrial/Vocational Education/Work

1129. Adams, Ezola B. The Role and Function of the Manual Training and
Industrial School at Bordentown [New Jersey] as an Alternative
School. Ed.D. Dissertation. Rutgers, the State University. 1977.
159 pp. DAI 38/11. (May 1978). Page 6587-A. Order # 7804581.

1130. Allen, Cameron K. The Development of Industrial Arts in the Inter-
mediate School, 1909-1971. Ed.D. Dissertation. Utah State University. 1974. 304 pp. DAI 36/1. (July 1975). Page 161-A. Order
75-14,408.

1131. Barrier, Lynn P. A History of Industrial Arts Education in North
Carolina, 1919-1977. Ed.D. Dissertation. North Carolina State Uni-
versity. 1977. 263 pp. DAI 39/3. (September 1978). Page 1382-
A. Order # 7811574.

1132. Burns, Elizabeth J. The Industrial Education Myth: Character Building at Penn School, 1900-1948. Ph.D. Dissertation. University of
North Carolina. 1974. 630 pp. DAI 35/10. (April 1975). Page
6612-A. Order # 75-4803.

1133. Carlin, Marianne B. Education and the Occupational Decisions of the
Children of Italian and Polish Immigrants to Rome, New York, 1900-
1950. Ph.D. Dissertation. Cornell University. 1978. 105 pp. DAI
39/7. (January 1979). Page 4088-A. Order # 7902263.

1134. Caster, Richard J. Curricular Changes in the Canton City Schools,
1895-1939: From Manual Training to Vocational Education. Ed.D.
Dissertation. Akron University. 1980. 200 pp. DAI 40/10.
(April 1980). Page 5340. Order # 8008413.

1135. Duffy, Nishima I. Tracing an Idea: The Genius and the Making of
the 1963 American Vocational Act. Ph.D. Dissertation. Florida
State University. 1977. 103 pp. DAI 38/5. (November 1977).
Page 2734-A. Order # 77-24,754.

1136. Dye, Charles M. Calvin Milton Woodward: A Leader of the Manual
Training Movement in American Education. Ph.D. Dissertation. Washington University (St. Louis). 1971. 393 pp. DAI 32/9. (March
1972). Page 5000-A. Order # 72-9327.

1137. Gadell, John. Charles Allen Prosser: His Work in Vocational and
       General Education. Ph.D. Dissertation. Washington University (St.
       Louis). 1972. 301 pp. DAI 33/8. (February 1973). Page 4140-
       A. Order # 73-5038.

1138. Gray, Kenneth C. Support for Industrial Education by the National
       Association of Manufacturers, 1895-1917. Ed.D. Dissertation. Vir-
       ginia Polytechnic Institute and State University. 1980. 223 pp.
       DAI 41/8. (February 1980). Page 3454-A. Order # 8101883.

1139. Greenwood, Katy L.B. A Philosophic Rationale for Vocational Educa-
       tion: Contributions of Charles A. Prosser and his Contemporaries
       from 1900 to 1917 [2 volumes]. Ph.D. Dissertation. University of
       Minnesota. 1978. 370 pp. DAI 39/12. (June 1979). Page 7306-
       A. Order # 7912012.

1140. Grignano, Innocenzio A. The Industrial and Training School Concept
       in Allegheny County [Pennsylvania]: An Historical Analysis. Ph.D.
       Dissertation. University of Pittsburgh. 1975. 367 pp. DAI 36/10.
       (April 1976). Page 6518-A. Order # 76-7347.

1141. Hall, Julia A.O. C. Van Woodward: An American Educator. Ph.D.
       Dissertation. University of Mississippi. 1977. 159 pp. DAI 38/12.
       (June 1978). Page 7170-A. Order # 7807982.

1142. Herschbach, Dennis R. Industrial Educator Ideology, 1876-1917: A
       Social and Historical Analysis. Ph.D. Dissertation. University of
       Illinois. 1973. 480 pp. DAI 34/1. (July 1973). Page 159-A.
       Order # 73-17,557.

1143. Johnston, Robert E. The History of Trade and Industrial Education
       in Ohio. Ph.D. Dissertation. The Ohio State University. 1971.
       312 pp. DAI 32/3. (September 1971). Page 1408-A. Order # 71-
       22,493.

1144. Jones, James L. Analysis of Decisions Establishing the Mandate of
       the South Carolina Technical Education System. Ed.D. Dissertation.
       North Carolina State University. 1978. 187 pp. DAI 39/5. (No-
       vember 1978). Page 2712-A. Order # 7820036.

1145. Lorenz, Edward C. Guidance and Work in the New York City Schools:
       A History of Vocational Guidance, 1898-1941. Ph.D. Dissertation.
       University of Chicago. 1978. n.p. DAI 39/1. (July 1978). Page
       428-A. No order #.

1146. Markle, Howard B. An Historical and Critical Review of Vocational
       Education in the United States and Pennsylvania with a Focus on the
       Development of Vocational Schools (AVTS) of Pennsylvania, and an
       Assessment of AVTS Directors' Opinions Related to a Selection of
       Problems and Issues that Confront Vocational Education. Ph.D. Dis-
       sertation. Pennsylvania State University. 1977. 369 pp. DAI
       39/1. (July 1978). Page 251-A. Order # 7808389.

1147. O'Connell, Kathryn D. Industrial Education in Boston, 1870-1890:
       A Case Study in Curricular Change. Ph.D. Dissertation. Univer-
       sity of Wisconsin. 1975. 157 pp. DAI 36/12. (June 1976). Page
       7842-A. Order # 76-6102.

1148. Phillips, Jean O.D. The Evolution of Federal Vocational Educational Legislation with Special Reference to Business Education (1862-1963). Ph.D. Dissertation. The Ohio State University. 1971. 209 pp. DAI 32/3. (September 1971). Page 1410-A. Order # 71-22,522.

1149. Richards, Norman W. Who's in Control? Industrial Education in the Boston Public Schools, 1870-1920. Ph.D. Dissertation. Boston College. 1976. 194 pp. DAI 37/7. (January 1977). Page 4174-A. Order # 76-30,176.

1150. Ringel, Paul Joseph. The Introduction and Development of Manual Training and Industrial Education in the Public Schools of Fitchburg, Massachusetts, 1893-1928. Ed.D. Dissertation. Columbia University. 1980. 324 pp. DAI 41/4. (October 1980). Page 1443-A. Order # 8022151.

1151. Romano, Louis A. Manual and Industrial Education at Girard College, 1831-1865: An Era in American Educational Experimentation. Ed.D. Dissertation. New York University. 1975. 414 pp. DAI 36/4. (October 1975). Page 2073-A. Order # 75-21,172.

1152. Shannon, Samuel H. Agricultural and Industrial Education at Tennessee State University During the Normal School Phase, 1912-1922: A Case Study. Ph.D. Dissertation. The George Peabody College for Teachers. 1974. 350 pp. DAI 35/6. (December 1974). Page 3656-A. Order # 74-29,188.

1153. Shinn, Marion L. History of Vocational Education in Idaho [1917-1971]. Ed.D. Dissertation. University of Idaho. 1972. 365 pp. DAI 33/5. (November 1972). Page 2054-A. Order # 72-30,520.

1154. Sola, Peter A. Plutocrats, Pedagogues and Plebes: Business Influences on Vocational Education and Extracurricular Activities in the Chicago High Schools, 1899-1925. Ph.D. Dissertation. University of Illinois. 1972. 283 pp. DAI 34/2. (August 1973). Page 594-A. Order # 73-17,431.

1155. Stoute, Floyd J. The Attitudes, Policies and Lobbying Activities of the AFL-CIO Concerning Federal Aid to Vocational Education, 1955-1970. Ed.D. Dissertation, University of Houston. 1974. 428 pp. DAI 35/7. (January 1975). Page 4216-A. Order # 75-1025.

1156. Verdile, Benjamin V. P. Vocational Education in New Jersey, 1946-1973. Ed.D. Dissertation. Rutgers, the State University. 1975. 280 pp. DAI 36/7. (January 1976). Page 4307-A. Order # 76-1137.

1157. Williams, Margaret C. An Interpretation of the Philosophy of the Wachovia Moravians, 1753-1822: How Their Way of Life Related to the Evolution of Industrial Arts [in the Southern United States]. Ed.D. Dissertation. North Carolina State University at Raleigh. 1979. 107 pp. DAI 41/4. (October 1980). Page 1447-A. Order # 8020517.

Juvenile Delinquency/Juvenile Justice

1158. Bondavelli, Bonnie J. A Socio-Historical Study of Juvenile Justice.
       Ph.D. Dissertation. University of Missouri, Columbia. 1977. 312
       pp. DAI 38/10. (April 1978). Page 6337-A. Order # 7803697.

1159. Curtis, George B. The Juvenile Court Movement in Virginia: The
       Child Savers, 1890-1973. Ph.D. Dissertation. University of Virginia.
       1973. 200 pp. DAI 34/7. (January 1974). Page 4145-A. Order #
       73-31,123.

1160. Jacobs, Janet L. An Intensive Study of the Late Nineteenth Century
       Treatment of Juvenile Delinquents in Buffalo, New York. Ed.D. Dis-
       sertation. State University of New York at Buffalo, 1980. 271 pp.
       DAI 41/3. (September 1980). Page 966-A. Order # 8021162.

1161. Ross, Catherine J. Society's Children: The Case of Indigenous
       Youngsters in New York City, 1875-1903. Ph.D. Dissertation. Yale
       University. 1977. 245 pp. DAI 39/3. (September 1978). Page
       1789-A. Order # 7817150.

1162. Salsgiver, Richard O. Child Reform in Pittsburgh, 1890-1915: The
       Development of the Juvenile Court and the Allegheny County Indiana
       Training School for Boys. D.A. Dissertation. Carnegie-Mellon Uni-
       versity. 1975. 120 pp. DAI 36/7. (January 1976). Page 4717.
       Order # 76-636.

1163. Schlossman, Steven L. Love and the American Delinquent: The
       Theory and Practice of "Progressive" Juvenile Justice, 1825-1920.
       Ph.D. Dissertation. Columbia University. 1976. 340 pp. DAI 39/1.
       (July 1978). Page 429-A. Order # 7811152.

1164. Severns, George W. An Historical Study of the Antecedents of the
       1974 Memorandum of Agreement Transferring Administrative Respon-
       sibility for Educational Programs for Delinquent Youth to the Penn-
       sylvania Department of Education. Ph.D. Dissertation. University
       of Pittsburgh. 1978. 288 pp. DAI 39/8. (February 1979). Page
       4772-A. Order # 7902724.

1165. Stewart, Joseph M. A Comparative History of Juvenile Correctional
       Institutions in Ohio. Ph.D. Dissertation. The Ohio State University.
       1980. 251 pp. DAI 41/4. (October 1980). Page 1738-A. Order #
       8022353.

1166. Wirkkala, John C. Juvenile Delinquency and Reform in Nineteenth
       Century Massachusetts: The Formative Era in State Care, 1846-
       1879. Ph.D. Dissertation. Clark University. 1973. 379 pp. DAI
       34/5. (November 1973). Page 2542-A. Order # 73-27,001.

Labor and Education

1167. Bowman, Robert Atkins. The National Committee for the Extension of
       Labor Education, 1942-1950: A Study of the Committee's Attempt to
       Establish a Labor Extension Service. Ed.D. Dissertation. Rutgers,
       the State University. 1979. 429 pp. DAI 40/2. (August 1979).
       Page 691-A. Order # 7917902.

1168. Brody, Doris C. American Labor Education Service, 1927-1962: An
       Organization in Workers' Education. Ph.D. Dissertation. Cornell
       University. 1973. 264 pp. DAI 34/10. (April 1974). Page 6556-
       A. Order # 74-7173.

1169. Close, William E. An Historical Study of the American Federation of
       Labor--Congress of Industrial Organization's Involvement in Higher
       Education with an Emphasis on the Period 1960-1969. Ph.D. Disser-
       tation. Catholic University of America. 1972. 173 pp. DAI 33/6.
       (December 1972). Page 2729-A. Order # 72-26,250.

1170. Jorgenson-Esmaili, Karen L. Schooling and the Early Human Rela-
       tions Movement: with Special Reference to the Foreman's Conference,
       1919-1939. Ph.D. Dissertation. 1979. 268 pp. DAI 41/1. (July
       1980). Page 133-A. Order # 8014751.

1171. Lee, Isabella J.W. A History of the Labor Union Movement Among
       New York City Public School Teachers [1916-1967]. Ph.D. Disserta-
       tion, New York University. 1971. 335 pp. DAI 32/10. (April
       1972). Page 5580-A. Order # 72-11,467.

1172. Mavrinac, Henry C. "Big" Labor and Education in Pennsylvania: A
       Study of the Educational Concerns of the American Federation of
       Labor, the Congress of Industrial Organizations, and the AFL-CIO,
       1920-1970. Ph.D. Dissertation. University of Pittsburgh. 1977.
       290 pp. DAI 38/9. (October 1978). Page 5295-A. Order # 7801815.

1173. Schultz, Dagmar. The Changing Political Nature of Workers' Educa-
       tion: A Case Study of the Wisconsin School for Workers [1930's to
       1970's]. Ph.D. Dissertation. University of Wisconsin. 1972. DAI
       33/12. (June 1973). Page 6706-A. Order # 73-9223.

1174. Shapiro, William. Public Educational Interests and Positions of the
       CIO During the Era of the New Deal: An Historical Overview.
       Ed.D. Dissertation. Columbia University. 1979. 437 pp. DAI
       41/4. (October 1980). Page 1737-A. Order # 8022181.

1175. Williams, Carolyn R.A. Education for Black Participation in the Labor
       Movement: A Case Study. Ph.D. Dissertation. Cornell University.
       1978. 252 pp. DAI 39/4. (October 1978). Page 2461-A. Order #
       7817780.

Legal Education

1176. Consalus, Charles E. The History of Legal Education in New Jersey.
      Ed.D. Dissertation. Columbia University. 1979. 563 pp. DAI
      40/4. (October 1979). Page 1918-A. Order # 7923578.

1177. Epstein, Sandra P. Law at Berkeley: The History of Boalt Hall.
      Ph.D. Dissertation. University of California, Berkeley. 1979.
      526 pp. DAI 40/7. (January 1980). Page 3807-A. Order # 8000334.

1178. Harms, Herman E. A History of the Concept In Loco Parentis in
      American Education. Ed.D. Dissertation. University of Florida.
      1970. 174 pp. DAI 31/7. (January 1971). Page 3309-A. Order #
      71-249.

1179. Jandura, Ronald M. An Interpretation of the United States Supreme
      Court Since 1954 as They Affect School Segregation. Ed.D. Disser-
      tation. University of Alabama. 1970. 97 pp. DAI 31/7. (January
      1971). Page 3216-A. Order # 71-1248.

1180. Laska, Lewis L. A History of Legal Education in Tennessee, 1770-
      1970. Ph.D. Dissertation. George Peabody College for Teachers.
      1978. 818 pp. DAI 39/8. (February 1979). Page 4771-A. Order
      # 7902503.

Medical Education

1181. Gifford, James F. A History of Medicine at Duke University, Volume
      I: Origins and Growth [one volume only]. Ph.D. Dissertation.
      Duke University. 1970. 330 pp. DAI 31/6. (December 1970).
      Page 2842-A. Order # 70-23,397.

1182. Harris, Jonathan. The Rise of Medical Science in New York, 1720-
      1870. Ph.D. Dissertation. New York University. 1971. 451 pp.
      DAI 33/5. (November 1972). Page 2286-A. Order # 72-24,742.

1183. MacLeish, Marlene Y.S. Medical Education in Black Colleges and Uni-
      versities in the United States of America: An Analysis of the Emer-
      gence of Black Middle Schools Between 1867 and 1976. Ed.D. Dis-
      sertation. Harvard University. 1978. 264 pp. DAI 39/11. (May
      1979). Page 6614-A. Order # 7909888.

1184. Maszkiewicz, Ruth A. The Presbyterian Hospital of Pittsburgh:
      From its Founding to the Affiliation with the University of Pittsburgh.
      Ph.D. Dissertation. University of Pittsburgh. 1977. 154 pp. DAI
      38/9. (March 1978). Page 5294-A. Order # 7801814.

1185. Matejski, Myrtle P. The Influence of Selected External Forces on
      Medical Education at the University of Maryland School of Medicine,

1910-1950. Ph.D. Dissertation. University of Maryland. 1977.
199 pp. DAI 38/7. (January 1978). Page 3980-A. Order # 77-
28,747.

1186. Smith, Dale C. The Emergence of Organized Clinical Instruction in
the Nineteenth Century American Cities of Boston, New York and
Philadelphia. Ph.D. Dissertation. University of Minnesota. 1979.
365 pp. DAI 40/6. (December 1979). Page 3497-A. Order #
7926175.

Military Education

1187. Allen, Lawrence C. The United States Naval Institute: Intellectual
Forum of the New Navy: 1873-1889. Ph.D. Dissertation. University
of Maine. 1976. 386 pp. DAI 37/6. (December 1976). Page 3844-
A. Order # 76-28,670.

1188. Baughman, Keith L. Educational Changes at the United States Army
Armor School, 1940-1973. Ed.D. Dissertation. University of Ken-
tucky. 1974. 166 pp. DAI 35/9. (March 1975). Page 5768-A.
Order # 75-5814.

1189. Cheslik, Helen E. Effect of World War II Military Educational Training on Black Colleges. Ed.D. Dissertation. Wayne State University.
1980. 219 pp. DAI 41/4. (October 1980). Page 1421-A. Order #
8022810.

1190. Dilliard, Walter S. The United States Military Academy, 1865-1900:
The Uncertain Years. Ph.D. Dissertation. University of Washington.
1972. 418 pp. DAI 33/5. (November 1972). Page 2281-A. Order #
72-28,589.

1191. Easterling, Jr., Henry W. Nonmilitary Education in the United States
Air Force with Emphasis on the Period 1945-1979. Ed.D. Dissertation. Indiana University. 1980. 210 pp. DAI 41/4. (October
1980). Page 1344-A. Order # 8022694.

1192. Heitzmann, William R. The United States Naval Institute's Contribu-
tion to the In-Service Education of Naval Officers, 1873-1973. Ph.D.
Dissertation. University of Delaware. 1974. 254 pp. DAI 35/5.
(November 1974). Page 2738-A. Order # 74-26,105.

1193. Hirshauer, Victor B. The History of the Army Reserve Officer's
Training Corps, 1916-1973. Ph.D. Dissertation. Johns Hopkins
University. 1975. 491 pp. DAI 39/6. (December 1978). Page
3774-A. Order # 7821968.

1194. Kennedy, Gerald J. The United States Naval War College, 1919-1941:
An Institutional Response to Naval Preparedness. Ph.D. Dissertation.
University of Minnesota. 1975. DAI 36/6. (December 1975). Page
3966-A. n.p. No Order #.

1195. Kershner, James W. Sylvanus Thayer: A Biography. Ph.D. Disser-
      tation. University of West Virginia. 1976. 426 pp. DAI 37/12.
      (June 1976). Page 7921-A. Order # 77-12,314.

1196. Kofmehl, Jr., William E. Non-Military Education and the United States
      Army: A History. Ph.D. Dissertation. University of Pittsburgh.
      1973. 327 pp. DAI 34/5. (November 1973). Page 2354-A. Order
      # 73-27,146.

1197. Nenninger, Timothy K. The Fort Leavenworth Schools: Post Grad-
      uate Military Education and Professionalization in the United States
      Army, 1880-1920. Ph.D. Dissertation. University of Wisconsin.
      1974. 391 pp. DAI 35/5. (November 1974). Page 2910. Order #
      74-18,946.

1198. O'Connor, Thomas J. The Community College of the Air Force: A
      History and a Comparative Organizational Analysis. Ph.D. Disserta-
      tion. University of Denver. 1974. 284 pp. DAI 35/7. (January
      1975). Page 4215-A. Order # 75-1329.

1199. Reynolds, Jon A. Education and Training for High Command: Gen-
      eral Hoyt S. Vandenberg's Early Career. Ph.D. Dissertation. Duke
      University. 1980. 235 pp. DAI 41/3. (September 1980). Page
      1189A. Order # 8019332.

1200. Rilling, Alexander W. The First Fifty Years of Graduate Education
      in the United States Navy, 1909-1959. Ph.D. Dissertation. University
      of Southern California. 1972. 404 pp. DAI 33/7. (January 1973).
      Page 3339. Order # 73-761.

1201. Sheppard, Charles P. An Analysis of Curriculum Changes at the
      United States Naval Academy During the Period 1959 through 1974.
      Ed.D. Dissertation. George Washington University, 1974. 520 pp.
      DAI 35/12. (June 1975). Page 7692-A. Order # 75-12,623.

1202. Telman, Hester E.H. Training and Education Programs in the United
      States Army--An Overview. Ed.D. Dissertation. University of South-
      ern California. 1976. DAI 37/3. (September 1976). Page 1438-A.
      n.p. No Order #.

1203. Vollmar, William J. The Issue of Compulsory Military Training at the
      Ohio State University, 1913-1973. Ph.D. Dissertation. The Ohio
      State University. 1976. 480 pp. DAI 37/2. (August 1976). Page
      1182-A. Order # 76-18,054.

1204. Zuersher, Dorothy J.S. Benjamin Franklin, Jonathan Williams and the
      United States Military Academy. Ed.D. Dissertation. University of
      North Carolina at Greensboro. 1974. 148 pp. DAI 35/2. (August
      1974). Page 812-A. Order # 74-17,969.

Minority Education--General

1205. Beck, Nicholas P. The Other Children: Minority Education in Cali-

fornia Public Schools from Statehood to 1890. Ed.D. Dissertation.
University of California, Los Angeles. 1975. 216 pp. DAI 36/5.
(November 1976). Page 2681-A. Order # 75-22,604.

1206.   Carrillo, Jess M. The Process of School Desegregation: The Case
of the Los Angeles Unified School District. Ph.D. Dissertation.
University of California, Los Angeles. 1978. 282 pp. DAI 39/7.
(January 1979). Page 4536-A. Order # 7901341.

1207.   Castellanos, Diego A. The History of Bilingual Education in New
Jersey: Its Implications for the Future of Educational Equity for
National Origin Students. Ed.D. Dissertation. Fairleigh Dickinson
University. 1979. 676 pp. DAI 40/5. (November 1979). Page
2525-A. Order # 7921073.

1208.   Davis, Yvonne H. The Genesis, Development and Impact of the United
States Defense Department's Race Relations Institute, 1940-1975.
Ph.D. Dissertation. University of Pittsburgh. 1975. 114 pp. DAI
36/9. (March 1976). Page 5855-A. Order # 76-5426.

1209.   Dekay, Della L. From Melting Pot to Cultural Pluralism: An Examination of the "New" Immigrants as Treated in Secondary American
History Textbooks, 1950-1978. Ed.D. Dissertation. Columbia University. 1979. 330 pp. DAI 40/4. (October 1979). Page 1919-A.
Order # 7923580.

1210.   Fischer, Nicholas A. Desegregation and Integrating the Minneapolis
Public Schools: The Politics of American Education as Seen from
Within [1967-1973]. Ed.D. Dissertation. Harvard University. 1977.
433 pp. DAI 38/8. (February 1978). Page 5022-A. Order # 773068.

1211.   Giarrusso, Alfred P. Desegregation of the Orleans Parish School System. Ed.D. Dissertation. University of Arkansas. 1969. 173 pp.
DAI 30/7. (January 1970). Page 2818-A. Order # 70-393.

1212.   Grant, Joyce M. Harvard University: A Partner in Urban School
Desegregation. Ed.D. Dissertation. 1979. 169 pp. DAI 40/6.
(December 1979). Page 3017-A. Order # 7927915.

1213.   Hardt, Annanelle. The Bi-Cultural Heritage of Texas. Ph.D. Dissertation. University of Texas. 1968. 315 pp. DAI 30/7. (January 1970). Page 2818-A. Order # 69-21,911.

1214.   Howard, Ronald W. Education and Ethnicity in Colonial New York,
1664-1763: A Study in the Transmission of Culture in Early America. Ph.D. Dissertation. University of Tennessee. 1978. 566 pp.
DAI 39/8. (February 1979). Page 5103-A. Order # 7903428.

1215.   Hudson, Jean S. Emmaus, Pennsylvania: Conflict and Stability in
an Eighteenth-Century Moravian Community. Ph.D. Dissertation.
Lehigh University. 1977. 214 pp. DAI 38/9. (March 1978). Page
5665-A. Order # 7800837.

1216.   Mackey, Louis H. The Pennsylvania Human Relations Commission and
Desegregation in the Public Schools of Pennsylvania, 1961-1978.
Ph.D. Dissertation. University of Pittsburgh. 1978. 197 pp.
DAI 39/8. (February 1979). Page 4796-A. Order # 7902715.

1217. Ment, David M. Racial Segregation in the Public Schools of New Eng-
       land and New York, 1840-1940. Ph.D. Dissertation. Columbia Uni-
       versity. 1975. 314 pp. DAI 36/5. (November 1975). Page 2684-A.
       Order # 75-25,702.

1218. Montalto, Nicholas V. The Forgotten Dream: A History of the Inter-
       Cultural Education Movement, 1924-1941. Ph.D. Dissertation. Uni-
       versity of Minnesota. 1977. 327 pp. DAI 39/2. (August 1978).
       Page 1061-A. Order # 7813436.

1219. Mulhern, Joseph R. Controversies over Racial Imbalance in the Pub-
       lic Schools of New York State from 1938 to 1975 and the Legal Rights
       of Pupils in Relation to School Integration. Ed.D. Dissertation. New
       York University. 1978. 611 pp. DAI 39/6. (December 1978).
       Page 3418-A. Order # 7824113.

1220. Nava, Alfonso R. A Political History of Bilingual Language Policy in
       the Americas. Ph.D. Dissertation. Claremont Graduate School.
       1977. 191 pp. DAI 38/3. (September 1977). Page 1944-A. Order
       # 77-22,492.

1221. Pieroth, Doris H. Desegregating the Public Schools, Seattle, Wash-
       ington, 1954-1968. Ph.D. Dissertation. University of Washington.
       1979. 562 pp. DAI 40/6. (December 1979). Page 3495-A. Order
       # 7927853.

1222. Williams, Henry C. The Status of Minority Public Education in Mis-
       souri from 1820 to 1954: A Legal History. Ph.D. Dissertation.
       St. Louis University. 1977. 198 pp. DAI 38/9. (March 1978).
       Page 5297-A. Order # 7800524.

Asian-Americans

1223. Fernandes, Norman A. The San Francisco Board of Education and
       the Chinese Community: Segregation-Desegregation, 1850-1975.
       Ed.D. Dissertation. University of Denver. 1976. 202 pp. DAI 37/
       7. (January 1977). Page 4197-A. Order # 77-447.

1224. Jorgensen, Richard E. The Honorable Bridge: An Historical Study
       of Japan's Cultural Reputation in America. Ph.D. Dissertation.
       Georgetown University. 1973. 693 pp. DAI 34/9. (March 1974).
       Page 5840-A. Order # 74-6421.

1225. Kim, Illsoo. Immigrants to Urban America: The Korean Community
       in the New York Metropolitan Area. Ph.D. Dissertation. City Uni-
       versity of New York. 1979. 618 pp. DAI 39/12. (June 1979).
       Page 7540-A. Order # 7913143.

1226. Liu, Sun C.Y. A Study of the Chinese Ph.D. Recipients at Southern
       Illinois University at Carbondale, 1963-1975. Ph.D. Dissertation.
       Southern Illinois University. 1977. 133 pp. DAI 38/10. (April
       1978). Page 5953-A. Order # 7804288.

1227. Mossman, Robert A. Japanese-American War Relocation Centers as
       Total Institutions with Emphasis on the Educational Program. Ed.D.
       Dissertation. Rutgers, the State University. 1978. 198 pp. DAI
       39/5. (November 1978). Page 3164-A. Order # 7820337.

1228. Waugh, Isami A.D.C. Hidden Crime and Deviance in the Japanese-
       American Community, 1920-1946. Ph.D. Dissertation. University
       of California, Berkeley. 1978. 288 pp. DAI 39/8. (February
       1979). Page 5159-A. Order # 7904347.

1229. Yumiba, Carole K. An Educational History of the War Relocation Cen-
       ters at Jerome and Rohiver, Arkansas, 1942-1945. Ph.D. Dissertation.
       University of Southern California. 1979. n.p. DAI 40/7. (January
       1980). Page 3832-A. No Order #.

Black-Americans

1230. Anderson, James D. Education for Servitude: The Social Purposes
       of Schooling in the Black South, 1870-1930. Ph.D. Dissertation.
       University of Illinois. 1973. 308 pp. DAI 34/1. (July 1973).
       Page 153-A. Order # 73-17,493.

1231. Anderson, John R. Negro Education in the Public Schools of Newark,
       New Jersey, During the Nineteenth Century. Ed.D. Dissertation.
       Rutgers, the State University. 1972. 583 pp. DAI 33/9. (March
       1973). Page 4900-A. Order # 73-6428.

1232. Baker, Odessa B. Metaphors of Self-Identity as Contained in the
       Black Press from 1827 to the Present. Ed.D. Dissertation. Harvard
       University. 1978. 173 pp. DAI 39/6. (December 1978). Page
       3422. Order # 7823668.

1233. Boggs III, Wade H. State Supported Higher Education for Blacks in
       North Carolina, 1877-1945. Ph.D. Dissertation. Duke University.
       1972. 310 pp. DAI 34/4. (October 1973). Page 1792-A. Order #
       73-22,976.

1234. Borgsdorf, Linda A.R. Ann Arbor Michigan: An Historical Analysis
       of Board of Education Decisions on School Desegregation Issues.
       Ph.D. Dissertation. University of Michigan. 1980. 283 pp. DAI
       41/5. (November 1980). Page 1994-A. Order # 8025652.

1235. Bouldin, Chapman W. An Analysis of How Black Americans are De-
       picted in Eleventh Grade United States History Textbooks Used in
       the Secondary Public Schools from 1930 to 1979. Ph.D. Dissertation.
       University of Pittsburgh. 1980. 149 pp. DAI 41/2. (August 1980).
       Page 761-A. Order # 8018290.

1236. Brody, Richard S. W.E.B. DuBois' Educational Ideas. Ed.D. Disser-
       tation. 1972. 295 pp. DAI 33/9. (March 1973). Page 4900-A.
       Order # 73-6430.

1237. Brown, Lena B. Black Newspapers and Black Education in America,

1960-1970: A Study of Editorial Opinion on Education in Three Black Newspapers. Ed.D. Dissertation. Rutgers, the State University. 1979. 141 pp. DAI 40/11. (May 1980). Page 5758-A. Order # 8011416.

1238. Bryant, Bradford C. With More than Deliberate Speed: A Historical Study of Six Major Issues in Secondary Education in Palm Beach County, Florida 1954-1972 from a Black Perspective. Ed.D. Dissertation. Florida Atlantic University. 1975. 216 pp. DAI 36/4. (October 1975). Page 2069-A. Order # 75-22,483.

1239. Butchart, Ronald E. Educating for Freedom: Northern Whites and the Origins of Black Education in the South, 1862-1875. Ph.D. Dissertation. State University of New York, Binghamton. 1976. 579 pp. DAI 37/3. (September 1976). Page 1716-A. Order # 76-21,114.

1240. Carrington, Joel A. The Struggle for Desegregation of Baltimore City Public Schools, 1952-1966. Ed.D. Dissertation. University of Maryland. 1970. 174 pp. DAI 31/8. (February 1971). Page 3912-A. Order # 71-4044.

1241. Cayton, Leonard B. A History of Black Public Education in Oklahoma. Ed.D. Dissertation. University of Oklahoma. 1976. 177 pp. DAI 38/9. (March 1978). Page 5647-A. Order # 7732851.

1242. Citro, Joseph F. Booker T. Washington's Tuskegee Institute: Black School-Community, 1900-1915. Ed.D. Dissertation. University of Rochester. 1973. 573 pp. DAI 34/1. (July 1973). Page 153-A. Order # 73-14,844.

1243. Conner, Malcolm. A Comparative Study of Black and White Public Education in Nineteenth-Century New Brunswick, New Jersey. Ed.D. Dissertation. Rutgers, the State University. 1976. 402 pp. DAI 37/6. (December 1976). Page 3820-A. Order # 76-27,312.

1244. Cooper, Zachery L. Blacks in American History Textbooks: An Analysis of Two Middle School Textbooks. Ph.D. Dissertation. University of Wisconsin. 1979. 219 pp. DAI 40/8. (February 1980). Page 4378-A. Order # 8001132.

1245. Cornelius, Janet D. God's Schoolmasters: Southern Evangelists to the Slaves, 1830-1860. Ph.D. Dissertation. University of Illinois. 1977. 326 pp. DAI 38/1. (July 1977). Page 436-A. Order # 77-14,939.

1246. Crayton, James E. Predominantly Black Colleges and Universities: Their Mission. Ph.D. Dissertation. Claremont Graduate School. 1980. 215 pp. DAI 41/1. (July 1980). Page 121-A. Order # 8015598.

1247. Curtis, Alexander E. Three Black Educators: A Study of the Educational Perspectives of Richard Allen, Elijah Muhammad, and Adam Clayton Powell, Jr. Ed.D. Dissertation. Columbia University. 1980. 165 pp. DAI 41/10. (April 1981). Page 4310. Order # 8105850.

1248. Davis, Gerald N. Massachusetts Blacks and the Quest for Education, 1638-1860. Ed.D. Dissertation. University of Massachusetts. 1977. 314 pp. DAI 38/6. (December 1977). Page 3332-A. No Order #.

1249. Davis, Samuel C. Education, Law, and the Negro. Ed.D. Disserta-
       tion. University of Illinois. 1970. 150 pp. DAI 31/9. (March
       1971). Page 4500-A. Order # 71-5079.

1250. Doughty, James J. A Historical Analysis of Black Education--Focusing
       on the Contemporary Independent Black School Movement. Ph.D. Dis-
       sertation. The Ohio State University. 1973. 293 pp. DAI 34/11.
       (May 1974). Page 7014-A. Order # 74-10,947.

1251. Eakins, Sue L. The Black Struggle for Education in Louisiana, 1877-
       1930's. Ph.D. Dissertation. University of Southwestern Louisiana.
       1980. 289 pp. DAI 41/9. (March 1981). Page 4132-A. Order #
       8100288.

1252. Fleming, Cynthia G. The Development of Black Education in Tennes-
       see, 1865-1920. Ph.D. Dissertation. Duke University. 1977. 226
       pp. DAI 38/12. (June 1978). Page 7510-A. Order # 7807595.

1253. Frank, Zelma A.L. The Portrayal of Black Americans in Pictures and
       Content in the Caldicott Award Books and Honor Books from 1938-
       1978. Ed.D. Dissertation. University of Missouri. 1979. 193 pp.
       DAI 40/8. (February 1980). Page 4398-A. Order # 8002358.

1254. Franklin, Vincent P. Educating an Urban Black Community: The
       Case of Philadelphia, 1900-1950. Ph.D. Dissertation. University
       of Chicago. 1975. n.p. DAI 36/7. (January 1976). Page 4305-
       A. No Order #.

1255. Gardner, Booker T. The Educational Philosophy of Booker T. Wash-
       ington and its Implications for Social Mobility. Ph.D. Dissertation.
       Southern Illinois University, 1972. 280 pp. DAI 33/9. (March
       1973). Page 4670-A. Order # 73-6206.

1256. Garrett, R. Thomas. A Study of the Bluefield State College from a
       Black Teacher Preparation College to a Predominantly White Liberal
       Arts College. Ed.D. Dissertation. Rutgers, the State University.
       1979. 111 pp. DAI 40/7. (January 1980). Page 3827-A. Order
       # 8000953.

1257. Goldstein, Stanley L. The Influence of Marxism on the Educational
       Philosophy of W.E.B. Dubois, 1897-1963. Ph.D. Dissertation. Uni-
       versity of Texas. 1972. 227 pp. DAI 33/9. (March 1973). Page
       4672-A. Order # 73-7554.

1258. Gregory, Clarence K. The Education of Blacks in Maryland: An
       Historical Survey. Ed.D. Dissertation. Columbia University. 1976.
       517 pp. DAI 37/3. (September 1976). Page 1729-A. Order # 76-
       21,019.

1259. Griggs, Guy P. The White American Social and Physical Scientists'
       Views of the Negro, 1877-1920. Ph.D. Dissertation. University of
       Kansas. 1971. 319 pp. DAI 32/4. (October 1971). Page 2028-A.
       Order # 71-27,150.

1260. Grundman, Adolph H. Public School Desegregation in Virginia from
       1954 to the Present [1972]. Ph.D. Dissertation. Wayne State Uni-

versity. 1972. 428 pp. DAI 33/11. (May 1977). Page 6272-A.
Order # 73-12,521.

1261. Haley, Charles T. To Do Good and Do Well: Middle Class Blacks
and the Depression, Philadelphia, 1929-1941. Ph.D. Dissertation.
State University of New York, Binghamton. 1980. 246 pp. DAI
41/2. (August 1980). Page 566-A. Order # 8016647.

1262. Hardy, Cynthia G. A Historical Review of the Secondary School
Study of the Association of Colleges and Secondary Schools for Negroes,
1940-1946. Ph.D. Dissertation. Ohio State University. 1977. 178 pp.
DAI 38/5. (November 1977). Page 2609-A. Order # 77-24,635.

1263. Hasson, Jr., Willie R. A Historical Analysis of the Barriers to Black
Academic Achievement in the United States. Ed.D. Dissertation.
University of Massachusetts. 1978. 202 pp. DAI 39/8. (February
1979). Page 4796-A. Order # 7902016.

1264. Herenton, Willie W. A Historical Study of School Desegregation in
the Memphis City Schools, 1954-1970. Ph.D. Dissertation. Southern
Illinois University. 1971. 147 pp. DAI 32/9. (March 1972). Page
5001-A. Order # 72-10,254.

1265. Hess, Tad G. The History of Black Education (1865-1896): A Unit
of Individualized Instruction. Ph.D. Dissertation. University of
Utah. 1972. 202 pp. DAI 33/7. (January 1973). Page 3337-A.
Order # 72-33,299.

1266. Hines, Linda E.O. Background to Fame: The Career of George Washington Carver, 1896-1916. Ph.D. Dissertation. Auburn University.
1976. 228 pp. DAI 37/7. (January 1977). Page 4530-A. Order #
76-30,086.

1267. Hogan, Lawrence D. A Black National News Service: Claude Barnett.
The Associated Negro Press, and Afro-American Newspapers, 1919-
1945. Ph.D. Dissertation. Indiana University. 1978. 320 pp.
DAI 39/9. (March 1979). Page 5667-A. Order # 7906700.

1268. Holland, Davis R. A History of the Desegregation Movement in South
Carolina Public Schools During the Period 1954-1976. Ph.D. Dissertation. Florida State University. 1978. 244 pp. DAI 39/6. (December 1978). Page 3448-A. Order # 7822177.

1269. Holland, Howard E. Black Administrators in the Philadelphia Public
Schools, 1864-1975. D.Ed. Dissertation. Pennsylvania State Uni-
versity. 1975. 88 pp. DAI 36/11. (May 1976). Page 7096-A.
Order # 76-10,737.

1270. Horst, Samuel L. Education for Manhood: The Education of Blacks
in Virginia During the Civil War. Ph.D. Dissertation. University
of Virginia. 1977. 361 pp. DAI 39/7. (January 1979). Page
4446-A. Order # 7901137.

1271. Howard, Michael E. The Social Scientists, the Courts, and The School
Segregation Cases: A Historical Review. Ph.D. Dissertation. Stanford University. 1972. 204 pp. DAI 33/8. (February 1973). Page
4141-A. Order # 73-4517.

1272. Hunt, Frankie L.C. A History of the Desegregation of the Fayette
       County School System: Fayette County, Tennessee, 1954-1980.
       Ed.D. Dissertation. University of Mississippi. 1981. 360 pp. DAI
       42/11. (May 1982). Page 4670-A. Order # 8207670.

1273. Jackson, Brenda F. The Policies and Purposes of Black Public School-
       ing in Louisville, Kentucky, 1890-1930. Ph.D. Dissertation. Indiana
       University. 1976. 279 pp. DAI 37/8. (February 1977). Page
       4912-A. Order # 77-2004.

1274. Jackson, Rose J. The Black Educational Experience in a Northern
       City: Albany, New York, 1830-1970. Ph.D. Dissertation. North-
       western University. 1976. 267 pp. DAI 37/11. (May 1977). Page
       6993-A. Order # 77-10,040.

1275. Johnson, Jr., Adolph. A History and Interpretation of the William
       Edward Burghardt Dubois-Booker Taliaferro Washington Higher Ed-
       ucational Controversy. Ph.D. Dissertation. University of Southern
       California. 1976. n.p. DAI 38/10. (April 1978). Page 5949-A.
       No Order #.

1276. Johnson, Oscar C. The Institute for Services to Education: An Ef-
       fort at Educational Reform to Ameliorate the Status of Black People
       in America. Ed.D. Dissertation. 1974. 153 pp. DAI 35/6. (De-
       cember 1974). Page 3479-A. Order # 74-27,310.

1277. Johnson, Elliot M. The Influence of Blacks on the Development and
       Implementation of the Public Education System in South Carolina,
       1863-1876. Ph.D. Dissertation. The American University. 1978.
       203 pp. DAI 39/2. (August 1979). Page 720-A. Order # 7813584.

1278. Jordan, Elizabeth C. The Impact of the Negro Organization Society
       on the Public Support for Education in Virginia, 1912-1950. Ed.D.
       Dissertation. University of Virginia. 1978. 248 pp. DAI 40/2.
       (August 1979). Page 1011-A. Order # 7916270.

1279. Kessen, Thomas P. Segregation in Cincinnati Public Education: The
       Nineteenth Century Black Experience. Ed.D. Dissertation. Univer-
       sity of Cincinnati. 1973. 170 pp. DAI 34/6. (December 1973).
       Page 3103-A. Order # 73-29,456.

1280. La Plante, Bernard R. The Negro at Jefferson High School [Portland,
       Oregon]: A Historical Study of Racial Change. Ph.D. Dissertation.
       University of Oregon. 1970. 251 pp. DAI 31/10. (April 1971).
       Page 5160-A. Order # 71-10,755.

1281. Lewinson, Barbara S.K. Three Conceptions of Black Education: A
       Study of the Educational Ideas of Benjamin Elijah Mays, Booker T.
       Washington, and Nathan Wright, Jr. Ed.D. Dissertation. Rutgers,
       the State University, 1973. 172 pp. DAI 34/7. (January 1974).
       Page 3914-A. Order # 73-32,224.

1282. Little, Jr., Monroe H. The Black Student at the Black College.
       Ph.D. Dissertation. Princeton University. 1977. 264 pp. DAI
       38/9. (March 1978). Page 5648-A. Order # 7800286.

1283. Marshall, William A. Education in the Nation of Islam During the

Leadership of Elijah Muhammad, 1935-1975. Ed.D. Dissertation. Loyola University, Chicago. 1976. 127 pp. DAI 37/11. (May 1977). Page 6993-A. Order # 77-7340.

1284. Martin, Josephine W. The Educational Effects of the Major Freedman's Aid Societies and Freedman's Bureaus in South Carolina, 1862-1870. Ph.D. Dissertation. University of South Carolina. 1971. 221 pp. DAI 32/10. (April 1972). Page 5581-A. Order # 72-12,020.

1285. Maskin, Melvin R. Black Education and the New Deal: The Urban Experience. Ph.D. Dissertation. New York University. 1973. 373 pp. DAI 34/3. (September 1973). Page 1213-A. Order # 73-19,948.

1286. Masters, Isabell. The Life and Legacy of Oliver Brown, The First Listed Plaintiff of Brown vs. Board of Education, Topeka, Kansas. Ph.D. Dissertation. University of Oklahoma. 1980. 195 pp. DAI 42/1. (July 1981). Page 112-A. Order # 8113243.

1287. Matthews, Carl S. After Booker T. Washington: The Search for a New Negro Leadership, 1915-1925. Ph.D. Dissertation. University of Virginia. 1971. 277 pp. DAI 32/8. (February 1972). Page 4532-A. Order # 72-7181.

1288. McCarthy, Joseph J. History of Black Catholic Education in Chicago, 1871-1971. Ph.D. Dissertation. Loyola University, Chicago. 1973. 206 pp. DAI 34/4. (October 1973). Page 1668-A. Order # 73-23,150.

1289. McGee, Leo. Adult Education for the Black Man in America, 1860-1880: An Historical Study of the Types. Ph.D. Dissertation. The Ohio State University. 1972. 245 pp. DAI 33/10. (April 1973). Page 5461-A. Order # 72-27,066.

1290. McGraw, Marie T. The American Colonization Society in Virginia, 1816-1832: A Case Study in Southern Liberalism. Ph.D. Dissertation. George Washington University. 1980. 250 pp. DAI 41/5. (November 1980). Page 2182-A. Order # 8023860.

1291. McIver, Isaiah. Puritanical Parallels in Afro-American Educational Thought [1619-1670]. Ph.D. Dissertation. Loyola University, Chicago. 1974. 697 pp. DAI 35/2. (August 1974). Page 943-A. Order # 74-16,959.

1292. McLaughlin, Andree N. Education for Black People: Instrument of Colonization or Mechanism for Liberation? Ed.D. Dissertation. University of Massachusetts. 1974. n.p. DAI 35/3. (September 1974). Page 1355-A. No Order #.

1293. Mielke, David N. W.E.B. Dubois: An Educational Critique. Ed.D. Dissertation. University of Tennessee. 1977. 208 pp. DAI 38/9. (March 1978). Page 5317-A. Order # 7802022.

1294. Mitchell, Robert L. Legislative Provisions and their Effects on Negro Public Education in Florida, 1869-1947. Ph.D. Dissertation. Florida State University. 1970. 112 pp. DAI 31/9. (March 1971). Page 4503-A. Order # 71-7070.

1295. Moniba, Harry F. Booker T. Washington, Tuskegee Institute, and Liberia: Institutional and Moral Assistance, 1908-1969. Ph.D. Dissertation. Michigan State University. 1975. 178 pp. DAI 36/9. (March 1976). Page 6251-A. Order # 76-5607.

1296. Moon, Mary C. Frederick Douglass Moon: A Study of Black Education in Oklahoma. Ed.D. Dissertation. University of Oklahoma. 1978. 437 pp. DAI 39/11. (May 1979). Page 6587-A. Order # 7911159.

1297. Morgan, Charlotte T. Ethnicity and Adult Education in Practice: Black Manhattan to 1961. Ed.D. Dissertation. Columbia University. 1979. 337 pp. DAI 40/9. (March 1980). Page 4849-A. Order # 8006838.

1298. Morris, Robert C. Reading, 'Riting and Reconstruction: Freedman's Bureau Education in the South, 1865-1870. Ph.D. Dissertation. University of Chicago. 1976. n.p. DAI 37/9. (March 1977). Page 5993-A. No Order #.

1299. Moss, Alfred A. The American Negro Academy: Voice of the "Talented Tenth." Ph.D. Dissertation. University of Chicago. 1977. n.p. DAI 38/12. (June 1978). Page 7491-A. No Order #.

1300. Murphy, Patricia G. The Education of the New World Blacks in the Danish West Indies, U.S. Virgin Islands: A Case Study of Social Transition (1732-1975). Ph.D. Dissertation. University of Connecticut. 1977. 194 pp. DAI 38/10. (April 1975). Page 5890-A.

1301. Muse, Clyde. The Education Philosophy of Martin Luther King, Jr. Ph.D. Dissertation. University of Oklahoma. 1978. 117 pp. DAI 39/10. (April 1979). Page 6017-A. Order # 7908832.

1302. Neverdon, Cynthia A.C. The Articulation and Implementation of Educational Goals for Blacks in the South, 1895-1925. Ph.D. Dissertation. Howard University. 1974. 272 pp. DAI 35/9. (March 1975). Page 6038-A. Order # 75-2185.

1303. Nicholes, Walter M. The Educational Development of Blacks in Cincinnati from 1800 to the Present. Ed.D. Dissertation. University of Cincinnati. 1977. 200 pp. DAI 39/2. (August 1978). Page 721-A. Order # 7812956.

1304. Oliver, Daily E. A Historic Perspective of the Emergence of Black Educational Aims and Purposes. Ph.D. Dissertation. University of Utah. 1978. 84 pp. DAI 39/12. (August 1978). Page 740-A. Order # 7812997.

1305. Olson, Margaret P. American Intellectuals and the Negro, 1909-1954. Ph.D. Dissertation. University of North Carolina. 1971. 596 pp. DAI 32/9. (March 1972). Page 5159-A. Order # 72-10,757.

1306. O'Wesney, Julia R. Historical Study of the Progress of Racial Desegregation in the Public Schools of Baltimore, Maryland. Ph.D. Dissertation. University of Maryland. 1970. 104 pp. DAI 31/5. (November 1970). Page 2141-A. Order # 70-23,310.

1307. Patton, June O. Major Richard Robert Wright, Sr. and Black Higher
      Education in Georgia, 1880-1920. Ph.D. Dissertation. University of
      Chicago. 1980. n.p. DAI 41/3. (September 1980). Page 968-A.
      No Order #.

1308. Posilkin, Robert S. An Historical Study of the Desegregation of the
      Montgomery County, Maryland, Public Schools, 1954-1977. Ed.D.
      Dissertation. George Washington University. 1979. 775 pp. DAI
      39/12. (June 1979). Page 7095-A. Order # 7914013.

1309. Quint, Catherine I. The Role of American Negro Women Educators in
      the Growth of the Common School. Ed.D. Dissertation. Boston Uni-
      versity. 1970. 267 pp. DAI 31/5. (November 1970). Page 2142-
      A. Order # 70-22,473.

1310. Ramsey, Berkley C. The Public Black College in Georgia: A History
      of Albany State College, 1903-1965. Ph.D. Dissertation. Florida
      State Universtiy. 1973. 528 pp. DAI 34/7. (January 1974). Page
      4167-A. Order # 73-31,528.

1311. Rathnun, Betty L.K. The Rise of the Modern American Negro Press,
      1880-1914. Ph.D. Dissertation. State University of New York, Buf-
      falo. 1979. 302 pp. DAI 39/12. (June 1979). Page 7486-A. Order
      # 7913918.

1312. Robbins, Faye W. A World Within a World: Black Nashville, 1880-
      1915. Ph.D. Dissertation. University of Arkansas. 1980. 362 pp.
      DAI 41/5. (November 1980). Page 2245-A. Order # 8026015.

1313. Rosen, Frederick B. The Development of Negro Education in Florida
      During Reconstruction: 1865-1877. Ed.D. Dissertation. University
      of Florida. 1974. 286 pp. DAI 35/8. (February 1975). Page
      5072-A. Order # 75-3523.

1314. Rosenbaum, Judy J. Black Education in Three Northern Cities [Chi-
      cago, Indianapolis, Philadelphia] in the Early Twentieth Century.
      Ph.D. Dissertation. University of Illinois. 1974. 262 pp. DAI
      35/12. (June 1975). Page 7849-A. Order # 75-11,741.

1315. Russell, Lester F. Secondary Schools Established and Supported by
      Black Baptists in Virginia, 1887-1957. Ed.D. Dissertation. Rutgers,
      the State University. 1976. 233 pp. DAI 37/6. (December 1976).
      Page 3821-A. Order # 76-27,343.

1316. Sapper, Neil G. A Survey of the History of the Black People of
      Texas, 1930-1954. Ph.D. Dissertation. Texas Tech University.
      1972. 555 pp. DAI 33/8. (February 1973). Page 4320-A. Order
      # 73-4071.

1317. Schultz, Harry R. Brown v. Topeka: A Legacy of Courage and
      Struggle. Ed.D. Dissertation. Ball State University. 1971. 347
      pp. DAI 32/1. (July 1971). Page 214-A. Order # 71-18,670.

1318. Shafer, Carlie J.C. A Study of Historical and Legal Factors Influ-
      encing the Desegregation Process of the Public Schools in Mississippi
      Ed.D. Dissertation. 1971. 174 pp. DAI 32/9. (March 1972). Page
      4904-A. Order # 72-9096.

1319. Silcox, Harry C. A Comparative Study in School Desegregation: The Boston and Philadelphia Experience, 1800-1881. Ed.D. Dissertation. Temple University. 1972. 350 pp. DAI 33/4. (October 1972). Page 1475-A. Order # 72-20,217.

1320. Smock, Raymond W. The Booker T. Washington Papers, September 1899-March 1901. Ph.D. Dissertation. University of Maryland. 1974. 765 pp. DAI 35/10. (March 1975). Page 6616-A. Order # 75-8522.

1321. Stitely, Thomas B. Bridging the Gap: A History of the Rosewald Fund in the Development of Rural Negro Schools in Tennessee, 1912-1932. Ph.D. Dissertation. George Peabody College for Teachers. 1975. 75 pp. DAI 36/4. (October 1975). Page 2074-A. Order # 75-22,292.

1322. Thomas, Gregory. Historical Survey of Black Education as a Means of Black Liberation. Ph.D. Dissertation. The Ohio State University. 1971. 171 pp. DAI 32/7. (January 1972). Page 3580-A. Order # 72-4669.

1323. Thomas, William H. An Assessment of Booker Taliaferro Washington's Educational Influence in the United States and West Africa Between the Years 1880 and 1925. Ph.D. Dissertation. Michigan State University. 1972. 272 pp. DAI 33/9. (March 1973). Page 4903-A. Order # 73-5501.

1324. Thompson, Lloyd K. The Origins and Development of Black Religious Colleges in East Texas. Ph.D. Dissertation. North Texas State University. 1976. 178 pp. DAI 37/11. (May 1977). Page 7276-A. Order # 77-11,122.

1325. Tucker, Thomas. An Historical Study of the Involvement of the Congress of Racial Equality in Public School Desegregation Actions Taken from 1954 through 1973. Ph.D. Dissertation. The Ohio State University. 1974. 158 pp. DAI 35/8. (February 1975). Page 4953-A. Order # 75-3211.

1326. Vandever, Elizabeth J. Brown v. Board of Education of Topeka: Anatomy of a Decision. Ph.D. Dissertation. University of Kansas. 1971. 457 pp. DAI 32/10. (April 1972). Page 5724. Order # 72-11,811.

1327. Vrame, William A. A History of School Desegregation in Chicago Since 1954. Ph.D. Dissertation. University of Wisconsin. 1970. 423 pp. DAI 31/12. (June 1971). Page 6534-A. Order # 71-328.

1328. Weaver, Billy L. The Educative Role of Black Newspapers, 1920-1930. Ph.D. Dissertation. Indiana University. 1979. 200 pp. DAI 40/4. (October 1979). Page 1924-A. Order # 7921336.

1329. Webber, Thomas L. The Education of the Slave Quarter Community: White Teaching and Black Learning on the Ante-Bellum Plantation. Ph.D. Dissertation. Columbia University. 1976. 526 pp. DAI 39/1. (July 1978). Page 415-A. Order # 7811161.

1330. White, Arthur O. Blacks and Education in Antebellum Massachusetts:

Strategies for Social Mobility. Ed.D. Dissertation. State University of New York, Buffalo. 1971. 416 pp. DAI 31/12. (June 1971). Page 6376-A. Order # 71-16,461.

1331. White, Jr., Clarence. Doctor Martin Luther King, Jr.'s Contributions to Education as a Black Leader (1929-1968). Ed.D. Dissertation. Loyola University, Chicago. 1974. 224 pp. DAI 35/4. (October 1974). Page 2927-A. Order # 74-23,079.

1332. William, Rush. Present Status and Future Prospects of the Negro High Schools in Arkansas, 1954-1969. Ed.D. Dissertation. University of Arkansas. 1969. 207 pp. DAI 30/7. (January 1970). Page 2820-A. Order # 70-394.

1333. Williams, Lea E. The United Negro College Fund: Its Growth and Development. Ed.D. Dissertation. Columbia University. 1978. 166 pp. DAI 39/1. (July 1978). Page 162-A. Order # 7810907.

1334. Wright, C.T. The Development of Education for Blacks in Georgia, 1865-1900. Ph.D. Dissertation. Boston University. 1977. 283 pp. DAI 37/12. (June 1977). Page 7901-A. Order # 77-11,433.

1335. Wye, Christopher G. Midwest Ghetto: Patterns of Negro Life and Thought in Cleveland, Ohio, 1929-1945. Ph.D. Dissertation. Kent State University. 1973. 520 pp. DAI 34/7. (January 1974). Page 4181-A. Order # 73-32,363.

1336. Wynetta, Devore. The Education of Blacks in New Jersey, 1900-1960: An Exploration in Oral History. Ed.D. Dissertation. Rutgers, the State University. 1980. 263 pp. DAI 41/9. (March 1981). Page 3933-A. Order # 8105216.

1337. Zellmer, Kathleen O. The Gray School: The Impact of de Facto Desegregation on a Selected School [1948-1968]. Ph.D. Dissertation. American University. 1972. 189 pp. DAI 33/8. (February 1973). Page 4144. Order # 72-30,120.

Hispanic-Americans

1338. Cameron, James W. The History of Mexican Public Education in Los Angeles, 1910-1930. Ph.D. Dissertation. University of Southern California. 1976. n.p. DAI 38/3. (September 1977). Page 1934-A. No Order #.

1339. Friedman, Marjorie S. An Appraisal of the Role of the Public School as an Acculturating Agency of Mexican Americans in Texas, 1850-1968. Ph.D. Dissertation. New York University. 1978. 277 pp. DAI 39/4. (October 1978). Page 2117-A. Order # 7818133.

1340. Gonzalez, Gilbert G. The System of Public Education and its Function within the Chicano Community, 1920-1930. Ph.D. Dissertation. University of California, Los Angeles. 1974. 232 pp. DAI 35/10. (April 1975). Page 6635-A. Order # 75-9392.

1341. San Miguel, Jr., Guadalupe. Endless Pursuits: The Chicano Educational Experiences in Corpus Christi, Texas, 1880-1960. Ph.D. Dissertation. Stanford University. 1979. 252 pp. DAI 40/4. (October 1979). Page 1922-A. Order # 7917277.

1342. Simmons, Thomas E. The Citizen Factories: The Americanization of Mexican Students in Texas Public Schools, 1920-1945. Ph.D. Dissertation. Texas A & M University. 1976. 214 pp. DAI 37/8. (February 1977). Page 4913-A. Order # 77-2668.

Native-Americans

1343. Balock, Qamar W. An Analysis of the Portrayal of American Indians in United States History Textbooks, 1860-1980. Ph.D. Dissertation. University of Pittsburgh. 1981. 81 pp. DAI 42/12. (June 1982). Page 5079-A. Order # 8210615.

1344. Brown, Richard W. Characteristics and Concepts of American Indians in Children's Fictional Literature Between 1963 and 1973. Ed.D. Dissertation. 1978. 144 pp. DAI 39/2. (August 1978). Page 737-A. Order # 7812259.

1345. Fischer, Frances J. The Third Force: The Involvement of Voluntary Organizations in the Education of the American Indian with Special Reference to California, 1880-1933. Ph.D. Dissertation. University of British Columbia. 1980. 269 pp. DAI 41/7. (January 1981). Page 2968-A. Order # 8029392.

1346. Fixico, Donald L. Termination and Relocation: Federal Indian Policy in the 1950's. Ph.D. Dissertation. University of Oklahoma. 1980. 328 pp. DAI 41/6. (December 1980). Page 2475-A. Order # 8027515.

1347. Gribskov, Margaret E. A Critical Analysis of Textbook Accounts of the Role of Indians in American History. Ph.D. Dissertation. University of Oregon. 1973. 152 pp. DAI 34/6. (December 1973). Page 3301-A. Order # 73-28,597.

1348. Hayes, Susanna A. The Resistance to Education for Assimilation by the Colville Indians, 1872-1972. Ph.D. Dissertation. University of Michigan. 1973. DAI 34/8. (February 1974). Page 4813-A. Order # 74-3641.

1349. Noley, Grayson B. The History of Education in the Choctaw Nation from Precolonial Times to 1830. Ph.D. Dissertation. Penn State University. 1979. 265 pp. DAI 40/11. (May 1980). Page 5760-A. Order # 8006034.

1350. Robbins, Webster S. The Administrative and Educational Policies of the United States Federal Government with Regard to the North American Indian Tribes of Nebraska from 1870 to 1970. Ed.D. Dissertation. University of Nebraska. 1976. 422 pp. DAI 37/5. (November 1976). Page 2687-A. Order # 76-25,906.

1351. Sanford, Gregory R. The Study of Nez Percé Indian Education.
       Ph.D. Dissertation. University of New Mexico. 1970. 245 pp.
       DAI 31/11. (May 1971). Page 5816-A. Order # 71-12,795.

1352. Satz, Ronald N. Federal Indian Policy, 1829-1849. Ph.D. Dissertation.
       University of Maryland. 1972. 368 pp. DAI 33/2. (August 1972).
       Page 708-A. Order # 72-21,132.

1353. Scheirbeck, Helen M. Education: Public Policy and the American
       Indian. Ed.D. Dissertation. Virginia Polytechnic Institute and State
       University. 1980. 461 pp. DAI 41/8. (February 1981). Page
       3455-A. Order # 8101898.

1354. Skelton, Robert H. A History of the Education System of the Cher-
       okee Nation, 1801-1910. Ed.D. Dissertation. University of Arkansas.
       1970. 291 pp. DAI 31/6. (December 1970). Page 2717-A. Order
       # 70-26,233.

1355. Spear, Eloise G. Choctaw Indian Education with Special Reference to
       Choctaw County, Oklahoma (1831-1977). Ph.D. Dissertation. Univer-
       sity of Oklahoma. 1977. 317 pp. DAI 38/9. (March 1978). Page
       5320-A. Order # 7732883.

1356. Stockman, Wallace H. Historical Perspectives of Federal Education
       Promises and Performance Among the Fort Berthold (North Dakota)
       Indians. Ed.D. Dissertation. University of Colorado. 1972. 364
       pp. DAI 33/4. (October 1972). Page 1475-A. Order # 72-25,221.

1357. Szasz, Margaret Ann C. American Indian Education, 1930-1970:
       From the Meriam Report to the Kennedy Report. Ph.D. Dissertation.
       University of New Mexico. 1972. 350 pp. DAI 34/1. (July 1973).
       Page 262-A. Order # 73-16,592.

1358. Thompson, Vernon R. A History of the Education of the Lumbee In-
       dians of Robeson County, North Carolina from 1885 to 1970. Ed.D.
       Dissertation. University of Miami. 1973. 114 pp. DAI 35/1.
       (July 1974). Page 149-A. Order # 74-14,331.

1359. Tingey, Joseph W. Indians and Blacks Together: An Experiment in
       Biracial Education at Hampton Institute (1878-1923). Ed.D. Disser-
       tation. 1978. 397 pp. DAI 40/4. (October 1979). Page 1923-A.
       Order # 7923636.

1360. Troy, Alice A. The Indian in Adolescent Literature, 1930-1940 vs.
       1960-1970. Ph.D. Dissertation. University of Iowa. 1972. 399 pp.
       DAI 34/1. (July 1973). Page 73-A. Order # 73-13,600.

1361. Weiner, Lilian R. Federal Legislation on Indian Education, 1819-1970.
       Ph.D. Dissertation. University of Maryland. 1972. 345 pp. DAI
       34/2. (August 1973). Page 522-A. Order # 73-18,272.

1362. Wiggin, Lexie O. A Critical History of the Southern Baptist Indian
       Mission Movement, 1855-1861. Ph.D. Dissertation. University of
       Alabama. 1980. 226 pp. DAI 41/7. (February 1981). Page 3698-
       A. Order # 8100597.

Music Education

1363. Baker, Barbara W. Black Gospel Music Styles, 1942-1975: Analysis and Implications for Music Education. Ph.D. Dissertation. University of Maryland. 1978. n.p. DAI 39/9. (March 1979). Page 5385-A. No Order #.

1364. Brault, Diana V. A History of the Ontario Music Education Association (1919-1974). Ph.D. Dissertation. University of Rochester/Eastman School of Music. 1977. 690 pp. DAI 38/6. (December 1977). Page 3352-A. Order # 77-26,618.

1365. Buckner, Reginald T. A History of Music Education in the Black Community of Kansas City, Kansas, 1905-1954. Ph.D. Dissertation. University of Minnesota. 1974. 347 pp. DAI 35/7. (January 1975). Page 4219-A. Order # 75-157.

1366. Fisher, James L. The Origin and Development of Public School Music in Baltimore [Maryland] to 1870. Ed.D. Dissertation. University of Maryland. 1970. 205 pp. DAI 31/11. (May 1971). Page 5810-A. Order # 71-13,198.

1367. Hancock, Paul C. A History of Music Education in Nashville and Davidson County Public Schools (1873-1975): Local Reflections of National Practices in Music Education. Ed.D. Dissertation. George Peabody College for Teachers. 1977. 315 pp. DAI 38/5. (November 1977). Page 2638-A. Order # 77-25,105.

1368. Mathison, Curtis J. The Teaching of the Theory of Music in American High Schools from 1900 to 1930. Ed.D. Dissertation. University of Michigan. 1972. 254 pp. DAI 34/4. (October 1973). Page 1671-A. Order # 73-24,734.

1369. Miller, Robert W. The North Texas State University Jazz Degree: A History and Study of its Significance. Ph.D. Dissertation. Michigan State University. 1979. 277 pp. DAI 40/8. (February 1980). Page 4465-A. Order # 8001565.

1370. Moore, Marvelene C. Multicultural Music Education: An Analysis of Afro-American and Native-American Folk Songs in Selected Elementary Music Textbooks of the Periods 1928-1955 and 1965-1975. Ph.D. Dissertation. University of Michigan. 1977. 286 pp. DAI 38/6. (December 1977). Page 3355-A. Order # 77-26,317.

1371. Podrovsky, Rosagitta. A History of Music Education in the Chicago Public Schools. Ph.D. Dissertation. Northwestern University. 1978. 319 pp. DAI 39/10. (April 1979). Page 6013-A. Order # 7907925.

1372. Reichmuth, Roger E. Price Doyle, 1896-1967: His Life and Work in Music Education. Ed.D. Dissertation. University of Illinois. 1977. 456 pp. DAI 38/10. (April 1978). Page 5981-A. Order # 7804123.

1373. Rideout, Roger R. Granville Stanley Hall and Music Education: 1880-

1924. Ed.D. Dissertation. University of Illinois. 1978. 154 pp. DAI 39/12. (June 1979). Page 7209-A. Order # 7913588.

1374. Yoder, Chris. Theodore Presser, Educator, Publisher, Philanthropist: Selected Contributions to the Music Teaching Profession in America [19th-20th centuries]. Ed.D. Dissertation. University of Illinois. 1978. 358 pp. DAI 39/12. (June 1979). Page 7211-A. Order # 7913668.

Nursing Education

1375. Allemang, Margaret M. Nursing Education in the United States and Canada, 1873-1950: Leading Figures, Forces, Views on Education. Ph.D. Dissertation. University of Washington. 1974. 316 pp. DAI 36/6. (December 1975). Page 3467-A. Order # 75-28,308.

1376. Ashley, Jo Ann. Hospital Sponsorship of Nursing Schools: Influence of its Apprenticeship and Paternalism on Nursing Education in America, 1893-1948. Ed.D. Dissertation. Columbia University. 1972. 337 pp. DAI 37/9. (March 1977). Page 5622-A. Order # 77-4181.

1377. Clayton, Bonnie C.W. Historical Perspectives of Psychiatric Nursing in Higher Education: 1946 to 1975. Ph.D. Dissertation. University of Utah. 1976. 174 pp. DAI 37/5. (November 1976). Page 2683-A. Order # 76-25,845.

1378. Kerr, Janet C.R. Financing University Nursing Education in Canada, 1919-1976. Ph.D. Dissertation. University of Michigan. 1978. 285 pp. DAI 39/6. (December 1978). Page 3403-A. Order # 7822930.

1379. Krampitz, Sydney D. The Historical Development of Baccalaureate Nursing Education in the American University: 1899-1935. Ph.D. Dissertation. University of Chicago. 1978. n.p. DAI 39/1. (July 1978). Page 152-A. No Order #.

1380. Lawrence, Cora J. University Education for Nursing in Seattle, 1912-1950: An Inside Story of the University of Washington School. Ph.D. Dissertation. University of Washington. 1972. 287 pp. DAI 33/5. (November 1972). Page 2141-A. Order # 72-28,622.

1381. Melosh, Barbara. "Skilled Hands, Cool Heads and Warm Hearts": Nurses and Nursing, 1920-1960. Ph.D. Dissertation. Brown University. 1979. 357 pp. DAI 40/11. (May 1980). Page 5980. Order # 8007047.

1382. Noroian, Elizabeth L. The School of Nursing at the University of Pittsburgh: 1939-1973. Ph.D. Dissertation. University of Pittsburgh. 1980. 452 pp. DAI 41/6. (December 1980). Page 2475-A. Order # 8028120.

1383. Paylor, Mary M. A History of Nursing Education in Florida from

1893-1970. Ph.D. Dissertation. Florida State University. 1975.
191 pp. DAI 36/4. (October 1975). Page 2059-A. Order # 75-
21,427.

1384. Sanders, Ruth E. History of the Illinois Association of School Nurses:
The Formative Years. Ph.D. Dissertation. Southern Illinois Univer-
sity. 1979. 184 pp. DAI 40/8. (February 1980). Page 4426-A.
Order # 8004090.

1385. Sheahan, Dorothy A. The Social Origins of American Nursing and its
Movement into the University: A Microscopic Approach. Ph.D. Dissertation. New York University. 1979. 620 pp. DAI 41/2. (August 1980). Page 623-A. Order # 8017528.

1386. Sloan, Patricia E. A History of the Establishment and Early Development of Selected Nurse Training Schools for Afro-Americans, 1886-
1906. Ed.D. Dissertation. Columbia University. 1978. 355 pp.
DAI 39/10. (April 1978). Page 6284-A. Order # 7909022.

1387. Smola, Bonnie K. A Study of the Development of Diploma and Baccalaureate Degree Nursing Education Programs in Iowa from 1907-1978.
Ph.D. Dissertation. Iowa State University. 1980. 323 pp. DAI
41/9. (March 1981). Page 3917-A. Order # 8106057.

1388. Story, Donna K. A Study of Practical and Associated Degree Nursing
Education in Iowa from 1918 to 1978. Ph.D. Dissertation. Iowa State
University. 1980. 311 pp. DAI 41/9. (March 1981). Page 3917-A.
Order # 8106061.

1389. Suhrie, Eleanor B. Evidence of the Influence of Ruth Perkins Kuehn
on Nursing and Nursing Education. Ph.D. Dissertation. University
of Pittsburgh. 1975. DAI 36/7. (January 1976). Page 4306-A.
Order # 76-375.

Organization, Structure and Finance

1390. Arrington, Alfred A. An Historical Analysis of the Development of
Supervision in the Public Schools of the United States from 1870 to
1970. Ed.D. Dissertation. George Washington University. 1972.
139 pp. DAI 33/6. (December 1972). Page 2628-A. Order # 72-
31,938.

1391. Barton, Ronald R. The Historical Study of the Organization and Development of the Junior High and Middle School Movement, 1920-1975.
Ed.D. Dissertation. University of Arkansas. 1976. 269 pp. DAI
37/5. (November 1976). Page 2682-A. Order # 76-26,371.

1392. Bury, John C. The Historical Role of Arizona's Superintendent of
Public Instruction. Ed.D. Dissertation. Northern Arizona Univer-
sity. 1975. 742 pp. DAI 36/12. (June 1976). Page 7906-A.
Order # 76-13,203.

1393. Chambers, Imogene K. The Evolution of School Finance Accounting:
       The United States from 1910 to 1980. Ed.D. Dissertation. 1980.
       365 pp. DAI 41/8. (February 1981). Page 3340-A. Order #
       8103288.

1394. Cuban, Larry. School Chiefs Under Fire: A Study of Three Big
       City Superintendents Under Outside Pressure. Ph.D. Dissertation.
       Stanford University. 1974. 282 pp. DAI 35/6. (December 1974).
       Page 3476-A. Order # 74-27,003.

1395. Dickson, David O. A History of the Indiana State Commission for the
       Reorganization of School Corporations and School Reorganization in
       Indiana Pursuant to the Acts of 1959, Chapter 202, and Amendments
       Thereto. Ph.D. Dissertation. Indiana State University. 1976.
       233 pp. DAI 38/3. (September 1977). Page 1935-A. Order # 77-
       20,664.

1396. Ekstrand, Laurie. Education Spending in the States: A 35 Year
       Perspective. Ph.D. Dissertation. Florida State University. 1978.
       DAI 39/6. (December 1978). Page 3799-A. Order # 7822157.

1397. Flora, Joseph C. The Centralization of Professional Administration in
       the Brooklyn, New York Public Schools, 1887-1902. Ed.D. Disserta-
       tion. Columbia University. 1971. 154 pp. DAI 32/3. (September
       1971). Page 1220-A. Order # 71-24,145.

1398. Gardner, Frank W. The History, Role and Operation of the Board of
       Examiners, Chicago Public Schools, 1917-1974. Ph.D. Dissertation.
       Northwestern University. 1975. 214 pp. DAI 36/7. (January
       1976). Page 4164-A. Order # 75-29,638.

1399. Gillies, III., William B. The Illinois Office of the Superintendent of
       Public Instruction: An Analysis of Effectiveness and Influence,
       1854-1920. Ph.D. Dissertation. University of Chicago. 1977. n.p.
       DAI 38/12. (June 1978). Page 7180-A. No Order #.

1400. Glanz, Jeffrey. Bureaucracy and Professionalism: An Historical In-
       terpretation of Public School Supervision in the United States, 1875-
       1937. Ed.D. Dissertation. Columbia University. 1977. 465 pp.
       DAI 38/3. (September 1977). Page 1935-A. Order # 77-22,255.

1401. Hentrel, Bobbie J.K. A History of Financing Public Schools in Mich-
       igan, 1933-1974. Ph.D. Dissertation. University of Michigan. 1975.
       230 pp. DAI 36/6. (December 1975). Page 3287-A. Order # 75-
       20,363.

1402. Jones, Donna R.C. An Historical Review of the Reorganization of
       School Districts in Colorado. Ed.D. Dissertation. University of
       Colorado. 1977. 168 pp. DAI 38/7. (January 1978). Page 3989-
       A. Order # 77-29,934.

1403. Kean, William W. Historical Trends in American Thought Concerning
       Preparation for the School Superintendency. Ph.D. Dissertation.
       University of Wisconsin. 1970. 481 pp. DAI 31/11. (May 1971).
       Page 5710-A. Order # 71-5646.

1404. Livesay, George B. A Status Study of the Public School Principal-
      ship in 1971, Viewed from the Historical Perspective. Ed.D. Disser-
      tation. Arizona State University. 1972. 204 pp. DAI 33/3. (Sep-
      tember 1972). Page 931-A. Order # 72-23,173.

1405. Lombart, George A. The Administration of Herbert S. Weet and James
      M. Spinning, Successive Superintendents of Schools in Rochester,
      New York, 1911-1954. Ed.D. Dissertation. University of Rochester.
      1969. 203 pp. DAI 30/8. (February 1970). Page 3241-A. Order #
      70-2938.

1406. Marenbach, Dieter. Rates of Return to Education in the United States
      from 1939 to 1959. Ph.D. Dissertation. Stanford University. 1973.
      189 pp. DAI 34/3. (September 1973). Page 1004-A. Order # 73-
      20,496.

1407. McClain, Kerry G. School Reorganization in Illinois During the Terms
      of Vernon L. Nickell, Illinois Superintendent of Public Instruction,
      1943-1959. Ph.D. Dissertation. Southern Illinois University. 1978.
      302 pp. DAI 39/10. (April 1979). Page 5849-A. Order # 7908055.

1408. Meulendyke, James E. Educational Leadership in a Time of Crisis,
      1932-1940. Ph.D. Dissertation. Michigan State University. 1970.
      255 pp. DAI 32/1. (July 1971). Page 136-A. Order # 71-18,255.

1409. Pacella, Anthony E. A History of the Louisiana School Boards Asso-
      ciation. Ed.D. Dissertation. Louisiana State University and Agri-
      cultural and Mechanical College. 1977. 131 pp. DAI 38/6. (De-
      cember 1977). Page 3334-A. Order # 77-25,395.

1410. Rice, Eileen K. The Superintendency and the Implementation of Pro-
      gressive Practices in the Ann Arbor Elementary Schools from 1921-
      1942. Ph.D. Dissertation. University of Michigan. 1977. 531 pp.
      DAI 38/11. (May 1978). Page 6573-A. Order # 7804801.

1411. Scarlette, Erma T. A Historical Study of Women in Public School Ad-
      ministration from 1900-1977. Ed.D. Dissertation. University of North
      Carolina, Greensboro. 1979. 160 pp. DAI 40/4. (October 1979).
      Page 1803-A. Order # 7922421.

1412. Seretny, Albert A. The Secondary School Principal's Role in Curric-
      ulum Development in New Haven, Connecticut, 1940-1970. Ph.D.
      Dissertation. University of Connecticut. 1971. 221 pp. DAI
      32/5. (November 1970). Page 2376-A. Order # 71-29,909.

1413. Simpson, Ronald P. Some Technical Aspects and Problems of the Ad-
      ministration of High School Facility Construction Projects in Wiscon-
      sin, 1900-1920. Ph.D. Dissertation. University of Wisconsin. 1979.
      385 pp. DAI 40/5. (November 1979). Page 24-1-A. Order #
      7918163.

1414. Spatz, Marshall C. New York City Public Schools and the Emergence
      of Bureaucracy 1868-1917. Ph.D. Dissertation. University of Chicago.
      1975. n.p. DAI 36/12. (June 1976). Page 8259-A. No Order #.

1415. Sterling, Mary E. Content Analysis of Elementary Administration

Textbooks, 1960-1975. Ph.D. Dissertation. University of Oklahoma. 1979. 67 pp. DAI 40/4. (October 1979). Page 1807-A. Order # 7921268.

1416. Sullins, Howard O. A History of the Public School Superintendency in Virginia. Ed.D. Dissertation. University of Virginia. 1970. 538 pp. DAI 31/9. (March 1971). Page 4505-A. Order # 70-26,591.

1417. Tinder, Thad N. An Econometric Approach to the Analysis of Enrollment Trend Variations of Five Year Old Public School Students in the United States, 1925-1975. Ed.D. Dissertation. University of Nebraska. 1979. 133 pp. DAI 40/2. (August 1979). Page 661-A. Order # 7918025.

1418. Wehrle, Richard I. The Voter, the Schools, and the Tax Dollar: A Study of School Tax Referenda, Rockford, Illinois, 1956-1977. Ed.D. Dissertation. Northern Illinois University. 1978. 196 pp. DAI 39/10. (April 1979). Page 5868-A. Order # 7902463.

1419. Wilson, Allan W. The Legal Pattern for Regionalization of School Districts in New Jersey from 1903 to 1966. Ph.D. Dissertation. University of Connecticut. 1969. 224 pp. DAI 30/8. (February Page 3267-A. Order # 70-1325.

1420. Wirtz, Thomas J. A History of the Indiana School Boards Association, 1964-1978. Ed.D. Dissertation. University of Indiana. 1979. 139 pp. DAI 40/8. (February 1980). Page 4445-A. Order # 8003835.

1421. Young, Harold S. In Pursuit of a Profession: A Historical Analysis of the Concept of "Professionalization" for the American School Superintendency, 1865-1973. Ed.D. Dissertation. Pennsylvania State University. 1976. 606 pp. DAI 37/11. (May 1977). Page 6894-A. Order # 77-9777.

Pre-School/Kindergarten

1422. Calkins, Joan S. Two Worlds of Early Childhood: Government-Sponsored Child Care Centers in the Soviet Union and California. Ph.D. Dissertation. Claremont Graduate School. 1976. 144 pp. DAI 37/5. (November 1976). Page 2725-A. Order # 76-23,922.

1423. Cavallo, Dominick J. The Child in American Reform: A Psychohistory of the Movement to Organize Children's Play, 1889-1920. Ph.D. Dissertation. State University of New York, Stony Brook. 1976. 338 pp. DAI 37/7. (January 1977). Page 4551-A. Order # 77-432.

1424. Davis, Sue Matthews. The Development of Public School Kindergartens in Virginia to 1975. Ed.D. Dissertation. Duke University. 1976. 306 pp. DAI 38/3. (September 1977). Page 1286-A. Order # 77-18,769.

1425. Dickason, Jerry G. The Development of the Playground Movement in the United States: A Historical Study. Ph.D. Dissertation. New York University. 1979. 281 pp. DAI 40/11. (May 1980). Page 5776-A. Order # 8010278.

1426. Hinitz, Blythe S.F. The Development of Creative Movement within Early Childhood Education, 1920-1970. Ed.D. Dissertation. Temple University. 1977. 266 pp. DAI 38/3. (September 1977). Page 1982-A. Order # 72-21,767.

1427. Jenkins, John Williams. Infant Schools and the Development of Public Primary Schools in Selected American Cities before the Civil War. Ph.D. Dissertation. University of Wisconsin. 1978. 213 pp. DAI 39/5. (November 1978). Page 2786-A. Order # 7815051.

1428. Lucey, Patricia A. Survey of the History and Major Improvements of Early Childhood Education in the United States Including the Rationale for these Movements. Ph.D. Dissertation. Marquette University. 1976. 184 pp. DAI 37/4. (October 1974). Page 2026-A. Order # 76-21,753.

1429. Metzow, Marion S. Thought and Practice in Early Childhood Education: 1900-1930. Ph.D. Dissertation. University of Illinois. 1977. 346 pp. DAI 38/6. (December 1977). Page 333-A. Order # 77-26,714.

1430. Oakes, Clifton R. Milton Bradley: An Historical Study of his Educational Endeavors in the Context of the Kindergarten Movement in America. Ed.D. Dissertation. University of the Pacific. 1975. 187 pp. DAI 36/6. (December 1975). Page 3364-A. Order # 75-26,105.

1431. Pattishall, Viola F. The Education of the Young Child in the Cincinnati Area, 1879-1926. Ed.D. Dissertation. University of Cincinnati. 1970. 245 pp. DAI 31/9. (March 1970). Page 4504-A. Order # 71-6405.

1432. Phifer, Betty T. The Origin and Development of the Kindergarten Idea in Newark, New Jersey, 1870-1915. Ed.D. Dissertation. Rutgers, the State University. 1977. 171 pp. DAI 38/7. (January 1978). Page 3989-A. Order # 77-27,955.

1433. Poole, Jr. David R. Bethesda: An Investigation of the Georgia Orphan House, 1738-1772. Ph.D. Dissertation. Georgia State University. 1978. 194 pp. DAI 39/4. (October 1978). Page 2100-A. Order # 7817582.

1434. Roland, Carol M. The California Kindergarten Movement: A Study in Class and Social Feminism. Ph.D. Dissertation. University of California, Riverside. 1980. 249 pp. DAI 41/3. (September 1980). Page 1190-A. Order # 8020619.

1435. Scadron, Arlene W. The Formative Years: Childhood and Childrearing in Eighteenth Century Anglo-American Culture. Ph.D. Dissertation. University of California, Berkeley. 1979. 341 pp. DAI 40/7. (January 1980). Page 4199-A. Order # 8000507.

1436. Sweiger, Jill D. Conceptions of Children in American Juvenile Periodicals: 1830-1870. Ed.D. Dissertation. Rutgers, the State

University. 1977. 285 pp. DAI 37/12. (June 1977). Page 7928-A.
Order # 77-13,474.

1437. Williams, Thomas C. The Dependent Child in Mississippi: A Social
History, 1900-1972. Ph.D. Dissertation. The Ohio State University.
1976. 307 pp. DAI 37/5. (November 1976). Page 3099-A. Order
76-24,708.

Press and Education

1438. Broissard, Walter R. An Isolation and Analysis of Educational Trends
Exhibited by the Lake Charles American Press Editorials, 1940-1975.
Ed.D. Dissertation. McNeese State University. 1977. 245 pp.
DAI 38/6. (December 1977). Page 3149-A. Order # 77-27,570.

1439. Carper, James C. The Published Opinions of Kansans Concerning
Education, 1854-1900. Ph.D. Dissertation. Kansas State University.
1977. 156 pp. DAI 38/6. (December 1977). Page 3331-A. Order
77-26,028.

1440. Hanrahan, Joanne M. Admonition and Nurture: Views of Childhood
and Youth in the American Periodical Press, 1820-1850. Ph.D. Dissertation. St. Louis University. 1979. 228 pp. DAI 40/5. (November 1979). Page 2762-A. Order # 7923826.

1441. Hartke, Leo M. Editorial Reaction of School Financing in Tucson and
Phoenix [Arizona] Metropolitan Daily Newspapers, 1950-1959. Ed.D.
Dissertation. University of Arizona, 1973. 264 pp. DAI 34/3.
(September 1973). Page 1000-A. Order # 73-20,647.

1442. MacLeod, James L. A Catalogue of References to Education in the
South Carolina Gazettres, Charleston, South Carolina, 1731-1770, and
Commentary. Ed.D. Dissertation. Mississippi State University.
1972. 240 pp. DAI 33/7. (January 1973). Page 3338-A. Order
73-150.

Private Schools

1443. Curry, Joseph R. Mount Hermon [Massachusetts] from 1881 to 1971:
An Historical Analysis of a Distinctive American Boarding School.
Ed.D. Dissertation. University of Massachusetts. 1972. 187 pp.
DAI 33/9. (March 1973). Page 4901-A. Order # 73-5238.

1444. Fuller, Lawrence B. Education for Leadership: The Emergence of
the College Preparatory School. Ph.D. Dissertation. Johns Hopkins
University. 1974. 465 pp. DAI 35/6. (December 1974). Page
3478-A. Order # 74-27,910.

1445. Heron, William J. The Growth of Private Schools and their Impact on
       the Public Schools of Alabama (1955-1975). Ed.D. Dissertation. Uni-
       versity of Alabama. 1977. 131 pp. DAI 39/1. (July 1978). Page
       80-A. Order # 7809859.

1446. Johnson, John J. A Historical Analysis of Attempts to Secure Public
       Funds for Nonpublic Schools in the State of New Jersey. Ed.D. Dis-
       sertation. Rutgers, the State University. 1978. 261 pp. DAI 39/5.
       (November 1978). Page 2746-A. Order # 7820326.

1447. Johnson, William B. A History of the Florida Council of Independent
       Schools, 1954-1972. Ed.D. Dissertation. University of Miami. 1976.
       236 pp. DAI 37/5. (November 1976). Page 2541-A. Order # 76-
       26,201.

1448. Mathis, Kenneth W. A Historical and Status Survey of Member Schools
       of the Mississippi Private School Association from 1957 until 1974.
       Ed.D. Dissertation. University of Mississippi. 1975. 143 pp. DAI
       36/7. (January 1976). Page 4661-A. Order # 76-458.

1449. McGrew, Elliott B. The Private School: A Study of an American
       Phenomenon [since the eighteenth century]. Ph.D. Dissertation.
       University of Minnesota. 1971. 366 pp. DAI 33/1. (July 1972).
       Page 177-A. Order # 72-14,416.

1450. McLeod II, John P. The New England Boarding School: An Analysis
       of its Historical Development and Contemporary Uncertainty of Pur-
       pose. Ed.D. Dissertation. University of Massachusetts. 1973.
       192 pp. DAI 34/10. (April 1974). Page 6315-A. Order # 74-8615.

1451. Steeley, Robert J. A History of Independent Education in South
       Carolina [eighteenth century to the present]. Ed.D. Dissertation.
       University of South Carolina. 1979. 122 pp. DAI 40/11. (May
       1980). Page 5760-A. Order # 8011247.

Psychology/Testing

1452. Behling, Calvin C. A History and Analysis of Educational Assessment
       in the United States. Ed.D. Dissertation. Wayne State University.
       1980. 185 pp. DAI 41/4. (October 1980). Page 1442-A. Order #
       8022807.

1453. Chapman, Paul Davis. Schools as Sorters: Louis M. Terman and the
       Intelligence Testing Movement, 1890-1930. Ph.D. Dissertation. Stan-
       ford University. 1980. 264 pp. DAI 40/11. (May 1980). Page
       5759-A. Order # 8011615.

1454. Echols, James P. The Rise of the Evaluation Movement, 1920-1942.
       Ph.D. Dissertation. Stanford University. 1973. 436 pp. DAI 34/3.
       (September 1973). Page 1108-A. Order # 73-20,471.

1455. Hainer, Frank T. A Critical Analysis of the Thought of Edward L.

Thorndike: The Logical Status of "Scientific" Claims in Education.
Ph.D. Dissertation. University of Pittsburgh. 1977. 290 pp. DAI
38/12. (June 1978). Page 7205-A. Order # 7809585.

1456. Hazlett, James A. A History of the National Assessment of Educational
Progress, 1963-1973: A Look at Some of the Conflicting Ideas and
Issues in Contemporary American Education. Ed.D. Dissertation.
University of Kansas. 1974. 423 pp. DAI 35/9. (March 1975).
Page 5887-A. Order # 75-6135.

1457. Marks, Russell. Testers, Trackers and Trustees: The Ideology of
the Intelligence Testing Movement in America, 1900-1954. Ph.D. Dissertation. University of Illinois. 1972. 193 pp. DAI 34/2. (August 1973). Page 593-A. Order # 73-17,311.

1458. McCormick, Dean R. The Controversial Development of the Michigan
Educational Assessment Program, 1969-1977. Ph.D. Dissertation.
Michigan State University. 1978. 195 pp. DAI 39/7. (January
1979). Page 4090-A. Order # 7900720.

1459. McDermott, Jr., John William. The Controversy Over Ability Group-
ing in American Education, 1916-1970. Ed.D. Dissertation. Temple
University. 1976. 360 pp. DAI 37/4. (October 1976). Page 2026-
A. Order # 76-22,056.

1460. McNasby, James J. Educational Testing Service and the Exercise of
Power and Influence in American Education, 1947-1977. Ed.D. Dissertation. Rutgers, the State University. 1978. 361 pp. DAI
40/1. (July 1979). Page 216-A. Order # 7914125.

1461. Merideth, Donald C. A Status Study of the Use of Ability Grouping
in American Schools Between 1867 and 1981. Ph.D. Dissertation.
University of Nebraska. 1981. 220 pp. DAI 42/11. (May 1982).
Page 4707-A. Order # 8208368.

1462. Noble, Gilbert L. Joseph Mayer Rice: Critic of the Public Schools
and Pioneer in Modern Educational Measurement. Ph.D. Dissertation.
State University of New York, Buffalo. 1970. 342 pp. DAI 31/9.
(March 1970). Page 4503-A. Order # 71-6100.

1463. Norton, Rita J. Private Foundations and the Development of Stand-
ardized Tests, 1900-1935. Ed.D. Dissertation. University of Massachusetts. 1980. 184 pp. DAI 41/8. (February 1981). Page 3455-
A. Order # 8101374.

1464. O'Donnell, John M. The Origins of Behaviorism: American Psychology,
1870-1920. Ph.D. Dissertation. University of Pennsylvania. 1979.
682 pp. DAI 40/6. (December 1979). Page 3493-A. Order #
7828159.

1465. O'Shea, Joseph A. An Inquiry into the Development of the University
of Chicago Evaluation Movement. Ph.D. Dissertation. University of
Illinois. 1979. 275 pp. DAI 40/8. (February 1980). Page 4444-A.
No Order #.

1466. Pozovich, Gregory J. Functional Psychology and its Influence upon

the Emergence of the Mental Measurement Movement, 1870-1910.
Ph.D. Dissertation. Southern Illinois University. 1978. 230 pp.
DAI 39/4. (October 1978). Page 2101-A. Order # 7817541.

1467. Sattar, Ellen M. A Half-Century of Ability Grouping: An Evaluation
of its Development in the United States. Ed.D. Dissertation. Boston
University. 1970. 246 pp. DAI 31/12. (June 1971). Page 6375-A.
Order # 71-3966.

1468. Slegeski, Ignatius J.M. A History of Behavioral Technology Prior to
1938. Ph.D. Dissertation. The Ohio State University. 1979.
170 pp. DAI 40/4. (October 1979). Page 1922-A. Order #
7922561.

1469. Sokal, Michael M. The Educational and Psychological Career of James
McKeen Cattell, 1860-1904. Ph.D. Dissertation. Case Western Reserve University. 1972. 683 pp. DAI 33/9. (March 1973). Page
5106-A.

1470. Sulman, A. Michael. The Freudianization of the American Child: The
Impact of Psychoanalysis in Popular Periodical Literature in the
United States, 1919-1939. Ph.D. Dissertation. University of Pitts-
burgh. 1972. 162 pp. DAI 33/8. (February 1973). Page 4322-A.
Order # 73-5007.

1471. Thigpen, Carole M. The Development and Evolution of the Eight Year
Study. Ph.D. Dissertation. University of North Carolina. 1978.
194 pp. DAI 39/7. DAI 39/7. (January 1979). Page 4091-A.
Order # 7900509.

1472. Thomas, William B. Black Education and Intelligence Testing: The
Case of the South and the Educational and Vocational Guidance of
Blacks, 1920-1950. Ph.D. Dissertation. State University of New
York, Buffalo. 1978. 373 pp. DAI 39/2. (August 1978). Page
722-A. Order # 7810668.

1473. Weinland, Thomas P. A History of the I.Q. in America, 1890-1941.
Ph.D. Dissertation. Columbia University. 1970. 364 pp. DAI
33/10. (April 1973). Page 5666-A. Order # 73-8991.

1474. Wyman, Sharon O. A History of the National Study of School Evaluation, 1933-1978. Ed.D. Dissertation. Indiana University. 1978.
147 pp. DAI 39/9. (March 1979). Page 5436-A. Order #
7905981.

Reading/Children's Literature

1475. Blue, Gladys F. The Aging as Portrayed in Realistic Fiction for Children, 1945-1975. Ph.D. Dissertation. University of Akron. 1977.
296 pp. DAI 38/5. (November 1977). Page 2711-A. Order # 77-
23,440.

1476. Bruton, Antoinette L. A Review of Reading Comprehension Research
       in Journals from 1900 through 1975. Ed.D. Dissertation. University
       of Tennessee. 1977. 271 pp. DAI 38/7. (January 1978). Page
       3903-A. Order # 77-27,645.

1477. DeLonas, John W. The Struggle for Reading as Seen in American
       Magazines (1741-1840). Ph.D. Dissertation. Michigan State Univer-
       sity. 1976. 259 pp. DAI 37/2. (August 1976). Page 705-A.
       Order # 76-18,610.

1478. Kasen, Jill H. Portraits from the Dream: The Myth of Success in
       the Comic Strip, 1925-1975. Ph.D. Dissertation. Rutgers, the State
       University. 1978. 441 pp. DAI 39/10. (April 1979). Page 6341-
       A. Order # 7901276.

1479. Koss, Helen G. A Comparison of Sexism in Trade Books for Primary
       Children, 1950-1953 and 1970-1973. Ph.D. Dissertation. University
       of Connecticut. 1979. 176 pp. DAI 40/2. (August 1979). Page
       647-A. Order # 7914166.

1480. Lee, Elaine J. A Comparative Thematic Categorical Survey of Chil-
       dren's Publications in England and America from 1744 to 1850. Ed.D.
       Dissertation. Temple University. 1976. 1357 pp. DAI 37/4. (Oc-
       tober 1976). Page 1975-A. Order # 76-22,051.

1481. Levstik, Linda S.T. Refuge and Reflection: American Children's
       Literature as Social History, 1920-1940. Ph.D. Dissertation. The
       Ohio State University. 1980. 339 pp. DAI 41/1. (July 1980).
       Page 98-A. Order # 8015900.

1482. Monaghan, Edith J. Noah Webster's Speller, 1783-1843: Causes of
       its Success as a Reading Text. Ed.D. Dissertation. Yeshiva Uni-
       versity. 1980. 603 pp. DAI 41/4. (October 1980). Page 2511-
       A. Order # 8021251.

1483. Nesteby, James R. The Tarzan Series of Edgar Rice Burroughs:
       Lost Races and Racism in American Popular Culture. Ph.D. Disser-
       tation. Bowling Green State University. 1978. 263 pp. DAI 39/7.
       (January 1979). Page 4347-A. Order # 7901450.

1484. Nist, Joan I.S. The Mildred L. Batcheldor Award Books, 1968-1977:
       A Decade of Honored Children's Literature in Translation. Ed.D.
       Dissertation. Auburn University. 1977. 156 pp. DAI 38/8.
       (February 1978). Page 4633-A. Order # 7730436.

1485. Pelosi, Peter L. The Origins and Development of Reading Diagnosis
       in the United States: 1896-1946. Ed.D. Dissertation. State Uni-
       versity of New York, Buffalo. 1977. 435 pp. DAI 39/3. (Septem-
       ber 1978). Page 1301-A. Order # 7813986.

1486. Wall, Margaret E. Puritanism in Education: An Analysis of the Tran-
       sition from Religiosity to Secular Morality as Seen in Primary Reading
       Materials, 1660-1775. Ph.D. Dissertation. Washington University.
       1979. 363 pp. DAI 40/7. (January 1980). Page 3831-A. Order #
       8002468.

1487. Williamson, Mary A.L. The History of the Henkel Press [early 19th century German-language newspaper near Baltimore--publisher of children's books] and Impact on Children's Literature. Ed.D. Dissertation. University of Virginia. 1977. 417 pp. DAI 39/7. (January 1979). Page 3935-A. Order # 7901144.

1488. Worth, Barbara S. Achievement and Affiliation Motives of Male and Female Characters in Realistic Fiction for Children, 1945-1975. Ph.D. Dissertation. New York University. 1977. 159 pp. DAI 38/10. (April 1978). Page 5917-A. Order # 7803045.

Religious Education

1489. Aldstadt, Robert H. A Documentary Analysis of Two Major Denominational Periodicals, The Lutheran and Presbyterian Life, on Issues in American Precollege Education, 1963-1970. Ph.D. Dissertation. University of Pittsburgh. 1975. 419 pp. DAI 36/12. (June 1976). Page 7906-A. Order # 76-14,101.

1490. Allen, Madeline M. An Historical Study of Moravian Education in North Carolina: The Evolution and Practice of the Moravian Concept of Education as it is Applied to Women. Ph.D. Dissertation. Florida State University. 1971. 223 pp. DAI 32/9. (March 1972). Page 4998-A. Order # 72-10,014.

1491. Archibald, Helen A. George Albert Coe: Theorist for Religious Education in the Twentieth Century. Ph.D. Dissertation. University of Illinois. 1975. 350 pp. DAI 36/5. (November 1975). Page 2680-A. Order # 75-24,247.

1492. Ballweg, George E. The Growth in the Number and Population of Christian Schools Since 1966: A Profile of Parental Views Concerning Factors which Led them to Enroll their Children in a Christian School. Ed.D. Dissertation. Boston University. 1980. 287 pp. DAI 41/5. (November 1980). Page 2040-A. Order # 8024075.

1493. Barger, Robert N. John Lancaster Spalding: Catholic Educator and Social Emissary. Ph.D. Dissertation. University of Illinois. 1976. 271 pp. DAI 37/10. (April 1977). Page 6311-A. Order # 77-8930.

1494. Barrick, William E. Field Education in Protestant Theological Seminaries in the United States: An Interpretation of Major Trends, 1920-1970. Ed.D. Dissertation. Columbia University. 1975. 190 pp. DAI 36/3. (September 1975). Page 1341-A. Order # 75-20,186.

1495. Benkart, Paula K. Religion, Family, and Community Among Hungarians Migrating to American Cities, 1880-1930. Ph.D. Dissertation. Johns Hopkins University. 1975. 255 pp. DAI 39/5. (November 1978). Page 3080-A. Order # 7821951.

1496. Benson, Warren S. A History of the National Association of Christian Schools During the Period of 1947-1972. Ph.D. Dissertation. Loyola University, Chicago. 1975. 199 pp. DAI 36/1. (July 1975). Page 158-A. Order # 75-14,500.

1497. Bittar, Helen. The Y.W.C.A. of the City of New York: 1870-1920. Ph.D. Dissertation. New York University. 1979. 267 pp. DAI 40/6. (December 1979). Page 3484-A. Order # 7925442.

1498. Blackburn, James C. The Role of the Church-Related College in Higher Education: An Analysis of Four Evangelical Christian Colleges in Central Indiana [Taylor, Goshen, Marion and Anderson]. Ph.D. Dissertation. Miami University. 1979. 199 pp. DAI 40/3. (September 1979). Page 1645-A. Order # 7920296.

1499. Blanchette, Claudia A. Social Justice: Mandate and Dilemma for Roman Catholic Religious Education in the Light of the Second Vatican Council. Ph.D. Dissertation. Boston University. 1979. 190 pp. DAI 40/5. (November 1979). Page 2574-A. Order # 7923919.

1500. Boylan, Anne M. The Nursery in the Church: Evangelical Protestant Sunday Schools, 1820-1880. Ph.D. Dissertation. University of Wisconsin. 1973. 366 pp. DAI 34/6. (December 1973). Page 3287-A. Order # 73-20,981.

1501. Brady, Brian J. The Congregation for Catholic Education, the Catholic School and the Thought of Jacques Maritain. Ed.D. Dissertation. Columbia University. 1979. 248 pp. DAI 39/12. (June 1979). Page 7260-A. Order # 7913183.

1502. Bruggemann, Reverend Walter O. Ethos and Ecumenism: The History of Eden [Missouri] Theological Seminary, 1925-1970. Ph.D. Dissertation. St. Louis University. 1974. 290 pp. DAI 35/5. (November 1974). Page 2737-A. Order # 74-24,051.

1503. Chanover, Hyman. A History of the National Board of License for Teachers and Supervisory Personnel in American Jewish Schools: The Struggle to Improve the Quality of Instruction in Jewish Schools in the United States. Ed.D. Dissertation. New York University. 1971. 449 pp. DAI 32/10. (April 1972). Page 5578-A. Order # 72-11,488.

1504. Clark, Carol L. The Effect of Secular Education upon Mormon Relief Society Curriculum, 1914-1940. Ph.D. Dissertation. University of Utah. 1979. 232 pp. DAI 40/11. (May 1980). Page 5759-A. Order # 8010658.

1505. Clement III, Stephen M. Aspects of Student Religion at Vassar College, 1861-1914. Ed.D. Dissertation. Harvard University. 1977. 292 pp. DAI 38/8. (February 1978). Page 4620-A. Order # 7732060.

1506. Coleman, Michael C. Presbyterian Missionaries and their Attitudes to the American Indians, 1837-1893. Ph.D. Dissertation. University of Pennsylvania. 1977. 319 pp. DAI 38/8. (February 1978). Page 5003-A. Order # 7730187.

1507. Combs Jr., Kermit S. The Course of Religious Education at the South-
       ern Baptist Theological Seminary, 1902-1953: A Historical Study.
       Ed.D. Dissertation. The Southern Baptist Theological Seminary.
       1978. 349 pp. DAI 39/2. (August 1978). Page 794-A. Order #
       7814243.

1508. Crandall, Robert A. The Sunday School as an Instructional Agency
       for Religious Instruction in American Protestantism, 1872-1922.
       Ph.D. Dissertation. Notre Dame University. 1977. 235 pp. DAI
       38/3. (September 1977). Page 1317-A. Order # 77-19,144.

1509. Croghan, Penelope P. Moral Universe as Portrayed in Third Grade
       Readers [1960's-1970's]. Ph.D. Dissertation. Northwestern Univer-
       sity. 1979. 200 pp. DAI 40/6. (December 1979). Page 3553-A.
       Order # 7927322.

1510. Davis, James M. Frontier and Religious Influences on Higher Educa-
       tion: 1796-1860. Ed.D. Dissertation. Northern Illinois University.
       1975. 226 pp. DAI 36/10. (April 1976). Page 6517-A. Order #
       76-8909.

1511. DeBolt, Thomas H. Presbyterian Educational Institutions in Virginia,
       1740-1785. Ph.D. Dissertation. George Peabody College for Teach-
       ers. 1976. 267 pp. DAI 37/4. (October 1976). Page 2381-A.
       Order # 76-21,623.

1512. Deschamps, Nello E. The Secularization of American Higher Educa-
       tion: The Relationship Between Religion and the University as Per-
       ceived by Selected University Presidents, 1867-1913. Ph.D. Disser-
       tation. University of Southern California. 1976. n.p. DAI 37/3.
       (September 1976). Page 1424-A. No Order #.

1513. DiMichele, Charles C. The History of the Roman Catholic Educational
       System in Mississippi. Ed.D. Dissertation. Mississippi State Univer-
       sity. 1973. 217 pp. DAI 34/8. (February 1974). Page 4813-A.
       Order # 74-2915.

1514. Dorr, Ronald F. Death Education in McGuffey's Readers, 1836-1896.
       Ph.D. Dissertation. University of Minnesota. 1979. 416 pp. DAI
       40/6. (December 1979). Page 3377-A. Order # 7926117.

1515. Eisikovits, Rikva A. The Sisters of Our Lady of Charity of the Good
       Shepherd, 1835-1977: A Study in Cultural Adaptation. Ph.D. Dis-
       sertation. University of Minnesota. 1978. 248 pp. DAI 39/2.
       (August 1978). Page 627-A. Order # 7813392.

1516. Engels, Leo J. A Study of Catholic Education in Oklahoma with Spe-
       cial Emphasis on the Dioceses of Oklahoma City and Tulsa (1875-1970).
       Ed.D. Dissertation. Tulsa University. 1971. 182 pp. DAI 32/8.
       (February 1972). Page 4277-A. Order # 72-6048.

1517. Epstein, David H. A Model for Educational Supervision Drawn from
       Classical Jewish Sources. Ph.D. Dissertation. 1978. 200 pp. DAI
       38/11. (May 1978). Page 6429-A. Order # 7804953.

1518. Freese, Doris A. The Role of the Sunday School Conventions in the

Preparation of Protestant Sunday School Teachers, 1832-1903. Ph.D. Dissertation. Loyola University, Chicago. 1979. 251 pp. DAI 40/4. (October 1979). Page 1920-A. Order # 7921786.

1519. Gabert, Glen H. A History of the Roman Catholic Parochial School System in the United States: A Documentary Interpretation. Ph.D. Dissertation. Loyola University, Chicago. 1971. 205 pp. DAI 32/5. (November 1971). Page 2451-A. Order # 71-28,121.

1520. Ganss, Karl P. American Catholic Education in the 1960's: A Study of the Parochial School Debate. Ph.D. Dissertation. Loyola University, Chicago. 1979. 177 pp. DAI 39/11. (May 1979). Page 6585-A. Order # 7910331.

1521. Harper, James C. A Study of Alabama Baptist Higher Education and Fundamentalism, 1890-1930. Ph.D. Dissertation. University of Alabama. 1977. 148 pp. DAI 39/6. (December 1978). Page 3399-A. Order # 7819177.

1522. Harris, Daniel S. Activism and [7th Day] Adventist Higher Education. Ed.D. Dissertation. University of Southern California. 1974. 313 pp. DAI 35/1. (July 1974). Page 216-A. Order # 74-14,444.

1523. Havner, Carter S. The Reaction of Yale to the Great Awakening, 1740-1766. Ph.D. Dissertation. University of Texas. 38/12. (June 1978). Page 7511-A. Order # 7807314.

1524. Hayes, Donald P. The Iowa Amish and their Education. Ph.D. Dissertation. University of Iowa. 1972. 113 pp. DAI 33/7. (January 1973). Page 3336-A. Order # 73-637.

1525. Higgins Jr., George L. The Louisiana Baptist Convention and Christian Education, 1893-1956. Ed.D. Dissertation. Oklahoma State University. 1971. 250 pp. DAI 33/2. (August 1972). Page 587-A. Order # 72-21,890.

1526. High, Juanita J. Black Colleges as Social Intervention: The Development of Higher Education within the African Methodist Episcopal Church [1786-1976]. Ed.D. Dissertation. Rutgers, the State University. 1978. 251 pp. DAI 39/1. (July 1978). Page 160-A. Order # 7810230.

1527. Hook, Milton R. The Avondale School and [7th Day] Adventist Educational Goals, 1894-1900. Ed.D. Dissertation. Andrews University. 1978. 357 pp. DAI 39/12. (June 1979). Page 7194-A. Order # 7912439.

1528. Hunt, Thomas C. Catholic Educational Policy and the Decline of Protestant Influence in Wisconsin's Schools During the Late Nineteenth Century. Ph.D. Dissertation. University of Wisconsin. 1971. 445 pp. DAI 32/8. (February 1972). Page 4389-A. Order # 72-1035.

1529. Jaffe, Bernette K. The Evolution of Jewish Religious Education in America in the Twentieth Century. Ph.D. Dissertation. Case Western Reserve University. 1980. 291 pp. DAI 41/4. (October 1980). Page 1516-A. Order # 8021698.

1530. Johnson, Tony W. The Old Moral Philosophy Course: Its Contemporary Legacy [1750-1870]. Ph.D. Dissertation. George Peabody College for Teachers. 1978. 182 pp. DAI 39/11. (May 1979). Page 6586-A. Order # 7909920.

1531. Kallam, James G. A History of the African Evangelical Fellowship from its Inception to 1917. Ph.D. Dissertation. New York University. 1978. 255 pp. DAI 39/12. (June 1979). Page 7261-A. Order # 7911247.

1532. Kearney, Anna R. James A. Burns, C.S.C.--Educator. Ph.D. Dissertation. Notre Dame University. 1975. 218 pp. DAI 36/3. (September 1975). Page 1344-A. Order # 75-19,940.

1533. Kincheloe, Joe L. The Antebellum Southern Evangelical and State-Supported Colleges: A Comparative Study. Ed.D. Dissertation. University of Tennessee. 1980. 225 pp. DAI 41/5. (November 1980). Page 1978-A. Order # 8024917.

1534. Klein, Christa R. The Jesuits and Catholic Boyhood in Nineteenth Century New York City: A Study of St. John's College and the College of St. Francis Xavier, 1846-1912. Ph.D. Dissertation. University of Pennsylvania. 1976. 410 pp. DAI 37/11. (May 1977). Page 7181-A. Order # 77-10,180.

1535. Kramer, Daniel Z. The History of the Impact of Torah Umesorah and Hebrew Day Schools in America. Ph.D. Dissertation. Yeshiva University. 1976. 392 pp. DAI 37/3. (September 1976). Page 1721-A. Order # 76-19,941.

1536. Kuhr, Nancy J.N. Catholic Parochial Schools in the Austin [Texas] Diocese: Background, Development Since 1849, and Present Status. Ph.D. Dissertation. University of Texas. 1974. 222 pp. DAI 35/5. (November 1974). Page 2739-A. Order # 74-24,888.

1537. Kunkel C.S.F.N., Sister Norlene M. Bishop Bernard J. McQuaid [1st Bishop of Rochester, N.Y. in late 19th and early 20th centuries] and Catholic Education. Ph.D. Dissertation. University of Notre Dame. 1974. 283 pp. DAI 35/4. (October 1974). Page 2025-A. Order # 74-20,588.

1538. La Monte, Ruth B. Early Maryland Educators: The Colonials, the Catholics and the Carrolls. Ph.D. Dissertation. The Ohio State University. 1976. 238 pp. DAI 37/2. (August 1976). Page 844-A. Order # 76-18,001.

1539. Loren, Morris J. Hebrew Higher Educational Institutions in the United States, 1830-1975. Ph.D. Dissertation. Wayne State University. 1976. 199 pp. DAI 37/2. (August 1976). Page 835-A. Order # 76-17,327.

1540. Leutmer O.S.B., Sister Nora. The History of Catholic Education in the Present Diocese of St. Cloud, Minnesota, 1855-1865. Ph.D. Dissertation. University of Minnesota. 1970. 561 pp. DAI 31/10. (April 1971). Page 5161-A. Order # 71-8180.

1541. Lukonic, Joseph L. "Evangelicals in the City": Evangelical Protes-
      tant Social Concerns in Early Chicago, 1837-1860. Ph.D. Dissertation.
      University of Wisconsin. 1979. 220 pp. DAI 40/6. (December
      1979). Page 3490-A. Order # 7922819.

1542. Malizia, Gennaro A. The Effects of Vatican Council II on Catholic
      Education. Ph.D. Dissertation. University of Arizona. 1972. 256
      pp. DAI 33/12. (June 1973). Page 6705-A. Order # 73-13,317.

1543. Mattice, Howard L. The Growth and Development of Roman Catholic
      Education in New York City, 1842-1875. Ed.D. Dissertation. New
      York University. 1979. 261 pp. DAI 39/12. (June 1979). Page
      7195-A. Order # 7911276.

1544. Mc Cord, David M. Sunday School and Public School: An Explora-
      tion of their Relationship with Special Reference to Indiana, 1790-
      1860. Ph.D. Dissertation. Purdue University. 1976. 206 pp.
      DAI 37/8. (February 1977). Page 4913-A. Order # 77-1744.

1545. Medlin, Stuart B. The Founding of the Permanent Denominational
      Colleges in Virginia, 1776-1861. Ed.D. Dissertation. College of
      William and Mary. 1976. 143 pp. DAI 36/11. (May 1976). Page
      7248-A. Order # 76-11,177.

1546. Meighan R.S.M., Sister Cecilia. Nativism and Catholic Higher Educa-
      tion, 1840-1860. Ed.D. Dissertation. Columbia University. 1972.
      138 pp. DAI 33/5. (November 1972). Page 2130-A. Order #
      72-30,340.

1547. Meyer, Paul W. History and Philosophy of Education in the Lutheran
      Church--Missouri Synod, 1920-1940. Ed.D. Dissertation. Wayne
      State University. 1972. 507 pp. DAI 33/5. (November 1972).
      Page 2141-A. Order # 72-28,466.

1548. Morriss, Barbara L. The Defense of a Catholic University: The 1965
      Crisis at St. John's. Ed.D. Dissertation. Columbia University.
      1977. 326 pp. DAI 38/10. (April 1978). Page 5965-A. Order #
      7804463.

1561. Schrag, Lester D. Elementary and Secondary Education as Practiced
      by Kansas Mennonites [1874- ca. 1974]. Ed.D. Dissertation. Uni-
      versity of Wyoming. 1970. 234 pp. DAI 33/3. (September 1972).
      Page 1002-A. Order # 72-13,046.

1562. Schuler, Paul J. The Reaction of American Catholics to the Founda-
      tions and Early Practices of Progressive Education in the United
      States, 1892-1917. Ph.D. Dissertation. University of Notre Dame.
      1971. 437 pp. DAI 32/1. (July 1971). Page 214-A. Order #
      71-19,087.

1563. Scott, Noel W. The Schools of the Church of God (Holiness): A
      Historical Study [1890's to ca. 1974]. Ph.D. Dissertation. Univer-
      sity of Missouri. 1973. DAI 35/2. (August 1974). Page 860-A.
      Order # 74-18,637.

1564. Shanabruck, Charles H. The Catholic Church's Role in the Americanization of Chicago's Immigrants: 1833-1928 (2 Vols.). Ph.D. Dissertation. University of Chicago. 1975. n.p. DAI 36/7. (January 1976). Page 4718-A. No Order #.

1565. Sicius, Francis J. The Chicago Catholic Worker Movement, 1936 to the Present. Ph.D. Dissertation. Loyola University, Chicago, 1979. 326 pp. DAI 39/11. (May 1979). Page 6922-A. Order # 7910350.

1566. Skirball, Henry F. Isaac Baer Berkson and Jewish Education [1891-1975]. Ed.D. Dissertation. Columbia University. 1977. 339 pp. DAI 38/3. (September 1977). Page 2022-A. Order # 77-22,300.

1567. Sohn, Frederick H. The Evolution of Catholic Education in the Diocese of Rochester, New York, 1868 to 1970. Ed.D. Dissertation. Indiana University. 1972. 234 pp. DAI 33/11. (May 1973). Page 6149-A. Order # 73-10,785.

1568. Stein, David T. The Evolution of Policy Development for Programs of Higher Education in the Lutheran Church, Missouri Synod, and its Relationship to Internal and External Governance, 1944-1975. Ph.D. Dissertation. St. Louis University. 1979. 375 pp. DAI 40/5. (November 1979). Page 2509-A. Order # 7923683.

1569. Stevens, Michael E. The Ideas and Attitudes of Protestant Missionaries to the North American Indians, 1643-1776. Ph.D. Dissertation. University of Wisconsin. 1978. 385 pp. DAI 39/3. (September 1978). Page 1791-A. Order # 7811743.

1570. Stewart, Sonja M. John Heyl Vincent: His Theory and Practice of Protestant Religious Education from 1855-1920. Ph.D. Dissertation. University of Notre Dame. 1977. 222 pp. DAI 38/3. (September 1977). Page 1319-A. Order # 77-19,153.

1571. Tappan, Richard E. The Dominance of Men in the Domain of Women: The History of Four Protestant Church Training Schools, 1880-1918. Ed.D. Dissertation. Temple University. 1979. 351 pp. DAI 40/5. (November 1979). Page 2516-A. Order # 7924082.

1572. Twedt, Edgar E. The Controversy Among Lutherans in the United States Over Public Funds to Church Schools, 1960-1969. Ph.D. Dissertation. Michigan State University. 1970. 259 pp. DAI 32/1. (July 1971). Page 216-A. Order # 71-18,312.

1573. Vandever, Jr., William T. An Educational History of the English and American Baptists in the Seventeenth and Eighteenth Centuries. Ph.D. Dissertation. University of Pennsylvania. 1974. 523 pp. DAI 36/1. (July 1975). Page 161-A. Order # 75-14,633.

1574. Van Dyke, Gerard. A Study of the History and Development of the Secondary School in the Reformed Church of America: An Examination of the Influences of Secular Educational Developments on Religious Education from 1870-1910. Ed.D. Dissertation. Rutgers, the State University. 1979. 284 pp. DAI 40/11. (May 1980). Page 5761-A. Order # 8011434.

1575. Walch, Timothy G. Catholic Education in Chicago and Milwaukee,

1840-1890. Ph.D. Dissertation. Northwestern University. 1975.
249 pp. DAI 36/12. (June 1976). Page 7908-A. Order # 76-12,170.

1576. Warlick, Kenneth R. Practical Religion and the Negro College in
North Carolina, 1880-1930. Ph.D. Dissertation. University of North
Carolina. Chapel Hill. 1980. 467 pp. DAI 41/4. (October 1980).
Page 1444-A. Order # 8022522.

1577. Welch, Eloise T. The Background and Development of the American
Missionary Association's Decision to Educate Freedmen in the South,
with Subsequent Repercussions for Higher Education. Ph.D. Dissertation. Bryn Mawr College. 1976. 205 pp. DAI 37/10. (April
1977). Page 6314-A. Order # 776542.

1578. White, Joseph M. Religion and Community: Cincinnati Germans,
1814-1870. Ph.D. Dissertation. University of Notre Dame. 1980.
391 pp. DAI 41/3. (September 1980). Page 1192-A. Order #
8020972.

1579. Wimberly III, Ware W. Missionary Reforms in Indiana, 1826-1860:
Education, Temperance, Antislavery. Ph.D. Dissertation. Indiana
University. 1977. 321 pp. DAI 38/3. (September 1977). Page
2313-A. Order # 77-22,682.

1580. Winkleman, Gerald G. Polemics, Prayers, and Professionalization:
The American Protestant Theological Seminaries from 1784 to 1920.
Ph.D. Dissertation. State University of New York, Buffalo. 1975.
412 pp. DAI 36/11. (May 1976). Page 7249-A. Order # 76-9132.

Special Education

1581. Cooper, Richard J. A Legislative History of Special Education in
Pennsylvania [early 20th century to present]. Ph.D. Dissertation.
University of Pittsburgh. 1979. 207 pp. DAI 40/5. (November
1979). Page 2514-A. Order # 7924706.

1582. Hildenbrand, Suzanne. Democracy's Aristocrat: The Gifted Child
in America, 1910-1960. Ph.D. Dissertation. University of California,
Berkeley. 1978. 347 pp. DAI 40/1. (July 1979). Page 132-A.
Order # 7914637.

Teachers, Teaching, Etc.

1583. Bain, George W. Liberal Teacher: The Writings of Max Lerner,
1925-1965. Ph.D. Dissertation. University of Minnesota. 1975.
315 pp. DAI 36/6. (December 1975). Page 3691-A. Order # 75-
27,132.

1584.   Berlowitz, Marvin J. Teachers--'Professionals' or Estranged Labor?
        A Study of the Career Patterns of Buffalo School Teachers During
        the Period 1956-1963. Ph.D. Dissertation. State University of New
        York, Buffalo. 1971. 62 pp. DAI 32/6. (December 1971). Page
        2896-A. Order # 72-210.

1585.   Bystyoziensk, Jill M. The Status of Public School Teachers in Amer-
        ica: An Unfilled Quest for Professionalism. Ph.D. Dissertation.
        State University of New York, Buffalo. 1979. 282 pp. DAI 40/5.
        (November 1979). Page 2918-A. Order # 7925076.

1586.   Capps, Barbara H. Composition Instruction in Elementary Teacher
        Training Programs, 1886-1926. Ed.D. Dissertation. Indiana Uni-
        versity. 1973. 323 pp. DAI 34/8. (February 1974). Page 4812-
        A. Order # 74-2629.

1587.   Clough, Dick B. A History of Teachers' Institutes in Tennessee,
        1875-1915. Ed.D. Dissertation. Memphis State University. 1972.
        249 pp. DAI 33/10. (April 1973). Page 5528-A. Order # 72-
        33,849.

1588.   Coles, James A. An Historical Study of the Teacher Evaluation Sys-
        tem of the Montgomery County Secondary Schools, 1953-1973. Ed.D.
        Dissertation. George Washington University. 1975. 404 pp. DAI
        36/4. (October 1975). Page 2071-A. Order # 75-23,404.

1589.   Donley, Marshall O. A Study of the Roots, Causes, and Directions
        of Teacher Miltancy in the United States. Ph.D. Dissertation.
        American University. 1971. 485 pp. DAI 32/3. (September 1971).
        Page 1216-A. Order # 71-24,944.

1590.   El-Bouhy, Farouk S.S. Secondary School Teachers' Perceptions of
        Pre-Service Teacher Education: A Comparative Study in the U.S.A.
        and Egypt. Ph.D. Dissertation. University of Pittsburgh. 1980.
        174 pp. DAI 41/3. (September 1980). Page 1027-A. Order #
        8018299.

1591.   Elmore, Kenneth C. Techniques Suggested for Teacher Evaluation,
        1890-1973. Ph.D. Dissertation. University of North Carolina. 1974.
        297 pp. DAI 35/6. (December 1974). Page 3477-A. Order # 74-
        26,872.

1592.   Englert, Richard M. California Policies for Teacher Employment Re-
        lations, 1930 to 1975. Ed.D. Dissertation. Universtiy of California,
        Los Angeles. 1976. 299 pp. DAI 37/3. (September 1976). Page
        1324-A. Order # 76-21,347.

1593.   Fagan, Rita A. A Social History of Teacher Militancy. Ph.D. Disser-
        tation. Marquette University. 1979. 304 pp. DAI 40/9. (March
        1980). Page 4927-A. Order # 8006527.

1594.   Farmaki, George L. The Role of the American Teacher: An Histor-
        ical View Through Readings [1776-1971]. Ph.D. Dissertation. Wayne
        State University. 1971. 661 pp. DAI 32/11. (May 1972). Page
        6163-A. Order # 72-14,553.

1595.   Finn, Richard P. An Historical Analysis of the Contributions of Samuel

Read Hall to Nineteenth Century Teacher Education. Ph.D. Dissertation. Boston College. 1970. 274 pp. DAI 31/6. (December 1970). Page 2714-A. Order # 70-24,600.

1596. Gould, David A. Policy and Pedagogues: School Reform and Teacher Professionalization in Massachusetts, 1840-1920. Ph.D. Dissertation. Brandeis University. 1977. 604 pp. DAI 37/12. (June 1977). Page 7919-A. Order # 77-13,372.

1597. Greenberg, Howard M. A History of the New York State Teachers Retirement System, 1960-1979. Ph.D. Dissertation. New York University. 1980. 527 pp. DAI 41/2. (August 1980). Page 566-A. Order # 8017501.

1598. Griffin, F.S.C., Brother Kevin J. A History of Teacher Education in the Seven Colleges Conducted by the American Christian Brothers. Ph.D. Dissertation. St. Louis University. 1976. 152 pp. DAI 37/4. (October 1976). Page 2121-A. Order # 76-22,542.

1599. Hale, James M. The Emergence of the Paraprofessional in America, 1950-1972. Ed.D. Dissertation. University of Georgia. 1973. 114 pp. DAI 34/9. (March 1974). Page 5563-A. Order # 74-4808.

1600. Hartzog, S.C., Sister Julia A. History of the Preparation of Teachers and Other Specialists in the Education of Exceptional Persons in the School of Education at the University of Pittsburgh. Ph.D. Dissertation. University of Pittsburgh. 1976. 304 pp. DAI 37/3. (September 1976). Page 1488-A. Order # 76-19,911.

1601. Heflin, William H. The Historical Development of Training Programs for Secondary Public School Teachers of Modern Foreign Languages in the United States to 1940. Ph.D. Dissertation. Florida State University. 1971. 282 pp. DAI 32/9. (March 1972). Page 5000-A. Order # 72-10,056.

1602. Homer, Patricia A.M. Rights of Teachers as Determined by Court Cases from 1970 to 1978. Ed.D. Dissertation. University of Pittsburgh. 1978. 168 pp. DAI 39/8. (February 1979). Page 4626-A. Order # 7902700.

1603. Jones, Jacqueline. The 'Great Opportunity': Northern Teachers and the Georgia Freedman, 1865-1873. Ph.D. Dissertation. University of Wisconsin. 1976. 475 pp. DAI 37/6. (December 1976). Page 3279-A. Order # 76-20,116.

1604. Landwermeyer, Francis M. Teacher Unionism--Chicago Style: A History of the Chicago Teachers Union, 1937-1972. Ph.D. Dissertation. University of Chicago. 1978. n.p. DAI 39/10. (April 1979). Page 5845. No Order #.

1605. LaPointe, Richard T. Ideology and Organization in Teacher Unionism. Ph.D. Dissertation. University of California, Los Angeles. 1976. 254 pp. DAI 37/1. (July 1976). Page 156-A. Order # 76-16,654.

1606. Mansfield, Betty. That Fateful Class: Black Teachers of Virginia's Freedmen, 1861-1882. Ph.D. Dissertation. The Catholic University of America. 1980. 391 pp. DAI 41/2. (August 1980). Page 773-A. Order # 8018356.

1607. Muraskin, Lana D. The Teacher Union of the City of New York from
        Inception to Schism, 1912-1935. Ph.D. Dissertation. University of
        California, Berkeley. 1979. 228 pp. DAI 40/7. (January 1980).
        Page 3828-A. Order # 8000454.

1608. Navarre, Jane P. The Female Teachers: The Beginnings of Teaching
        as a 'Women's Profession.' Ph.D. Dissertation. Bowling Green State
        University. 1977. 273 pp. DAI 38/11. (May 1978). Page 6571-A.
        Order # 7805370.

1609. Newman, Joseph W. A History of the Atlanta Public School Teacher's
        Association, Local 89 of the American Federation of Teachers, 1919-
        1956. Ph.D. Dissertation. Georgia State University. 1978. 308 pp.
        DAI 39/7. (January 1979). Page 4091-A. Order # 7900116.

1610. Price, Rebecca R. An Historical Analysis of the Concepts of Teachers
        in America Between the 1850's, 1930's and 1960's as Portrayed in the
        Writings of the Times. Ph.D. Dissertation. Miami University. 1974.
        194 pp. DAI 36/1. (August 1975). Page 751-A. Order # 75-14,317.

1611. Proctor, Jr., Ralph. Racial Discrimination Against Black Teachers
        and Black Professionals in the Pittsburgh Public School System, 1834-
        1973. Ph.D. Dissertation. University of Pittsburgh. 1979. 194 pp.
        DAI 40/5. (November 1979). Page 2819-A. Order # 7924678.

1612. Russell, Robert W. A Content Analysis of Models for Teacher Educa-
        tion Proposed in Selected Professional Journals, 1965-1975. Ph.D. Dis-
        sertation. University of Southern California. 1978. n.p. DAI
        39/2. (August 1978). Page 711-A. No Order #.

1613. Sanzare, James. A Study of Teacher Unionism in Philadelphia, 1941-
        1973: The Case of Local 3, Philadelphia Federation of Teachers.
        Ed.D. Dissertation. Temple University. 1977. 339 pp. DAI 37/12.
        (June 1977). Page 7676-A. Order # 77-13,523.

1614. Schweikert, Roman J. The Western Literacy Institute and College of
        Professional Teachers: An Instrument in the Creation of a Profession
        [1831-1845]. Ed.D. Dissertation. University of Cincinnati. 1971.
        167 pp. DAI 32/7. (January 1972). Page 3740-A. Order # 72-
        4313.

1615. Solley, Paul M. A Century of Elementary Teacher Education, 1875-
        1975 at Indiana University in Pennsylvania. D.ED. Dissertation.
        1976. 508 pp. DAI 38/9. (March 1978). Page 5296-A. Order #
        7720946.

1616. Stefanov, Jan (Joseph). The Training of Teachers at the University
        of Missouri Until 1930: A History. Ph.D. Dissertation. University
        of Missouri. 1972. 307 pp. DAI 33/9. (March 1973). Page 4902-
        A. Order # 73-7093.

1617. Stein, Sanford. A Study of the Activities of the Toledo Federation
        of Teachers in the Collective Bargaining Elections and Negotiations
        in 1967-1973. Ed.D. Dissertation. Toledo University. 1978. 137
        pp. DAI 39/6. (December 1978). Page 3419-A. Order # 7824530.

1618. Talbot, Alfred K. History of the Virginia Teachers Association, 1940-

1965. Ed.D. Dissertation. The College of William and Mary. 1981. 167 pp. DAI 42/11. (May 1982). Page 4745-A. Order # 8206544.

1619. Thompson, Richard L. A Historical and Legal Analysis of Textbook Certification in North Carolina. Ed.D. Dissertation. University of North Carolina, Greensboro. 1979. 231 pp. DAI 40/4. (October 1979). Page 2017-A. Order # 7922423.

1620. Trogdon, Ernest W. The Effect of the Civil Rights Law of 1871 on Teacher Dismissal. Ed.D. Dissertation. University of North Carolina, Greensboro. 1980. 119 pp. DAI 41/4. (October 1980). Page 1738-A. Order # 8021786.

1621. Twohy, David W. Harvey C. Minnick: An Historical Study of the Man and his Work as Influences on the Teacher Training Unit of Miami University. Ph.D. Dissertation. Miami University. 1979. 298 pp. DAI 40/7. (January 1980). Page 3831-A. Order # 8001431.

1622. Wagner, Lilya V. A Historical Base and Rationale for Peer Teaching. Ed.D. Dissertation. University of Florida. 1980. 235 pp. DAI 41/5. (November 1980). Page 2074-A. Order # 8025400.

1623. Weller, L. David. A History of Undergraduate Teacher Education at Iowa State University, 1869-1968. Ph.D. Dissertation. Iowa State University. 1975. 484 pp. DAI 36/10. (April 1976). Page 6520-A. Order # 76-9207.

1624. Wexler, Lillian K. Teacher Excellence in Oregon, 1955-1976: A Study of Selected Excellent Teachers. Ph.D. Dissertation. University of Oregon. 1977. 156 pp. DAI 38/10. (April 1978). Page 5900-A. Order # 7802575.

1625. White, Anita L. The Teacher in Texas: 1836-1879. Ed.D. Dissertation. Baylor University. 1972. 191 pp. DAI 33/9. (March 1973). Page 4904-A. Order # 73-7325.

1626. White, Woodie T. The Study of Education at the University of Chicago, 1892-1958. Ph.D. Dissertation. University of Chicago. 1977. n.p. DAI 38/8. (February 1978). Page 4987-A. No Order #.

1627. Wilson, Jr., Ben. History of Teacher Education at Southwest Texas State University. Ed.D. Dissertation. Baylor University. 1977. 206 pp. DAI 38/9. (March 1978). Page 5298-A. Order # 7801561.

1628. Williams, Shirley S. Student Teaching in the Chicago Public Schools, 1856-1964. Ed.D. Dissertation. George Peabody College for Teachers. 1972. 479 pp. DAI 33/7. (January 1973). Page 3171-A. Order # 72-34,198.

Tenure

1629. Ancell, Mary K.Z. Academic Tenure and the Courts: An Historical

and Legal Analysis of the Concept of Academic Tenure in United
States Higher Education. Ph.D. Dissertation. Stanford University.
1978. 174 pp. DAI 39/9. (March 1979). Page 5344-A. Order #
7905812.

1630. Ferguson, John A.M. The Development of Academic Tenure in Amer-
ican Higher Education, 1870-1915: Judicialization as a Response to a
Changing Academic Environment. Ph.D. Dissertation. University of
Michigan. 1976. 280 pp. DAI 37/10 (April 1977). Page 6298-A.
Order # 77-7913.

Textbooks

1631. Bicanichi, Thomas P. An Analysis of the Shorthand Textbook Used
in American High Schools Prior to 1900. Ed.D. Dissertation. University of Pittsburgh. 1970. 117 pp. DAI 31/5. (November 1970).
Page 2138-A. Order # 70-22,738.

1632. Durham, Jr., Kenneth R. A Survey of All American History Textbooks Adopted for the Public High Schools of Texas from 1919 to
1970. Ph.D. Dissertation. North Texas State University. 1971.
233 pp. DAI 32/7. (January 1972). Page 3737-A. Order # 74-
4073.

1633. Eichelman, Frederic R. A Study of the Virginia History and Government Textbook Controversy, 1948-1972. Ed.D. Dissertation. Virginia Polytechnic Institute. 1975. 164 pp. DAI 36/5. (November
1975). Page 2682. Order # 75-25,981.

1634. Emanuel, Gary L. An Analysis of the Textbook Treatment of the Re-
construction Period: Changes that Occurred Between Editions of
College Level Survey Textbooks. D.A. Dissertation. Carnegie-
Mellon University. 1979. 158 pp. DAI 40/5. (November 1979).
Page 2837-A. Order # 7925770.

1635. Fedyck, Micheline. Conceptions of Citizenship and Nationality in High
School American History Textbooks, 1913-1977. Ph.D. Dissertation.
Columbia University. 1980. 427 pp. DAI 41/2. (August 1980).
Page 565-A. Order # 8016945.

1636. Gill, Martin. Paul R. Hanna: The Evolution of an Elementary Social
Studies Textbook Series. Ph.D. Dissertation. Northwestern Univer-
sity. 1974. 178 pp. DAI 35/10. (April 1975). Page 6490-A.
Order # 75-7918.

1637. Milligram, Emerson. The Development of Business Communications
Textbooks Designed for American Undergraduate Schools. Ph.D.
Dissertation. University of Pittsburgh. 1973. 201 pp. DAI 34/7.
(January 1974). Page 3936-A. Order # 74-1534.

1638. Schipper, Martin C. The Rugg Textbook Controversy: A Study in
the Relationship Between Popular Political Thinking and Educational

Materials. Ph.D. Dissertation. New York University. 1979. 330 pp.
DAI 40/6. (December 1979). Page 3162-A. Order # 7925291.

1639. Schlereth, Wendy L.C. The Chap-Book: A Journal of American Intellectual Life in the 1890's. Ph.D. Dissertation. University of Iowa.
1980. 334 pp. DAI 41/4. (October 1980). Page 1736-A. Order #
8022068.

1640. Schmidt, Kenneth C. The Treatment of East Asia in World History
Textbooks. Ph.D. Dissertation. Syracuse University. 1974. 164
pp. DAI 36/10. (April 1976). Page 6519-A. Order # 76-7937.

1641. Shanoski, Theodore M. The Treatment of the Cold War in American
History Textbooks, 1960-1975. Ed.D. Dissertation. Temple Univer-
sity. 1977. 252 pp. DAI 38/3. (September 1977). Page 1938-A.
Order # 77-21,788.

1642. Stebbins, Gay. The School Publishing Industry and the Response of
Major Publishers to Curriculum Change in Selective Secondary Sub-
ject Matter Areas, 1958-1975: An Economic and Historical Analysis.
Ed.D. Dissertation. Columbia University. 1978. 263 pp. DAI
39/5. (November 1978). Page 2788-A. Order # 7821278.

1643. Tamashiro, Masamitsu. An Analysis of the Treatment of Selected As-
pects of United States-Japan Relation from 1905 to 1960 as Found in
High School History Textbooks of Both Nations. Ed.D. Dissertation.
New York University. 1972. 312 pp. DAI 33/4. (October 1972).
Page 1476-A. Order # 72-26,643.

1644. Voege, Herbert W. The Impact of Keynsian Ideas on Secondary
School Economics Textbooks of the United States. Ph.D. Dissertation.
University of Michigan. 1971. 445 pp. DAI 33/5. (November 1972).
Page 2092-A. Order # 72-29,233.

Theory and Philosophy

1645. Allen, Bernard L. John Dewey's Views on History, 1859-1952. Ph.D.
Dissertation. University of West Virginia. 1971. 238 pp. DAI 32/11.
(May 1972). Page 6325-A. Order # 72-14,060.

1646. Applebaum, Phyllis. The Growth of the Montessori Movement in the
United States, 1909-1970. Ph.D. Dissertation. 1971. New York University. 277 pp. DAI 32/10. (April 1972). Page 5578-A. Order
72-11,442.

1647. Appleton, Robert B. The Educational Thought of Sidney Hook: An
Interpretation of Major Themes. Ph.D. Dissertation. American Uni-
versity. 1974. 203 pp. DAI 35/8. (February 1975). Page 5048-
A. Order # 75-4697.

1648. Barney, Joseph A. The Educational Ideas of Irving Babbitt: Critical Humanism and American Higher Education. Ph.D. Dissertation.

Loyola University, Chicago. 1974. 256 pp. DAI 35/2. (August 1974). Page 856-A. Order # 74-16,934.

1649. Carew, Mary A. Selected Educational Ideas of Samuel L. Clemens [Mark Twain]. Ph.D. Dissertation. Michigan State University. 1972. 139 pp. DAI 33/5. (November 1972). Page 2138-A. Order # 72-29,940.

1650. Chai, Dong-Bai. Josiah Strong [1877-1916]: Apostle of Anglo-Saxonism and Social Christianity. Ph.D. Dissertation. 1972. 300 pp. DAI 33/9. (March 1973). Page 5080. Order # 73-6357.

1651. Cosgrove, C.S.S.R., Reverend Edward C. Contemplation for Education: Its Value Shown in the Life, Education, and Writings of Thomas Merton. Ph.D. Dissertation. Loyola University, Chicago. 1973. 251 pp. DAI 34/1. (July 1973). Page 154-A. Order # 73-16,803.

1652. Curtis, Jr. Dalton B. Boyd H. Bode and the Theory of Democracy: The Social Ideas of a Deweyan Educator. Ph.D. Dissertation. University of Oklahoma. 1979. 186 pp. DAI 40/4. (October 1979). Page 1919-A. Order # 7921228.

1653. Cywar, Alan S. An Inquiry into American Thought and the Determinate Influence of Political, Economic and Social Factors in the Early Twentieth Century: Bourne, Dewey, Dubois, Nearing, Veblen and Weyl. Ph.D. Dissertation. University of Rochester. 1972. 599 pp. DAI 33/7. (January 1973). Page 3529-A. Order # 72-28,738.

1654. Davis, Clifford. The Philosophy of Soren Kierkegaard and its Implications for Education. Ed.D. Dissertation. University of Southern California. n.p. DAI 38/10. (April 1978). Page 5984-A. No Order #.

1655. De Jong, Norman. Boyd H. Bode: A Study in the Relationship Between the Kingdom of God and Democracy. Ph.D. Dissertation. University of Iowa. 1972. 297 pp. DAI 33/4. (October 1972). Page 1470-A. Order # 72-26,669.

1656. Dienes, Barbara. John Dewey and the Messianic Tradition in America. Ph.D. Dissertation. University of Minnesota. 1976. 335 pp. DAI 37/6. (December 1976). Page 3462-A. Order # 76-27,886.

1657. Franzosa, Susan D. Continuity, Emergence and Sociality: A Study of George Herbert Mead's Epistomology. Ph.D. Dissertation. State University of New York, Buffalo. 1979. 290 pp. DAI 39/12. (June 1979). Page 7214. Order # 7913880.

1658. Gelbach, Robert A. Society, Education and Politics in the Philosophy of John Dewey. Ph.D. Dissertation. Yale University. 1975. 469 pp. DAI 36/5. (November 1975). Page 3087-A. Order # 75-24,534.

1659. Giarelli, James M. A Comparative Analysis of the Conceptions of Development in Dewey, Piaget and Kohlberg and their Implications for Educational Theory and Practice. Ph.D. Dissertation. University of Florida. 1977. 267 pp. DAI 39/1. (July 1978). Page 178-A. Order # 7810950.

1660. Hendon, Ursula S. Hebart's Concept of Morality in Education and its Role in America. Ph.D. Dissertation. University of Alabama. 1980. 297 pp. DAI 41/8. (February 1981). Page 3454-A. Order # 8104075.

1661. Holderied, Kurt W. Ivan Illich and Contemporaries: Comparing Views of School Reform. Ed.D. Dissertation. Marquette University. 1975. 383 pp. DAI 36/10. (April 1976). Page 6518-A. Order # 76-8639.

1662. Jara, Joselito B. The Educational Philosophy of Mortimor J. Adler. Ph.D. Dissertation. University of Illinois. 1976. 324 pp. DAI 37/1. (July 1976). Page 173-A. Order # 76-16,144.

1663. Johnson, Gregory S. Francis Wayland Parker: An Historical Study of the Influences of his Philosophy of Education as it Relates to Language Arts/Reading Instruction. Ed.D. Dissertation. University of the Pacific. 1974. 168 pp. DAI 34/11. (May 1974). Page 6945-A. Order # 74-9509.

1664. Kaplan, Thomas J. From Theory to Practice in American Educational Reform, 1900-1925. Ph.D. Dissertation. University of Wisconsin. 1979. 311 pp. DAI 40/8. (February 1980). Page 4716-A. Order # 8001150.

1665. Keenan, James P. The Public Educational Thought of Selected American Big-Business Leaders, 1860-1917. Ed.D. Dissertation. Columbia University. 1972. 549 pp. DAI 33/3. (September 1972). Page 1001-A. Order # 72-23,702.

1666. Keough, Jean A.V. American Writings on Maria Montessori: An Inquiry into Changes in the Reception and Interpretations Given to Writings on Maria Montessori and Montessori Educational Ideas, 1910-1915 and 1958-1970. Ph.D. Dissertation. 1973. 353 pp. DAI 35/1. (July 1974). Page 233-A. Order # 74-15,066.

1667. Kim, Soo-Chul. Human Nature and Education: A Comparative Study of Aristotle, Confucius and John Dewey. Ed.D. Dissertation. Oklahoma State University. 1977. 184 pp. DAI 39/1. (July 1978). Page 179-A. Order # 7811048.

1668. Knight, George R. An Analysis of the Educational Theory of George S. Counts. Ed.D. Dissertation. University of Houston. 1976. 424 pp. DAI 37/5. (November 1976). Page 2712-A. Order # 76-23,367.

1669. Kromenaker, Reverend Joseph G. The Philosophy of Education of Robert M. Hutchins: Its Development and Change. Ph.D. Dissertation. St. Louis University. 1973. 192 pp. DAI 35/5. (November 1974). Page 2738-A. Order # 74-24,106.

1669-A. Lang, Roger P. The Pedagogy of Gustave Moreau [art education]. Ph.D. Dissertation. University of Oklahoma. 1979. 167 pp. DAI 40/4. (October 1979). Page 1821-A. Order # 7921243.

1670. Leeb-Lundberg, Kristina A.M. Friedrich Froebel's Mathematics for the Kindergarten: Philosophy, Program and Implementation in the United States. Ph.D. Dissertation. New York University. 1972. 439 pp. DAI 33/1. (July 1972). Page 176-A. Order # 72-20,642.

1671. Liles, Jesse Stuart. Contributions of William Heard Kilpatrick and
       Theodore Brameld Toward a Definition of the Relationship Between
       Education and Social Change. Ed.D. Dissertation. 1970. 274 pp.
       DAI 32/1. (July 1971). Page 212-A. Order # 71-19,190.

1672. Luebbering, Kenneth H. Learning from Nowhere: Educational Thought
       in the Anarchist Tradition. Ph.D. Dissertation. University of Mis-
       souri. 1980. 224 pp. DAI 42/11. (May 1982). Page 4744-A.
       Order # 8202650.

1673. Matsuura, Shigeharu. Edward Bellamy as Educator: Implications of
       his Life and Writings for Educational Philosophy. Ed.D. Dissertation.
       1974. 250 pp. DAI 35/3. (September 1974). Page 1552-A. Order
       # 74-20,453.

1674. McFadden, John P. Consciousness and Social Change: The Pedagogy
       of Paulo Freire. Ph.D. Dissertation. University of California, Santa
       Cruz. 1975. 179 pp. DAI 37/12. (June 1977). Page 7578-A.
       Order # 77-11,889.

1675. Miletta, Maureen M. Dewey and Teaching: A Selection of Readings
       with Commentary. Ed.D. Dissertation. Columbia University. 1980.
       360 pp. DAI 41/1. (July 1980). Page 134-A. Order # 8015086.

1676. Miller, Melvin R. Education in the Harmony Society, 1805-1905.
       Ph.D. Dissertation. University of Pittsburgh. 1972. 349 pp. DAI
       33/12. (June 1972). Page 6705-A. Order # 73-13,165.

1677. Miller, Steven I. The Essentialist Movement in American Education:
       A Critical Analysis. Ph.D. Dissertation. Michigan State University.
       1970. 214 pp. DAI 31/7. (January 1971). Page 3310-A. Order #
       71-2125.

1678. Mirhassani, Akbar. Educational Outlook of Mehdi Nakosteen: His
       Career as Educator and Philosopher. Ph.D. Dissertation. University
       of Colorado. 1977. 436 pp. DAI 38/7. (April 1978). Page 4017-
       A. Order # 77-29,952.

1679. Nighan, Raymond A. Ayn Rand's Concept of the Educated Man.
       Ph.D. Dissertation. Loyola University, Chicago. 1974. 234 pp.
       DAI 35/2. (August 1974). Page 859-A. Order # 74-19,963.

1680. Nostrand, Geraldine S. The Education of "Man As Man" As a Contin-
       uous Theme in the History of Educational Theory: A Study of this
       Theme from Antiquity to the Present in the Educational Writings of
       Selected Scholars. Ed.D. Dissertation. Rutgers, the State University.
       1978. 135 pp. DAI 39/5. (November 1978). Page 2786-A. Order #
       7820340.

1681. Olsen, Wesley A. The Philosophy of Jonathan Edwards and its Sig-
       nificance for Educational Thinking. Ed.D. Dissertation. Rutgers,
       the State University. 1973. 191 pp. DAI 34/7. (January 1974).
       Page 3937-A. Order # 73-32,229.

1682. Olson, Wayne C. Emerson, Thoreau and Fuller: Transcendentalist
       Insights for Education. Ed.D. Dissertation. Columbia University.

1980. 192 pp. DAI 41/4. (October 1980). Page 1469-A. Order # 8022142.

1683. Pellicer, James O. A Comparative Study of Domingo F. Sarmiento's Social Thought and his Philosophy of Education to Determine the Degree to which they are Compatible or Incompatible. Ph.D. Dissertation. New York University. 1973. 492 pp. DAI 34/2. (August 1973). Page 594-A. Order # 73-19,442.

1684. Peters, Adelia M. Two Visions of the Good Society: Lester F. Ward and Albion W. Small. Ph.D. Dissertation. Rochester University. 1970. 270 pp. DAI 31/4. (October 1970). Page 1593-A. Order # 70-17,927.

1685. Psihalos, Teresia E. An Analysis of Mark Twain's Concepts of the Child and Education. Ph.D. Dissertation. Loyola University, Chicago. 1974. 182 pp. DAI 35/4. (October 1974). Page 2025-A. Order # 74-22,443.

1686. Reed, John E. The Nature of Man in the Works of Burrhus Frederic Skinner and George Herbert Mead. Ph.D. Dissertation. University of Texas. 1974. 425 pp. DAI 35/1. (July 1974). Page 108-A. Order # 74-14,753.

1687. Renger, III, Paul. The Educational Philosophy of George Herbert Mead. Ph.D. Dissertation. University of South Carolina. 1977. 219 pp. DAI 38/9. (March 1978). Page 5327-A. Order # 7801175.

1688. Riordan, Timothy M. The Thought of Karl Jaspers: A Perspective for Consideration in Examining the American University. Ph.D. Dissertation. Marquette University. 1979. 134 pp. DAI 40/9. (March 1980). Page 4952. Order # 4952-A.

1689. Ripley, David B. The Educational Ideas, Implementations and Influence of A. Bronson Alcott. Ph.D. Dissertation. University of Iowa. 1971. 183 pp. DAI 32/8. (February 1972). Page 4392-A. Order # 72-8313.

1690. Sears, Charles L. The Educational Influence of John Williston Cook. Ed.D. Dissertation. Northern Illionis University. 1978. 161 pp. DAI 39/6. (December 1978). Page 3506-A. Order # 7823121.

1691. Shaughnessy, Edward F. Lester Frank Ward: The Development of an Educational Theory. Ph.D. Dissertation. Boston College. 1971. 251 pp. DAI 32/3. (September 1971). Page 1312-A. Order # 71-24,586.

1692. Simpson, Douglas J. A Critical Analysis of the Educational Philosophy of T.S. Eliot. Ph.D. Dissertation. University of Oklahoma. 1970. 155 pp. 31/11. (May 1971). Page 5816-A. Order # 71-12,617.

1693. Smith, Michael C. Karl Marx's Philosophy of Education: A Reconstruction of Marx's Ideas on Education. Ph.D. Dissertation. Marquette University. 1979. 131 pp. 40/9. (March 1980). Page 4952-A. Order # 8006557.

1694. Stoltz, Gary R. Santayana and the American Mind: A Study of George Santayana's Pre-1912 Contributions to American Thought and Culture. Ph.D. Dissertation. University of Washington. 1973. 359 pp. DAI 34/5. (November 1973). Page 2535-A. Order # 73-27,689.

1695. Teicher, Barry J. James Bryant Conant and The American High School Today. Ph.D. Dissertation. University of Wisconsin. 1977. 287 pp. DAI 38/6. (December 1977). Page 3335-A. Order # 77-19,129.

1696. Teitsworth, K. Anne. Tarry Awhile: The Humanism of Howard Mumford Jones. Ph.D. Dissertation. University of Michigan. 1977. 257 pp. DAI 38/6 (December 1977). Page 3577-A. Order # 77-26,371.

1697. Vernon, Roger L. Andrew Carnegie: The Educational and Social Theories of a Self-Made Man. Ph.D. Dissertation. Loyola University, Chicago. 1971. 691 pp. DAI 32/5. (November 1971). Page 2453-A. Order # 71-28,140.

1698. Vlasek, Dale R. The Social Thought of E. Franklin Frazier. Ph.D. Dissertation. University of Iowa. 1978. 302 pp. DAI 39/12. (June 1979). Page 7473-A. Order # 7912915.

1699. Welch, Stuart. John Dewey's Position Respecting the Role of the American School in Achieving Social Change. Ed.D. Dissertation. Rutgers, the State University. 1971. 198 pp. DAI 32/6. (December 1971). Page 2928-A. Order # 72-1105.

1700. Westbrook, Robert B. John Dewey and American Democracy. Ph.D. Dissertation. Stanford University. 1980. 355 pp. DAI 41/8. (February 1981). Page 3697. Order # 8103575.

1701. Young, Alfred. The Educational Philosophies of Booker T. Washington and Carlton G. Woodson: A Liberating Praxis. Ph.D. Dissertation. Syracuse University. 1977. 189 pp. DAI 39/2. (August 1978). Page 1039-A. Order # 7813356.

1702. Young, C.D.P., Bernadette L. John Dewey and Selected American-Catholic Thinkers: 1900-1975: From Anathema to Dialogue. Ph.D. Dissertation. University of Pittsburgh. 1977. 178 pp. DAI 38/9. (March 1978). Page 5329-A. Order # 7801885.

Transatlantic Relations

1703. Bigham, Wanda Durrett. The Germanic Impact on the American Professor in the Late Nineteenth Century. Ed.D. Dissertation. University of Kentucky. 1978. 127 pp. DAI 39/6. (December 1978). Page 3391-A. Order # 7824379.

1704. Carter, John Paul. German Influence on the Common School Movement. Ph.D. Dissertation. University of Virginia. 1979. 364 pp. DAI 40/9. (March 1980). Page 4926-A. Order # 8004606.

1705. Darstek, Wesley Irwin. A Comparison of the Educational Theories of
      John Locke and Jean-Jacques Rousseau. Ed.D. Dissertation. Rut-
      gers University. 1980. 183 pp. DAI 41/4. (October 1980). Page
      1467-A. Order # 8023591.

1706. Diehl, Carl Christoffer. Vison and Vocation: The Assimilation of
      Modern Scholarship in the Humanities in Germany and America, 1770-
      1870. Ph.D. Dissertation. Yale University. 1975. 298 pp. DAI
      36/12. (June 1976). Page 8230-A. Order # 76,13707.

1707. DiNitto, Thomas. Education and the Philosophy of Jean-Paul Satre.
      Ph.D. Dissertation. Boston College. 1980. 175 pp. DAI 41/6.
      (December 1980). Page 2494-A. Order # 8027569.

1708. Duminuco, S.J., Vincent Joseph. The Prelection in Jesuit Education:
      Its Sources, Development, and a Modern Application. Ph.D. Disser-
      tation. Stanford University. 1969. DAI 30/8. (February 1970).
      Page 3293-A. Order # 70-1522.

1709. Fennell, Jon Michael Barbour. Rousseau, the Curriculum, and the
      Standard of Nature. Ph.D. Dissertation. University of Illinois.
      1976. 263 pp. DAI 37/5. (November 1976). Page 2712-A. Order
      # 76,24,078.

1710. Geffrey, William Edward. The Epistomology of John Amos Comenius.
      Ed.D. Dissertation. University of Pacific. 1980. 186 pp. DAI
      41/4. (October 1980). Page 1467-A. Order # 8021949.

1711. Hale, Jr., Matthew. Psychology and Social Order: An Intellectual
      Biography of Hugo Münsterberg. Ph.D. Dissertation. University
      of Maryland. 1977. 451 pp. DAI 39/2. (August 1978). Page
      1033-A. Order # 7814026.

1712. Harrington, III, John Edward. Weimar Educators' Views on American
      Educational Practices. Ph.D. Dissertation. University of North Caro-
      lina at Chapel Hill. 1979. 248 pp. DAI 41/1. (July 1980). Page
      133-A. Order # 8013950.

1713. Heironimus, Rick Edward. Johann Heinrich Pestalozzi: A Study of
      His Influence on American Sunday Schools. Ed.D. Dissertation. The
      Southern Baptist Theological Seminary. 1977. 179 pp. DAI 38/11
      (April 1978). Page 6631-A. Order # 78-05418.

1714. Heives, Dorothy W. W.N. Hailmann: Defender of Froebel. Ph.D.
      Dissertation. Union Graduate School. 1974. 332 pp. DAI 36/2.
      (August 1975). Page 750-A. Order # 75-15,939.

1715. Humphrey, Mary Raphael. The Visual Modalty in the Pestalozzian or
      Inductive Method as Presented in the United States Periodicals for
      Teachers in the First Half of the Nineteenth Century. Ed.D. Dis-
      sertation. Columbia University. 1980. 287 pp. DAI 41/1. (July
      1980). Page 70-A. Order # 8015073.

1716. Jones, David Earl. Existentialism and the Teacher-Pupil Relationship:
      Some Implications of Satre and Buber. Ph.D. Dissertation. Michigan
      State University. 1977. 227 pp. DAI 38/10. (April 1978). Page
      5985-A. Order # 7803510.

1717. Kipnis, William F. Propagating the Pestalozzian: The Story of William
       MacLure's Involvement in Efforts to Affect Educational and Social Re-
       forms in the Early Nineteenth Century. Ph.D. Dissertation. Loyola
       University, Chicago. 1972. 428 pp. DAI 33/4. (October 1972).
       Page 1473-A. Order # 72-25,099.

1718. Klappenberg, James T. Knowledge, Responsibility and Reform: Amer-
       ican and European Social Theory, 1870-1920. Ph.D. Dissertation.
       Stanford University. 1980. 711 pp. DAI 41/5. (November 1980).
       Page 2244-A. Order # 8024683.

1719. Shapiro, Michael S. Froebel in America: A Social and Intellectual
       History of the Kindergarten Movement, 1848-1918. Ph.D. Dissertation.
       Brown University. 1980. 551 pp. DAI 41/12. (June 1981). Page
       5224-A. Order # 8111180.

Unions and Professional Organizations

1720. Baldwin, Melvin R. History of the Wyoming Education Association,
       1945-1972. Ed.D. Dissertation. University of Wyoming. 1973.
       200 pp. DAI 34/5. (November 1973). DAI 34/5. (November 1973).
       Page 2350-A. Order # 73-25,540.

1721. Block, Lawrence E. The History of the Public School Teachers Asso-
       ciation of Baltimore City [1849-1972]: A Study of the Internal Pol-
       itics of Education. Ph.D. Dissertation. Johns Hopkins University.
       1972. 292 pp. DAI 33/11. (May 1973). Page 6146-A. Order # 73-
       12,115.

1722. Bronner, Michael B. The Business Education Association of Metropol-
       itan New York: An Investigation of its Role and Growth. Ph.D. Dis-
       sertation. New York University. 1973. 460 pp. DAI 35/1. (July
       1974). Page 231-A.

1723. Clancy Jr., Lynn R. The History of the American Federation of
       Teachers in Los Angeles: 1919-1969. Ph.D. Dissertation. Univer-
       sity of California, Los Angeles. 1971. DAI 32/2 (August 1971).
       Page 759-A. Order # 71-19,449.

1724. Claunck, Edna G.K. The Emergence of V.O.T.E. [Voice of Teachers
       in Education] the Political Action Arm of the New York State Teachers
       Association, 1967-1972. Ed.D. Dissertation. University of Rochester.
       1974. 172 pp. DAI 35/3. (September 1974). Page 1370-A. Order
       # 74-20,622.

1725. Dumais, Richard A. A Historical Study of the Establishment and De-
       velopment of the Montgomery County Education Association (MCEA),
       Montgomery County, Maryland, 1867-1961. Ed.D. Dissertation.
       George Washington University. 1972. 474 pp. DAI 34/1. (July
       1973). Page 155-A. Order # 73-16,724.

1726. Eaton, William E. The Social and Educational Position of the American

Federation of Teachers, 1929-1941. Ph.D. Dissertation. Washington University. 1971. 255 pp. DAI 32/9. (March 1972). Page 5000. Order # 72-9328.

1727. Glasser, Richard B. A Historical Investigation of the Pittsburgh Federation of Teachers. Ph.D. Dissertation. University of Pittsburgh. 1974. 263 pp. DAI 35/9. (March 1975). Page 5885-A. Order # 75-5129.

1728. Goulding, Joel A. The History of Unionism in American Higher Education. Ed.D. Dissertation. Wayne State University. 1970. 327 pp. DAI 31/7. (January 1971). Page 3290-A. Order # 71-409.

1729. Grimshaw, William J. Big City Politics in Transformation: The Emergence of Union Rule in the Schools. Ph.D. Dissertation. University of Illinois. 1978. 247 pp. DAI 39/12. (June 1979). Page 7498-A. Order # 7498-A.

1730. Harriman, Myles L. A Comparison of Selected Contractual Items in Michigan Public School Professional Bargaining Agreements in 1952 and 1980. Ph.D. Dissertation. 1980. 141 pp. DAI 41/12. (June 1981). Page 4909-A. Order # 8112089.

1731. Hronicek, Francis R. The Historical Development of Teachers' Unions in United States' Public Education (K-12). Ed.D. Dissertation. St. Louis University. 1980. 201 pp. DAI 41/7. (January 1981). Page 2857-A.

1732. Hubbell, Joe. A History of the Oklahoma Education Association, 1945-1965. Ed.D. Dissertation. Oklahoma State University. 1970. 395 pp. DAI 31/11. (May 1971). Page 5812-A. Order # 71-11,172.

1733. Kemp, Doris R. Some Aspects of the National Education Association's Emphases on Instruction. Ph.D. Dissertation. North Texas State University. 1977. 276 pp. DAI 38/12. (June 1978). Page 7181-A. Order # 7807839.

1734. Lembo, Diana L. A History of the Growth and Development of the Department of Audio-Visual Instruction of the National Education Association from 1923 to 1968. Ph.D. Dissertation. New York University. 1970. 1057 pp. DAI 31/7. (January 1971). Page 3310-A. Order # 70-26,431.

1735. Malafronte, Anthony F. A History of the Dade County Classroom Teachers Association in its Collective Negotiations with the Dade County School Board, 1961-1974. Ed.D. Dissertation. University of Miami. 1974. 371 pp. DAI 35/12. (June 1975). Page 7699-A. Order # 75-12,873.

1736. Moran, Eugene P. An Historical Study of the Working Relationships Between the Montgomery County Board of Education and the Montgomery County Education Association During the Ten Year Period, 1961-1971. Ed.D. Dissertation. 1973. 207 pp. DAI 34/5. (November 1973). Page 2355-A. Order # 73-26,995.

1737. Patterson, Charles E. History of the Texas Association of Secondary

School Principals, 1923-1973. Ed.D. Dissertation. Baylor University. 1974. 398 pp. DAI 35/11. (May 1975). Page 7094-A. Order # 75-10,781.

1738. Rees, Willard D. The Professional Education Association Movement and Utah: An Interpretative Movement. Ph.D. Dissertation. University of Utah. 1977. 179 pp. DAI 38/1. (July 1977). Page 132-A. Order # 77-15,357.

1739. Roald, Jerry B. Pursuit of Status: Professionalism, Unionism, and Militancy in the Evolution of Canadian Teachers' Organizations. Ed.D. Dissertation. University of British Columbia. 1970. n.p. DAI 31/12. (June 1971). Page 6374-A. No Order #.

1740. Shotts, Constance T. The Origin and Development of the National Education Association's Political Action Committee, 1969-1976. Ed.D. Dissertation. Indiana University. 1976. 155 pp. DAI 37/8. (February 1977). Page 4723-A. Order # 77-3311.

1741. Strumbeck, Ronald E. A Study of the Origins and Changing Functions of the Delaware State Education Association and the Wilmington Federation of Teachers in Delaware. Ed.D. Dissertation. Rutgers, the State University. 1975. 259 pp. DAI 36/10. (April 1976). Page 6520-A. Order # 76-8707.

1742. Watkins, Bari J. The Professors and the Union: American Academic Social Theory and Labor Reform, 1883-1915. Ph.D. Dissertation. Yale University. 1976. 358 pp. DAI 37/7. (January 1977). Page 4574-A. Order # 77-407.

1743. Webb, Eleanor E. The Development of the Louisiana Teacher's Association from 1952 to 1977. Ed.D. Dissertation. The Louisiana State University and Agricultural and Mechanical College. 1978. 333pp. DAI 39/11. (May 1979). Page 6588. Order # 7911605.

Women and Education

1744. Adix, Shauna M. Differential Treatment of Women at the University of Utah from 1850 to 1915. Ph.D. Dissertation. University of Utah. 1976. 192 pp. DAI 37/11. (May 1977). Page 6968-A. Order # 77-10,433.

1745. Albert, Judith S. Margaret Fuller: Educator, Her Principles and Practices of Education. Ph.D. Dissertation. St. Louis University. 1978. 353 pp. DAI 39/10. (April 1979). Page 6016-A. Order # 7908247.

1746. Alcott, Pouneh M. Women at the Ohio State University in the First Four Decades, 1873-1912. Ph.D. Dissertation. The Ohio State University. 1979. 235 pp. DAI 40/7. (January 1980). Page 3826-A. Order # 8001681.

1747. Antler, Joyce. The Educated Woman and Professionalization: The
       Struggle for a New Feminine Identity, 1890-1920. Ph.D. Disserta-
       tion. State University of New York at Stony Brook. 1977. 45 pp.
       DAI 38/7. (January 1978). Page 4320-A. Order # 77-28,142.

1748. Baker, Carol E. Superintendent Mildred E. Doyle: Educational Leader,
       Politician, Woman. Ed.D. Dissertation. University of Tennessee.
       1977. 266 pp. DAI 38/9. (March 1978). Page 5139-A. Order #
       7801980.

1749. Blemer, Linda B. The Transition from Dutch to English Law: Its
       Impact on Women in New York, 1643 to 1727. Ph.D. Dissertation.
       Syracuse University. 1979. 303 pp. DAI 40/5. (November 1979).
       Page 2514-A. Order # 7925548.

1750. Brand, Barbara E. The Influence of Higher Education Sex-Typing
       in Three Professions, 1870-1920: Librarianship, Social Work, and
       Public Health. Ph.D. Dissertation. University of Washington. 1978.
       467 pp. DAI 39/5. (November 1978). Page 2771-A. Order #
       7820705.

1751. Brandstadter, Dianne P. Developing the Coordinate College for Women
       at Duke University: The Career of Alice Mary Baldwin, 1924-1947.
       Ph.D. Dissertation. Duke University. 1977. 174 pp. DAI 38/3.
       (September 1977). Page 2297-A. Order # 77-21,863.

1752. Brenzel, Barbara M. The Girls at Lancaster [Massachusetts]: A
       Social Portrait of the First Reform School for Girls in North America,
       1856-1905. Ed.D. Dissertation. Harvard University. 1978. 257 pp.
       DAI 39/6. (December 1978). Page 3417. Order # 7823671.

1753. Cohen, Miriam J. From Workshop to Office: Italian Women and Strat-
       ification in New York City, 1900-1950. Ph.D. Dissertation. Univer-
       sity of Michigan. 1978. 360 pp. DAI 39/10. (April 1979). Page
       6276-A. Order # 7907048.

1754. Colucci, Jr., Nicholas D. Connecticut Academies for Females, 1800-
       1865. Ph.D. Dissertation. University of Connecticut. 1969. 416
       pp. DAI 30/8. (February 1970). Page 3293-A. Order # 70-1248.

1755. Connolly, Mary K. The Anomaly of Catholic Higher Education for
       Women. Ed.D. Dissertation. Columbia University. 1976. 269 pp.
       DAI 37/2. (August 1976). Page 843-A. Order # 76-17,277.

1756. Daniels, Mary A. The Historical Transition of Women's Sports at the
       Ohio State University, 1885-1975 and its Impact on the National
       Women's Intercollegiate Setting During that Period. Ph.D. Disser-
       tation. 1977. 410 pp. DAI 38/5. (November 1977). Page 2644-
       A. Order # 77-24,616.

1757. Deutsch, Lucille S. The Giles Sisters' Contributions Toward the Higher
       Education of Women in the South: 1874-1904. Ph.D. Dissertation.
       University of Pittsburgh. 1978. 95 pp. DAI 40/2. (August 1979).
       Page 694-A. Order # 7917418.

1758. Drachman, Virginia G. Women Doctors and the Women's Medical

Movement: Feminism and Medicine, 1850-1895. Ph.D. Dissertation. State University of New York at Buffalo. 1976. 250 pp. DAI 37/8. (February 1977). Page 5299-A. Order # 77-3530.

1759. Dye, Judith L. For the Instruction and Amusement of Women: The Growth, Development, and Definition of American Magazines for Women, 1780-1940. Ph.D. Dissertation. University of Pennsylvania. 1977. 246 pp. DAI 38/11. (May 1978). Page 6791-A. Order # 7806576.

1760. Edmonds, Charles H. An Historical Perspective: The History of the Kate Duncan Smith, Daughters of the American Revolution School, Grant, Alabama. Ed.D. Dissertation. University of Alabama. 1977. 192 pp. DAI 39/1. (July 1978). Page 160-A. Order # 7809852.

1761. Haddad, Gladys M. Social Roles and Advanced Education for Women in Nineteenth Century America: A Study of Three Western Reserve Institutions. Ph.D. Dissertation. Case Western Reserve University. 1980. 277 pp. DAI 41/4. (October 1980). Page 1664-A. Order # 8021692.

1762. Harris, Elizabeth S. California Women School Superintendents: Characteristics and Trends, 1874-1974. Ed.D. Dissertation. University of California at Los Angeles. 1976. 129 pp. DAI 37/11. (May 1977). Page 6871-A. Order # 77-9344.

1763. Herman, Debra. College and After: The Vassar Experiment in Women's Education, 1861-1924. Ph.D. Dissertation. Stanford University. 1979. 365 pp. DAI 40/2. (August 1979). Page 1027-A. Order # 7917241.

1764. Jardine, Lauren L. Educational Implications in the Writings of Certain Contemporary Feminist Theoreticians. [Virginia Woolf, Simone de Beauvoir, Kate Millett]. Ph.D. Dissertation. Arizona State University. 1978. 171 pp. DAI 39/10. (April 1979). Page 6016-A. Order # 7907715.

1765. Jennings, Robert B. A History of the Educational Activities of the Women's Educational and Industrial Union from 1877-1927. Ed.D. Dissertation. Boston College. 1978. 175 pp. DAI 39/3. (September 1978). Page 1383-A. Order # 7816105.

1766. Kaufman, Polly A.W. Boston Women and City School Politics, 1872-1905: Nurturers and Protectors in Public Education. Ed.D. Dissertation. Boston University. 1978. 537 pp. DAI 42/1. (July 1981) Page 111-A. Order # 8112276.

1767. Keller, Dorothy J. Maria Mitchell, an Early Woman Academician. Ed.D. Dissertation. Rochester University. 1975. 163 pp. DAI 36/1. (July 1976). Page 159-A. Order # 75-15,237.

1768. Kern, Louis J. Love, Labor and Self-Control: Sex Roles and Sexuality in Three Nineteenth-Century American Utopian Communities. Ph.D. Dissertation. Rutgers, the State University. 1977. 536 pp. DAI 38/11. (May 1978). Page 6895-A. Order # 7805092.

1769. Klotzburger, Katherine M. Politics in Higher Education: The Issue
       of the Status of Women at the City University of New York, 1971-
       1973. Ph.D. Dissertation. New York University. 1976. 584 pp.
       DAI 37/9. (March 1977). Page 6029-A. Order # 77-5419.

1770. Kransdorf, Martha. Julia Richman's Years in the New York City
       Public Schools, 1872-1912. Ph.D. Dissertation. University of Michi-
       gan. 1979. 244 pp. DAI 40/6. (December 1979). Page 3161-A.
       Order # 7926461.

1771. Lagemann, Ellen C. A Generation of Women: Studies in Educational
       Biography. Ph.D. Dissertation. Columbia University. 1978. 357
       pp. DAI 39/4. (October 1978). Page 2486-A. Order # 7819374.

1772. Lau, Estelle P.O. Ellen C. Sabin, President of Milwaukee-Downer
       College, 1895-1921: Proponent of Higher Education for Women.
       Ph.D. Dissertation. Marquette University. 1976. 142 pp. DAI
       37/4. (October 1976). Page 2026-A. Order # 76-21,752.

1773. Levy, Elyse. Susan Isaacs: An Intellectual Biography. Ph.D. Dis-
       sertation. Claremont Graduate School. 1977. 402 pp. DAI 38/3.
       (September 1977). Page 2002-A. Order # 77-22,483.

1774. McCrone, Kathleen E. The Advancement of Women During the Age of
       Reform, 1832-1870. Ph.D. Dissertation. New York University. 1971.
       466 pp. DAI 32/3. (September 1971). Page 1447-A. Order # 71-
       24,758.

1775. Mather, Linda L. The Education of Women: Images from Popular
       Magazines. Ed.D. Dissertation. University of Pennsylvania. 385 pp.
       DAI 38/5. (November 1977). Page 2611-A. Order # 77-24,171.

1776. Maskiell, Michelle G. Women's Higher Education and Family Networks
       in South Asia: Kinnaird College, Lahore [Pakistan], 1913-1960.
       Ph.D. Dissertation. University of Pennsylvania. 1979. 298 pp.
       DAI 40/6. (December 1979). Page 3472-A. Order # 7928154.

1777. Matthews, Emily P. Lucy Sprague Mitchell: A Deweyan Educator
       [at Bank Street College in New York City]. Ed.D. Dissertation.
       Rutgers, the State University. 1979. 209 pp. DAI 40/3. (Sep-
       tember 1979). Page 1310-A. Order # 7917913.

1778. Matthews, LaMoyne M. Portrait of a Dean: A Biography of Isabel
       Burns Lindsay, First Dean of the Howard University School of So-
       cial Work. Ph.D. Dissertation. University of Maryland. 1976. 262
       pp. DAI 37/11. (May 1977). Page 7064-A. Order # 77-10,287.

1779. Misenheimer, Helen E. Rousseau on the Education of Women. Ed.D.
       Dissertation. University of North Carolina at Greensboro. 1979.
       104 pp. DAI 40/4. (October 1979). Page 1946-A. Order # 7922415.

1780. Mouritsen, Russell H. A Study of Women at the University of Utah
       Between 1941 and 1953. Ph.D. Dissertation. University of Utah.
       1980. 153 pp. DAI 41/5. (November 1980). Page 1979-A. Order
       # 8025606.

1781.   Nuckols, Margaret L.   A Comparative Analysis of Selected United Na-
        tions Documents Related to Educational Opportunities for Women Dur-
        ing the First Development Decade (1960-1970). Ph.D. Dissertation.
        Florida State University. 1975. 135 pp. DAI 36/6. (December
        1975). Page 3454-A. Order # 75-26,802.

1782.   Palmer, Barbara H.   Lace Bonnets and Academic Gowns: Faculty
        Developments in Four Women's Colleges, 1875-1915. Ph.D. Disserta-
        tion. Boston College. 1980. 356 pp. DAI 41/6. (December 1980).
        Page 2476-A. Order # 8026752.

1783.   Perkins, Linda M.   Fanny Jackson Coppin and the Institute for Col-
        ored Youth: A Model of Nineteenth Century Female Educational and
        Community Leadership, 1837-1902. Ph.D. Dissertation. University
        of Illinois. 1978. 356 pp. DAI 39/5. (November 1978). Page 2786.
        Order # 7821222.

1784.   Pichanick, Valerie K.   The Conscience and Social Consciousness of
        Harriet Martineau. Ph.D. Dissertation. University of Massachusetts.
        1976. 480 pp. DAI 37/4. (October 1976). Page 2374-A. Order #
        76-22,289.

1785.   Pope, Christie F.   Preparation for Pedestals: North Carolina Ante-
        Bellum Female Seminaries. Ph.D. Dissertation. University of Chi-
        cago. 1977. DAI 38/5. (November 1977). Page 2976. No
        Order #.

1786.   Roysterhorn, Juana R.   The Academic and Extracurricular Undergrad-
        uate Experience of Three Black Women at the University of Washing-
        ton, 1935 to 1941. Ph.D. Dissertation. University of Washington.
        1980. 274 pp. DAI 41/5. (November 1980). Page 1979-A. Order
        # 8026297.

1787.   Sherrick, Rebecca L.   Private Visions, Public Lives: The Hull House
        Women in the Progressive Era. Ph.D. Dissertation. Northwestern
        University. 1980. 208 pp. DAI 41/6. (December 1980). Page
        2740-A. Order # 8026921.

1788.   Small, Sandra E.   The Yankee Schoolmarm in Southern Freedmen's
        Schools, 1861-1871:   The Career of a Stereotype. Ph.D. Dissertation.
        Washington State University. 1976. 244 pp. DAI 37/4. (October
        1976). Page 2268-A. Order # 76-21,398.

1789.   Stephens, Barbara J.   May Wright Sewall (1844-1920). Ph.D. Disser-
        tation. Ball State University. 1977. 236 pp. DAI 38/10. (April
        1978). Page 6275-A. Order # 7803672.

1790.   Tedesco, Marie.   Science and Feminism: Conceptions of Female Intel-
        ligence and Their Effect on American Feminism, 1859-1920. Ph.D.
        Dissertation. Georgia State University. 1978. 385 pp. DAI 39/2.
        (August 1978). Page 1028-A. Order # 7813488.

1791.   Wein, Roberta.   Educated Women and the Limits of Domesticity, 1830-
        1918. Ph.D. Dissertation. New York University. 1974. 180 pp.
        DAI 35/8. (February 1975). Page 5073-A. Order # 75-4277.

1792. Wuchenich, John G. The Social and Educational Advancement of the American Woman as Reflected in the Cookbook, 1776-1899. Ph.D. Dissertation. University of Pittsburgh. 1978. 192 pp. DAI 39/8. (February 1979). Page 4773-A. Order # 7902732.

Youth Organizations

1793. Linn, Howard F. A History of [Boy Scout] Camp Wisdom from 1922 through 1978. Ed.D. Dissertation. East Texas State University. 1980. 142 pp. DAI 41/3. (September 1980). Page 1212-A. Order # 8018368.

1794. Wagner, Carolyn D. The Boy Scouts of America: A Model and a Mirror of American Society. Ph.D. Dissertation. Johns Hopkins University. 1979. 414 pp. DAI 40/1. (July 1979). Page 325-A. Order # 7914312.

HISTORY OF CANADIAN EDUCATION

1795. Anderson, David F. A Synthesis of the Canadian Federal Government Policies in Amateur Sports, Fisheries and Recreation Since 1961. Ph.D. Dissertation. Northern Colorado University. 1974. 117 pp. DAI 35/9. (March 1975). Page 5897-A. Order # 75-5394.

1796. Andrews, Samuel D. Conceptual Influences in Teacher Education in the Province of Quebec: 1857 to 1916. Ph.D. Dissertation. University of Connecticut. 1971. 205 pp. DAI 32/11. (May 1972). Page 6162-A. Order # 72-14,212.

1797. Blenkinsop, Padraig J. A History of Adult Education on the Prairies: Learning to Live in Agrarian Saskatchewan, 1870-1914. Ph.D. Dissertation. 1979. n.p. DAI 40/8. (February 1980). Page 4351-A. No Order #.

1798. Burgess, Donald A. Education and Social Change: A Quebec Case Study. Ed.D. Dissertation. Harvard University. 1978. 267 pp. DAI 39/11. (May 1979). Page 6584-A. Order # 7909882.

1799. Cody, Howard H. Toward a Perspective on the Perpetuation of the Canadian Federal System: Federal-Ontario Relations in University Education, 1945-1970. Ph.D. Dissertation. McMaster University. 1977. n.p. DAI 38/11. (May 1978). Page 6906-A. No Order #.

1800. Darville, Richard T. Political Economy and Higher Education in the Nineteenth Century Maritime Provinces. Ph.D. Dissertation. University of British Columbia. 1978. n.p. DAI 39/9. (March 1979). Page 5745-A. No Order #.

1801. Davey, Ian E. Educational Reform and the Working Class: School Attendance in Hamilton, Ontario, 1851-1891. Ph.D. Dissertation. University of Toronto. 1975. n.p. DAI 38/6. (December 1977). Page 3331-A. No Order #.

1802. De Pencies, Marni F.L. Ideas of the University in English-Speaking Canada to 1920. Ph.D. Dissertation. University of Toronto. 1978. n.p. DAI 39/7. (January 1979). Page 4075-A. No Order #.

1803. Dixon, Robert T. The Ontario Separate School System and Section

93 of the BNA Act. Ph.D. Dissertation. University of Toronto.
1976. n.p. DAI 39/3. (September 1978). Page 1883-A. No Order #.

1804. Fiorino, Albert F. The Philosophical Roots of Egerton Ryerson's Idea
of Education as Elaborated in his Writings Preceding and Including
the Report of 1846. Ph.D. Dissertation. University of Toronto.
1975. n.p. DAI 38/9. (March 1979). Page 5292-A. Order #.

1805. Gaffield, Charles M. Cultural Challenges in Eastern Ontario: Land,
Family and Education in the Nineteenth Century. Ph.D. Dissertation.
University of Toronto. 1978. n.p. DAI 40/2. (August 1979).
Page 710-A. No Order #.

1806. Gregor, Alexander D. The Federated University Structure in Mani-
toba. Ph.D. Dissertation. Michigan State University. 1975. 387
pp. DAI 35/9. (March 1975). Page 5885-A. Order # 75-717.

1807. Jain, Genevieve L. Canadian History Textbooks and Nationalism in
Ontario and Quebec, 1867-1914. Ph.D. Dissertation. McGill Univer-
sity. 1970. n.p. DAI 32/7. (January 1972). Page 3923-A. No
Order #.

1808. Jones, David C. Agriculture, the Land, and Education: British
Columbia, 1914-1929. Ph.D. Dissertation. University of British
Columbia. 1978. n.p. DAI 39/9. (March 1979). Page 5367-A.
No Order #.

1809. Ketchum, John A.C. "The Most Perfect System": Official Policy in
the First Century of Ontario's Government Secondary Schools and its
Impact on Students Between 1871 and 1910. Ph.D. Dissertation.
University of Toronto. 1979. n.p. DAI 40/8. (February 1980).
Page 4443-A. No Order #.

1810. Lawr, Douglas A. Development of Agriculture Education in Ontario,
1870-1910. Ph.D. Dissertation. University of Toronto. 1972. n.p.
DAI 34/3. (September 1973). Page 1109-A. No Order #.

1811. Love, James H. Social Stress and Education Reform in Mid-Nineteenth
Century Upper Canada. Ph.D. Dissertation. University of Toronto.
1978. n.p. DAI 39/7. (January 1979). Page 4090-A. No Order #.

1812. Matthews, Barbara L.C. The Growth of Disagreement Among Teachers Over the Dual School System in the Province of Quebec (1868-
1973). Ph.D. Dissertation. University of Michigan. 1973. 323 pp.
DAI 34/8. (February 1974). Page 4814-A. Order # 74-3687.

1813. McDonald, Neil G. Forming the National Character: Political Socialization in Ontario Schools, 1867-1914. Ph.D. Dissertation. University of Toronto. 1980. n.p. DAI 42/1. (July 1981). Page 112-A.
No Order #.

1814. McLeod, Keith A. Education and Assimilation of the New Canadians
in the North-west Territories and Saskatchewan, 1885-1934. Ph.D.
Dissertation. University of Toronto. 1975. n.p. DAI 38/6. (December 1977). Page 3332-A. No Order #.

1815. MacMillan, Charles M. Majorities and Minorities: Henri Bourassa and Language Rights in Canada. Ph.D. Dissertation. University of Minnesota. 1979. 331 pp. DAI 41/3. (September 1980). Page 1200-A. Order # 8019546.

1816. Meikle, William D. "And Gladly Teach": G.M. Wrong and the Department of History at the University of Toronto. Ph.D. Dissertation. Michigan State University. 1977. 393 pp. DAI 38/3. (September 1877). Page 1583-A. Order # 77-18,518.

1817. Morley, Mary L. Home Economics in Canada, 1960-1970. Ph.D. Dissertation. Columbia University. 1973. 275 pp. DAI 34/7. (January 1974). Page 3936-A. Order # 73-31,288.

1818. Morrison, Terrence R. The Child and Urban Social Reform in Late Nineteenth Century Ontario, 1875-1900. Ph.D. Dissertation. University of Toronto. 1971. n.p. DAI 33/2. (August 1972). Page 608-A. No Order #.

1819. Moynes, Riley E. Teachers and Pteranodons: The Origins and Development of the Education Department of the Royal Ontario Museum (1914-1974). Ph.D. Dissertation. University of Toronto. 1978. n.p. DAI 40/3. (September 1979). Page 1310-A. No Order #.

1820. Nicholson, Norman L. The Evolution of Graduate Studies in the University of Ontario, 1841-1971. Ed.D. Dissertation. University of Toronto. 1975. n.p. DAI 38/9. (March 1979). Page 5281-A. No Order #.

1821. O'Driscoll, Denis C. Ontario Attitudes Toward American and British Education, 1792-1950: A Comparative Study of International Images. Ph.D. Dissertation. University of Michigan. 1974. n.p. DAI 35/7. (January 1975). Page 4054-A. Order # 74-25,282.

1822. Parr, Gwynth J. The Home Children: British Juvenile Immigrants to Canada, 1868-1924. Ph.D. Dissertation. Yale University. 1977. 317 pp. DAI 40/6. (December 1979). Page 3475-A. Order # 7926868.

1823. Pilkington, Gwendoline. A History of the National Conference of Canadian Universities, 1911-1961. Ph.D. Dissertation. University of Toronto. 1974. n.p. DAI 37/10. (April 1977). Page 6307-A. No Order #.

1824. Prentice, Alison L. The School Promoters: Education and Social Class in Mid-Nineteenth Century Upper Canada. Ph.D. Dissertation. University of Toronto. 1974. n.p. DAI 38/6. (December 1977). Page 3652-A. No Order #.

1825. Robinson, Roosevelt M. Communicators and Power Within the York Region System of Education During a Period of Transition, 1969-74. Ed.D. Dissertation. University of Toronto. 1975. n.p. DAI 38/9. (March 1978). Page 5296-A. No Order #.

1826. Sherrill, Peter T. The Imperial Factor in the Imperial School Question (1890-1897). Ph.D. Dissertation. Vanderbilt University. 1970. 425 pp. DAI 31/10. (April 1971). Page 5337-A. Order # 71-10,464.

1827. Silver, Arthur I. Quebec and the French-Speaking Minorities, 1864-
       1917. Ph.D. Dissertation. University of Toronto. 1973. n.p.
       DAI 38/6. (December 1977). Page 3654-A. No Order #.

1828. Smillie, Benjamin G. J.S. Woodworth, Civic Pedagogue, 1874-1942.
       Ed.D. Dissertation. Columbia University. 1970. 236 pp. DAI
       31/7. (January 1971). Page 3312-A. Order # 71-1118.

1829. Spencer, Hildrith H. To Nestle in the Mane of the British Lion: A
       History of Canadian Black Education, 1820-1870. Ph.D. Dissertation.
       Northwestern University. 1970. 345 pp. DAI 31/7. (January 1971).
       Page 3312-A. Order # 71-1975.

1830. Sutherland, John N. Children in English-Canadian Society: Framing
       the Twentieth-Century Consensus. Ph.D. Dissertation. University
       of Minnesota. 1973. 723 pp. DAI 34/5. (November 1973). Page
       2357-A. Order # 73-25,699.

1831. Wasteney, Hortense C.F. A History of the University Settlement of
       Toronto, 1910-1958: An Exploration of the Social Objectives of the
       University Settlement and Their Implementation. Ph.D. Dissertation.
       University of Toronto. 1975. n.p. DAI 38/6. (December 1977).
       Page 3736-A. No Order #.

HISTORY OF EUROPEAN EDUCATION

General

1832. Bark, Nathan. Plato's Educational Stance Views from the Perspective of Authority. Ph.D. Dissertation. Johns Hopkins University. 1973. 245 pp. DAI 34/11. (May 1974). Page 7013-A. Order # 74-10,389.

1833. Birchenall, Michael S.S. A Comparative Historical and Philosophical Study of the Educational Theories of John Amos Comenius (1592-1670), Friedrich Froebel (1782-1852), and Maria Montessori (1870-1952). Ph.D. Dissertation. University of Denver. 1970. 252 pp. DAI 31/9. (March 1971). Page 4500-A. Order # 71-6435.

1834. Burlingame, Leslie J. Lamarck's Theory of Transformism in the Context of the Views of Nature from 1776 to 1809. Ph.D. Dissertation. Cornell University. 1973. 442 pp. DAI 34/9. (April 1974). Page 6557-A. Order # 74-6372.

1835. Capernaros, George S. Literary Humanism in the Educational Theory of Isocrates. Ph.D. Dissertation. Boston College. 1970. 174 pp. DAI 31/6. (December 1970). Page 2714-A. Order # 70-24,598.

1836. DeBourg, Clyde E. A Study of Roles for the Teacher from an Historical Perspective. Ph.D. Dissertation. Michigan State University. 1980. 143 pp. DAI 41/3. (September 1980). Page 965-A. Order # 8020691.

1837. Ekdahl, Richard W. The Educational Ideas of Epictetus as Recorded by Arrian in the Discourses. Ed.D. Dissertation. University of Houston. 1970. 143 pp. DAI 31/3. (September 1970). Page 1136-A. Order # 70-16,013.

1838. Falkowitz, Robert S. The Sumerian Rhetoric Collections. Ph.D. Dissertation. University of Pennsylvania. 1980. 288 pp. DAI 41/3. (September 1980). Page 699-A. Order # 8018543.

1839. Fuchs, Sarel P. The Education of Princes: A Comparative Analysis of Desiderius Erasmus' Instituto Principis Christiani, Guillume Bude's De l'Institution Du Prince, and Thomas More's Utopia. Ph.D. Dissertation. Johns Hopkins University. 1972. 197 pp. DAI 33/4. (October 1972). Page 1471-A. Order # 72-24,963.

1840. Hibler, Richard W. The Life, Educational Work and School of Epicurus.

Ed.D. Dissertation. University of Wyoming. 1974. 272 pp. DAI
35/12. (June 1975). Page 7699-A. Order # 75-12,834.

1841. Innerd, Wilfred L. The Educational Thought of John of Salisbury.
Ph.D. Dissertation. University of Pittsburgh. 1971. 247 pp. DAI
32/7. (January 1972). Page 3738-A. Order # 72-3364.

1842. Kaczynski, Bernice M. Greek Learning in the Medieval West: A Study
of St. Gall, 816-1022. Ph.D. Dissertation. Yale University. 1975.
320 pp. DAI 37/1. (July 1876). Page 509-A. Order # 76-14,590.

1843. Lane, Mary C. An Early Medieval Latin Grammatical Text: Codex
Ambrosianus L22 Sup. Ed.D. Dissertation. University of Southern
California. 1974. 388 pp. DAI 35/6. (December 1974). Page
3480-A. Order # 74-28,447.

1844. Leeds, Jo Alice. The Workshop and the Academy: A Comparative
Historical Study of the Late Medieval Florentine Workshop and the
English Royal Academy as Art Learning Environments. Ph.D. Dis-
sertation. University of Oklahoma. 1974. 166 pp. DAI 35/9.
(March 1974). Page 5888-A. Order # 75-6532.

1845. Leigh, Mary H. The Evolution of Women's Participation in the Summer Olympic Games, 1900-1948. Ph.D. Dissertation. Ohio State University. 1974. 490 pp. DAI 35/8. (February 1975). Page 5098-
A. Order # 75-3121.

1846. Leverenz, Rev. Edwin W. Philipp Melanchthon: Beyond Humanism.
The Development of Humanism from Petrarch to Erasmus and Culmi-
nating in the Education of the Reformation. Ph.D. Dissertation.
Marquette University. 1971. 635 pp. DAI 33/1. (July 1972).
Page 176-A. Order # 72-20,391.

1847. Loader, Colin T. Karl Mannheim: An Intellectual Portrait. Ph.D.
Dissertation. University of California. Los Angeles. 1974. 439
pp. DAI 35/2. (August 1974). Page 1019-A. Order # 74-18,782.

1848. Mason, Carl B. Renaissance Business Attitudes Towards Academic
Learning. Ph.D. Dissertation. University of Southern California.
1974. 237 pp. DAI 35/7. (January 1975). Page 4357-A. Order #
75-1071.

1849. Overman, Steven J. The Student in the Medieval University. Ph.D.
Dissertation. Washington State University. 1971. 367 pp. DAI
32/8. (February 1972). Page 4391-A. Order # 72-7672.

1850. Provenzo, Jr., Eugene F. Education and the Aesopic Tradition.
Ph.D. Dissertation. Washington University. 1976. 416 pp. DAI
37/4. (October 1976). Page 2027-A. Order # 76-23,095.

1851. Sawdayee, Maurice M. The Impact of Western European Education on
the Jewish Millet of Baghdad, 1860-1950. Ph.D. Dissertation. New
York University. 1977. 320 pp. DAI 38/10. (April 1978). Page
6259-A. Order # 7803136.

1852. Schimmels, Cliff. Quintilian and the Great Ideas Concept: Cultural

Regressivism as an Educational Alternative in a Crisis Culture. Ph.D. Dissertation. University of Oklahoma. 1974. DAI 35/9. (March 1975). Page 5889-A. Order # 75-6553.

1853. Shubart, Robert F. From Socrates to Thomas: An Emblemic Epoch as Seen Through its Philosophy and its Visual Aesthetics. Ph.D. Dissertation. New York University. 1980. 1375 pp. DAI 41/2. (August 1980). Page 583-A. Order # 8017529.

1854. Verbal, Betty J. Youth Movements in Modern European History, 1815-1914. D.A. Dissertation. Carnegie-Mellon University. 1971. 326 pp. DAI 33/1. (July 1972). Page 263-A. Order # 72-17,887.

Austria

1855. Berls, Janet W. The Elementary School Reforms of Maria Theresa and Joseph II in Bohemia (1770's). Ph.D. Dissertation. Columbia University. 1970. 350 pp. DAI 31/9. (March 1971). Page 4663-A. Order # 71-6143.

1856. Dunne, John T. Between the Renaissance and Reformation; Humanism at the University of Vienna, 1450-1520. Ph.D. Dissertation. University of Southern California. 1974. 250 pp. DAI 35/7. (January 1975). Page 4373-A. Order # 75-1058.

1857. Markovits, Andrei S. The Austrian Student Right: A Study in Political Continuity. Ph.D. Dissertation. Columbia University. 1976. 581 pp. DAI 39/2. (August 1978). Page 1081-A. Order # 7809913.

1858. Singer, Walter E. A Study of the Early History of the University of Vienna from the Foundation through the Supremacy of Humanistic Thought, 1365-1500. Ed.D. Dissertation. University of Houston. 1971. 291 pp. DAI 32/5. (November 1971). Page 2453-A. Order # 71-29,549.

1859. Zeps, Michael J. The Politics of Education in Austria; Church, State and the Reform of Education, 1765-1962. Ph.D. Dissertation. Stanford University. 1979. 571 pp. DAI 40/2. (August 1979). Page 1021-A. Order # 7917292.

Belgium

1860. April, Miriam. Bilingualism in Belgium and the Linguistic Frontier. Ph.D. Dissertation. New York University. 1979. 172 pp. DAI 40/3. (September 1979). Page 1315-A. Order # 7918832.

1861. Curtis, Arthur E. New Perspectives on the History of the Language Problem in Belgium. Ph.D. Dissertation. University of Oregon.

1971. 599 pp. DAI 32/6. (December 1971). Page 3198-A. Order # 72-915.

1862. Gingrich, Newton L. Belgian Educational Policy in the Congo, 1945-1960. Ph.D. Dissertation. Tulane University. 1971. 307 pp. DAI 32/7. (January 1972). Page 3918-A. Order # 72-3881.

1863. Ndoma, Ungina. Some Aspects of Planning Language Policy in Education in the Belgian Congo, 1906-1960. Ph.D. Dissertation. Northwestern University. 1977. 406 pp. DAI 38/8. (February 1978). Page 4633-A. Order # 7732334.

1864. Nielsen, Francoise D. Linguistic Conflict in Belgium: An Ecological Approach. Ph.D. Dissertation. Stanford University 1978. 225 pp. DAI 38/12. (June 1978). Page 7604-A. Order # 7808819.

1865. Swing, Elizabeth S. Bilingualism and Linguistic Separation in the Schools of Brussels (1932-1971). Ph.D. Dissertation. University of Pennsylvania. 1979. 380 pp. DAI 40/6. (December 1979). Page 3169-A. Order # 7928178.

Bulgaria

1866. Heath, Ray E. The Establishment of the Bulgarian Ministry of Public Instruction and its Role in the Development of Modern Bulgaria, 1878-1885. Ph.D. Dissertation. University of Wisconsin. 1979. 479 pp. DAI 40/6. (December 1979). Page 3477-A. Order # 7926761.

Czechoslovakia

1867. Freeze, Karen A.J. The Young Progressives: The Czech Student Movement, 1887-1997. Ph.D. Dissertation. Columbia University. 1974. 387 pp. DAI 36/2. (August 1975). Page 1033-A. Order # 75-16,112.

1868. Green, Simon R. Thomas Garrigue Masaryk: Educator of a Nation. Ph.D. Dissertation. University of California, Berkeley. 1976. 445 pp. DAI 37/9. (March 1977). Page 6002-A. Order # 77-4469.

1869. Hacker, Paul. Political Education Under Socialism: The Case of Czechoslovakia. Ph.D. Dissertation. Columbia University. 1976. 317 pp. DAI 39/1. (July 1978). Page 444-A. Order # 7809904.

Denmark

1870. Canfield, Alvah T. Folk High Schools of Denmark and Sweden: Their Development and Present Status. Ph.D. Dissertation. State University of New York, Buffalo. 1979. 156 pp. DAI 41/1. (July 1980). Page 59-A. Order # 8016178.

1871. Weissman, Ann B. State, Church and Private Initiative as Influential Factors in Elementary School Teacher Preparation in Scandanavia, 1850-1900: A Comparative Study. Ph.D. Dissertation. University of Pennsylvania. 1978. 630 pp. DAI 39/7. (January 1979). Page 4092-A. Order # 7824769.

England

1872. Argent, Russell H. The English Utilitarians and the Movement for Educational Reform: 1800-1838. Ph.D. Dissertation. Catholic University of America. 1972. 180 pp. DAI 32/12. (May 1972). Page 6774-A. Order # 72-17,627.

1873. Babler, Alan M. Education of the Destitute: A Study of London Ragged Schools, 1844-1874. Ph.D. Dissertation. Northern Illinois University. 1978. 338 pp. DAI 39/8. (February 1979). Page 4771-A. Order # 7902437.

1874. Baxter, Brenda. A Guarded Education: A Study of Quaker Educational Theories and Practices in Nineteenth Century England. Ph.D. Dissertation. University of Toronto. 1979. n.p. DAI 40/8. (February 1980). Page 4442-A. No Order #.

1875. Behlmer, George K. The Child Protection Movement in England, 1860-1890. Ph.D. Dissertation. Stanford University. 1977. 349 pp. DAI 39/2. (August 1978). Page 1031-A. Order # 7814223.

1876. Birken, William J. The Fellows of the Royal College of Physicians of London, 1603-1643: A Social Study. Ph.D. Dissertation. University of North Carolina. 1977. 446 pp. DAI 38/11. (May 1978). Page 6869-A. Order # 7807115.

1877. Boulianne, Rial G. The Royal Institution for the Advancement of Learning: The Correspondence, 1820-1829, A Historical and Analytical Study. Ph.D. Dissertation. McGill University. 1970. n.p. DAI 31/10. (April 1970). Page 5158. No Order #.

1878. Brodhead, Frank M. Social Imperialism and the British Youth Movement, 1880-1914. Ph.D. Dissertation. Princeton University. 1978. 310 pp. DAI 39/9. (March 1978). Page 5672-A. Order # 7905621.

1879. Clatworthy, Frederick J. The Formulation of British Colonial Educational Policy, 1923-1948. Ph.D. Dissertation. University of Michigan. 1970. 222 pp. DAI 31/12. (June 1971). Page 6372-A. Order # 71-15,117.

1880. Cunningham, Michael H. The Triumph of Fantasy: Childhood and Children's Literature in Victorian England. Ph.D. Dissertation. New School for Social Research. 1978. 326 pp. DAI 39/7. (January 1979). Page 4522-A. Order # 7820599.

1881. Dixon, Thomas P. The Contributions of the English Baptists to Education, 1660-1820. Ph.D. Dissertation. Vanderbilt University. 1975. 236 pp. DAI 36/4. (October 1975). Page 2071-A. Order # 75-21,584.

1882. Enros, Philip C. The Analytical Society: Mathematics at Cambridge University in the Early Nineteenth Century. Ph.D. Dissertation. University of Toronto. 1979. n.p. DAI 40/12. (June 1980). Page 6396-A. No Order #.

1883. Fee, Elizabeth. Science and the "Woman Question," 1860-1920: A Study of English Scientific Periodicals. Ph.D. Dissertation. Princeton University. 1978. 360 pp. DAI 39/4. (October 1978). Page 2494-A. Order # 7818332.

1884. Feyerharm, William R. Education in Elizabethan East Anglia. Ph.D. Dissertation. University of Wisconsin. 1972. 249 pp. DAI 33/4. (October 1972). Page 1471-A. Order # 72-22,089.

1885. Fidler, Geoffrey C. Aspects of the History of the Labour Movement in Liverpool in Relation to Education. c. 1870-1920. Ph.D. Dissertation. McGill University. 1980. n.p. DAI 41/3. (September 1980). Page 966-A. No Order #.

1886. Fiduccia, Marilyn R. Rudyard Kipling: A Study in Popular Education During an Imperialist Era. Ph.D. Dissertation. Loyola University, Chicago. 1977. 236 pp. DAI 37/12. (June 1977). Page 7575-A. Order # 77-13,413.

1887. Filner, Robert E. Science and Politics in England, 1930-1945: The Social Relations of Science Movement (sic). Ph.D. Dissertation. Cornell University. 1973. 491 pp. DAI 34/10. (April 1974). Page 6563-A. Order # 74-6380.

1888. Frith, Simon W. Education, Industrialization and Social Change: The Development of Elementary Schooling in Nineteenth-Century Leeds, A Case Study in Historical Sociology. Ph.D. Dissertation. University of California, Berkeley. 1976. 520 pp. DAI 38/2. (August 1977). Page 1047-A. Order # 1047-A.

1889. Gabriel, Ruth. Learned Communities and British Educational Communities in North India, 1780-1830. Ph.D. Dissertation. University of Virginia. 1979. 287 pp. DAI 40/9. (March 1980). Page 5149-A. Order # 8004615.

1890. Garibaldi, David E. The Conservatives and the Development of the English Educational System, 1891-1902. Ph.D. Dissertation. Uni-

versity of Notre Dame. 1970. 271 pp. DAI 31/8. (February 1972).
Page 4085-A. Order # 71-5537.

1891. Garland, Martin M. A Liberal Education: The Development of an
Ideal at the University of Cambridge, 1800-1860. Ph.D. Dissertation.
Oregon State University. 1975. 327 pp. DAI 36/11. (May 1976).
Page 7582-A. Order # 76-9971.

1892. Geison, Gerald L. Michael Foster and the Rise of the Cambridge
(University) School of Physiology, 1870-1900. Ph.D. Dissertation.
Yale University. 1970. 542 pp. DAI 32/2. (August 1971). Page
880-A. Order # 71-16,240.

1893. Gelband, Spencer H. Mental Retardation and Institutional Treatment
in Nineteenth Century England, 1845-1866. Ph.D. Dissertation.
University of Maryland. 1979. 569 pp. DAI 41/2. (August 1980).
Page 765-A. Order # 8016711.

1894. Goering, Joseph W. The Popularization of Scholastic Ideas in Thir-
teenth Century England and an Anonymous Speculum Iuniorum.
Ph.D. Dissertation. University of Toronto. 1977. n.p. DAI 39/7.
(January 1979). Page 4417-A. No Order #.

1895. Greenlee, James G.C. Education and Imperial Unity, 1901-1926.
Ph.D. Dissertation. McMaster University. 1975. n.p. DAI 36/9.
(March 1976). Page 6242-A. No Order #.

1896. Griffin, Hazel M. Thomas Babington MaCauley and the Anglicist-
Orientalist Controversy in English Education, 1833-1837. Ph.D. Dis-
sertation. University of Pennsylvania. 1972. 603 pp. DAI 33/12.
(June 1973). Page 6703-A. Order # 73-13,408.

1897. Gusewelle, Jack K. The Board of Invention and Research: A Case
Study in the Relations Between Academic Science and the Royal Navy
in Great Britain During the First World War. Ph.D. Dissertation.
University of California, Irvine. 1971. 272 pp. DAI 32/11. (May
1972). Page 6340-A. Order # 72-14,659.

1898. Hall, Manson P. The Educational Policies of the British Labour
Party: A History of the Party's Influence and Achievement in Secondary Education (1900-1970). Ed.D. Dissertation. Columbia University. 1971. 442 pp. DAI 32/2. (August 1971). Page 669-A.
Order # 71-20,013.

1899. Hanneman, Robert A. Inequality and Development in Britain, France
and Germany from 1850-1870: A Political Sociological Approach.
Ph.D. Dissertation. University of Wisconsin. 1979. 388 pp. DAI
40/6. (December 1979). Page 3571-A. Order # 7919797.

1900. Hebrank, Helen G. Manchester and the Struggle for Nondenomina-
tional Education, 1847-1880. Ph.D. Dissertation. University of Minnesota. 1976. 182 pp. DAI 37/12. (June 1977). Page 7576-A.
Order # 77-12,813.

1901. Hewitt, James S. Oaks of Righteousness: Formation of Character in

British Higher Education. Ph.D. Dissertation. University of Massachusetts. 1980. 491 pp. DAI 41/4. (October 1980). Page 1427-A. Order # 8019467.

1902. Holland, Mary G. The British Catholic Press and the Educational Controversy, 1847-1865. Ph.D. Dissertation. Catholic University of America. 1875. 334 pp. DAI 36/3. (September 1975). Page 1723-A. Order # 75-19,884.

1903. Kane, Herman W. The Political Response to Student Radicalism in England During the 1960's. Ph.D. Dissertation. Columbia University. 1978. 418 pp. DAI 39/8. (February 1979). Page 5124-A. Order # 7904090.

1904. Karp, Alan. The Academic Corporations of England in the Middle Ages: Oxford and Cambridge, 1150-1509. Ed.D. Dissertation. Columbia University. 1977. 409 pp. DAI 38/2. (August 1977). Page 668-A. Order # 77-16,679.

1905. Kasbekar, Veena P. Power Over Themselves: The Controversy over Female Education in England, 1660-1820. Ph.D. Dissertation. University of Cincinnati. 1980. 389 pp. DAI 41/7. (January 1981). Page 3218-A. Order # 8029672.

1906. Keefe, Brian M. An Investigation of the Expressed Attitudes and Policies Towards Secondary Education and Relevant Sections of the 1944 Education Act in the House of Commons. Ph.D. Dissertation. Michigan State University. 1971. 149 pp. DAI 32/9. (March 1972). Page 5002-A. Order # 72-8717.

1907. Lagana, Loretta M. Toynbee Hall: Its Ideological Origins and Development. Ph.D. Dissertation. City University of New York. 1980. 214 pp. DAI 41/12. (June 1981). Page 5208-A. Order # 8112364.

1908. Lewis, Judith S. Manners and Medicine: Childbearing in the English Aristocracy, 1790-1840. Ph.D. Dissertation. Johns Hopkins University. 1979. 310 pp. DAI 40/1. (July 1979). Page 413-A. Order # 7914295.

1909. Lochhead, Elspeth N. The Emergence of Academic Geography in Britian in its Historical Context. Ph.D. Dissertation. University of British Columbia. 1980. 694 pp. DAI 41/7. (January 1981). Page 3237-A. Order # 8029481.

1910. Lyons, Charles H. "To Wash an Aethiop White": British Ideas about Black African Educability, 1530-1865. Ph.D. Dissertation. Columbia University. 1970. 408 pp. DAI 33/10. (April 1973). Page 5530-A. Order # 73-8970.

1911. Lytle, III, Gary F. Oxford Students and English Society: c. 1300-c. 1510. Ph.D. Dissertation. Princeton University. 1976. 354 pp. DAI 37/3. (September 1976). Page 1715-A. Order # 76-20,806.

1912. Madgwick, Gordon A. Charles Dickens--Gadfly for Educational Reform. Ph.D. Dissertation. University of Maryland. 1970. 322 pp. DAI 31/10. (April 1971). Page 5161-A. Order # 71-10,479.

1913. Mallea, John R. The Boys' Endowed Grammar Schools in Victorian
England: The Educational use of Sport. Ph.D. Dissertation. Columbia University. 1971. 276 pp. DAI 34/12. (June 1974). Page
7562-A. Order # 74-12,738.

1914. Mannion, Lawrence P. Sidney Smith: A Study of his Writings on
Education. Ph.D. Dissertation. State University of New York,
Albany. 1976. 327 pp. DAI 37/3. (September 1976). Page 1437-
A. Order # 76-19,669.

1915. Marshall, Phineas P. Evangelical Family Life and Child-Rearing,
Clapham, England, 1790-1830. Ph.D. Dissertation. University of
Chicago. 1979. n.p. DAI 40/1. (July 1979). Page 133-A. No
Order #.

1916. McClure, Ruth K. The Captain and the Children: Captain Thomas
Caram, 1668-1751, and the London Foundling Hospital, 1739-1799.
Ph.D. Dissertation. Columbia University. 1975. 562 pp. DAI
36/5. (November 1975). Page 3063-A. Order # 75-25,699.

1917. McConahey, Michael W. Sports and Recreation in Later Medieval
France and England. Ph.D. Dissertation. University of Southern
California. 1974. 504 pp. DAI 35/7. (January 1975). Page 4232-
A. Order # 75-1072.

1918. McPherson, Bruce I. Matthew Arnold and the Pursuit of Perfection.
Ed.D. Dissertation. Harvard University. 1975. 221 pp. DAI
36/11. (May 1976). Page 7248-A. Order # 76-10,566.

1919. Mickelson, Joan M. British Women in India, 1757-1857. Ph.D. Dissertation. University of Michigan. 1978. 398 pp. DAI 39/2. (August 1978). Page 1035-A. Order # 7813702.

1920. Mintz, Steven H. Studies in the Victorian Family. Ph.D. Dissertation.
Yale University. 1979. 206 pp. DAI 40/6. (December 1979). Page
3464-A. Order # 7926662.

1921. Moran, JoAnn H. Educational Development and Social Change in York
Diocese from the Fourteenth Century to 1548. Ph.D. Dissertation.
Brandeis University. 1975. 522 pp. DAI 36/5. (November 1975).
Page 3028-A. Order # 75-24,826.

1922. Newkirk, Thomas R. James Britton and the Teaching of Writing in
Selected British Middle and Secondary Schools. Ph.D. Dissertation.
University of Texas. 1977. 255 pp. DAI 38/5. (November 1977).
Page 2622-A. Order # 77-23,004.

1923. Olson, Barbara V. Philanthropic Educational Programs for Children
of the Poor: A Study of Objectives and in Methodology within the
Context of Eighteenth-Century British Society. Ph.D. Dissertation.
New York University. 1975. 373 pp. DAI 36/4. (October 1975).
Page 2073-A. Order # 75-21,156.

1924. Paz, Denis G. The Politics of Public Education in Britain, 1833-1848:
A Study of Policy and Administration. Ph.D. Dissertation. University of Michigan. 1974. 406 pp. DAI 35/7. (January 1975). Page
4398-A. Order # 75-773.

1925. Pope, Rhama D. The Development of Formal Higher Education for
       Women in England, 1862-1914. Ph.D. Dissertation. University of
       Pennsylvania. 1972. 615 pp. DAI 33/7. (January 1973). Page
       3338-A. Order # 73-1433.

1926. Robbins, David L. A Radical Alternative to Paternalism: Voluntary
       Associations and Popular Enlightenment in England and France, 1800-
       1840. Ph.D. Dissertation. Yale University. 1974. 347 pp. DAI
       35/5. (November 1974). Page 1741-A. Order # 74-24,563.

1927. Roberts, Gerrylynn K. The Royal College of Chemistry (1845-1853):
       A Social History of Chemistry in Early Victorian England. Ph.D.
       Dissertation. Johns Hopkins University. 1973. 489 pp. DAI 34/8.
       (February 1974). Page 5074-A. Order # 73-28,429.

1928. Ruggles, David P. The Contributions of James Mill and Robert Owen
       to a State Philosophy of Popular Education in England, 1800-1839.
       Ph.D. Dissertation. Michigan State University. 1971. 157 pp. DAI
       32/3. (September 1971). Page 1312-A. Order # 71-23,236.

1929. Schmitt, Jacob A. Aldous Huxley: An Analysis of Awareness in his
       Educational Philosophy. Ph.D. Dissertation. University of Minne-
       sota. 1974. 346 pp. DAI 35/12. (June 1975). Page 7700-A.
       Order # 75-12,198.

1930. Shapin, Steven A. The Royal Society of Edinburgh: A Study in the
       Social Context of Hanoverian Science. Ph.D. Dissertation. University
       of Pennsylvania. 1972. 396 pp. DAI 32/12. (June 1972). Page
       6868-A. Order # 72-17,423.

1931. Sher, Richard B. Church, University, Enlightenment: The Moderate
       Literati of Edinburgh, 1720-1793. Ph.D. Dissertation. University of
       Chicago. 1979. n.p. DAI 40/4. (October 1979). Page 2216-A.
       No Order #.

1932. Sherington, Geoffrey E. World War I and the National Educational
       Policy in England. Ph.D. Dissertation. McMaster University. 1975.
       n.p. DAI 36/9. (March 1976). Page 6247-A. No Order #.

1933. Short, Kenneth R.M. The Educational Foundation of Elizabethan Pur-
       itanism: With Special Reference to Richard Greenhans (1535-1594).
       Ed.D. Dissertation. University of Rochester. 1970. 269 pp. DAI
       31/7. (January 1971). Page 3311-A. Order # 71-1455.

1934. Siskin, Sidney S. The Skeptical Educator: Bertrand Russell's Edu-
       cational Views in the Light of his Intellectual Development. Ph.D.
       Dissertation. Cornell University. 1974. 291 pp. DAI 35/9. (March
       1975). Page 6011-A. Order # 75-6749.

1935. Smith, Steven R. The Apprentices of London, 1640-1660: A Study
       of a Revolutionary Youth Subculture. Ph.D. Dissertation. Vander-
       bilt University. 1971. 302 pp. DAI 32/7. (January 1972). Page
       3936-A. Order # 72-3236.

1936. Somers, Mary H. Irish Scholars in the Universities of Paris and Ox-
       ford Before 1500. Ph.D. Dissertation. City University of New York.

1979. 177 pp. DAI 40/9. (March 1980). Page 5145-A. Order #
8006473.

1937. Strauss, Claudia M. A Pedagogy for Independence in an age of Con-
straints: The Educational Thought of Mary Wollstonecraft. Ed.D.
Dissertation. Columbia University. 1979. 196 pp. DAI 40/9.
(March 1980). Page 4929-A. Order # 8006862.

1938. Tyler, Richard. Children of Disobedience: The Social Composition
of Emmanuel College, Cambridge, 1596-1645. Ph.D. Dissertation.
University of California, Berkeley. 1976. 358 pp. DAI 37/9.
(March 1979). Page 6015-A. Order # 77-4633.

1939. Washington, Judy U. The Frobelian Influence on the British Infant
School. Ph.D. Dissertation. Temple University. 1973. 63 pp.
DAI 34/8. (February 1974). Page 4817-A. Order # 74-1835.

1940. Welch, Sylvia. The Role of the Birmingham Reformers in the Movement for Change in the Educational System of England, 1840-1877.
Ph.D. Dissertation. New York University. 1970. 226 pp. DAI
32/1. (July 1971). Page 341-A. Order # 71-15,447.

1941. White, Jane F. An Historical Study of Business Letter Writing in
England from 1798 to 1900. Ph.D. Dissertation. University of
North Dakota. 1974. 215 pp. DAI 35/10. (April 1975). Page
6492-A. Order # 75-9104.

1942. Wilkes, John W. James Robertson, 1720-1795: An Anti-Enlightenment
Professor at the University of Edinburgh. Ph.D. Dissertation. New
York University. 1976. 351 pp. DAI 37/3. (September 1976).
Page 1736-A. Order # 76-19,490.

France

1943. Allen, James S. Toward a Social History of French Romanticism:
Authors, Readers, and the Book Trades in Paris, 1820-1840. Ph.D.
Dissertation. Tufts University. 1979. 287 pp. DAI 40/3. (Sep-
tember 1979). Page 1628-A. Order # 7920517.

1944. August, Thomas G. Colonial Policy and Propaganda: The Popularization of the "Idee Coloniale" in France, 1919-1939. Ph.D. Dissertation.
University of Wisconsin. 1978. 303 pp. DAI 40/5. (November
1979). Page 2813-A. Order # 7918135.

1945. Browning, Carol C. Democratization of Higher Education in France
During the DeGaulle Administration of the Fifth Republic. Ph.D.
Dissertation. Columbia University. 1971. 369 pp. DAI 34/12.
(June 1974). Page 7461-A. Order # 74-12,692.

1946. Bruneau, William A. The French Faculties and Universities, 1870-
1920. Ph.D. Dissertation. University of Toronto. 1977. n.p.
DAI 39/7. (January 1979). Page 4087-A. No Order #.

1947. Burton, June R.K. History and Historians under the First (French) Empire. Ph.D. Dissertation. University of Georgia. 1972. 149 pp. DAI 33/7. (January 1973). Page 3526-A. Order # 72-34,048.

1948. Casteel, Theodore W. The College and the University of Arts in Nimes: an Experiment in Humanistic Education in the Age of Reform. Ph.D. Dissertation. Stanford University. 1973. 288 pp. DAI 34/9. (March 1974). Page 5855-A. Order # 74-6455.

1949. Ceplair, Larry S. The Education of a Revolutionary Labor Union Minority: The French Railroad Workers and CGT (Confederation generale du travail), 1890-1922. Ph.D. Dissertation. University of Wisconsin. 1973. 361 pp. DAI 34/12. (June 1974). Page 7672-A. Order # 74-8995.

1950. Chase, George W. Ferdinand Buisson: A Study in Laicite in the Third Republic. Ph.D. Dissertation. University of Toronto. 1977. n.p. DAI 39/7. (January 1979). Page 4088-A. No Order #.

1951. Chisick, Harvey. Attitudes Toward the Education of the Peuple in the French Enlightenment, 1762-1789. Ph.D. Dissertation. Johns Hopkins University. 1974. 411 pp. DAI 35/7. (January 1975). Page 4367-A. Order # 74-29,003.

1952. Cohen, Elizabeth S. The Socialization of Girls and Young Women in Early Modern France (1560-1700). Ph.D. Dissertation. University of Toronto. 1978. n.p. DAI 40/12. (August 1979). Page 1017-A. No Order #.

1953. Cohen, Habida S. Decade of Change and Crisis: The New French Universities Since 1968. Ph.D. Dissertation. Indiana University. 1977. 471 pp. DAI 38/8. (February 1978). Page 4599-A. Order # 7730281.

1954. Contreni, John J. The School of Laon from 858 to 930: Its Manuscripts and Masters. Ph.D. Dissertation. Michigan State University. 1971. 339 pp. DAI 32/9. (March 1972). Page 5137-A. Order # 72-8651.

1955. Croal, Ralph F. The Idea of the Ecole Speciale Militare and the Founding of Saint-Cyr. Ph.D. Dissertation. University of Arizona. 1970. 345 pp. DAI 31/5. (November 1970). Page 2300-A. Order # 70-22,228.

1956. Donlon, Patric M. Five European Interpretations of Physical Education: Ignatius De Loyola, 1491-1566; Michel De Montaigne, 1533-1592; John Amos Comenius, 1592-1670; Jean Jacques Rousseau, 1712-1778; Johann Friedrich Guts-Muths, 1749-1839. Ph.D. Dissertation. University of Southern California. 1978. n.p. DAI 39/7. (January 1979). Page 4120-A. No Order #.

1957. Farge, James K. The Faculty of Theology at Paris, 1500-1536: Institutions, Personnel and Activity in Early Sixteenth-Century France. Ph.D. Dissertation. University of Toronto. 1976. n.p. DAI 39/4. (October 1978). Page 2453-A. No Order #.

1958.   Feeley, Francis M.   A Study of French Primary School Teachers
        (1880-1919), The Conditions and Events Which Led a Group of them
        into the Revolutionary Syndicaliste Movement.   Ph.D. Dissertation.
        University of Wisconsin.   1976.   539 pp.   DAI 37/7.   (January 1977).
        Page 4540-A.   Order # 76-23,315.

1959.   Felton, George N.   Popular Science and Philosophy in France, 1850-
        1875.   Ph.D. Dissertation.   Cornell University.   1974.   271 pp.
        DAI 35/2.   (August 1974).   Page 1005-A.   Order # 74-18,093.

1960.   Ferruolo, Stephen C.   Education and Society in the Twelfth Century:
        The Schools of Paris and their Critics.   Ph.D. Dissertation.   Prince-
        ton University.   1979.   533 pp.   DAI 40/8.   (February 1980).   Page
        4442-A.   Order # 8003780.

1961.   Fossati, William J.   Educational Influences in the Career of Marshal
        Ferdinand Foch of France.   Ph.D. Dissertation.   University of Kansas.
        1976.   246 pp.   DAI 37/8.   (February 1977).   Page 5285-A.   Order #
        77-2215.

1962.   Fuchs, Rachel G.   Abandoned Children in Nineteenth-Century France:
        Institutional Care and Public Attitudes.   Ph.D. Dissertation.   Indiana
        University.   1980.   412 pp.   DAI 41/1.   (July 1980).   Page 359-A.
        Order # 8016417.

1963.   Gelfand, Toby.   The Training of Surgeons in Eighteenth Century
        Paris and its Influence of Medical Education.   Ph.D. Dissertation.
        Johns Hopkins University.   1973.   522 pp.   DAI 34/5.   (November
        1973).   Page 2513-A.   Order # 73-28,400.

1964.   Halley, Anne M.   Arts, Law and Other Studies in Orleans in the
        Twelfth, Thirteenth and Fourteenth Centuries.   Ph.D. Dissertation.
        City University of New York.   1979.   228 pp.   DAI 39/12.   (June
        1979).   Page 7465-A.   Order # 7913132.

1965.   Harrigan, Patrick J.   Catholic Secondary Education in France, 1851-
        1882.   Ph.D. Dissertation.   University of Michigan.   1970.   315 pp.
        DAI 32/3.   (September 1971).   Page 1440-A.   Order # 71-23,770.

1966.   Hearn, Jana S.   The Schoolmaster of Liberty or the Political Views
        of Benjamin Constant De Rebecque.   Ph.D. Dissertation.   University
        of Indiana.   1970.   185 pp.   DAI 312/7.   (January 1971).   Page
        3470-A.   Order # 70-26,978.

1967.   Horvath, Sandra A.   Victor Duruy and French Education, 1863-1869.
        Ph.D. Dissertation.   Catholic University of America.   1971.   523 pp.
        DAI 34/2.   (October 1971).   Page 2030-A.   Order # 71-25,242.

1968.   Kates, Gary R.   The Cercle Social: French Intellectuals in the French
        Revolution.   Ph.D. Dissertation.   University of Chicago.   1978.   n.p.
        DAI 39/10.   (April 1979).   Page 6281-A.   No Order #.

1969.   Kselman, Claudia S.   The Modernization of Family Law: The Politics
        and Ideology of Family Reform in Third Republic France.   Ph.D.
        Dissertation.   University of Michigan.   1980.   330 pp.   DAI 41/5.
        (November 1980).   Page 2253-A.   Order # 8025712.

1970. Langdon, John W. Social Implications of Jesuit Education in France:
        The Schools of Varigirard and Sainte-Genevieve. Ph.D. Dissertation.
        Syracuse University. 1973. 234 pp. DAI 35/2. (August 1974).
        Page 1018-A. Order # 74-17,593.

1971. Langins, Janis. The Ecole Polytechnique (1794-1804): From Encyclo-
        paedic School to Military Institution. Ph.D. Dissertation. University
        of Toronto. 1979. n.p. DAI 40/12. (June 1980). Page 6396-A.
        No Order #.

1972. Martin, John E. French Universities: Reform for the Present and
        Future: La Loi D'Orientation De L'Enseignment Superieur, November
        12, 1968. Ph.D. Dissertation. Miami University. 1980. 210 pp.
        DAI 41/7. (January 1982). Page 2960-A. Order # 8100406.

1973. Maynes, Mary J. Schooling the Masses: A Comparative Social History
        of Education in France and Germany, 1750-1850. Ph.D. Dissertation.
        University of Michigan. 1977. 532 pp. DAI 38/11. (May 1978).
        Page 6886-A. Order # 7804768.

1974. Mayo, Jr., Frederic B. The Educational Ideas of the Marquis de
        Condorcet (1743-1794). Ph.D. Dissertation. Johns Hopkins Univer-
        sity. 1973. n.p. DAI 34/11. (May 1974). Page 7015-A. No
        Order #.

1975. McCarthy, Joseph M. Humanistic Emphases in the Educational Thought
        of Vincent of Beauvais. Ph.D. Dissertation. Boston College. 1972.
        266 pp. DAI 33/10. (April 1973). Page 5531-A. Order # 73-8241.

1976. Meyers, Peter V. The French Instituteur, 1830-1914: A Study of
        Professional Formation. Ph.D. Dissertation. Rutgers, the State Uni-
        versity. 1972. 316 pp. DAI 33/8. (February 1973). Page 4314-A.
        Order # 73-4765.

1977. Mindel, Adrianne R.S. Revolution, Liberty, and Order: A Study of
        the Views of Selected Members of the French Academy Active in the
        Political Life of the July Monarchy, 1830-1848. Ph.D. Dissertation.
        American University. 1976. 184 pp. DAI 37/3. (September 1976).
        Page 1723-A. Order # 76-19,783.

1978. Nelson, Douglas T. Academic Freedom and Subversion: Jules Mi-
        chelet and Edgar Quinet, 1838-1852. Ph.D. Dissertation. Columbia
        University. 1976. 269 pp. DAI 39/1. (July 1978). Page 420-A.
        Order # 7811147.

1979. Newell, Jr., John H. The Dignity of Man in William of Conches and
        the School of Chartres in the Twelfth Century. Ph.D. Dissertation.
        Duke University. 1978. 259 pp. DAI 39/9. (March 1979). Page
        5661-A. Order # 7905365.

1980. Ojala, James H. Education for Revolution: Pamphlets and the Po-
        liticization of French Society, 1787-1789. Ph.D. Dissertation. State
        University of New York, Binghamton. 1974. 270 pp. DAI 35/4.
        (October 1974). Page 21286-A. Order # 74-21,447.

1981. Osborne, Thomas R. The Recruitment of the Administrative Elite in the Third French Republic, 1870-1905: The System of the Ecole Libre Des Sciences Politique. Ph.D. Dissertation. University of Connecticut. 1974. 314 pp. DAI 35/4. (October 1974). Page 2186-A. Order # 74-21,804.

1982. Petix, Robert G. The Response of Educational Administration to Student-Initiated Revolt: A Case Study, Paris 1968. Ph.D. Dissertation. 1978. 262 pp. DAI 39/10. (April 1979). Page 5853-A. Order # 7908659.

1983. Potash, Janet R. The Foundling Problem in France, 1800-1869: Child Abandonment in Lille and Lyon. Ph.D. Dissertation. Yale University. 1979. 342 pp. DAI 40/6. (December 1979). Page 3464-A. Order # 7926865.

1984. Reitzel, Joan M. The Founding of the Earliest Secular Colleges within the Universities of Paris and Oxford. Ph.D. Dissertation. Brown University. 1971. 347 pp. DAI 39/11. (May 1979). Page 6896-A. Order # 7910648.

1985. Riemer, Reynold A. The National School Administration: Selection and Preparation of an Elite in Post-War France. Ph.D. Dissertation. Johns Hopkins University. 1977. 468 pp. DAI 41/3. (September 1980). Order # 8018384.

1986. Schwille, John R. Professional Perogatives and Consumer Interests: Political Demands on the French Ministry of National Education, 1951-1965. Ph.D. Dissertation. University of Chicago. 1975. n.p. DAI 36/4. (October 1975). Page 2074-A. No Order #.

1987. Spiegel, Sandra J. Education and Community in a French Village. Ph.D. Dissertation. University of California, Berkeley. 1978. 142 pp. DAI 40/1. (July 1979). Page 336-A. Order # 7914776.

1988. Stone, Judith F. Social Reform in France: The Development of its Ideology and Implementation, 1890-1914. Ph.D. Dissertation. State University of New York, Stony Brook. 1979. 480 pp. DAI 40/3. (September 1979). Page 1641-A. Order # 7919356.

1989. Sullivan, Larry E. The Burg of Sainte-Genevieve: Development of the University Quarter of Paris in the Thirteenth Centuries. Ph.D. Dissertation. Johns Hopkins University. 1975. 420 pp. DAI 36/7. (January 1976). Page 4666-A. Order # 76-1577.

1990. Taylor, Judith C. From Proselytizing to Social Reform: Three Generations of French Female Teaching Congregations, 1600-1720. Ph.D. Dissertation. Arizona State University. 1980. 740 pp. DAI 41/7. (January 1981). Page 3227-A. Order # 8029298.

1991. Telzrow, Thomas M. The Watchdogs: French Academic Philosophy in the Nineteenth Century--The Case of Paul Janet. Ph.D. Dissertation. University of Wisconsin. 1973. 201 pp. DAI 34/5. (November 1973). Page 2538-A. Order # 73-20,281.

1992. Thibodeau, Kenneth F. Science in an Urban Perspective: Social and Cultural Parameters of the Sciences in Sixteenth Century Strasbourg.

Ph.D. Dissertation. University of Pennsylvania. 1974. 342 pp.
DAI 35/4. (October 1974). Page 2158-A. Order # 72-22,919.

1993. Tobin, Josemary B. Vincent of Beauvais' De Erudition Filorum No-
bilium: The Education of Women. Ph.D. Dissertation. Boston College. 1972. 211 pp. DAI 33/2. (August 1972). Page 601-A.
Order # 72-22,889.

1994. Varney, Marsha. Education in Eighteenth-Century French and Eng-
lish Periodicals (1700-1789). Ph.D. Dissertation. University of
Arizona. 1978. 465 pp. DAI 39/6. (December 1978). Page 3419-
A. Order # 7824363.

1995. Vogt, William P. The Politics of Academic Sociological Theory in
France, 1890-1914. Ph.D. Dissertation. University of Indiana. 1976.
422 pp. DAI 37/4. (October 1976). Page 2376-A. Order # 76-
21,553.

1996. Wanner, Raymond E. Claude Fleury (1640-1723) as an Educational
Historiographer and Thinker. Ph.D. Dissertation. University of
Pennsylvania. 1971. 426 pp. DAI 32/12. (June 1972). Page
6793-A. Order # 77-17,432.

1997. Washington, Eric S. A Study of the Struggle in France Between
Church and State for Control of Secondary Education, 1789-1850.
Ph.D. Dissertation. University of Mississippi. 1979. 220 pp. DAI
40/4. (October 1979). Page 1923-A. Order # 7921528.

1998. Weber, John B. The Register of the Beadle (Receipts and Expenses)
of the Faculty of Theology of Paris from 1449-1465. Ph.D. Dissertation. University of Notre Dame. 1975. 500 pp. DAI 36/4. (October 1975). Page 2351-A. Order # 75-21,451.

1999. Weisz, George D. The Academic Elite and the Movement to Reform
French Higher Education, 1850-1885. Ph.D. Dissertation. State Uni-
versity of New York, Stony Brook. 1976. 450 pp. DAI 37/3.
(September 1976). Page 1728-A. Order # 76-19,696.

2000. Wheeler, Penny M. The Twelfth Century School of St. Victor. Ph.D.
Dissertation. University of Southern California. 1970. 202 pp.
DAI 31/9. (March 1971). Page 4661-A. Order # 71-7749.

Germany (Pre-War, East & West)

2001. Albisetti, James C. Kaiser, Classicists, and Moderns: Secondary
School Reform in Imperial Germany. Ph.D. Dissertation. Yale Uni-
versity. 1976. 338 pp. DAI 38/1. (July 1977). Page 423-A.
Order # 77-14,017.

2002. Beatus, Morris. Academic Proletariat: The Problem of Overcrowding
in the Learned Professions and Universities During the Weimar Republic, 1918-1933. Ph.D. Dissertation. University of Wisconsin.

1975. 321 pp. DAI 36/3. (September 1975). Page 1712-A. Order
75-16,295.

2003. Blachburn, Gilmer W. Education as Ideology: The Uses of History
in Promoting National Socialist Aims. Ph.D. Dissertation. University of North Carolina. 1975. 418 pp. DAI 37/3. (September 1976).
Page 1301-A. Order # 76-19,996.

2004. Bodenman, Paul S. Academic Reform in Selected Universities of the
Federal Republic of Germany. Ph.D. Dissertation. University of
Maryland. 1973. 329 pp. DAI 34/11. (May 1974). Page 6859-A.
Order # 74-9821.

2005. Carmon, Arye Z. The University of Heidelberg and National Socialism, 1930-1935. Ph.D. Dissertation. University of Wisconsin. 1974.
438 pp. DAI 35/3. (September 1974). Page 1589-A. Order # 74-
16,199.

2006. Caruso, Jr., John. Adolf Hitler's Concept of Education and its Implementation in the Third Reich. Ph.D. Dissertation. University
of Connecticut. 1974. 202 pp. DAI 35/4. (October 1974). Page
2023-A. Order # 74-21,754.

2007. Craig, John E. A Mission for German Education: The University of
Strasbourg and Alsatian Society, 1870-1918. Ph.D. Dissertation.
Stanford University. 1973. 874 pp. DAI 333/12. (June 1973).
Page 6853-A. Order # 73-14,883.

2008. Dougherty, Richard W. Eros, Youth Culture and Geist: The Ideology of Gustav Wyneken and its Influence Upon the German Youth
Movement. Ph.D. Dissertation. University of Wisconsin. 1978.
619 pp. DAI 39/1. (July 1978). Page 418-A. Order # 7806418.

2009. Garver, Karen K. German Influence of French Educational Theory
and Practice During the July Monarchy and the Second Republic.
Ph.D. Dissertation. University of California, Los Angeles. 1974.
344 pp. DAI 35/10. (April 1974). Page 6634-A. Order # 75-9391.

2010. Grothe, S.M.I.C., Sister Justina Mary. Cistercians and Higher Edu-
cation in the Late Middle Ages with Special Reference to Heidelberg.
Ph.D. Dissertation. Catholic University of America. 1976. 307 pp.
DAI 37/4. (October 1976). Page 2350-A. Order # 76-23,362.

2011. Hanshew, Terrel R. The German Volkschullehren and the Weimar
Republic: A Study of the Deutscher Lehrerverein. Ph.D. Dissertation. University of Nebraska. 1975. 316 pp. DAI 36/12. (June
1976). Page 8233-A. Order # 76-13,330.

2012. Hendel, Kurt K. Johannes Bugenhagen's Educational Contribution.
Ph.D. Dissertation. Ohio State University. 1974. 246 pp. DAI
35/11. (May 1975). Page 7223-A. Order # 75-11,358.

2013. Kelly, Reece C. National Socialism and German University Teachers:
The NSDAP's Efforts to Create a National Socialist Professoriat and
Scholarship. Ph.D. Dissertation. University of Washington. 1973.
506 pp. DAI 33/12. (June 1973). Page 6690-A. Order # 73-13,845.

2014. Kitzler, Werner E. The Development of Marxist Comparative Education in the German Democratic Republic: A Historic Analysis from 1945-1972. Ph.D. Dissertation. University of Nebraska. 1978. 264 pp. DAI 39/3. (September 1978). Page 1411-A. Order # 7814698.

2015. Kressman, John H. Development of Comprehensive Secondary Schools (gesamtschulen) in the Federal Republic of Germany. Ph.D. Dissertation. George Peabody College for Teachers. 1976. 588 pp. DAI 37/4. (October 1976). Page 2025-A. Order # 76-21,632.

2016. Kyle, Joseph D. St. Emmeram (Regensburg) as a Center of Culture in the Late Tenth Century. Ph.D. Dissertation. University of Pittsburgh. 1876. 163 pp. DAI 37/8. (February 1977). Page 5273-A. Order # 77-3018.

2017. La Vopa, Anthony J. From Schoolmaster to Schoolteacher: The Making of a Modern Professional Corporation in Prussia, 1763-1850. Ph.D. Dissertation. Cornell University. 1976. 545 pp. DAI 37/1. (July 1976). Page 519-A. Order # 76-15,893.

2018. Lickteig, Franz-Bernard. The German Carmelites at the Medieval Universities. Ph.D. Dissertation. Catholic University of America. 1977. 625 pp. DAI 38/5. (November 1977). Page 2968-A. Order # 77-24,836.

2019. Marks, Richard B. The Medieval Manuscript Library of the Charterhouse of St. Barbara in Cologne. Ph.D. Dissertation. Cornell University. 1973. 465 pp. DAI 34/10. (April 1974). Page 6554-A. Order # 74-6318.

2020. Maw, Robin J.C. Humanism and Legal Education During the Reception of Roman Law in Germany: A Case Study. Ph.D. Dissertation. Columbia University. 1974. 219 pp. DAI 37/6. (December 1976). Page 3836-A. Order # 76-28,324.

2021. Mueller, Hans E. Bureaucracy and Education: Civil Service Reforms in Prussia and England as Strategies of Modernization. Ph.D. Dissertation. University of California, Los Angeles. 1974. 369 pp. DAI 35/10. (April 1975). Page 6824-A. Order # 75-9303.

2022. Olesko, Kathryn M. The Emergence of Theoretical Physics in Germany: Franz Neumann and the Konigsberg School of Physics, 1830-1890. Ph.D. Dissertation. Cornell University. 1980. 556 pp. DAI 41/4. (October 1980). Page 1740-A. Order # 8020861.

2023. Olson, James M. The Prussian Volksschule, 1890-1914: A Study of the Social Implications of the Extension of Elementary Education. Ph.D. Dissertation. New York University. 1971. 297 pp. DAI 32/7. (January 1972). Page 3929-A. Order # 72-3109.

2024. Pauwels, Jacques R.M. Women and University Studies in the Third Reich, 1933-1945. Ph.D. Dissertation. York University. 1976. n.p. DAI 37/12. (June 1977). Page 7912-A. No Order #.

2025. Poteet, David C. The Nazi Youth Movement, 1920-1927. Ph.D. Dissertation. University of Georgia. 1972. 248 pp. DAI 33/7. (January 1973). Page 3554-A. Order # 72-34,127.

2026. Rewmpel, Gerhard. The Misguided Generation: Hitler Youth and SS,
       1933-1945. Ph.D. Dissertation. University of Wisconsin. 1971.
       771 pp. DAI 32/4. (October 1971). Page 2040-A. Order # 71-
       20,688.

2027. Rudnick, Helene M.W. The German Professor: From Charismatic
       Ordinarius to Bureaucrat. Ph.D. Dissertation. Southern Illinois
       University. 1978. 222 pp. DAI 39/4. (October 1978). Page 2094-
       A. Order # 7817545.

2028. Rutherford, James C. Interaction of the Social Forces Dominant in
       the Establishment of Friedrichs Universitat, 1743. Ph.D. Dissertation.
       University of Oklahoma. 1970. 243 pp. DAI 31/3. (September
       1970). Page 1047-A. Order # 70-14,428.

2029. Schneider, Joanne F. An Historical Examination of Women's Education
       in Bavaria: Madchenschulen and Contemporary Attitudes About Them,
       1799-1848. Ph.D. Dissertation. Brown University. 1977. 275 pp.
       DAI 38/8. (February 1978). Page 4997-A. Order # 7732628.

2030. Schroeder, Richard E. The Hitler Youth as a Paramilitary Organiza-
       tion. Ph.D. Dissertation. University of Chicago. 1975. n.p. DAI
       36/4. (October 1975). Page 2379-A. No Order #.

2031. Skopp, Douglas R. The Mission of the Volksschule: Political Tenden-
       cies in German Primary Education, 1840-1870. Ph.D. Dissertation.
       Brown University. 1974. 457 pp. DAI 35/11. (May 1975). Page
       7236-A. Order # 75-9240.

2032. Spidle, Jr., Jake W. The German Colonial Civil Service Organiza-
       tion, Selection and Training. Ph.D. Dissertation. Stanford Univer-
       sity. 1972. 374 pp. DAI 33/6. (December 1972). Page 2872-A.
       Order # 72-30,711.

2033. Stark, Gary D. Entrepreneurs of Ideology: New Conservative Pub-
       lishers in Germany, 1890-1933. Ph.D. Dissertation. Johns Hopkins
       University. 1974. 654 pp. DAI 35/12. (June 1975). Page 7850-A.
       Order # 75-12,962.

2034. Steinberg, Michael S. Sabres, Books and Brown Shirts: The Rad-
       icalization of the German Student, 1918-1935. Ph.D. Dissertation.
       Johns Hopkins University. 1971. 934 pp. DAI 34/1. (July 1973).
       Page 261-A. Order # 73-16,674.

2035. Stokes, William S. Politics and Ethics in West Germany: A Study of
       the Ethical Goals in West German Schools and Society. Ph.D. Dis-
       sertation. Claremont Graduate School. 1978. 334 pp. DAI 39/6.
       (December 1978). Page 3811-A. Order # 7823863.

2036. Turner, Roy S. The Prussian Universities and True Research Im-
       perative, 1806-1848. Ph.D. Dissertation. Princeton University.
       1973. 561 pp. DAI 34/4. (October 1973). Page 1842-A. Order #
       73-23,225.

2037. Waite, Roberg G. Juvenile Delinquency in Nazi Germany, 1933-1945.
       Ph.D. Dissertation. State University of New York, Binghamton.

1980. 333 pp. DAI 41/6. (December 1980). Page 2723-A. Order #
8027557.

2038. Wegner, Robert A. Dewey's Ideas in German: The Intellectual Response, 1901-1933. Ph.D. Dissertation. University of Wisconsin.
1979. 309 pp. DAI 40/5. (November 1979). Page 2517-A. Order #
7918174.

2039. Wernecke, Hanns B. Interprovincial Cooperation in Education in West
Germany and Canada, 1945-1969: The West German Conference of
Ministers of Education and the Council of Ministers of Education
(Canada). Ph.D. Dissertation. University of Pennsylvania. 1971.
654 pp. DAI 32/4. (October 1971). Page 1893-A. Order # 71-
26,108.

2040. Westhoff, Carl W. The Role of Leibesubung und Sport in the Third
Reich. Ph.D. Dissertation. Michigan State University. 1978. 278 pp.
DAI 40/2. (August 1979). Page 1010-A. Order # 7917810.

2041. White, David O. Hitler's Youth Leader: A Study of the Heroic
Imagery in the Major Public Statements of Baldur von Schirach.
Ph.D. Dissertation. University of Oregon. 1970. 356 pp. DAI
31/10. (April 1971). Page 5104-A. Order # 71-10,794.

Greece

2042. Chambers, Roger R. Greek Athletes and the Jews: 165 B.C.-A.D.
70. Ph.D. Dissertation. University of Miami, Ohio. 1980. 199 pp.
DAI 41/4. (October 1980). Page 1711-A. Order # 8023651.

2043. Doty, Lawrence T. Cuneiform Archives from Hellenistic Uruk. Ph.D.
Dissertation. Yale University. 1977. 449 pp. DAI 38/6. (December 1977). Page 3644-A. Order # 77-27,070.

2044. Lewis, Rosa B. Lifelong Learning as an Ideal in Fourth Century
Greece. Ph.D. Dissertation. University of Toledo. 1980. 131 pp.
DAI 41/4. (October 1980). Page 1469-A. Order # 8021985.

2045. Melikokis, George C. The Origin and Development of the Pedagogic
Academies in Greece, 1933-1972. Ed.D. Dissertation. New York Uni-
versity. 1980. 258 pp. DAI 41/3. (September 1980). Page 967-
A. Order # 8017540.

2046. Neidinger, William J. The Philosophical and Political Foundations of
the Rhetorical Ideal in Classical Greece. Ph.D. Dissertation. Rice
University. 1980. 213 pp. DAI 41/2. (August 1980). Page 766-
A. Order # 8018074.

2047. Polychronopoulis, Panos. Politics and Pedagogy in Greece: A Critical
and Creative Analysis and Evaluation of the Ideological and Knowledge
Functions of the Greek School System, 1950-1975. Ed.D. Dissertation.
Boston University. 1976. 76 pp. DAI 37/3. (September 1976).
Page 1309-A. Order # 76-21,250.

2048. Rasis, Eleftherios P. A Historical Analysis of the Organization and Development of Vocational-Technical Education in Greece. Ph.D. Dissertation. University of Illinois. 1974. 160 pp. DAI 35/7. (January 1975). Page 4326-A. Order # 75-411.

2049. Rasis, Spyridon P. Demetres Glenos and Educational Demoticism in Greece. Ph.D. Dissertation. University of Illinois. 1980. 185 pp. DAI 41/6. (December 1980). Page 2476-A. Order # 8026574.

2050. Sarf, Harold. Establishing a Framework for Conceptualizing Socrates as Plato's Theoretical Education. Ph.D. Dissertation. University of California, Berkeley. 1980. 485 pp. DAI 41/2. (August 1980). Page 790-A. Order # 8014866.

2051. Soupios, Michael A. Eros and Paideia: Plato's Theory of Love and Learning. Ph.D. Dissertation. State University of New York, Buffalo. 1979. 272 pp. DAI 40/9. (March 1980). Page 4952-A. Order # 8005717.

2052. Sgouris, Katherine P. A Comparative Study of Selected Areas in Greek (1827-1977) and Michigan Education. Ph.D. Dissertation. Michigan State University. 1978. 345 pp. DAI 39/10. (April 1979). Page 5986-A. Order # 7907399.

2053. Thompson, James G. Sport, Athletics and Gymnastics in Ancient Greece. Ph.D. Dissertation. Pennsylvania State University. 1971. 140 pp. DAI 32/5. (November 1971). Page 2584-A. Order # 71-28,736.

2054. Trilianos, Athannasios A. An Analysis of Modern Greek Educational Thought, 1925-1975. Ph.D. Dissertation. University of Connecticut. 1977. 333 pp. DAI 38/2. (August 1977). Page 691-A. Order # 77-16,727.

2055. Valliantos, Evaggelos G. Adamantios Koraes (1748-1833) and the Modernizing of Greek Education, 1782-1821. Ph.D. Dissertation. University of Wisconsin. 1972. 245 pp. DAI 33/5. (November 1972). Page 2310-A. Order # 72-23,080.

Hungary

2056. Friedman, Armin H. Major Aspects of Yeshiva Education in Hungary, 1848-1948 (With the Emphasis on the Role of the Yeshiva of Pressburg). Ed.D. Dissertation. Yeshiva University. 1971. 398 pp. DAI 32/11. (April 1972). Page 5467-A. Order # 72-11,158.

2057. Paulovits, Julius G. Foundation of the Eotvos Lorand University (Budapest) and its History under Jesuit Administration, 1635-1773. Ph.D. Dissertation. Iowa State University. 1977. 242 pp. DAI 38/6. (December 1977). Page 3334-A. Order # 77-26,003.

Iceland

2058. Hanson, George. Icelandic Education: Tradition and Modernization
       in a Cultural Perspective. Ed.D. Dissertation. Loyola University,
       Chicago. 1979. 415 pp. DAI 39/10. (April 1979). Page 5985-A.
       Order # 7907435.

Ireland

2059. Browne, Dorothea L. The Church and Learning in Ireland from 400
       to 800. Ph.D. Dissertation. New York University. 1975. 283 pp.
       DAI 36/6. (December 1975). Page 3910-A. Order # 75-28,512.

2060. Burke, Andrew. The Beginning and the End of the Catholic Ban on
       Trinity College, Dublin Ireland. Ph.D. Dissertation. Boston College.
       1974. 551 pp. DAI 35/10. (April 1975). Page 6490-A. Order #
       75-9716.

2061. Riordan, S.M.A., Rev. Eugene. The Religious Question in the Early
       Irish National Schools (1830's). Ph.D. Dissertation. Boston College.
       1970. 410 pp. DAI 31/11. (May 1971). Page 5815-A. Order #
       71-13,160.

Italy

2062. Argento, Elmiro. Italian Education from 1859 to 1923: A Study in
       Educational Expectations and Performance. Ph.D. Dissertation.
       University of Pennsylvania. 1975. 387 pp. DAI 36/12. (June
       1976). Page 8242-A. Order # 76-12,239.

2063. Bazzano, Carmelo. The Contributions of the Italian Renaissance to
       Physical Education. Ed.D. Dissertation. Boston University. 1973.
       194 pp. DAI 34/4. (October 1974). Page 1672-A. Order # 73-
       23,535.

2064. Brough, Theodore G. Diffusion of Italian Humanistic Education into
       Western Europe: A Multiple Regression Analysis. Ed.D. Disserta-
       tion. New Mexico State University. 1975. 195 pp. DAI 35/10.
       (April 1975). Page 6489-A. Order # 75-7864.

2065. Di Massa, Joseph F. The Origins and Social Antecedents of the Uni-
       versity of Bologna. Ph.D. Dissertation. University of Southern
       California. 1974. 161 pp. DAI 35/5. (November 1974). Page
       2714-A. Order # 74-26,024.

2066. Doviak, Ronald J. The University of Naples and the Study and Practice of Medicine in the Thirteenth and Fourteenth Centuries. Ph.D.
Dissertation. City University of New York. 1974. 291 pp. DAI
35/3. (September 1974). Page 1588-A. Order # 74-20,646.

2067. Hall, John R. Antonio Gramsci, Italian Communism and Education.
Ph.D. Dissertation. Michigan State University. 1980. 196 pp.
DAI 41/3. (September 1980). Page 966-A. Order # 8020704.

2068. Hoskin, Keith W. Education in Roman Society: 200 B.C.-100 A.D.
Ph.D. Dissertation. University of Pennsylvania. 1973. 460 pp.
DAI 34/4. (October 1974). Page 1666-A. Order # 73-24,158.

2069. Kidwell, Clara S. The Academia Dei Lincei and the Apiarium: A Case
Study of the Activities of a Seventeenth Century Scientific Society.
Ph.D. Dissertation. University of Oklahoma. 1970. 318 pp. DAI
31/6. (December 1970). Page 2847-A. Order # 70-22,993.

2070. Koon, Tracy H. Believe, Obey, Fight: Political Socialization of
Youth in Fascist Italy. 1922-1943. Ph.D. Dissertation. Stanford
University. 1977. 507 pp. DAI 38/9. (March 1978). Page 5640-
A. Order # 7802186.

2071. Ohl, Ronald E. The University of Padua, 1405-1509: An International
Community of Students and Professors. Ph.D. Dissertation. Uni-
versity of Pennsylvania. 1980. 244 pp. DAI 41/7. (January 1981).
Page 2970-A. Order # 8028877.

2072. Rosen, Richard L. The Academy of Science of the Institute of Bo-
logna, 1690-1804. Ph.D. Dissertation. Case Western Reserve University. 1971. 354 pp. DAI 32/6. (December 1971). Page 3225-
A. Order # 72-97.

2073. Wilbanks, Evelyn R. The Changing Images of Women in the Works of
Petrach Boccaccio, Alberti and Castiglione. Ph.D. Dissertation.
University of Chicago. 1977. n.p. DAI 38/12. (June 1978). Page
7483-A. No Order #.

Netherlands

2074. Ruestow, Edward G. Physics at Seventeenth-Century Leiden: The
Scientific Revolution and the University. Ph.D. Dissertation. Uni-
versity of Indiana. 1970. 277 pp. DAI 31/4. (October 1970).
Page 1738-A. Order # 70-17,960.

2075. Van Blankenstein, Steven. Dutch Secondary Schools: A Dilemma in
Democratization After the Mammoth Act of 1963. Ph.D. Dissertation.
University of Kansas. 1977. 234 pp. DAI 38/7. (January 1978).
Page 3989-A. Order # 77-28,921.

Norway

2076. Fain, Elaine. Norwegian Education and Cultural Nationalism, 1832-
1896. Ph.D. Dissertation. University of Wisconsin. 1972. 249 pp.
DAI 33/10. (April 1973). Page 5528-A. Order # 72-33,849.

2077. Larson, Karen A. Language and Socialization in Norwegian Village
and Town. Ph.D. Dissertation. University of California, Berkeley.
1978. 235 pp. DAI 40/1. (July 1979). Page 332-A. Order #
7914668.

Poland

2078. Brown, Jacqueline H. The Polish General Secondary School, 1961-
1971. Ph.D. Dissertation. University of Pittsburgh. 1973. 241
pp. DAI 34/8. (February 1974). Page 4811-A. Order # 74-1550.

2079. Cudnick, Ted M. The Reform and Development of Higher Education
in a Socialist Society: A Case Study of the Polish People's Republic.
Ed.D. Dissertation. University of Kentucky. 1979. 339 pp. DAI
40/6. (December 1979). Page 3139-A. Order # 7927669.

2080. Kulczycki, John J. Polish Society in Poznania and the School Strikes
of 1901-1907. Ph.D. Dissertation. Columbia University. 1973.
349 pp. DAI 34/6. (December 1973). Page 3307-A. Order # 73-
29,848.

2081. Ward, Barclay. Polish Provinces and Policy Outputs in Housing,
Health and Technical Education (1970-1972). Ph.D. Dissertation.
University of Iowa. 1978. 338 pp. DAI 39/12. (June 1979). Page
7515-A. Order # 7912916.

2082. Wolkowski, Leszek A. Polish Commission for National Education, 1773-
1794--Its Significance and Influence on Russian and American Education. Ph.D. Dissertation. Loyola University, Chicago. 1979.
216 pp. DAI 39/12. (June 1979). Page 7195-A. Order # 7910356.

Portugal

2083. Coufinho, Verissimo. GOA's History of Education: A Case Study of
Portuguese Colonialism. Ph.D. Dissertation. Loyola University,
Chicago. 1975. 515 pp. DAI 36/1. (July 1975). Page 158-A.
Order # 75-14,505.

Romania

2084. Deligiannis, Emmannel A.D. Education in the Socialist Republic of
      Romania. Ph.D. Dissertation. University of Southern California.
      1971. 325 pp. DAI 32/5. (November 1971). Page 2431-A. Order
      # 71-27,917.

2085. Neag, Marie. The Historical Development of the Romanian Educational
      System with a Comparison of the Organizational Structure and Cur-
      ricula During the Pre-Socialist (1800-1948) and Post-Socialist (1948-
      1974) Eras. Ph.D. Dissertation. University of Akron. 1974. 147
      pp. DAI 35/11. (May 1975). Page 7094-A. Order # 75-10,094.

Spain

2086. Bellak, George M. Recent Reforms in Spanish Education. Ed.D. Dis-
      sertation. Columbia University. 1973. 193 pp. DAI 34/8. (Feb-
      ruary 1974). Page 4811-A. Order # 74-2116.

2087. Bermudy, Andrea B. Influence of the Institution of Free Learning
      on Spanish Education. Ed.D. Dissertation. University of Houston.
      1974. 149 pp. DAI 35/7. (January 1975). Page 4214-A. Order
      # 75-1009.

2088. Brown, Thomas A. The Academy of San Carlos of New Spain (1784-
      1810). Ph.D. Dissertation. Duke University. 1970. 286 pp. DAI
      32/2. (August 1971). Page 858-A. Order # 71-21,535.

2089. Burke, Michael E. The Royal College of San Carlos: Surgery and
      Spanish Medical Reform in the Late Eighteenth Century. Ph.D. Dis-
      sertation. Duke University. 1971. 351 pp. DAI 32/8. (February
      1872). Page 4520-A. Order # 72-5348.

2090. Franzblau, Bettie B. Literacy in Spain. Ed.D. Dissertation. Uni-
      versity of West Virginia. 1976. 215 pp. DAI 37/12. (June 1977).
      Page 7576-A. Order # 77-12,293.

2091. Hernandez-Sanchez, Roberto. Ideas and Beliefs and their Implications
      for Education in Ortego's Thought. Ph.D. Dissertation. University
      of Illinois. 1975. 141 pp. DAI 36/12. (June 1976). Page 8334-A.
      Order # 76-6788.

2092. Holtby, David V. Society and Primary Schools in Spain, 1898-1936.
      Ph.D. Dissertation. University of New Mexico. 1978. 474 pp.
      DAI 39/7. (January 1979). Page 4089-A. Order # 7900939.

2093. Manuel, Azaria. The Ideological Foundations of Jose Ortega y Gas-
      set's Educational Thought: A Study of Ortega's Educational Philos-
      ophy and its Relationship to the Ideology of Modern Secularism.

Ph.D. Dissertation. University of Southern California. 1977. n.p.
DAI 38/10. (April 1978). Page 5964-A. No Order #.

2094. McClendon, Carmen C. Discurso Sobre la Educacion Fisca y Moral
de las Mugeres by Josepha Amar y Barbon: A Translation with
Introduction and Notes. Ph.D. Dissertation. Mississippi State University. 1976. 227 pp. DAI 37/3. (September 1976). Page 1711-
A. Order # 76-20,768.

2095. Sherwood, Joan M. Abandoned and Illegitimate Infants in Eighteenth
Century Spain: A History of the Foundling Hospital of the Inclusa.
Ph.D. Dissertation. University of Toronto. 1978. n.p. DAI
40/2. (August 1979). Page 1020-A. No Order #.

2096. Williams, George D. Governance at the University of Salamanca, 1200-
1500. Ph.D. Dissertation. University of Denver. 1970. 234 pp.
Dai 32/1. (July 1971). Page 346-A. Order # 71-15,511.

2097. Wilmath, Karl D. The Philosophy of Education of Baltasar Gracian.
Ph.D. Dissertation. University of Kansas. 1979. 346 pp. DAI
40/8. (February 1980). Page 4470-A. Order # 802807.

Sweden

2098. Bradshaw, Jr., Russell H. "Service House" Development in Sweden:
A Social Historical Description. Ed.D. Dissertation. Harvard Uni-
versity. 1977. 252 pp. DAI 38/8. (February 1978). Page 5072-
A. Order # 7730676.

2099. De Angelis, Ronald W. Ellen Key: A Biography of the Swedish Reformer. Ph.D. Dissertation. University of Connecticut. 1978. 309
pp. DAI 39/11. (May 1979). Page 6905-A. Order # 7911357.

Switzerland

2100. Martin, Janet L.R. Swiss Policy on Immigrant Workers and the
Ueberfremdung Initiative: A Study in Consociational Democracy and
Direct Democracy. Ph.D. Dissertation. Yale University. 1979.
467 pp. DAI 40/6. (December 1979). Page 3512-A. Order #
7927642.

2101. Stunden, Beverly J. Educational Problems Associated with the Guest
Workers in Western Europe, as Reflected in the Situation in Zurich,
Switzerland. Ph.D. Dissertation. University of Southern California.
1976. n.p. DAI 37/9. (March 1977). Page 5458-A. No Order #.

Turkey

2102. Anar, Suat. Social and Philosophical Foundations of Modern Turkish
       Education: The Impact of Ziya Gokalp's (1876-1924) Teaching on the
       Philosophy of Education. Ph.D. Dissertation. University of Mary-
       land. 1976. 303 pp. DAI 38/3. (September 1977). Page 1834-A.
       Order # 77-21,345.

Union of Soviet Socialist Republics

2103. Alexander, Hunter H. The Education of Alexei Kosygin (1924-1969).
       Ph.D. Dissertation. Georgetown University. 1971. 402 pp. DAI
       32/3. (September 1971). Page 1428-A. Order # 71-23,407.

2104. Allister, Steven H. The Reform of Higher Education in Russia Dur-
       ing the Reign of Nicholas I, 1825-2855. Ph.D. Dissertation. Prince-
       ton University. 1974. 310 pp. DAI 35/5. (November 1974). Page
       2887-A. Order # 74-25,937.

2105. Burch, Robert J. Social Unrest in Imperial Russia: The Student
       Movement at Moscow University, 1887-1905. Ph.D. Dissertation.
       University of Washington. 1972. 468 pp. DAI 33/5. (November
       1972). Page 2277-A. Order # 72-28,582.

2106. Dudgeon, Ruth O.F. Women and Higher Education in Russia, 1855-
       1905. Ph.D. Dissertation. George Washington University. 1975.
       454 pp. DAI 36/6. (December 1975). Page 3922-A. Order # 75-
       26,000.

2107. Eklof, Arthur B. Spreading the Word: Primary Education and the
       Zemstov in Moscow Province, 1864-1910. Ph.D. Dissertation. Prince-
       ton University. 1977. 521 pp. DAI 38/2. (August 1977). Page
       957-A. Order # 77-14,237.

2108. Epp, George. The Educational Policies of Catherine II. Ph.D. Dis-
       sertation. Manitoba University. 1976. n.p. DAI 37/6. (Decem-
       ber 1976). Page 3816-A. No Order #.

2109. Forgos, Silvia P. Estonian Nationalism and Primary Education, 1860-
       1905. Ph.D. Dissertation. University of Illinois. 1974. 326 pp.
       DAI 35/1. (July 1974). Page 362-A. Order # 74-14,535.

2110. Galskoy, Constantine. The Ministry of Education Under Nicholas I:
       (1826-1836). Ph.D. Dissertation. Stanford University. 1977.
       219 pp. DAI 37/12. (June 1977). Page 7909-A. Order # 77-12,636.

2111. Jones, Thomas A. Higher Education and Social Stratification in the
       Soviet Union. Ph.D. Dissertation. Princeton University. 1978.
       564 pp. DAI 38/9. (March 1978). Page 5275-A. Order # 7801977.

2112. Kassow, Samuel D. The Russian University in Crisis, 1899-1911.
       Ph.D. Dissertation. Princeton University. 1976. 773 pp. DAI
       37/5. (November 1976). Page 3090-A. Order # 76-23,858.

2113. Kimberlin, Jack K. Educational Methods for Dealing with Cultural
       Pluralism in the USSR, with Emphasis on Central Asia. Ed.D. Dis-
       sertation. University of Southern California. 1978. n.p. DAI
       38/12. (June 1978). Page 7206-A. No Order #.

2114. King, Elizabeth G. The Teaching of the Social Sciences as a Tool of
       Political Socialization in the Soviet Union. Ph.D. Dissertation.
       University of Missouri. 1978. 244 pp. DAI 39/8. (February 1979).
       Page 5125-A. Order # 7903918.

2115. Klabik-Lozovsky, Nora N. The Education of Russian Women: Evolu-
       tion or Revolution, a Comparative Analysis. Ed.D. Dissertation.
       University of British Columbia. 1972. n.p. DAI 33/8. (February
       1973). Page 4141-A. No Order #.

2116. Kyshakevytch, Tatiana. University Education in the Ukraine. Ph.D.
       Dissertation. University of Pittsburgh. 1976. 407 pp. DAI 37/3.
       (September 1976). Page 1437-A. Order # 76-20,182.

2117. Lehrman, Sara M. The Pedagogical Ideas of Anton Semenovitch Ma-
       karenko. Ph.D. Dissertation. University of Pittsburgh. 1971.
       279 pp. DAI 32/11. (May 1972). Page 6166-A. Order # 72-16,146.

2118. Marker, Gary J. Publishing and the Formation of a Reading Public
       in Eighteenth Century Russia. Ph.D. Dissertation. University of
       California, Berkeley. 1977. 485 pp. DAI 39/2. (August 1978).
       Page 1034-A. Order # 7812678.

2119. Markus, Roberta L. Teaching about the Westerner in the Soviet Un-
       ion. Ph.D. Dissertation. University of Toronto. 1976. n.p. DAI
       39/4. (October 1978). Page 2514-A. No Order #.

2120. McClelland, James C. Bolsheviks, Professors, and the Reform of
       Higher Education in Soviet Russia, 1917-1921. Ph.D. Dissertation.
       Princeton University. 1970. 446 pp. DAI 32/12. (June 1971).
       Page 6521-A. Order # 71-14,395.

2121. Mozes, George. Instructional Technology in the USSR as Reflected
       in Soviet Books and Periodicals, 1958-1975. Ed.D. Dissertation.
       Northern Illinois University. 1977. 459 pp. DAI 39/8. (February
       1979). Page 4668-A. Order # 7902456.

2122. Nash, Carol S. The Education of Women in Russia 1762-1796. Ph.D.
       Dissertation. New York University. 1978. 319 pp. DAI 40/1.
       (July 1979). Page 413-A. Order # 7912300.

2123. O'Connor, Mark F. Culture and Conflict: A Case Study in Russian-
       Polish Relations: The University of Wilno. Ph.D. Dissertation.
       Boston College. 1978. 345 pp. DAI 38/12. (June 1978). Page
       7505-A. Order # 7807241.

2124. O'Connor, Timothy E. The Politics of Soviet Culture: Anatoli V.

Lunacharskii--Revolutionary Romanticism and the Soviet Intelligentsia. Ph.D. Dissertation. University of Minnesota. 1980. 346 pp. DAI 41/5. (November 1980). Page 2254-A. Order # 8025495.

2125. Pogorelskin, Alexis E. Scholar and Journalist: The Career of M.M. Stasiulevitch, 1850-1882. Ph.D. Dissertation. Yale University. 1976. 326 pp. DAI 38/1. (July 1977). Page 415-A. Order # 77-14,302.

2126. Popovecz, Jr., Andrew. Higher Education in the Soviet Union: A Descriptive Study. Ph.D. Dissertation. Wayne State University. 1976. 353 pp. DAI 37/11. (May 1977). Page 6982-A. Order # 77-9438.

2127. Rader, Inge A. Krupskaya: Pioneer Soviet Educator of the Masses. Ph.D. Dissertation. Southern Illinois University. 1974. 227 pp. DAI 35/7. (January 1975). Page 4216-A. Order # 75-136.

2128. Russell, Sylvia J. The Philosophy of Education of Anatoli Vasil Evitch Lunacharsky, Commissar of Education, 1917-1929. Ph.D. Dissertation. University of Indiana. 1970. 195 pp. DAI 31/9. (March 1971). Page 4690-A. Order # 71-6897.

2129. Santa Maria, Philip. The Question of Elementary Education in the Third Russian State Duma, 1907-1912. Ph.D. Dissertation. Kent State University. 1977. 189 pp. DAI 38/5. (November 1977). Page 2988-A. Order # 77-23,619.

2130. Shapiro, Joel. A History of the Communist Academy, 1918-1936. Ph.D. Dissertation. Columbia University. 1976. 393 pp. DAI 37/6. (December 1976). Page 3839-A. Order # 76-29,044.

2131. Smith, Pinkney C. The Soviet State and Education, 1917-1918. Ph.D. Dissertation. University of North Carolina. 1974. 344 pp. DAI 35/6. (December 1974). Page 3658-A. Order # 74-26,942.

2132. Solomon, Susan G. Controversy in Social Science: Soviet Rural Studies in the 1920's. Ph.D. Dissertation. Columbia University. 1973. 461 pp. DAI 38/1. (July 1977). Page 460-A. Order # 77-15,294.

2133. Sydorenko, Alexander. The Kievan Academy in the Seventeenth Century: Scholastic Humanist and Baroque Strains in Orthodox Spirituality. Ph.D. Dissertation. University of Illinois. 1974. 356 pp. DAI 35/1. (July 1974). Page 387-A. Order # 74-14,625.

2134. Szekely, Beatrice B. The Establishment of the Academy of Pedagogical Sciences of the USSR. Ph.D. Dissertation. Columbia University. 1976. 239 pp. DAI 37/6. (December 1976). Page 3465-A. Order # 76-29,115.

2135. Von Frank, April A.J. Family Policy in the USSR Since 1944. Ph.D. Dissertation. University of Missouri. 1975. 144 pp. DAI 37/4. (October 1976). Page 2441-A. Order # 76-21,986.

2136. Youngblood, Denise J. On the Kino Front: The Evolution of the Soviet Cinema in the 1920's. Ph.D. Dissertation. Stanford University. 1980. 502 pp. DAI 41/5. (November 1980). Page 2245-A. Order # 8024764.

Yugoslavia

2137. Karanovitch, Milenko. The Development of Education in Serbia, 1838-
      1858. Ph.D. Dissertation. University of Wisconsin. 1974. 468 pp.
      DAI 35/11. (May 1975). Page 7225-A. Order # 75-7589.

2138. Pavichevich, Helen A. Education and Modernization in Montenegro,
      1831-1918. Ph.D. Dissertation. Loyola University, Chicago. 1976.
      290 pp. DAI 37/5. (November 1976). Page 2686-A. Order # 76-
      24,453.

2139. Sterdjevich, Boryanka A. The Influence of Historic Events and Social
      Agents of the Development of Serbian Education (1804-1970). Ph.D.
      Dissertation. University of Arizona. 1973. 225 pp. DAI 34/6.
      (December 1973). Page 2938-A. Order # 73-28,792.

HISTORY OF ASIAN EDUCATION

Afghanistan

2140. Zai, Baqui Y. The Goals of Kabul University: An Historical Approach. Ph.D. Dissertation. Indiana University. 1974. 158 pp. DAI 35/10. (April 1975). Page 6489-A. Order # 75-8964.

Hong Kong

2141. Law, David K.C. A History of Adult Education in Hong Kong: An Analysis of Role, Scope and Change from 1955 to 1975. Ph.D. Dissertation. Florida State University. 1979. 161 pp. DAI 40/9. (March 1980). Page 4848-A. Order # 8007473.

2142. Ng, Alice Lun N.H. Development of Government Education for the Chinese of Hong Kong, 1842-1913. Ph.D. Dissertation. University of Minnesota. 1976. 415 pp. DAI 38/16. (December 1977). Page 3652-A. Order # 77-26,142.

India

2143. Bhatnagar, Krishna M. Education of Rural Women and Fertility Decline in India: An Educational Policy Analysis. Ed.D. Dissertation. University of South Dakota. 1980. 262 pp. DAI 41/3. (September 1980). Order # 8021015.

2144. Cameron, Alexa G. Christian Missions and the Social Reform Movement in the City of Poona in Western India: The Relationships Between the Activities of Christian Missions Towards Social Reforms and the Activities of the Social Reform Movement in the City of Poona from 1880 to 1920. Ph.D. Dissertation. New York University. 1973. 353 pp. DAI 34/6. (December 1973). Page 3101-A. Order # 73-30,054.

2145. Gopalakrishnan, Malini. Higher Education in Post-Independent India (1947-1970): A Critical Evaluation in Terms of Selected Criteria of

199

Effectiveness. Ed.D. Dissertation. Montana State University. 1973.
154 pp. DAI 34/5. (November 1973). Page 2329-A. Order # 73-
27,486.

2146. Jalan, Rahda V. Tagore--His Educational Theory and Practice and
its Impact on Indian Education. Ph.D. Dissertation. University of
Florida. 1976. 163 pp. DAI 37/10. (April 1977). Page 6430-A.
Order # 77-8193.

2147. Lahiri, Krishna. Education of Women in Bengal, 1849-1882, with
Special Reference to Missionary Contributions. Ph.D. Dissertation.
University of Pennsylvania. 1979. 474 pp. DAI 40/10. (April
1980). Page 5340-A. Order # 8009432.

2148. Lelyveld, David S. Aligarh's First Generation: Muslim Solidarity
and English Education in Northern India, 1875-1900. Ph.D. Dissertation. University of Chicago. 1975. n.p. DAI 36/4. (October
1975). Page 2368-A. No Order #.

2149. McGreal, Shirley P. A History of Mayo College, Ajmer, India 1875-
1971. Ed.D. Dissertation. University of Cincinnati. 1971. 301 pp.
DAI 33/6. (December 1972). Page 2745-A. Order # 72-32,033.

2150. Periaswamy, Asirvatham. Rabindranath Tagore's Philosophy of International Education. Ph.D. Dissertation. University of Chicago.
1976. 241 pp. DAI 37/5. (November 1976). Page 2713-A. No
Order #.

2151. Sandhu, Man M.S. Student Unrest in Colleges and Universities in
India, 1947-1970. Ed.D. Dissertation. University of Tennessee.
1972. 159 pp. DAI 33/2. (August 1972). Page 595-A. Order #
72-21,366.

2152. Sebaly, Kim P. The Assistance of Four Nations (USSR, France, USA,
England) in the Establishment of the India Institute of Technology,
1945-1970. Ph.D. Dissertation. University of Michigan. 1973.
186 pp. DAI 34/12. (June 1974). Page 7471-A. Order # 74-12,294.

2153. Zobairi, Riaguddin H. The Educational and Social Ideas of Sir Syed
Ahmad Khan. Ph.D. Dissertation. Southern Illinois University.
1971. 294 pp. DAI 32/9. (March 1972). Page 5003-A. Order
72-10,314.

Indonesia

2154. Aanenson, Charles R. The Utility of (Indonesian) Training Overseas. Ph.D. Dissertation. Indiana University. 1980. 229 pp.
DAI 41/3. (September 1980). Page 857-A. Order # 8020239.

2155. Abdullah, Taufik. Schools and Politics: The Kaum Muda Movement
in West Sumatra (1927-1933). Ph.D. Dissertation. Cornell University.
1970. 425 pp. DAI 32/1. (July 1971). Page 346-A. Order # 71-
7347.

Japan

2156.   Backman, Earl L. International Politics and the Left Wing Student
         Movement in Japan, 1952-1970. Ph.D. Dissertation. University of
         Utah. 1970. 171 pp. DAI 31/8. (February 1971). Page 3909-A.
         Order # 71-3015.

2157.   Bang, Hung K. Japan's Colonial Educational Policy in Korea, 1905-
         1930. Ph.D. Dissertation. University of Arizona. 1972. 241 pp.
         DAI 33/7. (January 1973). Page 3522-A. Order # 72-31,848.

2158.   Bartholomew, James R. The Acculturation of Science in Japan:
         Kitasato Shibasaburo and the Japanese Bacteriological Community,
         1885-1920. Ph.D. Dissertation. Stanford University. 1972. 258
         pp. DAI 32/12. (June 1972). Page 6878-A. Order # 72-16,688.

2159.   Beauchamp, Edward R. William Elliot Griffis and Japan: Yatoi, His-
         torian and International Educator. Ph.D. Dissertation. University
         of Washington. 1973. 216 pp. DAI 34/4. (October 1973). Page
         1808-A. Order # 73-22,552.

2160.   Bender, Fred A. A Historical Study of the Structure and Function of
         the Junior College in Japan. Ph.D. Dissertation. University of
         Texas. 1978. 248 pp. DAI 39/12. (June 1979). Page 7125-A.
         Order # 7910934.

2161.   Bethel, Dayle M. The Life and Thought of Tsubesaburo Makiguchi:
         His Contributions to Education. Ph.D. Dissertation. Michigan State
         University. 1971. 176 pp. DAI 32/12. Page 6790-A. Order # 72-
         16,386.

2162.   Bonnallie, Dorothy A. Education in Early Meiji Japan: Fukuzawa
         Yukichi, Nijima Jo and Mori Arinori. Ph.D. Dissertation. Clare-
         mont Graduate School. 1976. 205 pp. DAI 37/5. (November 1976).
         Page 2682-A. Order # 76-23,919.

2163.   Bryant, Gladys E. American Congregational Missionaries and Social
         Reform in Meiji Japan (1870-1900). Ph.D. Dissertation. Vanderbilt
         University. 1971. 435 pp. DAI 32/11. (May 1972). Page 6330-A.
         Order # 72-15,469.

2164.   Collins, Kevin A. Teacher Education in the Ryukyu Islands (1945-
         1970). Ph.D. Dissertation. Michigan State University. 1973. 166
         pp. DAI 34/6. (December 1973). Page 3101-A. Order # 73-29,679.

2165.   Eckroade, Ginger A. Political Socialization and Schooling: American
         Views of Japanese Educational Policies from 1872 to 1952. Ph.D. Dis-
         sertation. University of Maryland. 1979. 247 pp. DAI 40/12.
         (June 1980). Page 6224-A. Order # 8012656.

2166.   Fisher, Jerry K. The Meirokusha. Ph.D. Dissertation. University
         of Virginia. 1974. 272 pp. DAI 35/4. (October 1974). Page
         2168-A. Order # 74-23,246.

2167. Fujitania, Hidenori. Education and Status Attainment in Modern Japan. Ph.D. Dissertation. Stanford University. 1978. 357 pp. DAI 39/6. (December 1978). Page 3240-A. Order # 7822505.

2168. Griesy, Paul V. The Doshisha, 1875-1919: The Indigenization of an Institution (2 Volumes). Ed.D. Dissertation. Columbia University. 1973. 580 pp. DAI 34/5. (November 1973). Page 2352-A. Order # 73-24,069.

2169. Halpin, Keum C. Reform in University Governance in Japan: Case of the University of Tsukuba. Ph.D. Dissertation. University of Washington. 1978. 196 pp. DAI 39/12. (August 1978). Page 698-A. Order # 7814438.

2170. Haslett, Jacqueline G. A History of Physical Education and Sport in Japan from 1868 through 1972. Ed.D. Dissertation. Boston University. 1977. 1104 pp. DAI 38/9. (March 1978). Page 5333-A. Order # 7732773.

2171. Hopper, Helen M. The Conflict Between Japanese Tradition and Western Learning in the Meiji Intellectual Mori Ogai (1862-1922). Ph.D. Dissertation. Washington University. 1976. 301 pp. DAI 37/8. (February 1977). Page 5282-A. Order # 77-4036.

2172. Kamiyama, Tamie. Ideology and Patterns of Women's Education in Japan. Ph.D. Dissertation. St. Louis University. 1977. 318 pp. DAI 39/3. (September 1978). Page 1195-A. Order # 7814588.

2173. Kim, Soon-Ja. Historical Development of Japanese Secondary Technical Education, 1870-1935. Ph.D. Dissertation. University of Pittsburgh. 1978. 254 pp. DAI 40/2. (August 1978). Page 711-A. Order # 7917428.

2174. Koizumi, Kenkichiro. The Development of Physics in Meiji Japan: 1868-1912. Ph.D. Dissertation. University of Pennsylvania. 1973. 295 pp. DAI 34/4. (October 1973). Page 1828-A. Order # 73-24,167.

2175. Krauss, Ellis S. Radicals Revisited: A Longitudinal Political Socialization Study of Japanese Student Activists. Ph.D. Dissertation. Stanford University. 1973. 365 pp. DAI 33/12. (June 1973). Page 6984-A. Order # 73-14,918.

2176. Lee, Kenneth B. The Postwar Reforms and Educational Development in Japan, 1945-1970. Ph.D. Dissertation. University of Southern California. 1974. 504 pp. DAI 35/5. (November 1974). Page 2739-A. Order # 74-23,596.

2177. Meynardie, Mary E.W. The Role of Education in the Modernization of Japan. Ed.D. Dissertation. Toledo University. 1973. 279 pp. DAI 34/9. (March 1974). Page 5674-A. Order # 74-6933.

2178. Miller, Ernest R. Mission to Japan. Ed.D. Dissertation. University of Cincinnati. 1977. 158 pp. DAI 38/5. (November 1977). Page 2462-A. Order # 77-22,802.

2179. Molony, Kathleen S. One Woman Who Dared: Ichikawa Fusae and the Japanese Woman's Suffrage Movement. Ph.D. Dissertation. University of Michigan. 1980. 389 pp. DAI 41/2. (August 1980). Page 763-A. Order # 8017323.

2180. Nishi, Toshio. Politics of Freedom: American Occupation of Japan 1945-1952. Ph.D. Dissertation. University of Washington. 1976. 350 pp. DAI 37/5. (November 1976). Page 2685-A. Order # 76-25,441.

2181. Nishihara, Isao. Western Influences on the Modernization of Japanese Education, 1868-1912. Ph.D. Dissertation. Ohio State University. 1972. 482 pp. DAI 33/4. (October 1972). Page 1474-A. Order # 72-27,071.

2182. Okachi, Katsuji. An Analysis of Economic Returns of Educational Investment: Its Role in Determining the Significance of Educational Planning in Japan. Ph.D. Dissertation. Florida State University. 1980. 219 pp. DAI 41/3. (September 1980). Page 855-A. Order # 8018843.

2183. Pempel, T.J. The Politics of Higher Education in Postwar Japan. Ph.D. Dissertation. Columbia University. 1975. 330 pp. DAI 36/6. (December 1975). Page 3993-A. Order # 75-27,452.

2184. Roden, Donald T. School-Days in Imperial Japan: A Case Study in Adolescence and Student Culture. Ph.D. Dissertation. University of Wisconsin. 1975. 719 pp. DAI 36/12. (June 1976). Page 8239-A. Order # 76-8230.

2185. Rubinger, Richard. Shijuku: Private Academies of the Tokugawa Period. Ph.D. Dissertation. Columbia University. 1979. 296 pp. DAI 42/6. (December 1981). Page 2808-A. Order # 8125379.

2186. Sardaky, Nick. International Politics and the Left Wing Student Movement in Japan, 1952-1970. Ph.D. Dissertation. University of Utah. 1970. 171 pp. DAI 31/8. (February 1971). Page 3909-OA. Order # 71-3015.

2187. Smith, II, Henry D. Student Radicals in Prewar Japan. Ph.D. Dissertation. Harvard University. 1970. No information available.

2188. Sweeney, Arlyn G. An Investigation into the Factors Contributing to the High Literacy Rate in Japan. Ed.D. Dissertation. University of Southern California. 1978. 110 pp. DAI 39/9. (March 1979). Page 5253-A. No Order #.

2189. Suzuki, Itoko. Administrative Reform in Japan During 1962-1964. Ph.D. Dissertation. New York University. 1980. 397 pp. DAI 41/6. (December 1980). Page 2763-A. Order # 8027927.

[No entry 2190]

2191. Thurston, Donald R. The Interests of Teachers: A Study of the Japan Teachers' Union. Ph.D. Dissertation. Columbia University. 1970. 469 pp. DAI 32/1. (July 1971). Page 514-A. Order # 71-17,551.

2192. Totero, Susan H. The Junior College in Japan. Ed.D. Dissertation.
       Nova University. 1975. 240 pp. DAI 37/10. (April 1977). Page
       6231-A. Order # 77-7791.

2193. Tsuchimori, Gary H. The Rapid Expansion of Universities in Postwar
       Japan with Particular Reference to Private Universities. Ed.D. Dis-
       sertation. Columbia University. 1980. 257 pp. DAI 41/4. (Oc-
       tober 1980). Page 1438-A. Order # 8022186.

2194. Tsuchiyama, Bokumin. An Analysis and Reconstruction of the Con-
       cept of "The Whole Man" in the Theory of Education of Kuniyoshi
       Obara. Ph.D. Dissertation. Northwestern University. 1978. 150
       pp. DAI 39/8. (February 1979). Page 4843-A. Order # 7903381.

2195. Tsurumi, Elisabeth P. Japanese Colonial Education in Taiwan, 1895-
       1945. Ph.D. Dissertation. Harvard University. 1971. No informa-
       tion available.

2196. Van Pelt, Jerry L. Kakushu Gakko: A Study of the Non-Formal
       Miscellaneous Schools of Japan. Ph.D. Dissertation. Michigan State
       University. 1975. 135 pp. DAI 36/9. (March 1976). Page 5746-A.
       Order # 76-5663.

2197. Westney, Dorothy E. Organizational Development in Meiji Japan: A
       Study of Perfectural Variation in Modernization, 1880-1915. Ph.D.
       Dissertation. Princeton University. 1978. 344 pp. DAI 39/4.
       (October 1978). Page 2577-A. Order # 7818362.

2198. Wheeler, Donald F. The Japanese Student Movement: Value Politics,
       Student Politics and the Tokyo University Struggle. Ph.D. Disser-
       tation. Columbia University. 1974. 453 pp. DAI 36/2. (August
       1975). Page 1129-A. Order # 75-16,149.

2199. Wray, Harry J. Changes and Continuity in Japanese Images of the
       Kokutai and Attitudes and Roles Toward the Outside World, A Con-
       tent Analysis of Japanese Textbooks, 1903-1945. Ph.D. Dissertation.
       University of Hawaii. 1971. 438 pp. DAI 32/6. (December 1971).
       Page 3235-A. Order # 72-294.

2200. Yamamura, Satoshi. Politics and Education in Early Meiji Japan: The
       Modern Military System and the Formation of Gakusei (The Funda-
       mental Code of Education in 1872). Ph.D. Dissertation. University
       of California, Berkeley. 1978. 251 pp. DAI 40/7. (January 1980).
       Page 3831-A. Order # 8000577.

2201. Yoshida, Tadashi. The Rangaku of Shizuki Tadao: The Introduction
       of Western Science into Tokugawa Japan. Ph.D. Dissertation.
       Princeton University. 1974. 433 pp. DAI 35/9. (March 1974).
       Page 6083-A. Order # 75-6697.

Korea, North and South

2202. Bang, Hung K. H. Japan's Colonial Educational Policy in Korea,

1905-1930. Ph.D. Dissertation. University of Arizona. 1972. 241 pp. DAI 33/7. (January 1973). Page 3522-A. Order # 72-31,848.

2203. Beack, Jong-ouk. Education for Librarianship in the Republic of Korea Since World War II: An Analysis of the Past and Present Status, and Proposed Standards for the Future. Ph.D. Dissertation. George Peabody College for Teachers. 1978. 357 pp. DAI 39/8. (February 1979). Page 4750-A. Order # 7902487.

2204. Choe, Byung S. The Impact of the Government Policy on the Development of Education in the First Republic of Korea, 1948-1960. Ph.D. Dissertation. University of Pittsburgh. 1971. 292 pp. DAI 32/9. (March 1972). Page 4998-A. Order # 72-7884.

2205. Choi, Sung C. Korean Christian Higher Education in Transition: The Impact of Western Philosophies. Ph.D. Dissertation. Graduate Theological Union. 1975. 207 pp. DAI 36/8. (February 1976). Page 5078-A. Order # 75-28,498.

2206. Chung, Joong-Gun. Japanese Colonial Administration in Korea, 1905-1919. Ph.D. Dissertation. Claremont Graduate School. 1971. 214 pp. DAI 32/4. (October 1971). Page 2150-A. Order # 71-21,661.

2207. Cole, Ross H. The Koreanization of Elementary Citizenship Education in South Korea: 1948-1974. Ed.D. Dissertation. Arizona State University. 1975. 468 pp. DAI 36/8. (February 1976). Page 5017-A. Order # 76-3762.

2208. Dodge, Herbert W. A History of U.S. Assistance to Korean Education: 1953-1966. Ed.D. Dissertation. George Washington University. 1971. 326 pp. DAI 32/6. (December 1971). Page 3067-A. Order # 72-456.

2209. Kim, Anthony H. The History of School Music Education in Korea from 1886 to the Present. Ed.D. Dissertation. University of Northern Colorado. 1976. 119 pp. DAI 37/4. (October 1976). Page 2045-A. Order # 76-23,179.

2210. Kim, Chung H. Changing Functions of Women's Higher Education in the Republic of Korea: A Study of Educational Equality Between Men and Women. Ph.D. Dissertation. George Peabody College for Teachers. 1975. 304 pp. DAI 36/4. (October 1975). Page 2052-A. Order # 75-22,275.

2211. Kim, Jin E. An Analysis of the National Planning Process for Educational Development in the Republic of Korea, 1945-1970. Ph.D. Dissertation. University of Wisconsin. 1973. 274 pp. DAI 34/12. (June 1974). Page 7490-A. Order # 74-9003.

2212. Kim, Uk H. An Examination of the Interplay of Culture and Education in Korea: A Comparative Study. Ph.D. Dissertation. Claremont Graduate School. 1972. 275 pp. DAI 33/5. (November 1972). Page 2075-A. Order # 72-30,559.

2213. Martin, James R. Institutionalization and Professionalization of the Republic of Korea Army: The Impact of United States Military

Assistance through Development of A Military School System. Ph.D. Dissertation. Harvard University. 1973. 265 pp. n.p. No Order #.

2214. Son, Ye S. Curriculum Changes in Korean Elementary Education Since the Korean War. Ed.D. Dissertation. University of Missouri. 1978. 313 pp. DAI 39/8. (February 1979). Page 4704-A. Order # 7903936.

2215. Song, Byung S. Comparative Study of Ideological Influences on Educational Theory and Practice in North and South Korea. Ph.D. Dissertation. Wayne State University. 1974. 181 pp. DAI 35/7. (January 1975). Page 4277-A. Order # 74-29,866.

2216. Sung, Ha W. Education and Political Ideology in North Korea: A Critical Analysis of Educational Policy, Aims and Nationalism (1945-1970). Ph.D. Dissertation. George Peabody College for Teachers. 1976. 336 pp. DAI 37/8. (February 1977). Page 5027-A. Order # 77-3121.

2217. Wayland, Corita A. The Development of Institutions of Higher Education of the Korea Mission, Presbyterian Chruch, U.S. Ed.D. Dissertation. University of Georgia. 1972. 476 pp. DAI 33/7. (January 1973). Page 3341-A. Order # 72-34,161.

Malaysia

2218. Ahmad, Zainal A.B. Educational Reform and Ethnic Response: An Historical Study of the Development of a National System of Education in West Malaysia. Ph.D. Dissertation. University of California, Los Angeles. 1980. 284 pp. DAI 41/4. (October 1980). Page 1441-A. Order # 8023263.

2219. Loh, Philip F.S. British Educational Strategy in the Malay States, 1874-1940. Ph.D. Dissertation. Stanford University. 1970. 265 pp. DAI 31/11. (May 1971). Page 5814-A. Order # 71-12,944.

Nepal

2220. Pande, Badri D. Development of Higher Education in Nepal, 1918-1976. Ph.D. Dissertation. Southern Illinois University. 1978. 237 pp. DAI 39/10. (April 1979). Page 5979-A. Order # 7908068.

People's Republic of China

2221. Bich, Tran-Huy. Political Qualifications and Academic Achievement

as Criteria to Access to Higher Education in the People's Republic
of China, 1949-1976. Ph.D. Dissertation. University of Texas.
1980. 361 pp. DAI 41/4. (October 1980). Page 1420-A. Order #
8021402.

2222. Bietz, Gary R. The Politics of Educational Reform in the People's
Republic of China, 1966-68. Ph.D. Dissertation. New York Univer-
sity. 1972. 340 pp. DAI 33/11. (May 1973). Page 6264-A.
Order # 73-11,672.

2223. Bratton, Dale L. The Politics of Educational Reform in the People's
Republic of China, 1966-1973. Ph.D. Dissertation. University of
California, Berkeley. 1978. 315 pp. DAI 40/2. (August 1979).
Page 1047-A. Order # 7914550.

2224. Burk, Paula E. Education in the People's Republic of China: A
Study of Continuity and Change in Educational Ethic, Policy and
Practice. Ph.D. Dissertation. Syracuse University. 1980. 622 pp.
DAI 42/1. (July 1981). Page 30-A. Order # 8114157.

2225. Chaffee, John W. Education and Examinations in Sung Society (960-
1279). Ph.D. Dissertation. University of Chicago. 1979. n.p.
DAI 40/4. (October 1979). Page 2209-A. No Order #.

2226. Che, Wai-Kin. The Modern Chinese Family, 1959-1975. Ph.D. Dissertation. North Texas State University. 1978. 308 pp. DAI 39/7.
(January 1979). Page 4522-A. Order # 7824640.

2227. Deal, David M. National Minority Policy in Southwest China, 1911-
1965. Ph.D. Dissertation. University of Washington. 1971. 427 pp.
DAI 323/8. (February 1972). Page 4510-A. Order # 72-7334-A.

2228. Franklin, Richard K. Conflict Among Chinese Elites Over Moderniza-
tion Values, Strategies and Educational Policies, 1957-1967. Ph.D.
Dissertation. University of Kentucky. 1976. 319 pp. DAI 37/6.
(December 1976). Page 3872-A. Order # 76-28,109.

2229. Ginsberg, Philip H. Higher Education and Development in the People's
Republic of China, 1958-1966. Ph.D. Dissertation. Brown University.
1976. 279 pp. DAI 38/1. (July 1977). Page 455-A. Order # 77-
14,117.

2230. Glassman, Joel. The Implementation of Educational Policy in Communist China (1949-1965). Ph.D. Dissertation. University of Michigan.
1974. 355 pp. DAI 35/7. (January 1975). Page 4636-A. Order
75-699.

2231. Harrell, Paula S. The Years of the Young Radicals: The Chinese
Students in Japan, 1900-1905. Ph.D. Dissertation. Columbia Uni-
versity. 1970. 250 pp. DAI 32/1. (July 1971). Page 358-A.
Order # 71-17,500.

2232. Kolkatch, Jonathon. The Development of Modern Sports and Physical
Culture in China (ca. 1900-1970). Ph.D. Dissertation. Columbia
University. 1970. 343 pp. DAI 33/10. (April 1973). Page 5655-
A. Order # 73-8961.

2233. Kwong, Chak-Sin (Julia). Economy and Educational Development in China. Ph.D. Dissertation. University of Toronto. 1976. n.p. DAI 39/3. (September 1978). Page 1384-A. No Order #.

2234. Lang, Ting-Chih. School Systems in Communist China (1949-1963). Ed.D. Dissertation. Utah State University. 1974. 182 pp. DAI 34/12. (June 1974). Page 7468-A. Order # 74-13,235.

2235. Lawrie, Bruce R. Educational Missionaries in China: A Case Study of the Canadian Methodist Mission in Szechuan, West China, 1891-1925. Ph.D. Dissertation. University of Toronto. 1979. n.p. DAI 40/12. (June 1980). Page 6172-A. No Order #.

2236. Lee, Byung-Joo. Rural Reconstruction Movement in Kiangsu Province, 1917-1937: Educators Turn to Rural Reform. Ph.D. Dissertation. University of Hawaii. 1978. 556 pp. DAI 39/5. (November 1978). Page 3091-A. No Order #.

2237. Lee, Kuo-Jow. The Treatment of China in American Comparative Education, 1911-1970. Ph.D. Dissertation. Loyola University, Chicago. 1976. 232 pp. DAI 37/5. (November 1976). Page 2514-A. Order # 76-24,446.

2238. Lee, Thomas H.C. Education in Northern Sung China. Ph.D. Dissertation. Yale University. 334 pp. 1974. DAI 36/1. (July 1975). Page 459-A. Order # 75-15,340.

2239. Letvin, Richard J. Work-Study Programs in the People's Republic of China. Ed.D. Dissertation. Rochester University. 1980. 240 pp. DAI 41/5. (November 1980). Page 1924-A. Order # 8025047.

2240. Lin, Yu-Tee. A Study of Hsuntzu's [most prominent exponent and defender of Confucianism during warring states period, 403-221 B.C.] Philosophy of Education. Ph.D. Dissertation. University of Iowa. 1974. 124 pp. DAI 36/1. (July 1975). Page 160-A. Order # 75-13,786.

2241. Mehta, Ganshyam D. The Politics of Student Protest in China—Blooming and Contending at Peking University, Spring 1957. Ph.D. Dissertation. University of Washington. 1976. 460 pp. DAI 37/5. (November 1976). Page 3157-A. Order # 76-25,435.

2242. Morcom, Agnes T. The Great Proletarian Cultural Revolution and Higher Education in China: 1966-1976. Ed.D. Dissertation. Fairleigh Dickinson University. 1979. 139 pp. DAI 41/4. (October 1980). Page 1434-A. No Order #.

2243. Proett, Polly-Ann B. A History of Libraries in the People's Republic of China, Including Some Aspects of College and University Library Development, 1949-1974. Ed.D. Dissertation. George Washington University. 1974. 231 pp. DAI 35/4. (October 1974). Page 1880-A. Order # 74-23,497.

2244. Ridley, Charles P. Educational Theory and Practice in Late Imperial China: The Teaching of Writing as a Special Case. Ph.D. Dissertation. Stanford University. 1973. 555 pp. DAI 34/3. (September 1973). Page 1110-A. Order # 73-20,512.

2245. Robinson, Jean C. Institutions, Charisma and Bureaucrats: Minbin
       Schools and the Leadership of Mao Zedong in the People's Republic
       of China. Ph.D. Dissertation. Cornell University. 1980. 372 pp.
       DAI 41/3. (September 1980). Page 1202-A. Order # 8020873.

2246. Schintz, Mary A. An Investigation of the Modernizing Role of the
       Maryknoll Sisters in China. Ph.D. Dissertation. University of Wis-
       consin. 1978. 571 pp. DAI 39/5. (November 1978). Page 3092-A.
       Order # 7815070.

2247. Singer, Martin. The Revolutionization of Youth in the People's Re-
       public of China. Ph.D. Dissertation. University of Michigan. 1977.
       570 pp. DAI 38/11. (May 1978). Page 6879-A. Order # 7804810.

2248. Sun, Rhoda S.L.L. Mao's Ideology and its Effects on Chinese Society:
       Focus on the Impact of Health Education and Health Care. Ed.D.
       Dissertation. Boston University. 1977. 176 pp. DAI 38/9. (March
       1978). Page 5266-A. Order # 77327786.

2249. Walton-Vargo, Linda A. Education, Social Change, and Neo-Confucianism
       in Sung-Yuan China: Academies and the Local Elite in Ming Prefec-
       ture (NINGPO). Ph.D. Dissertation. University of Pennsylvania.
       1978. 294 pp. DAI 39/7. (January 1979). Page 4434-A. Order
       # 7824765.

2250. Wan, Helena S.Y. The Educational Thought of Confucius. Ph.D.
       Dissertation. Loyola University, Chicago. 1980. 307 pp. DAI
       41/4. (October 1980). Page 1444-A. Order # 8020102.

2251. Wang, Chih-Yen. A Study of the Social Studies Program in Chinese
       Secondary Schools, 1929-1949. Ed.D. Dissertation. Temple Univer-
       sity. 1973. 234 pp. DAI 34/4. (October 1973). Page 1600-A.
       Order # 73-23,369.

2252. Yao, Katherine Y.B. The Development of Science and Technical Edu-
       cation in China: The Soviet Phase, 1949-1957. Ph.D. Dissertation.
       Columbia University. 1972. 228 pp. DAI 34/2. (August 1973).
       Page 522-A. Order # 73-9057.

Philippines

2253. Acierto, Maria G. American Influence in Shaping Philippine Secondary
       Education: An Historical Perspective, 1898-1978. Ed.D. Dissertation.
       Loyola University, Chicago. 1980. 300 pp. DAI 41/3. (September
       1980). Page 1012-A. Order # 8019009.

2254. Ang, Ma. Milda L. A Study of Philippine Higher Education: Its De-
       velopmental Role. Ph.D. Dissertation. Boston College. 1971. 154
       pp. DAI 32/6. (December 1971). Page 3046-A. Order # 72-692.

2255. Apilado, Mariano C. Revolution, Colonialism and Mission: A Study
       of the Role of Protestant Churches in the United States Rule of the

Philippines, 1898-1928. Ph.D. Dissertation. Vanderbilt University.
1976. 545 pp. DAI 37/9. (March 1977). Page 5985-A. Order #
77-6092.

2256. Bantug, Victoria P. Elements of Propagandistic Bias in the Philippine
History Textbooks Used in Philippine Schools During the American
Era and the Era of the Philippine Republic--A Comparative Analysis.
Ph.D. Dissertation. New York University. 1976. 249 pp. DAI
37/9. (March 1977). Page 5999-A. Order # 77-5287.

2257. Bowler, Francis L. The Beliefs of Educational Philosophers in Philippine Teacher Training Institutions. Ed.D. Dissertation. University
of Southern California. 1973. 200 pp. DAI 34/6. (December 1973).
Page 3230-A.

2258. De La Cruz, Leonardo D. An Analysis of Philippine Social Studies
Textbooks. Ph.D. Dissertation. Stanford University. 1971. 188
pp. DAI 32/2. (August 1971). Page 665-A. Order # 71-19,669.

2259. Douglas, Donald E. American Education and the Creation of an Inde-
pendent Philippines: The Commonwealth Period, 1935-1941. Ph.D.
Dissertation. University of Michigan. 1979. 334 pp. DAI 40/5.
(November 1979). Page 2514-A. Order # 7925139.

2260. Dufault, David V. Francis B. Sayre and the Commonwealth of the
Philippines, 1936-1942. Ph.D. Dissertation. University of Oregon.
1972. 517 pp. DAI 33/5. (November 1972). Page 2282-A. Order
72-28,135.

2261. Fritz, David. The Philippine Question: American Civil/Military Policy
in the Philippines, 1898-1905. Ph.D. Dissertation. University of
Texas. 1977. 768 pp. DAI 38/7. (January 1978). Page 4325-A.
Order # 77-29,029.

2262. Gott, OFM Conv., Reverend Camillus. William Cameron Forbes and
the Philippines, 1904-1946. Ph.D. Dissertation. Indiana University.
1974. 257 pp. DAI 35/4. (October 1974). Page 2171-A. Order #
74-22,734.

2263. Hill, David L. Theological Education in Missions as a Factor in Bap-
tist Church Growth with Special Emphasis on the Philippines. D.
Mn. Dissertation. Fuller Theological Seminary. 1979. 174 pp.
DAI 40/10. (April 1980). Page 5478-A. Order # 8001425.

2264. Horner, Layton. Japanese Military Administration in Malaysia and the
Philippines. Ph.D. Dissertation. University of Arizona. 1973.
322 pp. DAI 34/3. (September 1973). Page 1209-A. Order # 73-
20,637.

2265. Lepper, John A. Philippine Student Politics: With Special Emphasis
on the University of the Philippines. Ph.D. Dissertation. Georgetown University. 1971. 301 pp. DAI 32/5. (November 1971).
Page 2759-A. Order # 71-30,353.

2266. Manalang, Priscila S. A Philippine Rural School: Its Cultural Dimen-
sions. Ph.D. Dissertation. University of Pittsburgh. 1971. 464
pp. DAI 12/1. (June 1972). Page 6838-A. Order # 72-16,948.

2267. Maniago, Jo Anne B. The First Peace Corps: The Work of American Teachers in the Philippines, 1900-1910. Ph.D. Dissertation. Boston University. 1971. 324 pp. DAI 32/4. (October 1971). Page 2013-A. Order # 71-26,450.

2268. Martin, James D. American Influence in the Philippines as a Factor in Philippine National Development. Ph.D. Dissertation. Southern Illinois University. 1974. 425 pp. DAI 36/2. (August 1975). Page 1067-A. Order # 75-16,274.

2269. May, Glenn A. America in the Philippines: The Shaping of a Colonial Policy, 1898-1913. Ph.D. Dissertation. Yale University. 1975. 396 pp. DAI 36/6. (December 1975). Page 3932-A. Order # 75-27,024.

2270. Oades, Rizalino A. The Social and Economic Background of Philippine Nationalism, 1830-1892. Ph.D. Dissertation. University of Hawaii. 1974. 580 pp. DAI 35/6. (December 1974). Page 3650-A. Order # 74-27,686.

2271. Rambo, David L. The Christian Missionary Alliance in the Philippines, 1901-1970. Ph.D. Dissertation. New York University. 1975. 322 pp. DAI 36/4. (October 1975). Page 2118-A. Order # 75-21,160.

2272. Recana, Jaime R. Student Activism and Implications for Academic Governance in the Bicol University, Legazpi City, Philippines. Ed.D. Dissertation. Western Michigan University. 1973. 282 pp. DAI 34/7. (January 1974). Page 3924-A. Order # 73-32,497.

2273. Resposo, Epifania R.C. The Role of Universities in the Developing Philippines. Ed.D. Dissertation. Columbia University. 1970. 222 pp. DAI 31/7. (January 1971). Page 3301-A. Order # 70-26,800.

2274. Reyes, Amelia L.B. Impact of Centralized Political Authority on Higher Educational Organizations: The Philippine Case. Ph.D. Dissertation. Stanford University. 1977. 189 pp. DAI 38/9. (March 1978). Page 5285-A. Order # 7802222.

2275. Salas, Dominador J. Selected Relationships Between Education and Economic Development with Special Reference to the Philippines. Ed.D. Dissertation. Rutgers, the State University. 1972. 130 pp. DAI 33/4. (October 1972). Page 1331-A. Order # 72-26,795.

2276. Tovera, David G. A History of English Teaching in the Philippines: From Unlilingualism to Bilingualism. Ph.D. Dissertation. Northwestern University. 1975. 192 pp. DAI 36/7. (January 1976). Page 4191-A. Order # 75-29,771.

2277. Treadway, Sandra G. Terra Incognita: The Philippine Islands and the Establishment of American Colonial Policy, 1898-1904. Ph.D. Dissertation. University of Virginia. 1978. 295 pp. DAI 40/2. (August 1979). Page 1034-A. Order # 7916292.

Singapore

2278. Ahmad, Zahoor. Analysis of the Effects of Changes in Administrative
       Policies of the Singapore Ministry of Education on the Operation of
       the Singapore School System, 1960-1972. Ph.D. Dissertation. Uni-
       versity of Kansas. 1973. 206 pp. DAI 34/12. (June 1974). Page
       7477-A. Order # 74-12,515.

2279. Wilson, Harold E. Educational Policies in a Changing Society: Singa-
       pore, 1918-1959. Ph.D. Dissertation. University of British Columbia.
       1975. n.p. DAI 36/7. (January 1976). Page 4693-A. No Order #.

Sri Lanka (Ceylon)

2280. Bowles, Lawrence T. A History of Medical Education in Ceylon, 1942-
       1967. Ph.D. Dissertation. New York University. 1971. 117 pp.
       DAI 32/5. (November 1971). Page 2450-A. Order # 71-28,523.

Thailand

2281. Bhuapirom, Ladtongbai. A History of the Reorganization and Exten-
       sion of Thai Public Elementary Education, 1946-1975. Ed.D. Disser-
       tation. Loyola University, Chicago. 1978. 228 pp. DAI 38/10.
       (April 1978). Page 5962-A. No Order #.

2282. Kanthawongs, Charoen. Bangkok College: History, Evaluation and
       Projection. Ph.D. Dissertation. Syracuse University. 1978. 285 pp.
       DAI 39/6. (December 1978). Page 3402-A. Order # 7823570.

2283. Zack, Stephen J. Buddhist Education Under Prince Wachirayan
       Warorot. Ph.D. Dissertation. Cornell University. 1977. 277 pp.
       DAI 38/12. (June 1978). Page 7503-A. Order # 7807772.

Vietnam

2284. Bong, Vu Duc. The Vietnam Independent Education Movement (1900-
       1908). Ph.D. Dissertation. University of California, Los Angeles.
       1971. 307 pp. DAI 32/12. (June 1972). Page 6672-A. Order #
       72-13,591.

2285. Duong, Nhu Duc. Education in Vietnam Under the French Domination,

Vietnam 213

1862-1945. Ph.D. Dissertation. Southern Illinois University. 1978.
285 pp. DAI 39/10. (April 1978). Page 5984-A. Order # 7908021.

2286. Hess, David L. The Educated Vietnamese Middle Class of Metropolitan
Siagon and their Legacy of Confucian Authority. Ph.D. Dissertation.
New York University. 1977. 577 pp. DAI 38/10. (April 1978).
Page 6264-A. Order # 7803101.

2287. Kelly, Gail P. Franco-Vietnamese Schools, 1918 to 1938. Ph.D. Dissertation. University of Wisconsin. 1975. 424 pp. DAI 36/12.
(June 1976). Page 7907-A. Order # 76-8211.

2288. Lewis, Jr., Robert J. A Study of the Elementary Teacher Education
Programs in South Vietnam with Emphasis on the Participation of
Southern Illinois University, 1961-1971. Ph.D. Dissertation. South-
ern Illinois University. 1972. 582 pp. DAI 33/9. (March 1973).
Page 4883-A. Order # 73-6224.

2289. Phuoc, Nguyen H. Contemporary Educational Philosophies in Vietnam,
1954-1974: A Comparative Analysis. Ph.D. Dissertation. University
of Southern California. 1975. 184 pp. DAI 36/1. (July 1975).
Page 48-A. Order # 75-15,564.

HISTORY OF AFRICAN EDUCATION

General

2290. Livingston, Thomas W. Edward Wilmot Blyden, West African Cultural
Nationalist: His Educational Activities and Ideas. Ph.D. Dissertation.
Columbia University. 1971. 504 pp. DAI 35/7. (January 1975).
Page 4215-A. Order # 74-29,618.

2291. Sabatier, Peggy R. Educating a Colonial Elite: The William Ponty
School and its Graduates (1903-1950). Ph.D. Dissertation. University of Chicago. 1977. n.p. DAI 38/8. (February 1978). Page
4985-A. No Order #.

Cameroon

2292. Booth, Bernard F. A Comparative Study of Mission and Government
Involvement in Educational Development in West Cameroon, 1922-1969.
Ph.D. Dissertation. University of California, Los Angeles. 1973.
362 pp. DAI 34/7. (January 1974). Page 3932-A. Order # 73-32,051.

Congo, Democratic Republic of

2293. Rideout, William M. Education and Elites: The Making of the New
Elites and the Formal Educational System in the Congo. Ph.D. Dissertation. Stanford University. 1971. 562 pp. DAI 32/10. (April
1972). Page 5581-A. Order # 72-11,648.

Ethiopia

2294. Engu, Gebeyehu. Educational Planning and Educational Development in Ethiopia: 1957-1973. Ph.D. Dissertation. University of Wisconsin. 1980. 296 pp. DAI 41/9. (March 1981). Page 3796-A. Order # 8020558.

Ghana

2295. Ampiaw, Joseph A. The Post-Colonial Nationalization of Elementary School Programs and Policies in Ghana. Ph.D. Dissertation. University of Connecticut. 1977. 340 pp. DAI 38/8. (February 1978). Page 4565-A. Order # 7731052.

Ivory Coast

2296. Hamilton, Karen E. The Ivorienzation of the National University of the Ivory Coast, 1958-1977. Ph.D. Dissertation. University of Pennsylvania. 1979. 376 pp. DAI 40/10. (April 1980). Page 5333-A. Order # 8009410.

Kenya

2297. Corry, Joseph J. The History of Agricultural Education in Kenya, 1922-1954. Ph.D. Dissertation. University of Wisconsin. 1971. 154 pp. DAI 32/2. (August 1971). Page 876-A. Order # 71-16,067.

2298. Fischer, Heinz. The Influence of Jomo Kenyatta and Julius K. Nyerere on Education and Development in Kenya and Tanzania. Ph.D. Dissertation. University of Southern California. 1977. n.p. DAI 38/10. (April 1978). Page 5963-A. No Order #.

2299. Kay, Stafford. The Southern Abaluyia, the Friends African Mission, and the Development of Education in Western Kenya, 1902-1965. Ph.D. Dissertation. University of Wisconsin. 1973. 330 pp. DAI 34/6. (December 1973). Page 3103-A. Order # 73-21,003.

2300. Kinyanjui, Kabiru. The Political Economy of Educational Inequality: A Study of the Roots of Educational Inequality in Colonial and Post-Colonial Kenya. Ed.D. Dissertation. Harvard University. 1979. 350 pp. DAI 40/11. (May 1980). Page 6021-A. Order # 8010533.

2301. Kiteme, Kamuti. The Impact of A European Education upon Africans in Kenya: 1846-1940. Ph.D. Dissertation. Yeshiva University. 1970. 234 pp. DAI 31/9. (March 1971). Page 4502-A. Order # 71-5687.

2302. Kovar, Michael. The Kikiyu Independent School Movement: Inter-
      action of Politics and Education in Kenya (1923-1953). Ed.D. Dis-
      sertation. University of California, Los Angeles. 1970. 369 pp.
      DAI 31/5. (November 1970). Page 21240-A. Order # 70-22,810.

2303. Lohrentz, Kenneth P. The Politics of Educational Development in
      Central and Southern North Nyanza, Kenya, 1904-1939. Ph.D. Dis-
      sertation. Syracuse University. 1977. 422 pp. DAI 38/8. (Feb-
      ruary 1978). Page 4989-A. Order # 7730741.

2304. Mambo, Robert M. Challenges of Western Education in the Coast
      Province of Kenya, 1890-1963. Ph.D. Dissertation. Columbia Uni-
      versity. 1980. 341 pp. DAI 41/2. (August 1980). Page 566-A.
      Order # 8017089.

2305. Nguru, Godfrey M. A Study of Educational Expenditures in Kenya,
      1963-1975. Ed.D. Dissertation. University of Tennessee. 1977.
      163 pp. DAI 38/7. (January 1978). Page 3945-A. Order # 77-
      27,682.

2306. Njoroge, Nganga. An Outline of the Historical Development of Ele-
      mentary Education in Kenya, 1884-1970. Ph.D. Dissertation. Ohio
      University. 1972. 249 pp. DAI 33/2. (August 1972). Page 536-
      A. Order # 72-22,063.

2307. Schilling, Donald G. British Policy for African Education in Kenya,
      1895-1939. Ph.D. Dissertation. University of Wisconsin. 1972.
      559 pp. DAI 33/7. (January 1973). Page 3559-A. Order # 72-
      23,334.

2308. Truman, Robert H. The Origins and Development of Racial Pluralism
      in the Educational System of Kenya from 1895 to 1925. Ph.D. Dis-
      sertation. University of Illinois. 1973. 366 pp. DAI 34/2. (Au-
      gust 1973). Page 595-A. Order # 73-17,657.

Liberia

2309. Nguma, Fawoni. Missions and Education in Liberia: A Check List of
      Annotated Writings (1824-1977) on Western Education in Liberia with
      Emphasis on its Mission Origins. Ph.D. Dissertation. University of
      Missouri, Kansas City. 1979. 598 pp. DAI 40/10. (April 1980).
      Page 5393-A. Order # 8009372.

Malawi

2310. Harawa, Bernard A. The Teachers Union of Malawi: Its Emergence,
      Development and Activities from 1943-1973. Ed.D. Dissertation.
      Columbia University. 1974. 248 pp. DAI 35/6. (December 1974).
      Page 3478-A. Order # 74-26,594.

2311. Lange, Harold M. The Development of Higher Education in an Emer-
gent Country: Malawi, Africa, 1960-1967. Ed.D. Dissertation. University of Southern California. 1973. 237 pp. DAI 34/7. (January
1974). Page 3912-A. Order # 73-31,653.

Mali

2312. Saad, Elias N. Social History of Timbuktu, 1400-1900: The Role of
Muslim Scholars and Notables. Ph.D. Dissertation. Northwestern
University. 1979. 449 pp. DAI 40/6. (December 1979). Page '^
3468-A. Order # 7927437.

Nigeria

2313. Adesina, Sylvester A. An Analysis of Nigeria's Educational Plans
and Actual Educational Development between 1945 and 1970. Ed.D.
Dissertation. Columbia University. 1974. 303 pp. DAI 35/1.
(July 1975). Page 115-A. Order # 74-15,960.

2314. Ajala, Oyewole O. A Historical Review of Secondary Education in
Western Nigeria: 1842-1976. Ph.D. Dissertation. North Texas
State University. 1977. 238 pp. DAI 38/3. (September 1977).
Page 1321-A. Order # 77-19,655.

2315. Alafe-Aluko, Michael O. The Historical Development of the Comprehensive High School Aiyetoro, Nigeria: A Case Study in Educational
Development (1962-1972). Ph.D. Dissertation. University of Washington. 1973. 772 pp. DAI 34/12. (June 1974). Page 7478-A.
Order # 74-13,759.

2316. Anwukah, Anthony G. A History of the Development of Nigerian Education, 1960-1970. Ph.D. Dissertation. University of Washington.
1978. 236 pp. DAI 39/2. (August 1978). Page 633-A. Order #
7814401.

2317. Boyan, Douglas R. Educational Policy Formulation in the North of
Nigeria, 1900-1969. Ph.D. Dissertation. University of Wisconsin.
1972. 431 pp. DAI 33/9. (March 1973). Page 4708-A. Order #
72-31,665.

2318. Chamberlain, John W. The Development of Islamic Education in Kano
City, Nigeria, with Emphasis on Legal Education in the 19th and 20th
Centuries. Ph.D. Dissertation. Columbia University. 1875. 275 pp.
DAI 36/5. (November 1975). Page 2681-A. Order # 76-25,261.

2319. Ekam, Anna G. The Contributions of the Holy Child Sisters to
Women's Education in the Cross River State of Nigeria from 1930 to
1967. Ph.D. Dissertation. Catholic University of America. 1980.
196 pp. DAI 41/12. (June 1981). Page 4902-A. Order # 8111645.

2320. Emeji, Michael J. Art and National Policy Development: The Role of Government in the Arts and a Pre-Plan Toward Artistic Policy in Southern Nigeria. Ph.D. Dissertation. Florida State University. 1980. 247 pp. DAI 41/3. (September 1980). Page 905-A. Order # 8019595.

2321. Enyia, Dike O. Higher Education in Nigeria from the Earliest Times to 1972. Ph.D. Dissertation. University of Michigan. 1975. 206 pp. DAI 36/6. (December 1975). Page 3442-A. Order # 75-29,214.

2322. Ettang, Domenic A.U. An Historical Analysis of Higher Education in Nigeria. Ph.D. Dissertation. University of Alabama. 1977. 395 pp. DAI 39/4. (October 1978). Page 1947-A. Order # 7818863.

2323. Eze, Linus C.I. A History of Elementary Education in Nigeria. 1870-1970. Ed.D. Dissertation. University of North Dakota. 1979. 234 pp. DAI 40/9. (March 1980). Page 4823-A. Order # 7928063.

2324. Hubbard, James P. Education Under Colonial Rule: A Short History of Katsina College, 1921-1942. Ph.D. Dissertation. University of Wisconsin. 1973. 422 pp. DAI 34/7. (January 1974). Page 4158-A. Order # 73-21,162.

2325. Mohammed, Abdullahi. A Hausa Scholar-Trader and His Library Collection: The Case Study of Umar Falke of Kano, Nigeria. Ph.D. Dissertation. Northwestern University. 1978. 581 pp. DAI 39/8. (February 1979). Page 5088-A. Order # 7903326.

2326. Njoku, Simeon E. The Emergence of Nigeria's First Land-Grant University: A Study of Higher Educational Policy Formulation, 1955-1975. Ph.D. Dissertation. Catholic University of America. 1977. 317 pp. DAI 38/3. (September 1977). Page 1161-A. Order # 77-17,517.

2327. Oduyale, Amos T. Twenty-Five Year History of the Olympic Movement in Nigeria, 1951-1976. Ph.D. Dissertation. Pennsylvania State University. 1979. 200 pp. DAI 40/11. (May 1980). Page 5778-A. Order # 8006035.

2328. Ogbulafor, Simeon O. The Appropriateness of Deweyan Democracy and Nyerere's Ujaama for Nigerian Education and Development. Ph.D. Dissertation. University of Kansas. 1978. 298 pp. DAI 39/12. (June 1979). Page 7217-A. Order # 7910602.

2329. Ogunsola, Albert F. An Historical Study of the Impact of Education Ordinances on Education in Northern Nigeria, 1916-1966. Ph.D. Dissertation. Ohio University. 1970. 157 pp. DAI 32/1. (July 1971). Page 138-A. Order # 71-16,489.

2330. Olutimayin, Mary A. The Interrelationship Between Schools and Political and Economic Institutions in the Development of Nigeria, 1900-1975 (A Case Study of Change and Modernization). Ed.D. Dissertation. Rutgers, the State University. 1978. 322 pp. DAI 39/1. (July 1978). Page 154-A. Order # 7810232.

2331. Rhodes, Barbara A. The Genesis of the 1959 Ashby Commission Report on Education in Nigeria. Ph.D. Dissertation. University of Southern California. 1973. 206 pp. DAI 33/10. (April 1973). Page 5415-A. Order # 73-9320.

2332. Taiwo, Emmanuel O. Nigerian Education Since Independence: Its Achievements, Challenges and Promises for the Future. Ph.D. Dissertation. University of Pittsburgh. 1976. 156 pp. DAI 38/2. (August 1977). Page 669-A. Order # 77-15,225.

Rwanda

2333. Kambandu, Deogratias. A Descriptive Case Study of the Evolution of Education in Rwanda (1962-1973). Ph.D. Dissertation. University of Maryland. 1979. 165 pp. DAI 40/9. (March 1980). Page 4927-A. Order # 8006695.

Senegal

2334. Maack, Mary N. A History of Libraries, Archives and Documentation Centers in Senegal from their Colonial Beginnings to 1975. D.C.S. Dissertation. Columbia University. 1978. 589 pp. DAI 39/8. (February 1979). Page 4569-A. Order # 7904099.

Sierra Leone

2335. Corby, Richard A. Western Educated Sons of Chiefs, District Commissioners, and Chiefdom: The Role of Bo School and its Graduates in the Local-Level Development in Sierra Leone, 1906-1961. Ph.D. Dissertation. University of Indiana. 1976. 321 pp. DAI 37/8. (February 1977). Page 5280-A. Order # 77-1878.

2336. Williams, Joy E.S. The Educated and Professional Elite in the Gold Coast and Sierra Leone, 1885-1914. Ph.D. Dissertation. University of California, Los Angeles. 1980. 176 pp. DAI 41/8. (February 1981). Page 3689-A. Order # 8104046.

South Africa

2337. Davies, John L. Christian National Education in South Africa: A Study of the Influence of Calvinism and Nationalism on Educational

Policy. Ph.D. Dissertation. University of Wisconsin. 1978. 392 pp.
DAI 39/3. (September 1978). Page 1382-A. Order # 7811716.

2338. Martin, Joseph P. Educating the Sotho, 1833-1884. Ph.D. Dissertation.
Columbia University. 1973. 253 pp. DAI 34/12. (June 1974).
Page 7562-A. Order # 74-12,739.

2339. Mbere, Aggrey M. An Analysis of the Role Between Bantu Education
and Christian Nationalism: A Study of the Role of Ideology and Education. Ed.D. Dissertation. Harvard University. 1979. 357 pp.
DAI 40/7. (January 1980). Page 3828-A. Order # 7927954.

2340. Msomi, James E.B. The Development of African Education in South
Africa: 1954-1977. Ph.D. Dissertation. Syracuse University. 1978.
255 pp. DAI 39/6. (December 1978). Page 3287-A. Order #
7823581.

Tanzania (Tanganyika)

2341. Nystrom, Bradley H. Schooling and its Introduction Among the Chagga
of Northern Tanzania. Ph.D. Dissertation. University of Wisconsin.
1977. 404 pp. DAI 38/8. (February 1978). Page 4621-A. Order
7719779.

2341. Johnson, Lathan O. The Role of Education in Western Culture: Tan-
zania as a Model of Education for Self-Reliance. Ph.D. Dissertation.
Brandeis University. 1980. 378 pp. DAI 41/5. (November 1980).
Page 2293-A. Order # 8024553.

2343. Van Onselen, Jurgens J. The Social, Economic and Political Influences
on Higher Education in Tanganyika Since Independence (1961-1970).
Ed.D. Dissertation. University of Houston. 1970. 188 pp. DAI
31/7. (January 1971). Page 3306-A. Order # 71-1464.

Uganda

2344. Battle, Vincent M. Education in Eastern Uganda, 1900-1939: A Study
of Initiative and Response During the Early Colonial Period. Ph.D.
Dissertation. Columbia University. 1974. 255 pp. DAI 35/6.
(December 1974). Page 3476-A. Order # 74-28,482.

2345. Morgan, Izola P. Education in Uganda: Historical Perspective. Ed.D.
Dissertation. University of Arkansas. 1980. 178 pp. DAI 41/5.
(November 1980). Page 1979-A. Order # 8025997.

2346. Muyanda-Mutebi, Peter. The History Curricula for Uganda Secondary
Schools, 1940-1970: A General Evaluative Study, Focusing on Attempts to Use History as a Factor in Developing National Consciousness

and a Sense of African Dignity. Ph.D. Dissertation. University of
California, Los Angeles. 1973. 425 pp. DAI 35/3. (September
1974). Page 1431-A. Order # 73-32,071.

2347. Van Lutsenburg Maas, Jacob. Education and Social Stratification in
Colonial Societies: The Case of Uganda. Ph.D. Dissertation. Co-
lumbia University. 1975. 190 pp. DAI 36/5. (November 1975).
Page 2685-A. Order # 75-25,737.

Zambia

2348. Christensen, James E. Occupational Education in Zambia: Obstacles
to the Development of Technical and Vocational Education Programs in
Zambia, 1885-1970. Ph.D. Dissertation. University of California,
Los Angeles. 1972. 189 pp. DAI 33/10. (April 1973). Page
5527-A. Order # 73-10,413.

2349. Guthrie, Charles C. The Emergence and Decline of Mission-Educated
Elite in Northeast Zambia, 1895-1964. Ph.D. Dissertation. University
of Indiana. 1978. 317 pp. DAI 39/2. (August 1978). Page 1040-
A. Order # 7813190.

2350. Peters, Harold E. The Contributions of Education to the Development
of Elites Among the Plateau Tonga of Zambia: A Comparative Study
of School-Leavers from Two Mission Schools, 1930-1965. Ph.D. Dissertation. University of Illinois. 1976. 174 pp. DAI 37/1. (July
1976). Page 47-A. Order # 76-16,181.

2351. Ragsdale, John P. The Educational Development of Zambia as Influ-
enced by Protestant Missions from 1880-1954. Ed.D. Dissertation.
Lehigh University. 1973. 410 pp. DAI 34/4. (October 1974).
Page 1669-A. Order # 73-23,815.

Zimbabwe (Rhodesia)

2352. Kumbula, Tendayi J.S. Education and Social Control in Southern
Rhodesia, 1946-1974. Ph.D. Dissertation. University of Southern
California. 1976. n.p. DAI 38/8. (February 1978). Page 4459-A.
No Order #.

2353. Mungazi, Dickson A. The Change of Black Attitudes Toward Educa-
tion in Rhodesia, 1900-1975. Ph.D. Dissertation. University of
Nebraska. 1977. 343 pp. DAI 38/12. (June 1978). Page 7182-A.
Order # 7809160.

2354. Siyakwazi, Ben J. A History of Church-Related Teacher Education
Colleges in Zimbabwe, 1928 to 1976. Ed.D. Dissertation. Rutgers,
the State University. 1979. 231 pp. DAI 40/2. (August 1979).
Page 712-A. Order # 7917917.

HISTORY OF MIDDLE EASTERN EDUCATION

General

2355. Beavers, Tedd D. Arabic Contributions to Educational Thought. Ph.D. Dissertation. Oklahoma State University. 1972. 197 pp. DAI 33/2. (August 1972). Page 599-A. Order # 72-22,434.

2356. Koloti, Sami A. The Reformation of Islam and the Impact of Jamal Al-Din Al Afghan (1839-1897) and Mohammad Abduhl (1849-1905) on Islamic Education. Ph.D. Dissertation. Marquette University. 1974. 166 pp. DAI 35/4. (October 1974). Page 2025-A. Order # 74-22,293.

2357. Yousif, Abdelwahid A. Muslim Learning During the Earlier Abbasid Era, 749-861 A.D. Ph.D. Dissertation. University of Toronto. 1978. n.p. DAI 39/7. (January 1979). Page 3989-A. No Order #.

Bahrain

2358. Al-Arrayed, Thuraya E. An Analysis of the Development of Administrative Structures in the Bahraini System of Education, 1919-1974. Ph.D. Dissertation. University of North Carolina. 155 pp. DAI 36/6. (December 1975). Page 3251-A. Order # 75-29,002.

Egypt

2359. Aroian, Lois A. Education, Language and Culture in Modern Egypt: Dar 'Ulum and its Graduates (1872-1923). Ph.D. Dissertation. University of Michigan. 1978. 427 pp. DAI 39/6. (December 1978). Page 3754-A. Order # 7822852.

2360. Wahaib, Abdul A. Education and the Status of Women in the Middle East with Special Reference to Egypt, Tunisia and Iraq. Ph.D. Dissertation. Southern Illinois University. 1970. 99 pp. DAI 31/8. (February 1971). Page 3915-A. Order # 71-2414.

Iran

2361. Hosseini-Fouladi, Fereydon. A Study of Educational Policy Translation in Iran, 1962-1977: Establishment of Education Corps and Educational Revolution Decrees. Ed.D. Dissertation. Catholic University of America. 1979. 192 pp. DAI 40/4. (October 1979). Page 1785-A. Order # 7922587.

2362. Mowahed-Ardabillie, Medhi. Education and the Pattern of Modernization in Iran, 1945-1974. Ph.D. Dissertation. Arizona State University. 1975. 193 pp. DAI 36/6. (December 1975). Page 3241-A. Order # 75-27,085.

2363. Sadeghy, Ghafur. An Historical Analysis of the Development of the Administrative Structure of Higher Education in Iran from 1900 to 1971. Ph.D. Dissertation. University of Oklahoma. 1972. 287 pp. DAI 33/3. (September 1972). Page 937-A. Order # 72-23,111.

2364. Safavi-Hemami, Sayed-Reyhan. An Historical Perspective of the Cultural Influences on Curriculum in Iranian Education with Emphasis on the Period 1900-1980. Ph.D. Dissertation. George Peabody College for Teachers. 1980. 91 pp. DAI 41/9. (March 1981). Page 3916-A. Order # 8105525.

Iraq

2365. Diskin, S.J., Rev. John J. The "Genesis" of the Government Educational System in Iraq (1793-1920). Ph.D. Dissertation. University of Pittsburgh. 1971. 527 pp. DAI 32/8. (February 1972). Page 4388-A. Order # 72-7885.

2365a. Goodblatt, David M. Rabbinic Academic Institutions in Sasanian Babylonia. Ph.D. Dissertation. Brown University. 1972. 310 pp. DAI 33/8. (February 1973). Page 4288-A. Order # 73-2274.

Israel

2366. Al-Agah, Reyad F. Arab-Jewish Public Education in Israel from 1948 to 1967: And Implications for Palestinian Arab Minority Children. Ph.D. Dissertation. University of Kansas. 1978. 206 pp. DAI 39/11. (May 1979). Page 6403-A. Order # 7910592.

2367. Apsel, Joyce A.F. The Kibbutz: An Historical Perspective. Ph.D. Dissertation. University of Rochester. 1977. 419 pp. DAI 38/6. (December 1977). Page 3647-A. Order # 77-25,428.

2368. Aquil, Ismail A. Trends in Palestinian Higher Education Under Is-
       raeli Occupation. Ph.D. Dissertation. United States International
       University. 1980. 268 pp. DAI 41/3. (September 1980). Page
       955-A. Order # 8019772.

2369. Fine, Judith T. Education in an Israeli Immigrant Town. Ph.D. Dis-
       sertation. University of Pittsburgh. 1978. 303 pp. DAI 40/2.
       (August 1979). Page 935-A. Order # 7917468.

2370. Gordon, Macy A. Collegial Relationships Among Ashkenazuc Jewish
       Scholars: 1100-1300. Ed.D. Dissertation. Yeshiva University. 1977.
       258 pp. DAI 38/9. (March 1978). Page 5293-A. Order # 7732519.

2371. Lewis, Justin H. The Educational Philosophy of Abraham Kook (1865-
       1935) in Historical Perspective. Ph.D. Dissertation. New York Uni-
       versity. 1975. 281 pp. DAI 36/4. (October 1975). Page 2072-A.
       Order # 75-21,153.

2372. Manneberg, Eliezer. The Evolution of Jewish Educational Practices
       in the Sancak (Eyalet) of Jerusalem Under Ottoman Rule. Ph.D.
       Dissertation. University of Connecticut. 1976. 397 pp. DAI 37/2.
       (August 1976). Page 845-A. Order # 76-18,994.

       No entry 2373.

2374. Schwartz, Joseph H. The Ideological Development of the Kibbutz:
       From its Intellectual Antecedents in the Diaspora to the Socialization
       of the Adolescent Generation in Kibbutz Shoval. Ph.D. Dissertation.
       University of Toronto. 1979. n.p. DAI 40/9. (March 1980).
       Page 4928-A. No Order #.

Jordan

2375. Dirani, Eid H. The History of Education in the Hashemite Kingdom
       of Jordan (1921-1975). Ed.D. Dissertation. University of Arkansas.
       1977. 276 pp. DAI 38/5. (November 1977). Page 2445-A. Order #
       77-23,380.

2376. Shubbak, Musa I. The Development of the Jordanian Educational Sys-
       tem, 1952-1967. Ph.D. Dissertation. Southern Illinois University.
       1971. 218 pp. DAI 32/8. (February 1972). Page 4254-A. Order
       # 75-5392.

Kuwait

2377. Zalatimo, Farouk R. The Development of the Educational System in
       the State of Kuwait Since 1961. Ph.D. Dissertation. Southern Illi-
       nois University. 1977. 158 pp. DAI 38/10. (April 1978). Page
       5966-A. Order # 7804326.

Lebanon

2378. Ghusayni, Ra'uf S. Staudent Activism at Lebanon's Universities, 1951-1971. Ph.D. Dissertation. Stanford University. 1974. 423 pp. DAI 35/3. (September 1974). Page 1459-A. Order # 74-20,192.

Libya

2379. El-Mogherbi, Mohammed Z. The Socialization of School Children in the Socialist People's Libyan Arab Jamahirya. Ph.D. Dissertation. University of Missouri. 1978. 170 pp. DAI 40/1. (July 1979). Page 431-A. Order # 7915229.

2380. Hnetish, El-Hadi A. Educational Charts (1940-1975) and Projections (1975-2000) of the Libyan Arab Republic. Ph.D. Dissertation. University of Kansas. 1976. 171 pp. DAI 38/7. (January 1978). Page 3844-A. Order # 77-28,880.

Saudi Arabia

2381. Jammaz, Saud I. Riyadh University: Historical Foundations, Current Status, Critical Problems, and Suggested Solutions. Ph.D. Dissertation. University of Southern California. 1973. 205 pp. DAI 34/7. (January 1974). Page 3910-A. Order # 73-31,354.

2382. Shoaib, Mohammed S. Development of Social Studies Education in Saudi Arabia Since 1926. Ph.D. Dissertation. University of Missouri. 1980. 157 pp. DAI 42/8. (February 1982). Page 3423-A. Order # 8202665.

Syria

2383. Al-Doughill, Tarek A.H. A Historical Review of Education in Syria with Special Emphasis on the Effects of Arab Nationalism on Education from 1920 to 1962. Ph.D. Dissertation. East Texas State University. 1970. 202 pp. DAI 32/1. (July 1971). Page 210-A. Order # 71-18,621.

HISTORY OF LATIN AMERICAN EDUCATION

General

2384. Fisher, Julie H. Political Learning in the Latin American Barriadas: The Role of the Junta de Vecinos. Ph.D. Dissertation. Johns Hopkins University. 1977. 438 pp. DAI 41/3. (September 1980). Page 1205-A. Order # 8018385.

Barbados

2385. Blouet, Olwyn M. Education and Emancipation in Barbados, 1823-1846: A Study in Cultural Transference. Ph.D. Dissertation. University of Nebraska. 1977. 280 pp. DAI 38/7. (January 1978). Page 4306-A. Order # 77-29,476.

Belize (British Honduras)

2386. Herrmann, Eleanor K. The Development of Nursing Education in Belize (British Honduras), Central America, 1920-1970. Ed.D. Dissertation. Columbia University. 1979. 190 pp. DAI 39/12. (June 1979). Page 7173-A. Order # 7913199.

Bolivia

2387. Tolbert, Michael L. Problems of Educational Decentralization: A Bolivian Case Study: 1952-1980. Ph.D. Dissertation. University of Texas. 1980. 197 pp. DAI 41/7. (January 1981). Page 2875-A. Order # 8100973.

Brazil

2388. Dalbey, Richard O. The German Private Schools of Southern Brazil During the Vargas Years, 1930-1945. Ph.D. Dissertation. University of Indiana. 1970. 306 pp. DAI 31/3. (September 1970). Page 924-A. Order # 70-14,963.

2389. Hendricks, Howard C. Education and Maintainance of the Social Structure: The Faculdade De Direito Do Recife and the Brazilian Northeast, 1870-1930. Ph.D. Dissertation. State University of New York, Stony Brook. 1977. 246 pp. DAI 38/9. (March 1978). Page 5659-A. Order # 7800548.

2390. Johnson, Philip B. Ruy Barbosa and Educational Reform in Brazil, 1868-1970. Ph.D. Dissertation. Tulane University. 1971. 245 pp. DAI 32/4. (October 1972). Page 2932-A. Order # 71-27,288.

2391. O'Neil, Charles F. The Search for Order and Progress: Brazilian Mass Education, 1915-1935. Ph.D. Dissertation. University of Texas. 1975. 432 pp. DAI 36/5. (November 1975). Page 3064-A. Order # 75-24,931.

2392. Sisk, Lorie C. The History of the Agnes Erskine College in Brazil, 1904-1970. Ph.D. Dissertation. George Peabody College for Teachers. 1973. 307 pp. DAI 34/8. (February 1974). Page 4816-A. Order # 74-4630.

2393. Zevallos, Fania C.A. Contributions of Education to Economic Growth: The Brazilian Case, 1950-1970. Ph.D. Dissertation. University of Pittsburgh. 1978. 148 pp. DAI 39/8. (February 1979). Page 4608-A. Order # 7902736.

Chile

2394. Acosta-Gonzalez, Carolina T. Chile's Educational Reform Movement, 1865-1970. Ed.D. Dissertation. Pennsylvania State University. 1974. 215 pp. DAI 35/12. (June 1975). Page 7697-A. Order # 75-12,714.

2395. Fischer, Kathleen B. Political Ideology and Educational Reform in Chile, 1964-1976. Ph.D. Dissertation. University of California, Los Angeles. 1977. 292 pp. DAI 38/5. (November 1977). Page 2428-A. Order # 77-23,857.

2396. Sywak, William W. Values in Nineteenth-Century Chilean Education: The German Reform of Chilean Public Education, 1885-1910. Ph.D. Dissertation. University of California, Los Angeles. 1977. 369 pp. DAI 38/10. (April 1978). Page 6268-A. Order # 7802607.

2397. Thomas, Sandra C. The Women of Chile and Education for a Contemporary Society: A Study of Chilean Women, Their History and Present Status and the New Demands of a Society in Transition. Ph.D. Dissertation. St. Louis University. 1973. 378 pp. DAI 35/5. (November 1974). Page 2799. Order # 74-24,150.

Colombia

2398. Farrell, Robert V. The Catholic Church and Colombian Education: 1886-1930, in Search of a Tradition. Ph.D. Dissertation. Columbia University. 1974. 347 pp. DAI 35/9. (March 1975). Page 5885-A. Order # 75-5216.

2399. Kalenson, Martin W. A Study of Public Primary School Education in the Republic of Colombia, South America (1820-c.1970). Ph.D. Dissertation. New York University. 1972. 225 pp. DAI 33/5. (November 1972). Page 2140-A. Order # 72-26,599.

2400. Mendelson, Johannes S.R. The Jesuit Haciendas of the College of Papayan: The Evolution of the Great Estate in the Cauca Valley. Ph.D. Dissertation. Washington University. 1978. 450 pp. DAI 39/8. (February 1979). Page 5098-A. Order # 7904196.

2401. Suarz, Carlos A. Evolution of the Colombian Educational System During the Third Quarter of the Twentieth Century. Ph.D. Dissertation. Boston College. 1977. 184 pp. DAI 37/10. (April 1977). Page 6313-A. Order # 77-8681.

2402. Young, John L. University Reform in New Granada, 1820-1850. Ph.D. Dissertation. Columbia University. 1970. 218 pp. DAI 31/9. (March 1971). Page 4698-A. Order # 71-6271.

Cuba

2403. Puroff, Thomas C. The Cuban National Literacy Campaign, 1961. Ed.D. Dissertation. University of Tennessee. 1972. 166 pp. DAI 33/9. (March 1973). Page 4806-A. Order # 73-2487.

Guatamala

2404. Hernandez, Roberto E. Public Education and University Reforms in Guatamala, 1831-1920. Ph.D. Dissertation. University of Miami. 1977. 257 pp. DAI 38/3. (September 1978). Page 2296-A. Order # 77-21,895.

Guyana

2405. Mattai, Rudolph P. Education and Colonialism in a Plantation Society: Guyana, 1914-1967. Ph.D. Dissertation. University of Pittsburgh. 1977. 280 pp. DAI 38/3. (September 1977). Page 1936-A. Order # 77-21,224.

Haiti

2406. Clement, Job B. History of Education in Haiti, 1804-1915. Ph.D. Dissertation. University of Florida. 1977. 124 pp. DAI 38/11. (May 1978). Page 6570-A. Order # 7806683.

Jamaica

2407. Abbot, Marion E. Education for Development: A Case Study of Curricular Change, Jamaica, W.I. Ed.D. Dissertation. Columbia University. 1980. 287 pp. DAI 41/4. (October 1980). Page 1364-A. Order # 8022092.

2408. Archer, Douglas K. The Educational System and Nation-Building in Jamaica (1944-1970). Ph.D. Dissertation. Northwestern University. 1973. 159 pp. DAI 34/6. (December 1973). Page 2945-A. Order # 73-30,518.

2409. Jervier, Wills S. A Study of Educational Change in Post-Colonial Jamaica. Ed.D. Dissertation. State University of New York, Buffalo. 1976. 229 pp. DAI 37/9. (March 1977). Page 5647-A. Order # 77-6140.

2410. Turner, Trevor A. Social Objectives in the Thought of Jamaicans, 1870-1920. Ph.D. Dissertation. University of Toronto. 1975. n.p. DAI 38/9. (March 1978). Page 5297-A. No Order #.

Mexico

2411. Barrett, James A. Adult Education in Mexico (1920-1924): A Derivation of the Principles and Philosophy Underlying an Effective Educational Program for the Masses. Ph.D. Dissertation. Florida State University. 1970. 233 pp. DAI 35/2. (August 1974). Page 783-A. Order # 74-18,008.

2412. Britton, John A. The Mexican Ministry of Education, 1931-1940:
       Radicalism and Institutional Development. Ph.D. Dissertation. Tu-
       lane University. 1971. 313 pp. DAI 32/7. (January 1972). Page
       3909-A. Order # 72-3867.

2413. Farias, Hector. Nemesio Garcia Naranjo: Mexico's First Minister
       of Education, 1913-1914. Ph.D. Dissertation. Northwestern Univer-
       sity. 1971. 174 pp. DAI 32/6. (December 1971). Page 3068-A.
       Order # 71-30,795.

2414. Goldstein, Nancy G. Americanization and Mexicanization: The Mex-
       ican Elite and Anglo-Americans in the Gasden Purchase Lands, 1853-
       1880. Ph.D. Dissertation. Case Western Reserve University. 1977.
       342 pp. DAI 38/3. (December 1977). Page 1572-A. Order # 77-
       18,855.

2415. Gordon, Sally J.W. The Inca Empire: A Test Case for the Hypothe-
       sis of Schooling in Civilizational States. Ph.D. Dissertation. Univer-
       sity of Illinois. 1978. 174 pp. DAI 39/5. (November 1978). Page
       2785-A. Order # 7820946.

2416. Heller, George N. Music Education in the Valley of Mexico During
       the Sixteenth Century. Ph.D. Dissertation. University of Michigan.
       1974. 200 pp. DAI 35/5. (November 1974). Page 2746-A. Order
       # 74-15,744.

2417. Johnson, Clark V. Mormon Education in Mexico: The Rise of the
       Sociedad Educativa y Cultural. Ph.D. Dissertation. Brigham Young
       University. 1977. 342 pp. DAI 38/1. (July 1977). Page 133-A.
       Order # 77-13,808.

2418. Lee, James H. Nationalism and Education in Mexico, 1821-1861.
       Ph.D. Dissertation. Oregon State University. 1974. 288 pp. DAI
       35/2. (August 1974). Page 1018-A. Order # 74-17,791.

2419. Llinas-Alvarez, Edgar. Revolution, Education and Mexicanidad: The
       Quest for National Identity in Mexican Educational Thought. Ph.D.
       Dissertation. Columbia University. 1977. 338 pp. DAI 38/5. (No-
       vember 1977). Page 26109-A. Order # 77-24,105.

2420. Machlis, Michael. The Educational Philosophy of Ignacio Manuel Alta-
       mirano and his Contributions to the Public Primary Education in
       Nineteenth-Century Mexico. Ph.D. Dissertation. New York Univer-
       sity. 1974. 178 pp. DAI 35/5. (November 1974). Page 2740-A.
       Order # 74-25,006.

2421. Multerer, Raymond T. The Socialist Movement and its Impact on
       Mexican Education, 1930-1948. Ph.D. Dissertation. State University
       of New York, Buffalo. 1974. 436 pp. DAI 35/7. (January 1975).
       Page 4396-A. Order # 75-1503.

2422. Partin, Emmett M. The Life, Educational Ideas, and Work of Jose
       Vasconcelos (1882-1959). Ph.D. Dissertation. University of Penn-
       sylvania. 1973. 553 pp. DAI 34/8. (February 1974). Page 4815-
       A. Order # 74-2443.

2423. Rosser, Harry E. Beyond Revolution: The Social Concerns of Moises Saenz, Mexican Educator (1888-1941). Ph.D. Dissertation. American University. 1970. 437 pp. DAI 32/1. (July 1971). Page 214-A. Order # 71-19,092.

2424. Traboulay, David W. An Institutional and Intellectual History of the Universities of Mexico and San Marcos, Peru (1553-1800): Influences of the Medieval University Tradition in Europe. Ph.D. Dissertation. University of Notre Dame. 1970. 405 pp. DAI 31/9. (March 1971). Page 4661-A. Order # 71-5561.

2425. Vandenbergh, Marie. James Torres Bodet, Mexican Educator and Existentialism. Ph.D. Dissertation. Southern Illinois University. 1975. 325 pp. DAI 36/12. (June 1976). Page 7908-A. Order # 76-13,294.

2426. Vaughn, Mary K. Schools for Social Control: Mexican Educational Policy and Programs, 1880-1928. Ph.D. Dissertation. University of Wisconsin. 1973. 395 pp. DAI 34/5. (November 1975). Page 2539-A. Order # 73-20,283.

Panama (including canal zone)

2427. DeWitt, Donald L. Social and Educational Thought in the Development of the Republic of Panama, 1903-1946: An Intellectual History. Ph.D. Dissertation. Arizona State University. 1972. 249 pp. DAI 33/3. (September 1972). Page 1105-A. Order # 72-23,354.

2428. Harper, Francis A.A. Tracing the Course of Growth and Development in Educational Policy for the Canal Zone Colored Schools, 1905-1955. Ph.D. Dissertation. University of Maryland. 1974. 301 pp. DAI 35/9. (March 1975). Page 5886-A. Order # 75-7333.

2429. Smith, Michael E. The Growth and Development of the Canal Zone College (1933-73). Ph.D. Dissertation. North Texas State University. 1973. 220 pp. DAI 34/8. (February 1974). Page 4816-A. Order # 74-4054.

2430. Swain, Robert J. The Role of Education in the Independence of Panama, 1850-1903: A Cause of Revolution. Ph.D. Dissertation. Temple University. 1973. 337 pp. DAI 34/7. (January 1974). Page 4175-A. Order # 73-30,175.

Peru

2431. Osberg, James A. Centro De Altos Estudios Militaires: Education for Change in the Peruvian Military, 1950-1973. Ph.D. Dissertation.

Southern Illinois University. 1976. 190 pp. DAI 37/6. (December
1976). Page 3464-A. Order # 76-28,767.

Venezuela

2432. Mulino-Betancourt, Freddy A.   Historical Development of Mathematical
Education in Venezuela During the Eighteenth and Nineteenth Centuries. Ed.D. Dissertation. Oklahoma State University. 1974.
146 pp. DAI 35/12. (June 1975). Page 7700-A. Order # 75-8842.

West Indies

2433. Caaesar, Francis G.B.   Planning and Educational Development in the
West Indies, 1952-1972. Ph.D. Dissertation. University of Wisconsin.
1977. 181 pp. DAI 38/6. (December 1977). Page 3166-A. Order
77-17,816.

HISTORY OF AUSTRALASIAN EDUCATION

General

2434. Albinger, Donald E. The South Pacific System: A Focus on the South Pacific Commission. Ph.D. Dissertation. University of Colorado. 1976. 742 pp. DAI 37/11. (May 1977). Page 7297-A. Order # 77-11,280.

2435. Herr, Richard A. Regionalism in the South Pacific: The Impact of the South Pacific Commission, 1947-1974. Ph.D. Dissertation. Duke University. 1976. 398 pp. DAI 37/12. (June 1977), Page 7939-A. Order # 77-11,819.

Australia

2436. Brennan, Mary B. A Socio-Histoical Examination of Education Policies and Practices from [sic] Immigrant Children in the London Borough of Ealing and for Migrant Children in the Catholic Education Authority in Western Australia. Ph.D. Dissertation. University of California, Los Angeles. 1977. n.p. DAI 38/12. (June 1978). Page 7197-A. Order # 7806457.

Melenesia

2437. Brown, Harold E. The Story of Education in Lutheran Missions and the Evangelical Lutheran Church of New Guinea, 1886-1970. Ph.D. Dissertation. Ohio State University. 1972. 232 pp. DAI 33/4. (October 1972). Page 1470-A. Order # 72-26,983.

2438. Singh, Silas P. British Influences on Education in Fiji: Emerging Patterns. Ph.D. Dissertation. Southern Illinois University. 1972. 297 pp. DAI 33/5. (November 1972). Page 1993-A. Order # 72-28,556.

Micronesia

2439. Brown, Richard G. Germany, Spain, and the Caroline Islands, 1885-
       1899. Ph.D. Dissertation. University of Southern Mississippi. 1976.
       259 pp. DAI 37/9. (March 1977). Page 5987-A. Order # 77-5926.

2440. Ehrlich, Paul M. "The Clothes of Men": Ponape Island and German
       Colonial Rule, 1899-1914. Ph.D. Dissertation. State University of
       New York, Stony Brook. 1978. 275 pp. DAI 39/3. (September
       1978). Page 1769-A. Order # 7813929.

2441. Thomas, Mary D. Transmitting Culture to Children on Namonuito
       Atoll, Caroline Islands. Ph.D. Dissertation. University of Hawaii.
       1978. 178 pp. DAI 39/8. (February 1979). Page 5020-A. Order
       # 7903503.

Polynesia

2442. Harrigan, Norwell E. Higher Education in the Micro-State: A Theory
       of Raritan Society. Ph.D. Dissertation. University of Pittsburgh.
       1972. 196 pp. DAI 33/2. (August, 1972). Page 580-A. Order #
       72-22,716.

2443. Rolff, Karla. Fa'a Samoa: Tradition in Transition. Ph.D. Dissertation.
       University of California, Santa Barbara. 1978. 307 pp. DAI 40/1.
       (July 1979). Page 335-A. Order # 7911657.

INDEX

Index